THE MEDIAEVAL ACADEMY OF AMERICA
PUBLICATION NO. 63

STUDIES IN THE LIFE AND WORKS OF PETRARCH

STUDIES IN
THE LIFE AND WORKS
OF PETRARCH

by

ERNEST HATCH WILKINS

*Fellow of the Mediaeval
Academy of America*

THE MEDIAEVAL ACADEMY OF AMERICA
CAMBRIDGE, MASSACHUSETTS
1955

Printed at Crimson Printing Company
Cambridge, Massachusetts, U.S.A.

Preface

For the two years of Petrarch's last stay in Provence it is possible, through use of the many extant letters that he then wrote and of other relevant evidence of various kinds, to construct a more complete account of his outer and inner experience —his dwellings, his comings and goings, his personal associations, his personal enterprises, his participation in matters of public concern, his ideas, his hopes, his fears, his antipathies, his troubles, and the conditions under which he carried on his literary work—than could be constructed for any other period of similar length in Petrarch's life. Such construction is attempted in the fifth and main chapter of this book. Chapters 1–4 and 6–10 are related to the main chapter; but their subjects are treated not merely in the respects that are related to that chapter, but in their entirety.

The only two other Petrarchan studies that I have completed since the preparation of *The Making of the "Canzoniere" and Other Petrarchan Studies* are included as Chapters 11 and 12; and my translation of Petrarch's Coronation Oration is included as an Appendix.

Chapters 1–3, Section II of Chapter 5, Chapters 11 and 12, and the Appendix have been published previously, as follows: Chapter 1 in *Speculum*, xxviii (1953), 754–775; Chapter 2 in *Modern Philology*, li (1953), 9–17; Chapter 3 in *Medievalia et Humanistica*, viii (1954), 22–31; Section II of Chapter 5 (under the title "The Dates of Petrarch's Last Journey to Provence") in *Modern Language Notes*, lxix (1954), 92–96; Chapter 11 in *Speculum*, xxv (1950), 374–378; Chapter 12 in *Comparative Literature*, ii (1950), 327–342; and the Appendix in *PMLA*, lxviii (1953), 1242–1250. They reappear in this book with many slight alterations, but without substantial change.

E.H.W.

Newton Centre, Massachusetts

Table of Contents

Introductory Notes

Petrarch's Changes of Residence

In view of the frequency of Petrarch's changes of residence after 1326 the following list, which includes also two of his major journeys, may be convenient for reference:

1326 May–1337 Summer	Avignon
1337 Summer–1341 February	Vaucluse and Avignon
1341 February–May	Coronation Journey
1341 May–1342 early	Parma
1342 Spring–1343 September	Vaucluse and Avignon
1343 September–December	Journey to Naples
1343 December–1345 early	Parma
1345 Summer and Autumn	Verona and Parma
1345 late–1347 November	Vaucluse and Avignon
1347 December–1351 Summer	Parma and Padua
1351 Summer–1353 May	Vaucluse and Avignon
1353 May–1358 late	Milan
1358–1359 Winter	Padua
1359 Spring–1361 Spring	Milan
1361 Spring–1362 September	Padua
1362 September–ca 1367 end	Venice
ca 1367 end–1370 Summer	Padua
1370 Summer–1374 July	Arquà

Petrarch's Popes

The following list of Petrarch's popes may also be convenient for reference:

Benedict XII	20 December 1334–25 April 1342
Clement VI	7 May 1342–6 December 1352
Innocent VI	18 December 1352–12 September 1362
Urban V	28 September 1362–19 December 1370
Gregory XI	30 December 1370–26–27 March 1378

Petrarchan Editions

Quotations from the works of Petrarch are taken from the following editions:

Canzoniere

Rerum vulgarium fragmenta, ed. by Gianfranco Contini (Paris, 1949).

Triumphs

In general: *Le rime sparse e i trionfi,* ed. by Ezio Chiòrboli (Bari, 1930).

Poi che la bella e gloriosa donna: ed. by Roberto Weiss in his *Un inedito petrarchesco: la redazione sconosciuta di un capitolo del "Trionfo della fama"* (Rome, 1950). Referred to as Weiss 1.

Bucolicum carmen

Ed. by Antonio Avena (Padua, 1906).

Epistolae metricae

In general: *Poëmata minora,* ed. by Domenico Rossetti, Vols. II–III (Milan, 1831–1834). Referred to as Rossetti.

I 1, II 16,[1] and III 3, 18, 19, and 33: ed. by Enrico Bianchi, in *Rime, Trionfi e poesie latine,* ed. by F. Neri, G. Martellotti, Bianchi, and N. Sapegno (= Vol. 6 in the series *La letteratura italiana, storia e testi*) (Milan, 1951). Referred to as Bianchi.

Exul ab Italia

In Rossetti, II, 60–66.

Valle locus Clausa

In Bianchi, p. 852.

Epistolae familiares

Le familiari, Vols. I–III ed. by V. Rossi and Vol. IV ed. by Rossi and Umberto Bosco (= *Edizione nazionale,* Vols. X–XIII) (Florence, 1933–1942). Referred to as Rossi 1.[2] Rossi's section numbers are given, in general, for quotations from the longer letters, and in certain other cases.

---

[1] Wrongly numbered by Rossetti as II 17.

[2] Rossi's numeration of the *Familiares* is followed in all cases. For a Table showing the respects in which his numeration differs from the now superseded numeration followed by Fracassetti in his edition and in his translation of the *Familiares,* see the manual listed on p. xiv as Wilkins 2, pp. 5–6.

Epistolae sine nomine

Ed. by Paul Piur, in his *Petrarcas "Buch ohne Namen" und die Päpstliche Kurie* (Halle, 1925). Referred to as Piur 1.

Epistolae seniles

In general, in *Librorum Francisci Petrarche impressorum annotatio*, Vol. II (Venice, 1501).[3]

I 2: in Piur, *Petrarcas Briefwechsel mit deutschen Zeitgenossen* (= *Konrad Burdach, Vom Mittelalter zur Reformation*, VII) (Berlin, 1933), pp. 233–236.

X 2: in *Lettere autobiografiche*, ed. and trans. by Enrico Carrara (Milan, 1929), pp. 87–121. Referred to as Carrara 1.

XVIII 1: in Carrara, "L'epistola 'Posteritati' e la leggenda petrarchesca," in Istituto Superiore di Magistero del Piemonte, *Annali* (1929), 309–324.

Epistolae variae

In *Epistolae de rebus familiaribus et variae*, ed. by Giuseppe Fracassetti, Vol. III (Florence, 1863). Referred to as Fracassetti 1.

Miscellaneous Letters [4]

Misc. 5 and 6: ed. by Faraglia on p. 155 of the article listed on p. xiii.

Misc. 9 and 11: ed. by Marco Vattasso in his *Del Petrarca e di alcuni suoi amici* (= *Studi e testi*, 14) (Rome, 1904), pp. 17 and 31.

Misc. 16: ed. Weiss on pp. 65–66 of the article listed on p. xiv.

Invective contra medicum

Ed. by P. G. Ricci (Rome, 1950). Referred to as Ricci.

———————

Reference is made occasionally to *Le rime*, ed. by Giovanni Mestica (Florence, 1896). Referred to as Mestica.

Reference is made occasionally to *Lettere . . . delle cose familiari . . . lettere varie*, ed. and trans. by Fracassetti, 5 vols. (Florence, 1863–1867), referred to as Fracassetti 2; also to *Lettere senili*, 2 vols. (Florence, 1869–1870), referred to as Fracassetti 3.

---

[3] The 1501 numeration of the *Seniles* is followed in all cases. For a Table showing the respects in which this numeration differs from the incorrect numeration of the editions of 1554 and 1581 and (in a very few cases) from the numeration followed by Fracassetti in his translation of the *Seniles*, see the same manual, pp. 6–8.

[4] For a numbered list of these letters see the same manual, pp. 11–14.

Letters Addressed to Petrarch

For a list of these letters, with references to their places of publication, see the manual listed on p. xiv as Wilkins 2, pp. 115–122. In the present book such letters are referred to both by the name of the writer and by the letters LAP (standing for "Letters Addressed to Petrarch") followed by the numbers they bear in that list. That list should now be supplemented by these two additional entries:

Benedict XII.
   One letter is published by J. F. P. A. de Sade in his *Mémoires pour la vie de François Pétrarque*, iii (Amsterdam, 1767), as No. xv among the "Pièces justificatives" at the end of the volume, and is republished on pp. 6–7 of the present book.
   5a.   Litterarum scientia, morum honestas. *1335 Jan. 25.*

Under Clement VI the introductory paragraph should begin thus:

   One letter is published by G. Livi in his "Nuovi documenti relativi a Francesco Petrarca," in RR. Deputazioni di Storia patria per le Provincie dell' Emilia, *Atti e memorie*, N.S., iii (1878), Part II, 295–296; and three letters are published by C. Cipolla . . .

The first entry following this paragraph should be:

   11a.   Vita ac morum honestas. *1342 May 23.*

Periodicals

The *Archivio storico italiano* is referred to as *ASI*.
The *Giornale storico della letteratura italiana* is referred to as *GSLI*.

Other Books and Articles

The other books and articles that are referred to in two or more chapters, with the abbreviated references that will be used for them, are as follows:

Appel 1. Carl Appel, *Zur Entwickelung italienischer Dichtungen Petrarcas* (Halle, 1891).

Avena. Antonio Avena, "Guglielmo da Pastrengo e gli inizii dell'umanesimo in Verona," in Accademia d'Agricoltura Scienze Lettere Arti e Commercio di Verona, *Atti*, Ser. IV, VII (1907), 229–290.

Baldasseroni. F. Baldasseroni, "La guerra tra Firenze e Giovanni Visconti," in *Studi storici*, XII (1903), 41–94.

Baluze. Étienne Baluze, *Vitae paparum avenionensium*, ed. by Guillaume Mollat, Vol. II (Paris, 1927).

Billanovich. Giuseppe Billanovich, *Petrarca letterato*, I: *Lo scrittoio del Petrarca* (Rome, 1947).

Bosco. Umberto Bosco, "Particolari petrarcheschi," in *Studi petrarcheschi*, I (1948), 97–109.

Burdach. Konrad Burdach, *Vom Mittelalter zur Reformation*, 11 vols. (Berlin, 1912–1939).

Burdach-Piur. *Briefwechsel des Cola di Rienzo* (= Burdach, II), 5 Parts (1913–1928).

Calcaterra. Carlo Calcaterra, "La prima ispirazione dei 'Trionfi,'" in his *Nella selva del Petrarca* (Bologna, 1942), pp. 145–208.

Carrara 2. Enrico Carrara, *La poesia pastorale* (Milan, 1909).

Carrara 3. *Idem*, "I commenti antichi e la cronologia delle egloghe petrarchesche," in *GSLI*, XXVIII (1896), 123–153.

Cesareo 1. G. A. Cesareo, *Su le "poesie volgari" del Petrarca: nuove ricerche* (Rocca S. Casciano, 1898).

Cochin 1. Henry Cochin, *Un ami de Pétrarque: lettres de Francesco Nelli à Pétrarque* (Paris, 1892).

Cochin 2. *Idem, Un amico di Francesco Petrarca: le lettere del Nelli al Petrarca* (Florence, 1901). A translation of Cochin 1, embodying some revisions.

Eubel. Conrad Eubel, *Hierarchia catholica medii aevi*, 2d ed., Vol. I (Münster, 1913).

Faraglia. N. F. Faraglia, "Barbato da Sulmona e gli uomini di lettere della corte di Roberto d'Angiò," in *ASI*, Ser. V, III (1889), 313–360.

Flamini. Francesco Flamini, *Tra Valchiusa ed Avignone* (= *GSLI*, Supplemento No. 12) (Turin, 1910).

Foresti 1. Arnaldo Foresti, *Aneddoti della vita di Francesco Petrarca* (Brescia, 1928).

Ginori Conti. Piero Ginori Conti, *Vita ed opere di Pietro di Dante Alighieri* (Florence, 1939).

Gregorovius. Ferdinand Gregorovius, *Geschichte der Stadt Rom im Mittelalter*. Cited by Book, Chapter, and Section, which apply to all editions and translations.

Léonard 1. E-G. Léonard, *La jeunesse de Jeanne Ire*, 2 vols. (Monaco, 1932).

Léonard 2. *Idem*, "Un ami de Pétrarque, sénéchal de Provence:

Giovanni Barrili," in *Études italiennes*, ix (1927), 109–142.

Livi. Giovanni Livi, "Nuovi documenti relativi a Francesco Petrarca," in RR. Deputazioni di Storia Patria per le Provincie dell'Emilia, *Atti e memorie*, N.S., iii (1878), Part II, 289–299.

Magrini. Diana Magrini, *Le epistole metriche del Petrarca* (Rocca S. Casciano, 1907).

Martellotti. Guido Martellotti, "Linee di sviluppo dell'umanesimo petrarchesco," in *Studi petrarcheschi*, ii (1949), 51–80.

Mascetta-Caracci. Lorenzo Mascetta-Caracci, *Dante e il "Dedalo" petrarchesco* (Lanciano, 1910).

Melodia. Giovanni Melodia, *Studio su i Trionfi del Petrarca* (Palermo, 1898).

Mollat. Guillaume Mollat, *Les papes d'Avignon*, 9th ed. (Paris, 1949).

Paganini. Pagano Paganini, "Delle relazioni di Messer Francesco Petrarca con Pisa," in R. Accademia Lucchese di Scienze, Lettere ed Arti, *Atti*, xxi (1882), 149–214.

Piur 2. Piur, *Cola di Rienzo* (Vienna, 1931). Cited by Chapter.

Rizzi 1. Fortunato Rizzi, *Francesco Petrarca e il decennio parmense (1341–1351)* (Turin, 1934).

Rizzi 2. *Idem*, "Spes magna boni (il Petrarca cardinale?)," in *Scuola e cultura*, xiv (1938), 38–48.

De Sade. J. F. P. A. de Sade, *Mémoires pour la vie de François Pétrarque*, 3 vols. (Amsterdam, 1764–1767).

E. H. R. Tatham, *Francesco Petrarca*, 2 vols. (London, 1925–1926).

Volpi 1. Guglielmo Volpi, *Il trecento*, 1st ed. (Milan, 1897–1898).

Volpi 2. *Idem, Il trecento*, 2d ed. (Milan, 1907).

Weiss 2. Roberto Weiss, "Some New Correspondence of Petrarch and Barbato da Sulmona," in *Modern Language Review*, xliii (1948), 60–66.

Wilkins 1. E. H. Wilkins, *The Making of the "Canzoniere" and Other Petrarchan Studies* (Rome, 1951).

Wilkins 2. *Idem, The Prose Letters of Petrarch: a Manual* (New York, 1951). In cases in the present book in which the dates of letters are stated without argument they correspond to the dates assigned to the letters in question in the latest discussions reported in this manual.

STUDIES IN
THE LIFE AND WORKS
OF PETRARCH

CHAPTER I

Petrarch's Ecclesiastical Career

Petrarch's father at his death in 1326 left a considerable estate, and for a time his sons Francesco and Gherardo lived, in Avignon, a life of fashionable gayety. Soon, however, the dishonesty of the father's executors rendered the sons "de divitibus inopes," as Petrarch says in *Fam.* x 3, written long afterward to Gherardo. The malversation of the executors is referred to also in *Sen.* xvi 1.

It became necessary for Petrarch, therefore, to enter a profession. He had been trained for the law, but disliked it too much to make it the means of earning his livelihood. He was living in what was then the papal city; he was befriended by the young Giacomo Colonna, who held the bishopric of Lombez; and he decided, very naturally, to enter the clerical profession. He must, then, have taken the tonsure. There is no evidence, however, that he took even the minor orders: theoretically only one who had taken those orders could hold benefices, but in Petrarch's time this requirement was not enforced. He certainly never took the major orders. No one of the benefices he received involved the cure of souls. His own religious observances, referred to in *Fam.* x 5 (written in 1347 or somewhat later), were clearly a matter rather of personal piety than of formal obedience.[1]

His ecclesiastical appointments, however, constituted the main source of his livelihood, and they and various experiences related thereto were of vital concern to him throughout his mature life: yet the relevant data have never hitherto been completely assembled; some of them have been misinterpreted; and

---

[1] Vigenio Soncini, "Petrarca canonico e arcidiacono a Parma," in *Archivio storico per le province parmensi*, N.S., xxxiv (1934), 140–146.

3

the importance of his ecclesiastical career as an essential phase of his total experience has never been duly recognized.

In the normal process of papal appointment to a benefice four documents were involved (the next two paragraphs apply also to petitions regarding other matters):

(1) The candidate's own petition, which served only as the basis for the preparation of

(2) A formalized petition, prepared by a papal secretary. In such formalized petitions, designed to simplify the task of the Pope, the candidate's own petition was recast in standard formulas, but in some instances preserved some of the candidate's own wording (instances of such preservation are noted below, in Sections X and XIII of the present chapter). The formalized petition was presented to the Pope, who, if he approved it, endorsed it with the word "Fiat" (sometimes followed by qualifying or directing words, such as "ad biennium" or "motu proprio") and an initial constituting his signature (Clement VI used the letter R, the initial of his family name, Roger). The approved petition then passed to a *datator* (later called *datarius*) who, after adding the date of the Pope's approval, transmitted it to a *registrator supplicationum*, whose task it was to see to it that an exact copy of the formalized petition, with its endorsement and its date, be entered in a Register of Petitions. This done, the *datator* took the formalized petition itself to the chancellery, where it served as the basis for the preparation of the two types of letter (both to be issued as papal bulls) next to be mentioned. The formalized petition itself, having served its function, was then destroyed: it is only through the copies entered in the Register that the petitions have survived. The Register copy bears, as has been said, the date of the Pope's approval of the petition, but it does not bear the date of the presentation of the petition. It is therefore impossible to generalize as to the usual lapse of time between presentation and approval: scattered minor indications, however, tend to strengthen the natural supposition that the lapse of time was, at least in many cases, considerable.

(3) A letter of notification addressed by the Pope to the appointee.

(4) A letter addressed by the Pope to three clerics, commissioning them to see to it that the appointee be given possession of the benefice and protected in his rights thereto.

If however the appointment was made actually (or nominally) on papal initiative, the formalized petition was replaced (or supplemented) by a memorandum (presumably drafted, under direction, by a papal secretary) indicating that the appointment was to be considered as made *motu proprio* (such memoranda are referred to in Sections IX and XXII of the present chapter). This memorandum, duly endorsed, then followed the same course as an endorsed formalized petition.[2]

I. Chaplain to Cardinal Colonna

In 1330 Petrarch entered the service of Cardinal Giovanni Colonna, on the recommendation of Bishop Giacomo. In a document of 25 January 1335 (presently to be quoted) he is referred to as the Cardinal's "capellanus continuus commensalis." With Petrarch's removal to Vaucluse in 1337 his service to the Cardinal became discontinuous, and with his year in Parma in 1341–1342 and his longer residence there in 1343–1345 it became hardly more than occasional; but it did not cease until 1347. Petrarch is referred to as the Cardinal's "capellanus" in a document of 22 May 1342 (to be quoted in part in Section IV). His mission to Naples in 1343 (to be mentioned in Section VIII) was undertaken as a representative of the Cardinal. Relations between the two men continued to be cordial until 1347. In 1345, when Petrarch had been in Italy for nearly two years, Sennuccio del Bene, doubtless on behalf of the Cardinal, sent Petrarch a pleasant sonnet, beginning "Oltra l'usato modo si rigira," in which it is said in the octave and in the first tercet that Laura and the Cardinal desire Petrarch's return. The first tercet reads:

> E 'l signor nostro in desir sempre abonna
> di vedervi seder nelli suoi scanni:
> e 'n atto et in parlar questo distinsi.

---

[2] See Ursmer Berlière, *Suppliques de Clément VI* (Rome, 1906), Introduction, and *Lettres de Clément VI* (Rome, 1924) (= *Analecta Vaticano-Belgica*, i and vi).

The first two of the three lines certainly mean: "And our lord [the Cardinal] still, as always, desires very much to see you sitting at his board." [3]

Petrarch's Eclogue VIII, entitled *Divortium*, written in or as of 1347, indicates clearly, under the pastoral veil, that Petrarch's service with the Cardinal came definitely to an end when Petrarch, in that year, determined to return to Italy. Relations between Petrarch and the Cardinal were evidently strained at this time; but the strain did not prevent Petrarch from writing, in his last letter to the Cardinal, *Fam.* VII 13: "Fatebor ingenue . . . me tibi omnia debere, ingenium scilicet et corpusculum hoc quod peregrinus inhabito, et siquid externorum obtigit bonorum. Neque enim minus aula tua animo meo contulit quam corpori, quam fortunis; sub te nutritus a iuventute mea, sub te auctus et eruditus sum. . . ." Nor did it prevent the Cardinal—if the reconstruction of events attempted below in Section XIII is correct—from supporting the request made by Petrarch for the Parmese archdeaconate when it became probable that the tenure of that office by Dino da Urbino would soon come to an end. The Cardinal died, of the Black Death, on 3 July 1348.

II. Lombez: a Canonry

On 25 January 1335 Benedict XII appointed Petrarch, on the recommendation of Cardinal Colonna, to a canonry in the cathedral of Lombez. The letter of notification (LAP 5a),[4] which has not been reprinted since the eighteenth century, is the earliest document in which the name of Petrarch appears, and it is a good specimen of the form used in general in giving notice of papal appointments to benefices. As printed by De Sade,[5] it is as follows (I make no attempt to indicate apparent errors in this document or in the other documents quoted in this study, and I break this document into paragraphs for the sake of clarity):

Dilecto Filio Francisco Petrachi de Florentiâ, canonico Lomberiensi, salutem.

Litterarum scientia, morum honestas, & alia multiplicia merita

---

[3] On this sonnet see below, pp. 63–65.
[4] For the meaning of LAP see above, p. xii.
[5] III, "Pièces justificatives," No. xv, pp. 47–48.

probitatis super quibus apud nos fide digno commendaris testimonio nos inducunt ut tibi reddamus ad gratiam liberales.

Volentes itaque nullum, ut asseris, beneficium Ecclesiae assecuto praemissorum meritorum tuorum intuitu, nec non consideratione dilecti filii nostri Joannis sancti Angeli Diaconi Cardinalis pro te, Capellano continuo commensali suo, nobis super hoc humiliter suplicantis, gratiam facere specialem, Canonicatum Ecclesiae Lomberiensis cum plenitudine Juris Canonici, Apostolicâ tibi auctoritate conferimus, & de illo providemus.

Praebendam verò, si quae in ipsâ Ecclesiâ vacat ad praesens, vel cum vacaverit, quam tu per te vel per Procuratorem tuum ad hoc legitimè constitutum infrà unius mensis spatium, postquam tibi vel tuo Procuratori vacatio illius innotuerit, duxeris acceptandam, conferendam tibi per acceptationem hujus cum omnibus juribus & pertinentiis suis dictâ Auctoritate Apostolicâ reservamus; districtius inhibentes Venerabili Filio nostro Episcopo & Dilecto Filio Capitulo Lomberiensi, ac illi vel illis ad quem vel ad quos in eâdem Ecclesiâ praedicta collatio vel provisio seu quaevis alia dispositio pertinet, communiter vel divisim, de illâ ante acceptationem hujusmodi, nisi postquam eis constiterit quod tu vel Procurator tuus praedictam illam nolueritis acceptare, disponere quoquo modo praesumat;

decernentes ex tunc irritum & inane, si secus super iis à quoquam quavis auctoritate contigerit attentari, non obstantibus, &c.

Nulli ergo, &c.

Avenione, 8. Calend. Februar. anno primo.

This document is essentially a form letter, the "Volentes" paragraph and the reference to the Bishop and the Chapter of Lombez being the only portions specific to this particular appointment. The laudation and the references to a trustworthy witness, to the present or future vacancy of the prebend, to a possible procurator, to acceptance, to the possibility of non-acceptance, and to the invalidity of any action inconsistent with the appointment appear in virtually the same language in several of the other documents to be referred to in this study. The "Volentes" paragraph indicates (in its "ut asseris") that a petition had been submitted; also that the petition had been supported by Cardinal Colonna. No corresponding commissioning letter is known to exist.

Petrarch never took personal possession of this benefice: doubtless he received its income through a procurator, as he did in the case of the Pisan canonry presently to be mentioned. In *Fam.* iv 12, written on 5 January 1342, he refers, but merely in passing, to the fact of his holding a canonry in Lombez. He continued to hold this canonry until 1355, when he exchanged it for the church of S. Maria de Capellis in the diocese of Teano, previously held by his friend "Socrates" (Ludwig van Kempen). This exchange will be discussed in Section XVIII.

III. Chaplain to King Robert

On 2 April 1341, Petrarch being then in Naples for his pre-coronation examination, King Robert appointed him to a chaplaincy. The appointing document [6] reads in part:

Ipsum in Presbyterum, & Familiarem nostrum domesticum, ac de nostro hospitio duximus de certa nostra scientia, tenore praesentium retinendum. Recepto prius ab eo solito in talibus Iuramento; Volentes & expressè mandantes, vt illis honoribus, fauoribus, priuilegiis & praerogatiuis alijs potiatur, & gaudeat, quibus caeteri Clerici, & Familiares nostri domestici potiuntur, & gaudent. . . .

Despite the implications of the sentence just quoted, this chaplaincy can hardly have been more than honorary.

IV. Pisa: a Canonry

On 22 May 1342 Clement VI appointed Petrarch, on the recommendation of Cardinal Colonna, to a canonry in the cathedral of Pisa. The letter of notification (LAP 12) is addressed "Dilecto filio Francisco Petraccho de Florentia canonico Pisano;" begins with the words "Licterarum scientia, vita et morum honestas;" and contains the clause "nec non consideratione dilecti filij nostri Johannis Sancti Angeli diaconi cardinalis pro te, capellano suo." On the same day there was issued a corresponding commissioning letter,[7] addressed to the Bishop of Teano and the abbots of the Pisan monasteries of S. Savino and S. Zeno. Petrarch seems never to have taken personal possession of this benefice. That he re-

---

[6] Published by G. F. Tomasini, *Petrarcha redivivus* (Padua, 1635), pp. 77–78. Republished by De Sade, No. xvi, p. 48.

[7] Both documents are published by Carlo Cipolla in his "Francesco Petrarca canonico di Pisa," in R. Accademia delle Scienze di Torino, *Atti,* xli (1905–06), 178–179.

ceived its income through a procurator is proved by a document of 1 September 1352,[8] whereby he appoints one Ugolino Martelli as his procurator for this purpose.

V. Papal Commissioner for a Parmese Appointment

On 23 May 1342, the day after Clement had appointed Petrarch to a canonry in Pisa, he appointed him also to be one of three clerics designated to carry out the installation of Romanello Baratta in a Parmese canonry. The commissioning letter [9] is addressed "dilectis filiis Agapito de Colupna archidiacono, et Francisco Petracche canonico lumberiensis et Meruello de Benedictis canonico parmensis ecclesiarum," and begins with the words (which refer to Romanello) "Vite ac morum honestas."

On 17 September 1350, trouble having arisen with regard to Romanello's tenure of his canonry, Petrarch, who was about to leave Parma for a journey to Rome, appointed two Parmese clerics to act in his stead. The document [10] of appointment begins with the words "Nos Franciscus Petracca, canonicus lumberiensis, executor una cum quibusdam aliis colegis. . . ." Its essential provision is indicated in the words "cum circa executionem huiusmodi non possimus presentialiter interesse . . . dominis Iacobino de Albertuciis canonico parmensi, et Hugolino de Maramo archipresbitero de Cusignano parmensi . . . committimus vices nostras."

VI. Pisa: a Priorate Lost

On 6 October 1342 Clement appointed Petrarch to the priorate of S. Nicola di Migliarino, near Pisa—a rich benefice. The letter of notification has not been found. The commission-

---

[8] Published by Paganini, pp. 212–214. Republished in part below, on p. 133.

[9] Published by Livi, pp. 295–296. This letter (LAP 11a) is preserved through its complete inclusion in a document of 17 September 1350 published by Livi.

[10] Livi, pp. 293–294. Livi publishes also, on pp. 294–295, a document of 3 December 1351, bearing on the same case and drawn up in Petrarch's house, but during his absence.

ing letter [11] is addressed to the Bishop of Teano, the abbot of the monastery of S. Zeno, and the abbot of the monastery of S. Porziano (near Lucca). It turned out, however, that this priorate was claimed by one Lotto del Nicchio degli Orlandi. Petrarch did his best to have Lotto's claim annulled, and took the matter to the papal court; but Lotto was sustained, and the appointment brought Petrarch nothing but trouble. Lotto entered into possession on 12 February 1344.[12]

Petrarch refers to this experience at length, but allegorically, in *Fam.* VII 3, written on 14 January 1343, and briefly in *Fam.* V 18, written later in the same year, and in *Met.* III 27, written apparently in 1344; [13] and it is presumably to this experience that he refers in *Fam.* VII 10, written on 7 or 8 April 1348, in this passage:

> Super negotio litis nostre, nil aliud dico: res in curia vertitur. Spero fore ut illius predonis insidie detegantur; in omnes tamen casus paratus est animus: victor gaudebo, victus victa cum iustitia solabor. . . . De lite igitur sit quicquid esse potest; michi paupertas mea non molesta nec sordida, sed multis plus etiam quam vellem invidiosa, sufficiet.[14]

VII. *Castiglione Fiorentino: a Rectory*

In view of the difficulty with regard to the Pisan priorate, Clement awarded to Petrarch, by a letter of notification dated 24 August 1343, the rectory of S. Angelo in Castiglione Fiorentino. The letter contains the clause, which refers to the Pisan

---

[11] Published by De Sade, III, "Pièces justificatives," No. XXI, p. 54; by Paganini, pp. 199–200; and by Cipolla, *op. cit.*, pp. 179–180.

[12] Documents in the case are published by Paganini, pp. 200–211, and by Arnaldo Della Torre in his "Un nuovo documento su un benefizio toscano del Petrarca (il priorato di Migliarino)," in *ASI*, N.S. V, XLII (1908), 129–136. Della Torre discusses the case at length on pp. 118–128. It is discussed also by Mascetta-Caracci, pp. 126–140.

[13] See Foresti 1, pp. 142–143 and 147–151.

[14] An entry in one of the indexes (prepared by Umberto Bosco) in Rossi 1, IV, 348, implies a belief that the reference is to the contest for the Pisan priorate. There is indeed no other known experience in Petrarch's life to which it could refer. If it does refer to the Pisan contest, it affords our only indication that Petrarch continued the contest after 1344.

priorate: "pro quo adhuc litigat necdum eius possessionem nescitur assecutus." [15] This letter (preserved in the Vatican Archives), of which only the clause just quoted has been printed, is to be published by Giuseppe Billanovich in a forthcoming article.[16]

VIII. Envoy to Naples and Chaplain to Queen Joan

In September 1343 Petrarch left Provence for Naples, with missions from Cardinal Colonna and from the Pope. He remained in Naples from early October to about the middle of December.[17] On behalf of the Cardinal, he presented and urged an appeal for the release of the three Pipini brothers, who were being held in prison in Naples: reports of his unavailing efforts are contained in *Fam.* v 3 and 6. That he considered himself an envoy from the Pope is made clear by the opening lines of *Met.* ii 15, written either while he was still in Naples or shortly afterward:

> Nuper ab aetherii, qui temperat astra, Tonantis
> Missus habente vices, dulcem claramque revisi
> Parthenopem.[18]

In *Fam.* v 3, which contains a black picture of conditions in Naples, he urges the Cardinal to inform the Pope "de singulis, que aliis secretioribus ad te literis latius scripsi."

On 26 November Queen Joan appointed Petrarch to a chaplaincy, as her grandfather had done two years before. The appointing document,[19] after referring to that previous appointment, continues with language almost identical with that of King Robert's document quoted above. Petrarch, however, is

---

[15] See a note by Pietro Fedele in his review of Burdach–Piur, in *GSLI*, lxiv (1916), 397, n. 4.

[16] See Billanovich, p. 274. For his forthcoming article, "Documenti di curia per la biografia del Petrarca," see his Preface, p. xiii. It is to Professor Billanovich that I owe the reference to Fedele's mention of this benefice.

[17] See Guido Persico, "Il Petrarca a Napoli," in *Napoli nobilissima*, xiii (1904), 113–120, and Léonard 1, i, 311–323.

[18] Rossetti, iii, 162.

[19] Published by Tomasini, pp. 78–79. Republished by De Sade, No. xvii, p. 49.

now referred to specifically as "Capellanus." This chaplaincy
can hardly have been more than honorary.

IX. *Parma: a Canonry*

In 1346 Pietro Marini, canon and archdeacon of the cathedral
of Parma, died; and Petrarch (who now owned a house in Parma,
but was in Provence at the time) petitioned the Pope for the
canonry and the archdeaconate.[20] It was presumably while his
petition was pending that he wrote from Vaucluse to his friend
"Laelius" (Angelo or Lello di Pietro Stefano dei Tosetti)—who
was also in the service of Cardinal Colonna and was then in
Avignon—a letter, *Fam.* III 20, which contains these passages:

> queso ne pigeat apud comunem dominum pro felici rerum me-
> arum exitu intercedere; voco autem quemlibet felicem, modo aliquis
> sit . . .

> hanc ipse michi legem statui: altiora me non querere, paria vero
> pauca quidem et modeste, quo scilicet et obtentis sobrie gaudeam et
> amissa feram fortiter et repulse dolore non torquear. . . . Quam-
> obrem per omnes te celicolas, frater, oro ab hac quamprimum
> perplexitate dissolvi; auferte michi expectationem; quicquid erit,
> equanimiter feram.

It seems altogether probable that the matter with regard to which
he was asking Laelius to prod the Cardinal was this matter of the
double Parmese appointment.[21]

---

[20] On Petrarch's canonry and his (later) archdeaconate in Parma,
see Soncino, *op. cit.* in n. 2; Rizzi 1: see index, s. vv. "canonico" and
"arcidiacono"; and Cipolla, "Note petrarchesche desunte dall'Archivio
Vaticano," in the *Memorie* of the Turin Academy, Ser. II, LIX (1909),
Scienze morali, storiche e filologiche, 27–32.

[21] Book III ends with four letters, 19–22, all addressed to Laelius, and
all written from Vaucluse. Nos. 19 and 20 bear no dates; 21 is dated
26 April; and 22 is dated 29 April. The dates of 19 and 20 have never
been discussed. Fracassetti 2 assigns 21 and 22 to 1347; but Tatham, II,
378, n. 4, is clearly right in assigning them to 1346: on 18 January 1347
Laelius was about to leave Avignon for Naples; and it is very unlikely
that he could have fulfilled his mission there and been back in Avignon
by April. The location of 19 and 20 just before 21 and 22 creates a
strong presumption that they were written about the same time (Rizzi 1,
p. 249, n. 133, so assumes, but he follows Fracassetti as to the year of
21 and 22). The perfect appropriateness of 20 to a time when the Pope's
decision on Petrarch's petition for the double Parmese appointment was
delayed serves to confirm the probability that all four letters are of 1346.

On 29 October Clement approved a memorandum that begins thus: "Motu proprio providemus Francisco Petracho clerico florentino de canonicatu et prebenda et archidiaconatu Parmensis ecclesie. . . ." Clement's approval was limited, however, to appointment to the canonry and the prebend: the endorsement reads "Fiat de canonicatu et prebenda." On the same day Clement sent to Petrarch a letter of notification (LAP 13) addressed "Dilecto filio Francisco Petraccho, canonico Parmensi" and beginning with the words "Litterarum scientia ac morum honestas"; and sent a corresponding commissioning letter to the Archbishop of Ravenna and the Abbots of S. Benedetto Polirone and S. Maria di Valserena.[22] The archdeaconate was given to Dino da Urbino, chaplain to the Pope and papal auditor, evidently—in view of the offers referred to in Section XI—not because of any dissatisfaction with Petrarch on Clement's part, but presumably because of prior commitment to Dino. The prebend assigned to Petrarch was that of Coloreto, which had previously been assigned to the archdeaconate.[23]

On his return to Parma in December 1347 Petrarch took personal possession of his canonry. His attention to its duties is mentioned thus, in passing, in *Met.* II 18, addressed to Guglielmo da Pastrengo:

> Nunc ubi sim? Parmae. Quae sit mea tota diaeta?
> Hortulus, aut templum, nisi me nemus extrahat urbe.[24]

X. *Proposed Retirement to Montrieux?*

Early in 1347 Petrarch spent a day and a night in the Carthusian monastery of Montrieux, where his brother Gherardo had been living as a monk for several years. Petrarch was very deeply impressed by the serene piety of the life at Montrieux, as he states in the Preface of the *De otio religiosorum*, which he wrote at Vaucluse soon after his return.

---

[22] The three documents regarding the canonry are published by Cipolla, "Note petrarchesche," pp. 28–29. The letter of notification had been published by Ireneo Affò in his *Memorie degli scrittori e letterati parmigiani,* II (Parma, 1789), xxix–xxx.

[23] Soncino, pp. 153–154.

[24] Rossetti, II, 184.

In the spring or summer he presented to the Pope a petition containing five items, of which only the first two bear on his own career. These items, in which—especially in the second—traces of his own wording remain, are as follows, the passage here italicized being cancelled, but legible, in the Register:[25]

Supplicat S. V. devotus et humilis servus vester Franciscus Petracchus de Florentia, quatenus sibi in altero beneficiorum suorum *non mutato ac prioris loci ipsius obtenta licentia ad quem ordinem, precipue propter germanum suum in eo professum vehementer afficitur* residendo, beneficiorum suorum omnium, que nunc habet vel habebit in posterum, fructus, honores, redditus ac proventus . . . perinde percipiat ac si in eis et quolibet eorundem residentiam faceret personalem, concedere dignemini. . . .

Item quod similem sibi per omnia gratiam facientes in personam Ludovici Sanctus . . . precarissimi socij et confamiliaris sui in domo domini Cardinalis et qui semper sibi extitit loco fratris et secum usque ad mortem inseparabiliter esse cupit, sed id neutri eorum potest contingere sine huiusmodi gratia et vestre clementie largitate.

On 9 September 1347 Clement approved this petition, with the endorsement "Fiat ad biennium."

The meaning of the two items quoted and of the cancelled passage in particular is obscure. The cancellation must have been made before the petition was approved, but as it stands in the Register, the cancelled passage is unintelligible. Three things, however, are clear: (a) that Petrarch desired for himself and for his Socrates permission to receive income from benefices in which they did not reside; (b) that the cancelled passage refers to Montrieux and to Gherardo; and (c) that Petrarch was trying to effect an arrangement by which he and Socrates could live together.

Berlière interprets the two items as meaning that Petrarch, already planning to return to Italy, wanted to take Socrates with

---

[25] Published by Berlière in his *Un ami de Pétrarque, Louis Sanctus de Beeringen* (Rome, 1905), pp. 40–41, and discussed on pp. 14–15 and p. 40, n. 1. Published independently and discussed by Cipolla, "Note petrarchesche," pp. 23–25. I quote from Cipolla. The three other items of the petition, all of them approved, are requests for legitimation of Barriano da Correggio and of Petrarch's son Giovanni, and a request that a benefice be granted to Filippo di Benvegna da Verona.

him, and to have Gherardo assigned to another Carthusian monastery. One does not see why papal permission for Socrates to go to Italy should have been necessary; and the idea that the Pope should order the transfer of a Carthusian monk from one monastery to another would seem to be untenable. The petition had presumably been presented long before the date on which it was approved; and there is no evidence that Petrarch had determined long before that date to return to Italy. Cipolla, studying the matter in much more detail, suggests a very different explanation, which, however, involves the asking of questions that cannot be answered with assurance:

Francesco Petrarca chiede di poter godere di tutti i benefici ecclesiastici, risiedendo in un solo di essi, col permesso del priore del convento al quale era stretto da vivo affetto, perchè vi aveva fatto professione il fratello. Aveva dunque egli un beneficio a Montrieux? E col beneplacito del priore monastico, voleva messer Francesco fermarsi colà, per stare vicino a Gerardo? . . . Viene quindi facile il dubbio che, attratto dall'amor del fratello, dalla sacra pace del sito, volesse egli stabilirsi colà o nei dintorni, e intendesse di condurre seco il suo Socrate. . . . Uniti essi avrebbero passato serenamente la vita.

I am inclined to think that Cipolla is right in his inference that Petrarch desired to settle, with Socrates, at Montrieux, in some special kind of quasi-monastic retirement. I see no evidence that a benefice at Montrieux was involved. These, however, are merely opinions. In any case, Petrarch had decided, by November, to return to Italy.

XI. Papal Offers Declined

On 25 November 1347 Petrarch wrote "ex itinere" to Socrates a letter, *Fam.* VII 6, which is, in its entirety, of major importance for the understanding of his attitude toward high ecclesiastical office: he disclaims any ambition for such office, states his unwillingness to accept such office, and closes with a statement which implies that Clement, while making him an offer or offers that he could not accept, had refused him a small favor for which he had asked. Particularly noteworthy are these passages:

. . . magne fortune appetens numquam fui. . . .

. . . omnis enim michi altitudo suspecta est, et precipitii admonet omnis ascensus. . . .

si optata michi mediocritas . . . ut pridem promittebatur, obvenerit, est quod grata intentione suscipiam, et perliberaliter mecum agi dicam; sin invisum illud et grave maioris officii honus imponitur, renuo, excutio. Pauper esse malim quam solicitus, quamvis, ut res eunt . . . pauper esse non possim. . . . non est vera liberalitas dura, non lenta, non difficilis; nichil respicit nisi quem complexa est; illi morigera est. Non iubet illa sed obsequitur, et implet vota, non limitat; scimus ergo quia petenti modicum immensa porrigere, species est negandi.

Passages in *Fam.* IX 5 and *Var.* 15 make it clear that Clement repeatedly offered him a bishopric, which he refused. *Fam.* IX 5, written on 28 December 1351 to Ugolino dei Rossi, Bishop of Parma, disclaiming jealousy of Ugolino's office, contains, in sections 29 and 35, these passages:

Si status tui desiderio tangerer, quid nunc possem nescio, sed sepe per hos annos potui non modo tue parem sed opulentiorem sedem scandere, quem ascensum semper non dicam sprevi sed exhorrui et . . . splendide servituti libertatem humilem pretuli. Quod ipsum forsitan siluissem, nisi superesset adhuc qui me illa sede dignum credidit, neve ipse me indignum crederem clementissime deprecatus est, non rogare solitus sed rogari ab ipsis etiam regibus affusis similiterque supplicibus. . . .

Postea vero, neglectis maioribus que ultro sepe michi obtulit superna largitas, archidyaconus tuus esse volui.

Var. 15, written in 1371 to Francesco Bruni, contains, in a passage relating to Clement VI, the clause: "Cum enim sui gratia . . . me saepe, licet indignum, Episcopum facere voluisset." The phrase "per hos annos" and the repeated "sepe" of *Fam.* IX 5, and the "saepe" of *Var.* 15, taken in connection with the general references in *Fam.* VII 6 and with the fact that Petrarch had been back in Provence only six months when he wrote *Fam.* IX 5, serve to indicate that at least one offer of a bishopric had been made to Petrarch before his departure from Provence in 1347. The "sepe" and the "saepe" serve also to indicate that Clement renewed the offer after Petrarch's return to Provence in 1351.

Passages in *Fam.* XIII 5 and XX 14, *Sen.* I 2, 3, and 4, and

Var. 15, taken together, show that Clement offered Petrarch an apostolic secretaryship in 1347, that on his refusal it was given to Francesco Calvo, that Clement again offered him an apostolic secretaryship in 1351, that Innocent VI made the same offer to Petrarch on Calvo's death in 1359, that on his refusal it was given to Zanobi da Strada, and that on Zanobi's death two years later Innocent again offered it to Petrarch, who again declined.

One of the opening paragraphs of Book I—written originally as a letter early in 1352—of the *Invective contra medicum* contains this reference to offers made by Clement: "Percontare ipsum illum de quo loquimur [*i.e.*, Clement], et dicet tibi sepe ultro se michi obtulisse quantum tu optare, licet sic importúnissimus, non auderes, meque propter amorem libertatis, quod tibi inexpertum et incognitum bonum est, omnia recusasse."

The last words of *Fam.* VII 6, quoted above, are "scimus ergo quia petenti modicum immensa porrigere, species est negandi." What was the "modicum" for which Petrarch had petitioned? At the time when he wrote this letter his only unsatisfied petition, as far as we know, was that for the archdeaconate of Parma: he might well have termed the archdeaconate "modicum" in comparison to offers of a bishopric or an apostolic secretaryship. It is then probably to this denied request that he refers in *Fam.* VII 6— either to the original request or to a subsequent and unrecorded request, perhaps oral, for the reversion of the archdeaconate when next it should become vacant. It is, however, not impossible that the reference is to a request for a reopening of the case of the Pisan priorate, or to a request for the removal of the limitation "ad biennium" of Clement's approval of the petition discussed in the previous Section, or to some other request as to which we have no knowledge.

XII. Papal Envoy to Verona

In November 1347 Clement VI was greatly troubled by the intention of King Louis of Hungary to invade the Kingdom of Naples, and was doing his best to stir up opposition to Louis among Italian rulers. Knowing that Petrarch was planning to return to Italy, and knowing apparently that he was intending to go to Verona, Clement entrusted him with a special message to Mastino della Scala, lord of Verona, and wrote on 13 November a letter addressed to Mastino establishing Petrarch's status as papal envoy. The letter ends thus: ". . . rogamus, quatenus . . . ea que dilectus filius magister Franciscus Petrachi, clericus florentinus, tibi pro parte nostra retulerit, fidem cum grate prosecutionis effectu adhibere procures." Before Petrarch could reach Verona, however, Louis had passed through that city, where he had been received with high honor, had been assured of Mastino's approval of his enterprise, and had been given a troop of 300 Veronese horsemen. Any attempt on Petrarch's part to carry out his mission would, therefore, have been utterly futile.[26]

XIII. Parma: the Archdeaconate

At some time after the appointment of Dino da Urbino to the archdeaconate of Parma, it became probable that he would for some reason give up his office. The course of events, as I reconstruct it on the basis of the obscure document of 23 August 1348, presently to be quoted, seems to have been as follows. When it became probable that the archdeaconate would become vacant, Petrarch, with the support of Cardinal Colonna (who died on 3 July 1348), petitioned for the appointment, and received some sort of reply indicating that the appointment would be given to him when the archdeaconate should actually become vacant. Then Dino died; and Petrarch (then in or near Parma) sent Clement a new petition. The corresponding formalized petition,[27] which retains some traces of Petrarch's wording, reads thus:

Supplicat S. V. devota creatura vestra Franciscus Petracchus quod eadem Vestra Sanctitas de archidiaconatu ecclesie Parmensis, qui tunc vacare sperabatur in brevi per consecracionis munus suscipiendum

---

[26] On this episode see Cipolla, "Sui motivi del ritorno di Francesco Petrarca in Italia nel 1347," in *GSLI*, XLVII (1906), 253–265. The letter exists in two forms, written on the same day, printed by Cipolla on pp. 256–257. My quotation is from the earlier form. The later and longer form is more explicit as to Clement's desires: the reference to Petrarch reappears without variation.

[27] Published by Cipolla, "Note petrarchesche," 30.

per dominum Dynum de Urbino . . . aut alio quovis modo eidem Francisco ad bo. me. domini Johannis de Columpna quondam Sancti Angeli diaconi cardinalis instanciam generose providit prout in supplicatione annexa presenti cedula continetur. Verum quia idem dominus Dynus antequam munus prefatum susciperet . . . viam est universe carnis ingressus et archidiaconatus predictus . . . vacare noscitur in presenti, supplicat idem Franciscus quatenus eidem motu proprio eundem archidiaconatum sic vacantem, cum omnibus iuribus et pertinentijs suis, conferre dignemini. . . .

On 23 August 1348 Clement approved this petition, with the endorsement "Fiat motu proprio." No corresponding letter of notification or commissioning letter is known to exist.

Affò refers to the archdeaconate as "un assai pingue Benefizio," and quotes this item from a document of 1302: "Ecclesiae autem Archidiaconatus sunt istae: In Civitate, Ecclesia Sancti Gervasii; extra Civitatem, Plebes de Cuxiliano cum Capellis suis, Ecclesia de Vixilliano, Ecclesia de Vicofertulis, Ecclesia de Vicomandulis." [28] A document of 1354 has this entry with regard to the yield of the archdeaconate and the prebend together: "Archidiaconatus cum Canonicatu sibi unito in Ecclesia Parmensi, cujus Canonicatus Praebenda sita est principaliter in terra de Coloreto lib. triginta octo, sold. tredecim, denar. quatuor imperial. L. 370." [29] The archdeacon had also a house, which, however, Petrarch, preferring to live in his own house, did not occupy.[30]

There exists one document that records an action taken by Petrarch as archdeacon. Early in 1351, while Petrarch was living temporarily in Padua, there fell vacant a benefice in Parma to which he had the right of presentation; and he authorized two clerics in Parma to carry through the appointment of one Giacomo degli Amadei. The document [31] was notarized on 9 April in Padua "in vicinia majoris Ecclesie in domo habitationis dicti domini Francisci Archidiaconi."

Petrarch's appointment as archdeacon brought him into con-

---

[28] *Vol. cit.*, pp. xxvii–xxviii.

[29] G. M. Allodi, *Serie cronologica de' vescovi di Parma*, I (Parma, 1856), 193, n. 1.

[30] See Rizzi 1, pp. 491–492, and *Per la casa parmense del Petrarca: Lettera aperta al Prof. O. Masnovo* (Parma, 1936).

[31] Published by Affò, *vol. cit.*, pp. xxxix–xli.

tact and into conflict with Ugolino dei Rossi, who had been bishop of Parma since 1323.[32] In a long letter written in May 1349 to Luca Cristiani, proposing that Luca and two other friends come to Parma and make their home with him (in the archdeacon's house), Petrarch writes, in a portion of the letter in which he is speaking of the persons whom they might meet in Parma:

> Neque nunc de dominis loquor, quorum benivolentia sperari potest, conversatio non potest. Obstat enim mutuo convictui disparitas fortunarum; alioquin aliquos dinumerem, atque in primis dominum epyscopum, de quo utinam aliquando videamus quot quotidie videor videre, quod et valde possibile est, Deo simul et glorie ipsius et quieti nostre misericorditer providente.[33]

A few years later, when Petrarch was gathering his letters into the collection of the *Epistolae familiares,* he broke this long letter into four separate letters, *Fam.* viii 2–5. The passage just quoted reappears in *Fam.* viii 4: the first part of it, from "Neque" through "fortunarum" remains virtually unchanged; but the rest is replaced by the words "et amicitiarum virus, insolentia, dum vilescere metuentes adorari expetunt, non amari."

The rift grew more serious as time passed. Late in 1351, when Petrarch was in Avignon, word came to him that the Bishop had been led to believe that he, Petrarch, had come to Avignon with the intention of harming the Bishop, about whom he was preparing to spread calumnies. Against this charge Petrarch defended himself in *Fam.* ix 5, written on 28 December. In the course of the year 1352, however, Petrarch felt it necessary to petition Clement for aid against the Bishop; and on 15 September Clement sent to Petrarch an extraordinary letter (LAP 14), addressed "dilecto filio Francisco Petracho archidiacono ecclesie Parmensis" and beginning with the words "Literarum sciencia tuorumque grandium excellentia meritorum," in which he decrees that in order that "plena tranquillitas" may ensue to Petrarch, both he [Petrarch] and the archdeaconate

---

[32] On Petrarch's relations with Ugolino see Soncino, pp. 157–168, and Rizzi 1, pp. 475–481.
[33] Rossi, ii, 196.

shall be exempt, immune, and free "ab omni iurisdicione dominio ac ordinaria potestate episcopi Parmensis, qui est et erit pro tempore, ac metropolitani ipsius." On the same day, Clement sent a corresponding commissioning letter to the Bishop of Verona, the abbot of the Monastery of San Giovanni, and the archdeacon of the cathedral of Genoa.[34] There is no evidence to indicate that the breach was ever healed.

Petrarch's last word on his archdeaconate is found in his Will. If he should die in Parma, he says, he wishes to be buried in the cathedral, "ubi per multos annos archidiaconus fui inutilis et semper fere absens."[35]

XIV. Padua: a Canonry

In the long letter to Luca Cristiani referred to in the previous Section—a letter written in May 1349—Petrarch gives this account of his receipt of a canonry in Padua (the "spiritus generosus" is Jacopo da Carrara, lord of Padua):

Siquidem generosus ille spiritus et artificiosissime liberalis, mores meos atque animum solicite contemplatus, ut me ad trahendum interdum Padue moram honorificis quibusdam, ut ita dixerim, compedibus alligaret, iuvenem quendam canonicum paduanum sanguine sibi coniunctum ad resignandam prebendam suam, quedam sibi maiora pollicitus, induxit; et ita per manus domini Legati, assistente epyscopo paduano et grande michi nimis atque humeris meis utinam tolerabile testimonium perhibente, prebendam ipsam Padue per viam permutationis obtinui, cumque ingenti totius ecclesie letitia possessionem eius sum pacificam consecutus die sabati post Pascha.[36]

This passage does not appear in any one of the four letters into which the long original letter was eventually broken up.

The first form of a letter written to Socrates on 20 June 1349 contains this passage, in which Petrarch, deploring his absence from Parma earlier in the year, seems to be referring to the gift

[34] These two documents are published by Cipolla, "Note petrarchesche," 31–32.

[35] The Will is printed in Fracassetti 1, pp. 537–544.

[36] Rossi 1, II, 194–195. Easter fell, in 1349, on 12 April: it was therefore on 18 April that Petrarch took possession of this canonry. The Legate was Cardinal Gui de Boulogne. The Bishop of Padua was Ildebrandino Conti.

of the Paduan canonry: "illud impie molita est [i.e., *fortuna*], ut qui iam recurso anni spatio pedem Parma non moveram, nunc abessem sub obtentu magni nescio cuius boni." [37] This passage does not appear in the final form of the letter (*Fam.* VIII 7–9).

This Paduan benefice was well endowed. A papal letter of 1390, regarding the award of the same benefice, in that year, to Antonio Loschi, speaks thus of the canonry and its prebend: "Canonicatum et Praebendam praedictos, quorum fructus, redditus et proventus ducentorum et sexaginta ducatorum auri, secundum communem extimationem, valorem annuum, ut asseritur, non excedunt." [38]

When in residence in Padua Petrarch occupied a house, owned by the cathedral, in the cathedral close: it was in such a house that the document of 9 April 1351, referred to in Section XIII, was executed.[39]

In June 1351, when Petrarch was leaving Italy for Provence, he appointed Corradino Corradi to act in his absence as his procurator to receive the income from his Paduan canonry, and to act for him in other matters as well. The document [40] begins thus:

Item eodem millesimo, indictione et die xxv iunii, reverendus vir dominus Franciscus Petraccus, canonicus paduanus etc., fecit, constituit et ordinavit suum certum nuncium, actorem, procuratorem et negotiorum gestorem, legiptimum defensorem Corradinum Corradi de Vuratislavia, absentem tamquam presentem ad omnes caussas, lites et questiones quas habet vel habiturus est cum quibuscumque personis et coram quocumque iudice et officiali ecclesiastico vel seculari, ordinario vel delegato, tam ad agendum quam ad defendendum.

---

[37] Rossi 1, II, 204.

[38] Published by Antonio Medin, in his "Il successore del Petrarca nel canonicato di Padova," in *Padova in onore di Francesco Petrarca* (Padua, 1904), II (*Miscellanea di studi critici e ricerche erudite*), 50. F. S. Dondi dall'Orologio states, in his *Serie cronologico-istorica dei canonici di Padova* (Padua, 1805), p. 149, that this prebend was the one known "sotto il titolo di S. Giacomo."

[39] See Andrea Gloria, *Documenti inediti intorno al Petrarca, con alcuni cenni della casa di lui in Arquà e della reggia dei Da Carrara in Padova* (Padua, 1878), pp. 16–18; and Antonio Zardo, *Il Petrarca e i Carraresi* (Milan, 1887), pp. 70–74.

[40] Published by Livi, pp. 298–299. The "eodem millesimo" refers to the year 1351. On the date of this document see below, pp. 87–89.

On his return to Padua late in 1358, Petrarch approved formally, in a document of 24 December—signed in the palace of Francesco da Carrara, then the lord of Padua—the administration of the income of his canonry by two successive procurators, Aldrighetto di Olmo and Jacopo di Villarazzo.[41]

On 31 May 1364 the chapter of the canons of the cathedral, at a meeting held in the sacristy of the cathedral, at which Petrarch was present, invested the heirs of Niccolò da Torre with a tithed leasehold of property owned by the cathedral.[42]

His relations with the cathedral of Padua remained happy to the end of his life. To the cathedral, "unde percepi et commoda et honores," he leaves by his Will 200 gold ducats "ad emendum aliquantulum terrae . . . de cuius proventibus perpetuum anniversarium animae meae fiat"; and he provides that his great Breviary, bought in Venice for a hundred pounds, shall go ultimately to the cathedral sacristy, "ad obsequium perpetuum presbyterorum, ut . . . orent . . . pro me."

XV. Recall to Avignon

From *Fam.* XIII 5, written to Nelli on 9 August 1352, we learn that Petrarch (presumably in Padua, and presumably in the winter of 1350–1351 or early in the spring of 1351) received from two friendly cardinals, writing with the approval of the Pope, an urgent request that he return to Avignon, for a purpose not stated. Petrarch, feeling that he could not refuse this request, returned to Provence in the early summer of 1351, to find that he had been recalled in order that he might be prevailed upon to accept appointment as an apostolic secretary. His account of the pressures brought to bear upon him and of his final success in avoiding the appointment constitutes, in the words with which the letter opens, "Flebilem ridiculamque rem." His interview with Clement regarding the appointment is reported thus: "Veneram interea ad illius pedes qui digito celum pandit et temperat

---

[41] This document is published and discussed by Gloria, pp. 11 and 27, and discussed by Zardo, pp. 59–60.

[42] The document recording this meeting is published and discussed by Gloria, pp. 15 and 28–29, and discussed by Zardo, p. 70.

astra galero; is equidem adventu meo letari visus, multa dixit quibus satis apparet non libertati mee illum sed opinioni omnium favere."

It is apparently to this same interview, or to some other interview held soon afterward, that Petrarch refers in *Var.* 15, in a vivid passage that will be quoted below, on p. 72.

It was at this time, if ever, that the idea that he might be made a cardinal was active in Petrarch's mind. A detailed study of this difficult and interesting question will be undertaken in Chapter IV.

XVI. *Canonries Resigned*

In *Fam.* xiv 4, written on 19 October 1352 to Luca da Piacenza, Petrarch writes as follows, in Section 24, in the course of a refutation of a charge of avarice brought against him by his enemies:

> Nosti quidem equis fere portionibus quadripartitam michi ab olim hereditatem ecclesiasticam contigisse, quando ut hinc vivamus sors nostra est, et seu parentum seu nostris auspiciis a primis annis id vite genus elegimus. Huius igitur hereditatis duas partes michi suffecturas ratus, duas reliquas inter duos veteres et benemeritos amicos ita partitus sum, ut cum usque ad hoc tempus ambobus ditior fuerim, nunc me ditior sit uterque. . . .

To this same resignation Petrarch refers, long afterward, in *Sen.* iii 7 and xi 17. In iii 7, written to Neri Morando on 25 April 1363, he says that Urban V, on the basis of a report of his [Petrarch's] death, had assigned to insistent applicants not only a benefice that he had been intending to give to Petrarch (as will appear in Section XX), but also "reliqua que dudum teneo insuper: & que ante decennium hoc quibusdam amicis tunc egentibus nunc defunctis cesseram." In xi 17, written to Urban on 8 May 1370, he says, referring to the same incident, that the applicants "Petierunt autem non hec duo tantum que tunc temporis habebam queue nunc habeo sed illa quoque que ante longum tempus amicis egentibus sponte concesseram."

The four benefices referred to in *Fam.* xiv 4 were clearly those of Lombez, Pisa, Parma, and Padua. He held the Lombez canonry, as will appear in Section XVIII, until 1355, when he exchanged it for a "ruralem ecclesiam" previously held by Socrates. On 1 September 1352 he had appointed a procurator for the receipt of income from the Pisan canonry; but he may of course have resigned it within the next month and a half: he had certainly resigned it before 4 March 1355, since the papal document relating to his exchange of benefices with Socrates refers to his tenure of a canonry and the archdeaconate in Parma and a canonry in Padua, and does not mention the Pisan canonry, as it certainly would have done if he had still held it. It would seem that by 19 October 1352 he had decided to cede or exchange the Lombez and Pisan canonries to the advantage of two of his friends, and that sooner or later he carried out his intentions. It may be noted that the income from the rural church was presumably less than that of the Lombez canonry; also, in connection with the last words quoted from *Sen.* III 7, that Socrates died in 1361.

XVII. *Modena: Another Canonry Resigned*

After the sentence quoted in part at the beginning of Section XVI, *Fam.* XIV 4 continues: "Accesserat hereditatis huiusce de qua loquor quinta quedam particula, reliquis quidem impar, sed que locorum vicinitate tibi convenientior visa sit. Hanc nuper oblatam michi eripiens, tibi dedi; itaque per hunc ipsum nuntium apostolicas literas recipies, in quibus te Mutinensem canonicum factum leges." As to this canonry we have no other information.

XVIII. *The Church of S. Maria de Capellis*

In a petition [43] approved on 4 March 1355 Petrarch and Socrates request an exchange of benefices, Petrarch yielding to Socrates his canonry at Lombez and receiving in its stead the rural church of S. Maria de Capellis in the diocese of Teano. The petition reads:

---

[43] Published by Berlière in his *Suppliques d'Innocent VI, 1352–1362* (Rome, 1911) (= *Analecta Vaticano-Belgica*, v), p. 256. This petition has not been referred to in any previous Petrarchan study.

Sanctissime pater. Cum Ludovicus Sanctus per se ecclesiam ruralem S. Marie de Capellis, Theanensis diocesis, valoris 40 florenorum
annuatim, et Franciscus Petrarcus canonicatum et prebendam ecclesie
Lomberiensis per Guidonem Septem, archidiaconum Januensem
ydoneum procuratorem suum . . . causa permutationis . . . in manibus . . . archiepiscopi Tholosani, libere resignavit, iidem supplicant
. . . quatenus Ludovico de canonicatu et prebenda, et Francisco pre-
dictis de ecclesia rurali prefatis dignemini providere; non obstante
quod idem Ludovicus canonicatum et prebendam ac cantoriam in
ecclesia S. Donatiani Brugensis . . . et Franciscus in Paduana et Parmensi ecclesiis canonicatus et prebendas ac archidiaconatum ejusdem
ecclesie Parmensis obtineant. . . .

On 20 June of the same year Innocent approved an exchange
of benefices between Socrates and one Raymond Mancipi, Socrates yielding to Mancipi the canonry at Lombez and receiving
in its stead the church of Notre Dame de Courtrai. The ap-
proving document [44] refers to the previous exchange between
Petrarch and Socrates, and repeats, with merely verbal variation,
the statement contained in the document of 4 March as to the
value of the church of S. Maria de Capellis.

XIX. Benefices Conferred by Innocent VI

Sen. i 2, written to Nelli in 1361 or early in 1362, contains
this passage: "Nouissime uerum summus Pontifex . . . me altis
uocibus ad se uocat, duobus iam nunc beneficiis collatis pluribusque si pareram oblatis." As to the two benefices here said to have
been received from Innocent we have no other information. It
may be that one of them was the canonry at Monselice, to be
referred to in Section XXI. They may have been given as a result
of the desire for some moderate benefaction expressed by Petrarch in 1361, in connection with his refusal of an apostolic
secretaryship, as indicated in *Var. 55*.

XX. Carpentras: a Canonry Lost

From *Sen.* iii 7, written on 25 April 1363, and from *Sen.* ix 2,
written to the Apostolic Secretary Francesco Bruni in 1367 or
1368, we learn that Urban V had hoped to attract Petrarch to

---

[44] Published by Berlière in his *Un ami de Pétrarque*, pp. 49–50.

his court by giving him a small benefice at Carpentras, where Petrarch had spent four of his boyhood years; that the matter had gone so far that Bruni had written to Petrarch asking how he would like to have the official letters written (the clause "ut . . . tu . . . id mihi uoti mei conscius nunciasses: querens qualiter literas executorias fieri uellem" occurs in IX 2); and that a false report of Petrarch's death was then brought to Urban, who not only made other disposition of the benefice at Carpentras, but made new assignments (which were of course invalid) of the benefices then held by Petrarch (and of those that he had resigned).

XXI. Monselice: a Canonry

The *motu proprio* of 27 April 1365, to be quoted in the next Section, shows that on that date Petrarch held a canonry at Monselice—which is only five miles from Arquà, where, in and after 1370, he was to make his home. When and by whom this canonry was awarded to Petrarch we do not know. It is apparently referred to in *Var.* 15, written at Arquà on 24 May 1371, in the sentence: "Habeo hic praebendam, quae mihi panem et vinum dat non solum ad utendum, sed etiam ad vendendum."

XXII. A Florentine Effort

In 1365 the city of Florence tried to attract Petrarch by getting the Pope to provide him with a canonry.[45] Maestro Rinaldo da Romena was to be sent on a mission to Avignon, primarily for another purpose, but the last item in the Instructions drawn up for him on 30 March reads thus:

Item, essendo in Vignone, benchè per la principale cagione non haveste a essere col papa, vogliamo il visitiate et dopo raccomandationi humilissime gli direte che la celebre fama et sufficientia del maestro Francescho Petraccho nostro cittadino con grande desiderio ci ha indocti et induce di riducerlo ad habitare in Firenze sì per

[45] On this effort see Billanovich, *Restauri boccacceschi* (Rome, 1947), pp. 170–174. This effort is referred to scornfully by Scipione Ammirato il Giovane, in Scipione Ammirato, *Istorie fiorentine con l'aggiunte di Scipione Ammirato il Giovane*, Part I (Florence, 1647), II, 650–651.

honore della nostra città et sì per riposo suo. Il quale con molta
faticha di corpo et studio scientifico per varie parti del mondo s'è
affaticato. Et perochè patrimonio non ha in Firenze nè facultà
d'acquistare, et secolarmente non si dilecta d'abitare, acciò che ri-
cepto ecclesiastico possa avere, dengni concedergli di gratia il canonicato di Firenze prima vacante, nonobstante alcuna concessione; sì che
sia preferito a ongni altro canonico expectante, et nullo il preceda,
et di questo v'informate co' periti dello stile della corte, sì che concessione sia la più larga ch'essere può.[46]

There exists also a brief Latin petition of the same tenor, dated
8 April 1365, published by Luigi Bandini in the "Vita di Francesco Petrarca" contained in his edition of the *Rime* of Petrarch.[47]

   The Pope acted favorably and promptly, conditioning his
approval, however, on Petrarch's relinquishment of his canonry
at Monselice. The following *motu proprio* was approved on
27 April:

   Motu proprio providemus Francisco Petrachi clerico florentino
de canonicatu ecclesie florentine cum reservatione prebende in ea
vacantis vel vacature. . . . Volumus autem quod quampridem dictam
prebendam fuerit assecutus, canonicatum et prebendam quos obtinet
in ecclesia Montissilicis paduane diocesis omnino dimittat. . . .[48]

But a cancelling line is drawn through this *motu proprio* as it
appears in the Register, and a marginal note reads: "Sic erat
cassum orig. + I."

   Billanovich is doubtless right both in thinking that Boccaccio
was the prime mover in this effort and in thinking that the cancellation must have been due to a refusal by Petrarch.

XXIII. *Petrarch and Gregory XI*

   Our knowledge of Petrarch's relations with Gregory XI
comes mainly from three letters written by Petrarch to Francesco Bruni (still serving as Apostolic Secretary): *Var.* 15,

---

   [46] Attilio Hortis, *Scritti inediti di Francesco Petrarca* (Trieste, 1874),
p. 308.
   [47] On p. xxxvi of the first edition (Florence, 1748; there are many reprints). A French translation of this petition appears in De Sade, III, 661–
662. The petition is to be republished by Billanovich in the forthcoming
article referred to in n. 16.
   [48] Billanovich, p. 171.

written on 24 May 1371; *Sen.* XIII 13 (Fracassetti's XIII 12), written later in 1371 or early in 1372 (the last part of this letter, as prepared for inclusion in the collection of the *Seniles*, is taken from *Var.* 15 [49]); and *Sen.* XIII 14 (Fracassetti's XIII 13), written on 28 June 1372. From these letters we learn that Gregory, not long after his election, sent to Petrarch a letter of which, and of his reply, Petrarch speaks thus in XIII 14: "que quamvis & spei magne & pollicitationis multiplicis pena (*lege* plena) esset: non me tamen ulterius perpulit quam ut ei per litteras gratias agens & penitus nihil petens totum sue permitterem sanctitati." In his reply, however, according to *Var.* 15, "in fine remisi eum ad has tuas litteras"—namely, to *Var.* 15 itself, in which Petrarch indicates his desires to Bruni, as a basis for Bruni's presentation to the Pope.

According to this letter, Petrarch was maintaining at Arquà a considerable household, and found his income hardly sufficient to satisfy his needs. He had tried often to reduce expenses, but he felt that he had to keep servants, five or six copyists (if he could get them), and at least two horses. A venerable priest also lived with him; and visitors eager for food or for conversation often arrived at dinnertime. Moreover—though Petrarch does not mention the fact in this letter—his daughter Francesca, her husband Francescuolo da Brossano, and their little daughter Eletta were living with him. It would be possible for him, he writes, to live out the rest of his life as he has been living it, but it would be increasingly difficult, since the burden seems constantly to increase while his strength decreases. He hopes and intends also to build a little oratory to the Blessed Virgin, even if he has to pledge or sell his books in order to do so.

Under the circumstances, he asks Bruni to do what he can to

---

[49] This fact seems not to have been noted. The passage taken from *Var.* 15 begins with the words "Nam si roget in hunc modum" and continues to the end of the letter. The corresponding passage in *Sen.* XIII 13 begins with the words "Quod si forte quoniam hoc in dubium venire potest" and continues to the end of the letter. The two selections quoted at the end of *Var.* 15 from the second and third of the Penitential Psalms of Petrarch are replaced, at the end of *Sen.* XIII 13, by a brief reference, which however utilizes the last words of the second selection.

ments to the same effect, stressing now his recognition of the substantial adequacy of what he already holds, now his readiness either to receive or not to receive supplements thereto, now his lack of any desire for wealth, and now his aversion to high ecclesiastical office, will be quoted in Chapter IV.

His ecclesiastical status did not prevent him from writing his "Babylonian" sonnets, certain eclogues and *Epistolae metricae* that might equally well be called Babylonian, and his *Epistolae sine nomine.*

Of the freedom secured through his ecclesiastical income Petrarch made admirable use. The high and honorable distinction he attained constituted in fact an ample return to the Church for all the support it had given him.

CHAPTER II

Petrarch's Epistola Metrica to Pietro Alighieri

I

Dante's son Pietro, to whom Petrarch's *Met.* III 7 is addressed, was born in Florence in or before 1300, and presumably spent his boyhood there. By 1315 he was sharing his father's exile. In January, 1323, and again in January, 1324, he was in Florence (perhaps on the basis of special safe-conducts). In August, 1327, he was in Bologna. In 1332 he was serving in Verona as a judge and as delegate general of the *podestà*. His presence in Verona is attested for the years 1332–1362 by some forty documents, most of them concerned with legal or administrative activities. He appeared in Florence in July, 1341, in connection with a contest over the division of the family property—a contest that came to an end only in 1347. There is no evidence that he ever returned to Florence after 1341. He died in 1364. By one of the provisions of his will he left half the house in Florence that had been his father's to the Society of Orsammichele and to the hospital of the Misericordia. He wrote an erudite commentary, in Latin, on his father's *Commedia*, and a few poems in Italian.[1]

Petrarch and Pietro may have met as students at the University of Bologna, but there is no evidence that they did so. They must have met during Petrarch's stay in Verona in the spring

---

[1] On Pietro's life see Ginori Conti. On his commentary see Luigi Rocca, *Di alcuni commenti della Divina commedia composti nei primi vent'anni dopo la morte di Dante* (Florence, 1891), pp. 343–406; Remigio Sabbadini, *Le scoperte dei codici latini e greci ne' secoli XIV e XV*, II (Florence, 1914), 97–105; and J. P. Bowden, *An Analysis of Pietro Alighieri's Commentary on the "Divine Comedy"* (New York, 1951). On his Italian poems see his *Rime*, ed. by Giovanni Crocioni (Città di Castello, 1903).

and summer of 1345. They had much in common: both were Florentines; both were sons of men who had been banished in 1302, their property being confiscated; and both—Pietro in a minor degree—were men of letters.

II

Petrarch's *Met.* III 7 is as follows:

AD PETRUM DANTIS

Si sapientis habent aliquid phantasmata certi,
Spes mihi magna boni; longos Deus ille labores
Forsitan aetherea spectans miseratur ab arce,
Et lachrymis iam finis adest. Oh sera quietis
Tempora, grata tamen! sed, quod prior ista videres,
Fecit amor patriae, quam, quo melioribus astris
Nascimur, hoc animo colimus meliore parentem.
Et tua nunc igitur vigilantia pectora curae
Sollicitant; memoremque sopor suspendit amantem.
Tu mihi da veniam: brevior sum; dextra dolore
Segnis hebet, calamumque movens sibi fessa videtur
Nodosam versare trabem: tibi cognita causa est.[2]

The general meaning of this *epistola*, in so far as it may be stated with strict adherence to the text and with careful avoidance of any controversial interpretation, is as follows:

If there is anything reliable in the prognostications "sapientis," I have strong hope of a coming "bonum." God is perhaps taking pity on long labors, and the ending of tears is at hand. Oh "quietis tempora," belated but welcome! But that you should have beheld "ista" before I did is due to your love of "patria," which we cherish filially in proportion to the auspiciousness of the stars under which we are born. And now, in consequence, cares occupy your waking breast, and "sopor suspendit" (you), mindful and loving. Forgive my brevity: my right hand is slow and sluggish with pain, and as it wearily moves the pen it seems to be wielding a knotty beam: the cause is known to you.

The *epistola* has been discussed, with widely varying opin-

---

[2] Rossetti, III, 96. The reading "hebet" in line 11 is taken from Rossetti's note on p. 243.

ions, by De Sade, Rossetti, Crocioni, Friedersdorff, Miss Magrini, Lo Parco, Mascetta-Caracci, Tatham, Foresti, Rizzi, and Ginori Conti.[3] The one and only point on which all are in agreement is that the *epistola* is a reply to some communication received from Pietro. The "sapiens" has been identified as Petrarch, as Pietro, and as an astrologer of the Visconti; the hoped-for "bonum" as a return to Florence, as a restoration of Petrarch's Florentine patrimony, as a continuance of peace, as a Paduan canonry, and as a cardinal's hat; the labors, the tears, and the "quietis tempora" as personal and as general; the "patria" as Florence, as Verona, and as Italy; the "curae" as personal (on behalf of Petrarch) and as public; the "sopor" as sleep and as a period of calm; and the "dolor" as due to fever, as due to the failure of plans for a return to Florence, and as due to the accident suffered in Petrarch's escape from Parma in 1345. Pietro is thought to have been in Florence and to have been in Verona; and the *epistola* has been dated as of 1345, as of 1348, as of late 1348 or early 1349, and as of 1355. Of all the several discussions, however, only those of Mascetta-Caracci, Tatham, Foresti, and Rizzi have any continuing importance. The erroneous ideas of the discussions prior to that of Mascetta-Caracci have been sufficiently refuted by Mascetta-Caracci and Foresti; and Ginori Conti's discussion consists simply of a review of earlier discussions, followed by a single sentence in which he merely states that Rizzi's hypothesis seems to him "ragionevole e sensata."

---

[3] De Sade, II, 440–441 (De Sade does not discuss the *epistola* itself, but what he says serves to indicate his opinion as to the date and circumstances of its composition); Rossetti, III, 77 and 242–243; Crocioni, pp. 15–21; Franz Friedersdorff, *Franz Petrarcas Poetische Briefe* (Halle, 1903), p. 204; Magrini, pp. 133–138; Francesco Lo Parco, "Il Petrarca e Piero di Dante," in *Giornale dantesco*, XVI (1908), 205–207; Mascetta-Caracci, pp. 475–480; Tatham, II, 347–348; Foresti 1, pp. 221–225; Rizzi 1, pp. 195–201 and 245–260, and Rizzi 2, pp. 38–48; Ginori Conti, pp. 122–128. The *epistola* is mentioned in Fracassetti 2, II, 212–213. Carducci mentions it in the *Nuova antologia*, IV (1867), 471 (near the end of the second *discorso* of his essay "Della varia fortuna di Dante"), as being "breve, ansiosa, misteriosa, come una speranza di esule." Della Torre, in a review in *Bullettino della Società dantesca italiana*, XIII (1906), 41–42, merely refutes one of the arguments of Crocioni.

III

On the basis of the last three lines of the *epistola*, Mascetta-Caracci, Tatham, and Rizzi assign it to 1345; but Foresti believes it to have been written late in 1348 or early in 1349. The case for the earlier date, stated only summarily by the three scholars who have supported it, calls for a somewhat fuller statement.

On the night of 23 February 1345, Petrarch, with a few companions, made his escape from Parma, then besieged, but suffered a serious injury to his right arm: his horse fell, carrying him down, so that he was "confractus ac pene exanimatus." During most of the night he lay on the ground, "cum interea magis magisque lesi brachii tumor ac dolor ingravesceret." On the next day, "alligatus pro tempore," he reached Modena and on the following day Bologna. There, a few days later, unable either to raise his hand to his mouth or to write, he dictated an account of this experience in a letter to Barbato da Sulmona—a letter preserved as *Fam.* v 10. At the end of the letter he says:

Circa curam corporis, fit quantum humano ingenio fieri potest; spes est potius certa, quam velox. Estatis opem medici, ego Dei omnipotentis auxilium expecto; interim torpens mihi dextra non obsequitur, animus fit promptior in adversis.

From Bologna Petrarch soon went on to Verona—then first visited—and there he must have met Pietro, either for the first time or for the first time since student days. Pietro, it may be noted, appears in documents of 1333, 1337, and 1353 as associated, in some sense, with Guglielmo da Pastrengo, also a Veronese judge and a writer, whose warm friendship with Petrarch dated from 1339.[4] Before the end of the summer Petrarch returned to Parma; and late in the year, presumably passing through Verona on his way, he started for Provence.

We do not know with certainty how long Petrarch's arm continued to trouble him seriously. Such evidence as we have indicates that before he left Verona he was able, though with

---

[4] See Ginori Conti, pp. 41, 55, and 69, and Avena, pp. 237–241.

difficulty, to do some copying[5] and that when he started for Provence he was in good physical condition.[6]

There is no other known occasion in Petrarch's life when he suffered a serious injury to an arm. The correspondence of the character of the injury, as reported in *Fam.* v 10, with the manual pain and difficulty reflected in the *epistola*—the correspondence between the "torpens mihi dextra non obsequitur" of the prose letter and the "dextra dolore segnis hebet" of the *epistola* is particularly to be noted—and the fact that the *epistola* is addressed to Pietro, whom he must have met in Verona soon after his accident, suffice together to establish a virtually conclusive case for 1345 as the date of the *epistola*.

Foresti, however, argues for a later date, his argument running thus: The *epistola* to Pietro (III 7) is intimately related to an *epistola* to Guglielmo da Pastrengo (III 11); this *epistola* to Guglielmo was written in the second half of 1348; consequently, the *epistola* to Pietro must have been written about the same time.

The twelve-line *epistola* to Guglielmo begins and ends thus:

> Febribus obsideor validis, mortemque propinquam
> Suspicor. Haec inter turri vigil improbus alta
> Excubat.
>
> . . . .
>
> Singula dum premerent, celsam rationis in arcem
> Evasi; fateorque, libens haec tempora linquo.
> Hactenus hic animi status est mihi; cetera morbo
> Si requeam victus, pro me vaga fama loquetur.

---

[5] In Verona, at this time, Petrarch discovered Cicero's letters to Atticus; and either at this time or, less probably, on one of his three later visits to Verona he made a copy of those letters. To this copy he refers thus in *Fam.* xxi 10 (written in 1359): "Est michi volumen epystolarum eius ingens, quod ipse olim manu propria . . . scripsi, adversa tunc valitudine, sed corporis incommodum et laborem operis magnus amor et delectatio et habendi cupiditas vincebant."

[6] This we know from a letter written to Petrarch by Guglielmo da Pastrengo: recalling their parting, Guglielmo says that he quieted his misgivings as to Petrarch's ability to stand the winter journey over the Alps by these considerations: "viget aetas, valent membra pernicia, robur adest, valitudo suffragatur." Guglielmo's letter (LAP 62) is printed by Avena, pp. 288–289.

The lines omitted are devoted exclusively to the portrayal of a city in the grip of a militant tyranny—presumably Parma, in 1348, as Foresti thinks.

Foresti's first premise, more fully stated, is that III 7 is related to III 11 "non solo per l'accenno alla debolezza della mano che scrive a fatica, in conseguenza della malattia, ma per tutto il contenuto." But III 11 contains no mention of any manual difficulty. It is quite true that a severe fever might have made writing difficult; but III 7 speaks not of mere manual weakness but of a definite "dolor" in the right hand and of a difficulty that would appear to be very great indeed. The assumptions that the fever reported in III 11 must have had the effect described in the last three lines of III 7 and that Pietro must have known that Petrarch's difficulty in writing was caused by that fever, and the preference of these assumptions to the natural connection of these lines with the accident of February, 1345, followed so soon by a visit to Pietro's Verona, seem strangely aberrant.

Again, the correspondence of the two poems "per tutto il contenuto" simply does not exist. Foresti expands his idea of such a correspondence by saying that in III 7 Petrarch "confronta la sua con la vita dell'amico, tranquilla e onorata, utilmente spesa nell' esercizio delle cariche pubbliche, tenute con amore di patria, e sospira contro il suo destino che lo forza a una vita randagia, senza un nido suo, senza tranquillità, sicché egli è ovunque un forestiero." Foresti's "confronta la sua con la vita dell'amico" is not justified by the text of III 7; and in any case there is no corresponding contrast in III 11. Neither is there anything whatsoever in the text of III 7 that justifies Foresti's "sospira ... forestiero"; nor is there any reference in III 11 to a desired change of abode. The specific elements of III 7 are a "spes magna boni," labors and tears, a promise of better times, a foresight due to love of "patria," Pietro's cares and dreams resulting from such love, and a painful hand: not one of these elements appears in III 11. The specific elements of III 11 are a fever, a prospect of death, circumstances of militant tyranny, a recourse to reason, and the prospective spread of the news of Petrarch's death, if he succumbs: not one of these elements appears in III 7. Foresti's first premise, therefore, is invalid, and with it his entire argument.[7]

We may then rest assured that the *epistola* was in fact written in 1345, after the accident suffered in Petrarch's escape from Parma and after he had met Pietro Alighieri in Verona.

IV

I shall next set forth what seems to me to be a sound interpretation of the first nine lines of the *epistola*, combining ideas of my own with ideas that have been previously advanced, and shall then comment on certain previous discussions.

The first line of the *epistola*,

> Si sapientis habent aliquid phantasmata certi,

is derived from Ovid's

> Si quid habent veri vatum presagia [*Metam.* xv 878].

Petrarch had already used this line in the *Canzoniere* in the last line of No. CI (written in 1341):

> S'anime son qua giù del ben presaghe.

The first line of the *epistola* is then general rather than specific in its reference, and the meaning is: "if there is anything valid in the fantasies [*i.e.*, the imagined fulfilments of desire] of a wise man." The "sapientis" itself appears to be generic; but, in view of the fact that the *epistola* is a reply to a communication from Pietro, one is justified in hearing in the "sapientis" a courteous overtone suggesting that Pietro himself is to be considered as a wise man.

The "bonum" for which Petrarch hopes is obviously one that will benefit him; but this does not preclude the possibility that it may be such as to benefit others also. The nature of the "bonum" is indicated only by what follows, and in the light of what follows it is clear that the "bonum" must be (1) something coming

---

[7] Foresti's argument as to the nature of the hoped-for "bonum" will be examined below, in Section V.

after long labors, (2) something that will put an end to tears, (3) something that will produce "quietis tempora," (4) something that Pietro had beheld before Petrarch did, and (5) something that Pietro had been enabled so to behold because of his love for his "patria." [8]

It would seem probable that Petrarch was thinking of the long labors as his own. The reference to them follows close upon the "mihi"; and, if he had been thinking of them as Pietro's or as shared by several persons, he would presumably have indicated the fact by the introduction of an appropriate possessive adjective.

If the long labors are Petrarch's alone, the reference would seem to be not to particular labors undertaken by him for the purpose of obtaining the "bonum" in question—we have no knowledge of any such particular labors on his part, and our knowledge of his activities is very extensive—but rather to his unremitting labors as a man of letters. He might well have felt that the extent and the character of his literary labors were such as to qualify him for the receipt of a "bonum" that was not in itself of a literary nature. The implication of the "miseratur," in this case, is not that his labors were in themselves pitiable but simply that God might feel that the time had come when they deserved the "bonum" in question.

If the long labors are not Petrarch's alone, they must have been either Pietro's alone or else labors undertaken by a group of persons, including Pietro—who otherwise would hardly have been in a position to foresee their approaching outcome. They cannot have been shared by Petrarch and Pietro alone: there is no evidence that the acquaintance of the two men had begun before 1345 or that they ever shared any labors. Nor can the long labors have been labors undertaken in behalf of Petrarch

---

[8] The phrase "sub obtentu magni nescio cuius boni" occurs in the first form of the letter written by Petrarch on 20 June 1349 to Socrates (Rossi 1, II, 194–195); the phrase does not appear in the final form of that letter, *Fam.* VIII 7–9). In this case the reference is presumably to Petrarch's receipt of his Paduan canonry. In *Sen.* XII 14, written in 1372, Petrarch speaks of a letter received from the newly elected Gregory XI as being "spei magne & pollicitationis multiplicis plena."

alone: there is no reason to suppose that Pietro, with or without associates, should have carried on long labors on Petrarch's personal behalf. If, then, the labors are not Petrarch's alone, they must have been labors carried on for the benefit of a group of persons.

The fact that the "quietis tempora" had been long in coming proves that the tears must have been due to some distress that had lasted for a long time. (There was indeed nothing in Petrarch's general status in 1345 that could have furnished a serious cause for tears: he was deriving income from two canonries, one in Lombez and one in Pisa, and from a rectory in Castiglione Fiorentino; and he still enjoyed the patronage of Cardinal Colonna and of Azzo da Correggio.) The tears are linked, in the text, with the long labors, and Petrarch, accordingly, was presumably thinking of them as his own—though this does not preclude the possibility that others suffered from the same distress.

The exclamation

> Oh sera quietis
> Tempora, grata tamen!

may have reference either to prospects personal to Petrarch himself or to prospects opening before a group of persons, including Petrarch. The words in themselves naturally suggest the latter alternative, but they do not suffice to establish it.

In the clause "quod prior ista videres" the "ista" presumably refers to "tempora," but it may also be taken as a neuter collective, referring to the various elements of the general prospect; no substantial difference of meaning is involved. The "videres" in itself might mean either "seen"—that is, actually seen—or "foreseen"; but, since the whole tone of the *epistola* is one of prophetic expectation, since for Petrarch the "bonum" lies clearly in the future, and since there is no indication that Pietro has actually beheld anything that Petrarch has not yet beheld, it is clearly probable that the "videres" has the meaning "foreseen."

The general character of the prospect—and, consequently, of the hoped-for "bonum"—is first indicated in the words

> sed, quod prior ista videres,
> Fecit amor patriae,

"but that you should behold 'ista' before I did is due to your love of your 'patria.' " The prospect reported to Petrarch by Pietro had therefore something to do with Pietro's "patria." The word "patria" in itself might be either local or national in reference, might refer either to Florence or to Italy.[9] But in this instance a Florentine is writing to a Florentine, which creates a presumption that the reference is local. Moreover, Pietro's foreseeing, since it was due to love of his "patria" and preceded any such foreseeing on the part of Petrarch, must have been due to a love of his "patria" greater than Petrarch's love of that same "patria"—and it is exceedingly improbable that Petrarch could have thought or suggested that Pietro's love of Italy was greater than his own, whereas he could hardly help recognizing that Pietro's love of Florence was greater than his own.

The words

> quam, quo melioribus astris
> Nascimur, hoc animo colimus meliore parentem—

"which ('patria') we cherish filially in proportion to the favorableness of the stars under which we are born"—are apparently intended as a mild justification of the fact that Petrarch's love of Florence was less than Pietro's. Petrarch indeed had been born under the stars of exile; his parents (both now long since dead) had never returned to Florence after the beginning of their exile; Florence still held Petrarch's patrimony; and Petrarch himself, at this time, had never entered Florence.

Pietro's current preoccupations—his "curae"—are characterized thus:

> Et tua nunc igitur vigilantia pectora curae
> Sollicitant; memoremque sopor suspendit amantem.

In view of the presence of the word "vigilantia" in the first of these two clauses and the word "sopor" in the second, it is clear that "sopor" has here its first and natural sense of "sleep" and that Petrarch is contrasting Pietro's daytime preoccupations with his

---

[9] Petrarch uses the word in both senses. In *Fam.* vii 10, for instance, he refers to Florence as his "patria" (in a clause that is to be quoted below); and in *Met.* iii 24 he refers to Italy as his "patria."

corresponding dreams. The literal meaning of the second clause appears to be: "and sleep holds you in suspense, mindful and loving"—that is, "your 'curae' persist in your mind and heart, even in your sleep, although your actual activity is then in abeyance." The "nunc," emphatically placed, indicates that there is now something new about these preoccupations—a newness that can hardly be anything other than a newness in intensity: the "curae" are now so intense as to call for the use of the word "sollicitant" to indicate their insistence by day and for the assertion that they persist even at night. The intensity of Pietro's "curae" is linked with what precedes, both by the causal "igitur" and by the "amantem," which has relevance only if it resumes the idea of the "amor patriae": it is because of his "amor patriae" that his "curae" are now so insistent and persistent. And the sequence of thought requires also that the "curae" should be related, as the "amor patriae" is related, to the foreseeing by Pietro that is reflected in the opening lines of the *epistola*.

The foregoing analysis points to the conclusion that the occasion and the general implications of the *epistola* are, in all probability, as follows: Pietro, because of activities resulting from his love of Florence, believes, and has reported to Petrarch, that there is a good prospect of some Florentine action that will constitute for Petrarch (and presumably for others also) a "bonum" (which in Petrarch's case would be a recognition of his long labors), putting an end to a cause of long-continued distress and bringing in a period of quiet; and Pietro is now working harder than ever to bring this prospect to realization. If this conclusion is sound, it follows also that Pietro's activities must have been activities undertaken, presumably with others, on behalf of Florentine exiles and their heirs. Such activities would be perfectly natural on Pietro's part and would seem to Petrarch to constitute work not only for the group of exiles and their heirs but also for the general good of Florence.[10]

---

[10] That Florentine treatment of exiles was still severe and severely judged even in Florence is indicated by Giovanni Villani's discussion of the matter, under the year 1345, in his *Cronaca*, Book XII, Chap. XLIV.

For Petrarch personally the particular "bonum" in prospect, under these circumstances, would be the restoration of his confiscated patrimony, together with the removal of the bitterness resulting from the fact that Florence, far from honoring him hitherto, had left him in the status of an exile. To his treatment by Florence, Petrarch refers in *Fam.* vii 10 (written in 1348), in the words "mala, nisi fallor, et iniqua michi patrie tractatio." An actual Florentine invitation to Petrarch to settle in Florence and to receive a full restoration of his confiscated patrimony came in 1351, when he was called to lecture in the newly founded University of Florence. When that offer was made, however, Petrarch had new sources of income in Parma and in Padua; he was being urgently recalled to Avignon; and he was as reluctant as ever to incur any obligation that would interfere with his personal liberty. He acknowledged the invitation graciously (in *Fam.* xi 5), but he never accepted it—and the confiscated patrimony was never restored to him.

V

Mascetta-Caracci was the first to recognize the generic character and the classic source of the opening line of the *epistola*, the first to realize that the tears are not necessarily those of Petrarch alone and that the "quietis tempora" are presumably to be enjoyed by a considerable number of persons, and the first to recognize the relationship of the last lines to the accident suffered in the escape from Parma and to draw the conclusion that the *epistola* was written in 1345. He is wrong, however, in taking the "sapientis" to refer to Petrarch, in assuming that the "quietis tempora" have already arrived, in assuming that the "videres" means "(actually) seen" rather than "foreseen" and that it implies Pietro's presence in Florence, and in thinking that the "sopor" means "bonaccia" and that it is used with reference to a period of calm that has already arrived.

Tatham recognizes the implication that Pietro was "more favourably disposed towards Florence" than Petrarch was, connects the *epistola* with the accident suffered in 1345, and approaches my own conclusion in this sentence: "The natural meaning of this would be that Pietro had been telling our poet that Florence would welcome him back with open arms—perhaps restore to him his confiscated patrimony—if he would make some advance to the ruling party there." Tatham is wrong, however, in taking the tears to be those of Petrarch alone and in thinking the *epistola* to have been written in Bologna, before Petrarch had actually made Pietro's acquaintance.

Foresti's refutation of erroneous ideas advanced by De Sade, Crocioni, and Miss Magrini is thorough; but his own positive argumentation is very weak—a rare occurrence in the admirable and indispensable series of his Petrarchan studies. His primary argument, which concerns the date of the *epistola*, has been refuted above, in Section III. Assuming the validity of that argument, Foresti constructs this secondary argument: since *Met.* III 11 (with which Foresti wrongly considers III 7 to have been intimately associated) was written in the second half of 1348, the hoped-for "bonum" must have been one that came to Petrarch soon thereafter; the only known "bonum" that came to Petrarch soon thereafter was Jacopo da Carrara's gift of a Paduan canonry; the hoped-for "bonum" was therefore the receipt of that canonry. But even if Foresti's primary argument had been valid, this secondary argument would have been invalid. Its first premise is in itself invalid: hope is not always realized. Given the actual content of the *epistola* to Pietro, Foresti's secondary argument could in any case be valid only upon the exceedingly improbable assumption that, because of his love for his "patria" (wrongly assumed to be Italy rather than Florence), Pietro, a judge in Verona, foresaw, before Petrarch did, that Petrarch was to receive an ecclesiastical award in Padua; also, upon the equally improbable assumption that Petrarch would think that this award would put an end to a long-continued distress and usher in belated "quietis tempora" for him. As Rizzi points out, since Petrarch by 1348 held not only canonries in Lombez and Pisa but also a canonry and the archdeaconate in Parma, the prospect of the receipt of an additional canonry could hardly have aroused in him a hope so stirring as that manifested in this *epistola*.

Rizzi recognizes the relation of the *epistola* to the accident of

1345 and dates the poem accordingly, pointing out that it may well have been written while both Pietro and Petrarch were in Verona; [11] and Rizzi, as has just been said, points out the erroneous character of Foresti's secondary argument. But Rizzi's own positive argument, like that of Foresti, represents a weak spot in a work that as a whole is admirable and indispensable. He assumes that the tears are Petrarch's alone, that the "patria" is Italy, and that Pietro is already enjoying "quietis tempora" such as those that Petrarch still desires.

In the *epistola*, Rizzi says, Petrarch

ritorna col pensiero al suo Elicona transalpino, a Laura e al suo cardinale. . . . e dice: Dio ha guardato dall'alto i miei dolori, e le lagrime stan per finire: oh finalmente la quiete! Ma tu, o Piero, già godi questa pace, essendoti lasciato guidare dall'amor della patria: quanto più si nasce fortunati. . . . e con tanto miglior animo la veneriamo come madre (tu sei stato più fortunato di me giacchè hai potuto vivere sempre in Italia, perciò hai potuto amar la patria meglio di me). . . . Quell'accenno alla patria, e quel confronto a tal proposito fra Piero e sè. . . . si spiegano agevolmente se si pensa che il poeta, che lungamente ha vissuto in terra straniera, sta per ritornarvi.

There is, however, nothing in the *epistola* that suggests that Petrarch was contemplating a return to Provence; the assumption that, in speaking of Pietro's "patria," Petrarch was referring to Italy rather than to Florence has already been shown to be unsound; and the corollary assumption that the inferiority of Petrarch's love of Italy to Pietro's is due to Petrarch's absences from Italy is quite untenable: Petrarch himself—as in *Fam.* xi 15— speaks in general terms of absence as serving to increase love.

Taking up the question of the hoped-for "bonum," Rizzi says that it seems to him "che si possa pensare a qualche lusinghiera offerta venutagli d'oltr'Alpe. . . . Forse qualche alto posto nella corte del cardinale o anche nella curia stessa." There is, however, nothing in the *epistola* or in any other Petrarchan writing that suggests that Petrarch was at this time in receipt of "qualche lusinghiera offerta" from Provence.

---

[11] Rizzi cites two known instances in which Petrarch addressed an *epistola metrica* to a friend in the same city in which Petrarch was then staying.

Rizzi then makes use of the several arguments, drawn from sources other than the *epistola*, that are the basis of his theory (which I shall examine in Chapter IV) that Petrarch desired a cardinalate, and concludes that the "spes magna boni" of the *epistola* must have been a hope that an offer of a cardinalate was soon to be made to him. But, even if the theory that Petrarch desired a cardinalate should prove to be valid, it does not follow that the "spes magna boni" of the *epistola* is a hope that that desire was soon to be fulfilled. There is nothing to indicate that in 1345 Petrarch had the slightest reason to hope for a cardinalate. At that time he held canonries in Lombez and in Pisa, but he had no ecclesiastical position of any greater importance. In 1346 he was to petition for a canonry and the archdeaconate in Parma: he was to be given the canonry but not the archdeaconate. In 1346 or 1347, but not previously, he was to receive offers (which he declined) of a bishopric and of an apostolic secretaryship. If the idea that he might be made a cardinal was ever active in his mind, the time of that activity (as I shall show in Chapter IV) was in the period 1351–1352. Furthermore, given the text of the *epistola*, acceptance of Rizzi's theory as to the hoped-for "bonum" would involve acceptance of a combination of improbabilities very similar to that already pointed out in the case of Foresti's theory: for it would mean that, because of his love for his "patria" (wrongly assumed to be Italy), Pietro, a judge in Verona, foresaw, before Petrarch himself did, the prospect that a cardinalate was to be offered to Petrarch. It would involve also the very improbable assumption that Petrarch could have thought of a cardinalate as something that would put an end to a distress that he had suffered for a long time and as something that would bring him "quietis tempora."

No argument advanced by either Foresti or Rizzi seems to me, therefore, to impugn the validity of the conclusions as to the occasion and the meaning of the *epistola* that have been set forth above, at the end of Section IV.

CHAPTER III

Petrarch's Seventh Eclogue

The Sixth and Seventh Eclogues of Petrarch [1] are violent attacks, in terms of pastoral allegory, on the corruption of the papal court in Avignon under Clement VI. In the Sixth—written in 1347, and before November 20, when Petrarch left Provence for Italy—the interlocutors are the former shepherd Pamphilus, who represents St. Peter, and the shepherd Mitio, who represents Clement. Pamphilus reproaches Mitio vehemently for the sorry state of his flock, for his traffic in holy things, and for his shameful way of life. There are references to Mitio's paramour Epy, who represents the Avignonese papal court. Mitio's insolent defense is in effect a shameless confession. At the end, Pamphilus warns Mitio that there will yet come One who will turn his joys into mourning.

The Seventh Eclogue is a continuation of the Sixth. Entitled *Grex infectus et suffectus*, it is a bitter review of the personnel of the College of Cardinals. The interlocutors are Mitio and Epy. Mitio, after referring to the reproaches and the warning of Pamphilus, proposes that they review the flock. Epy says that it has been reduced by death and pestilence, and that, for the rest, all Mitio has to do is to look about him. Mitio, however, requests her to proceed; and in her first long speech (ll. 29–79) she characterizes twelve cardinals (goats, in the terms of the Eclogue),

---

[1] The text of *Ecl.* VII appears on pp. 127–131 of Avena's edition, which contains also three fourteenth-century commentaries: an anonymous commentary that covers only *Ecl.* I-V; the portion of the commentary of Benvenuto da Imola that covers *Ecl.* VI-XII; and the complete commentary (derived largely from that of Benvenuto) of Francesco Piendibeni da Montepulciano. It contains also a large number of anonymous early glosses. On Petrarch's Eclogues in general, see Carrara 2, pp. 87–111. On their chronology, see Carrara 3, pp. 138–153.

48

and ends by offering to give advice. Mitio asks for that advice; in her second long speech (ll. 98-128), planning to deceive Pamphilus, she proposes and characterizes twelve candidates: Mitio agrees to add them to the flock. There follows a brief discussion of one unacceptable candidate. The last lines of the Eclogue contain a reference to the possible return of Pamphilus.

I. Grex infectus

Epy's reference to the pestilence that is infecting the flock is as follows (ll. 19-26):

> Lanigerum quodcunque pecus servare solebas
> Mors rapuit, vel morbus habet; per gramina ripe
> Pascitur alterius quicquid superesse dedit fors.
> Febris iners, scabiesque tenax, violentaque tussis
> Iam vacuos populantur agros; premit horrida sudor
> Mucidus, et rigidi configunt tergora dumi.
> Tutius abfuerint, ne furtim leta pererret
> Mesta lues capita, et serpens per ovilia pestis.

The reference is clearly to the Black Death of 1348, which was to be the main theme of Petrarch's Ninth Eclogue.

Throughout the year 1347 the College of Cardinals contained 25 members (21 Frenchmen, three Italians, and one Spaniard).[2] Epy characterizes just twelve of the 25, dealing first with seven cardinals individually, then with two pairs of cardinals—all eleven being charged with one or another vice—and finally with one cardinal who is characterized less unfavorably (and with special mention of his former rivalry with a thirteenth cardinal, now deceased).

No attempt has been made hitherto to identify as many as possible of the cardinals referred to in Epy's two long speeches: nearly all of the men concerned, indeed, are characterized only in terms of vices, which are not a matter of official record.

The last two cardinals mentioned in Epy's first long speech are, however, readily identifiable. Lines 69-79 are as follows:

---

[2] Those designated by Eubel, pp. 15-18, as xxi 3, 4, 7, 12, 18 and 24-28, xxii 1, 2, 4, 5 and 7, and xxiii 1-3, 5, 7 and 9-13. On these cardinals, see Baluze, pp. 220-387.

Ille quidem, toto quem cernis ab agmine solum,
Natura generosus erat; sed, non sua tondens
Gramina, sollicito tacitus terit avia gressu.
Huic hostis generosus item, sed fractior evo,
Contigerat; mors alterius certamen utrinque
Conclusit. Non ille vadum torrentis aquosi,
Nec iuga saxosi timuisset carpere montis.
Dux gregis ille fuit, dum nostra reliquimus olim
Pascua; primus iter rapidum per lubrica flexit,
Hortatus sotios; mox cetera turba secuta est,
Unde diu letos vacui deduximus annos.

Benvenuto da Imola [3] comments thus on ll. 76–78:

et ille fuit dux civitatis romane quando nos dimissimus ytaliam et ipsam romam. iste de orsinis cardinalis flexit iter ut cardinales transirent ultra montes. mox tota curia secuta est ipsum.

Benvenuto is mistaken in equating the "ille" of l. 76 with the "Ille" of l. 69 rather than with the "hostis" of l. 72, and in his assertion that the "ille" of l. 76 "fuit dux civitatis romane": the "ille" of l. 76 is "dux gregis" (that is, the leader of the flock of cardinals), not "dux civitatis." But Benvenuto is certainly right in identifying the cardinal who "led the way over the mountains" as an Orsini. Petrarch's reference is clearly to Napoleone Orsini (1263–1342), a cardinal since 1288—the "Tu pre omnibus, Urse" of Dante's letter to the Italian cardinals—who in the conclave of 1304–1305, held in Perugia, headed the pro-French party, originated the candidacy of Bertrand de Got, brought about his election as Clement V, and was thus primarily responsible for the transfer of the papal court to France.[4]

Francesco Piendibeni [5] in his commentary on ll. 69–79 identifies the "primus" of l. 77 as "Ursinus," and the other cardinal in question as a Colonna: "Isti duo fuerunt cardinales duo de Ursinis et columnensibus." In this he is certainly right, though he confuses the two men in the rest of his commentary on the passage.

---

[3] Benvenuto's commentary on *Ecl.* vii appears on pp. 220-223 of Avena's edition.

[4] See C. A. Willemsen, *Kardinal Napoleon Orsini (1263–1342)* (= *Historische Studien*, 172) (Berlin, 1927), esp. pp. 13–24.

[5] Piendibeni's commentary on *Ecl.* vii appears on pp. 276–278 of Avena's edition.

The "Illo" of l. 69 is clearly Petrarch's own patron of many years, Cardinal Giovanni Colonna; and the characterization in ll. 69—71 clearly reflects Petrarch's feeling toward the cardinal after their break in 1347—the break that is the subject of the Eighth Eclogue, *Divortium*. In that Eclogue the Cardinal's earlier and later attitudes are contrasted thus (ll. 6–7):

> Tibi letior annis
> Tunc animus fuerat; nunc intractabilis, asper.

The Cardinal's later manner is also indicated thus (ll. 23–24):

> Adde supercilij pondus, quod non gravis equet
> Ethna iugis, non Ossa rigens, non altus Olimpus.

And his prospective loneliness is foretold thus (ll. 120–121):

> ipse meis . . .
> Te sine—quod nollem—iam solus pascar acervis.

The break accounts also for Petrarch's use of the imperfect tense "erat" with reference to the Cardinal's generous nature. As to the hostility here ascribed to the two cardinals it may be noted that while Cardinal Orsini had soon found reason to regret his action at Perugia, and had become in Avignon the recognized leader of the Italian cardinals, actual leadership of the group had passed by 1335 to Cardinal Colonna.[6] The usual rivalry of the Colonna and Orsini families may also have been involved.

No other cardinal referred to in this speech is identified by either Benvenuto or Piendibeni: two others, however, may be identified with a considerable degree of assurance, and a third with somewhat less assurance. The first of the twelve cardinals is characterized at some length (ll. 29–39) as old, but still actively vicious. An unknown glossator [7] identifies him as "cardinalis de burgundia," and speaks of him as "remotum tunc de curia." One cannot be certain as to the sense in which the glossator used the term "burgundia": but among the 25 cardinals there were only

---

[6] This was evident in the conclave that resulted in the election of Benedict XII: see G. Marchal, "Le premier conclave d'Avignon," in *Mémoires de l'Académie de Vaucluse*, 2d ser., xix (1919), 27–36, and Willemsen, p. 130.

[7] The glosses appear as footnotes on the pages referred to in n. 5.

three who, it would seem, might have been termed Burgundians, and one of these was still a young man. The other two were Pierre Bertrand, a native of Annonay, and Bertrand de Déaulx (commonly called Bertrand de Deux), a native of Uzès. There is no record of the absence of Pierre Bertrand from the Curia in 1347 or in the first half of 1348 (he died at the end of June). Bertrand de Déaulx is indeed the only cardinal for whom a long absence at this time is a matter of official record: as a papal legate for affairs in Italy he was absent from 26 August 1346 to 17 November 1348. During the first part of this time he served in Naples (which was held by the House of Anjou as a fief under papal sovereignty), seeking ineffectively to control the situation resulting from the assassination of Andrew of Hungary, the first husband of Queen Joan. In the autumn of 1347 he was transferred to Rome with instructions to dissuade Cola di Rienzo, using drastic means if necessary, from his intention of allying himself with the King of Hungary, expelling Queen Joan from Naples, and subjecting the Kingdom of Naples and the County of Provence to the Roman People. In this he failed; but when public opinion turned against Cola, Bertrand excommunicated him, fostered a rising against him, and, after his flight, restored the previous form of senatorial government. Bertrand's activities in Italy were such as to make him widely known and such as might well have stirred the wrath of many Italians, and of Petrarch in particular.[8]

The sixth of the twelve cardinals is characterized thus (ll. 61–62):

> Esurit ille rubos, fulgentibus imminet undis,
> Nec toto satianda Tago sitis arida fervet.

The reference to the Tagus suggests a Spanish cardinal: the only Spanish cardinal living in 1347 was Pedro Gomez, a native of Toledo—by which city the Tagus flows over its golden sands.

The fourth of the twelve is characterized thus (ll. 56–58):

---

[8] Baluze, pp. 316–319; Gregorovius, Book XI, Chap. III, Sect. 3, Chap. VI, Sects. 3 and 4, and Chap. VII, Sect. 1; Burdach-Piur, Part I, pp. 449 and 618; Léonard 1, *passim* (see index); and Mollat, pp. 190–191, 201, 245–246, and 283–286.

Ille, piger senio, torpet; tamen integer olim
Ludere clam solitus, virides nec spernere frondes.
Nunc iacet et celum spectat.

Benvenuto interprets the third of these lines as meaning "iacet et
expectat mortem." Since the Seventh Eclogue is so closely related to the Sixth, it is inherently probable that the Seventh was
at least begun while Petrarch was working on the Sixth, or immediately afterward: it is then inherently probable that the first
part of the Seventh was written—as was the Sixth—in 1347, and
before 20 November, when Petrarch left Provence for Italy. No
cardinal died in 1347. The only cardinal who died within the
first four months of 1348 was Elias de Nabilanis, of Périgord,
who died on 13 January.

As to the dating of the first part of the Seventh Eclogue, it is
inherently probable—as has just been said—that it was written in
1347, and before 20 November. An impassable *terminus ante
quem* is afforded by the fact that ll. 69–79 must have been written
while Petrarch knew or supposed Cardinal Giovanni Colonna to
be still living: he died on 3 July 1348, and Petrarch must have
heard of his death within a few weeks afterward. Lines 19–26,
which refer to the Black Death, can hardly have been written
before 1348, since the plague (which had appeared before the
end of 1347 in Sicily and in Marseilles) did not reach Northern
Italy until 1348. In January it appeared in Genoa and in Venice,
whence it soon spread to Padua and to Verona. In March it appeared in Florence, and in April in Siena. It seems not to have
reached Parma until June. Meanwhile, it had broken out in
Avignon in January 1348.[9] Petrarch on his return to Italy had
gone to Parma; but he was in Verona for a few days, at least, in
April. His first datable reference to the plague occurs in *Fam.*
VII 10, written in Verona on 7 or 8 April, in the words "pestis
anni huius universum orbem sed cunta presertim litora proterens
atque consumens." Petrarch's lines on the plague in the Seventh
Eclogue are general rather than specific: they may well have
been written before he had had occasion to see the effects of the

---

[9] Georg Sticker, *Abhandlungen aus der Seuchengeschichte und
Seuchenlehre*, I (Giessen, 1908), 42–74.

plague for himself. All in all, the most likely date for the writing of these lines would seem to be the Spring of 1348. If then these lines appeared in the first draft of the Eclogue, it would follow that Epy's first long speech was not written until the Spring of 1348. That is possible, despite the inherent probability, already mentioned, of an earlier date; but it would seem to be more probable that that speech was written in 1347, before Petrarch left Provence, and that ll. 19–26 are an insert—the Eclogues are known to contain other inserts.

II. Grex suffectus

Of the 25 cardinals living in 1347 seven died in 1348, one in 1349, and two in 1350, before December; and the number of cardinals was thus reduced to fifteen. At a consistory held on 17 December 1350, Clement created twelve new cardinals—nine Frenchmen, two Italians, and one Spaniard. The two Italians, both Romans, were Niccola Capocci, who had been Bishop of Urgel, and Rinaldo Orsini, who had been an apostolic notary.[10] The news of this consistory must have reached Petrarch, in Parma or in Padua, late in December 1350, or in January 1351. He must have been intensely interested, and very indignant at the continued packing of the College with Frenchmen and at the slight recognition given to Italians.

In Epy's second long speech (ll. 98–128) she proposes twelve, or almost exactly twelve, candidates: Petrarch probably counted them as twelve, but there are two points at which his numeration is uncertain.[11] The pattern of this speech is in general similar to that of Epy's first long speech: she deals at first with individuals and then with pairs, at first with persons charged with vices and then with persons not so charged, and ends, as will presently appear, with the characterization of two Italians. This speech,

---

[10] On these twelve cardinals see Eubel, pp. 18–19, and Baluze, pp. 403–420.

[11] The "ille" of l. 106 is probably, but not certainly, identical with the "ille" of l. 105. The "Mitior" of l. 109 is probably, but not certainly, identical with the "ille" of that same line. The "Hi" of l. 114 probably constitute a pair, but their number is not specified.

however, is much shorter than her first long speech, and the new characterizations are therefore in general briefer and slighter than those of the first long speech. The longest characterization, that of the final pair, is as follows (ll. 121–126):

> En quoque par longe varium; pratum ille modesto
> Dente metit, ramos patulos vorat alter hiatu,
> Teque tuumque gregem rauca qui voce fatiget,
> Meque fugare locis informi murmure possit,
> Spumeus ac frendens, tunsoque simillime urso.
> Hos tibi romulei miserunt gramina saltus.

The "urso," the "romulei," and the pairing of the two candidates suffice to identify them as Niccola Capocci and Rinaldo Orsini.[12] This identification, in turn, suffices to prove that the group characterized in this speech is the group named on 17 December 1350.

The other characterizations are too slight or too cryptic to afford tangible clues for identification.[13] It is however worth noting that one of the newly named cardinals here in question was Jean de Caraman, who was within a few years to become the target of Petrarch's fierce *Invectiva contra quendam magni status hominem sed nullius scientie aut virtutis*.[14]

At the conclusion of Epy's speech, Mitio, indicating his acceptance of all the candidates who have been reviewed, says to her (ll. 129–131):

> O pecudum decus eximium, reginaque silve,
> Perge, age, iunge greges, et cornua flore rubenti
> His quoque circumda; grex esse videbitur unus.

---

[12] The obvious identification of Orsini is made by Benvenuto, Piendibeni, and the unknown glossator. The other member of the pair is wrongly called a Colonna by Piendibeni and a Neapolitan by the glossator. Rizzi 2, p. 46, fails to realize that the person characterized in ll. 122-125 is Rinaldo Orsini and that he is accepted by Mitio, and confuses him with the rejected candidate referred to in ll. 132-137.

[13] Neither Benvenuto nor Piendibeni attempts any other identifications. The unknown glossator says that the "hic" of l. 103 was "de Burgundis" and that those mentioned in ll. 109–115 were "de Flandia": but no one of the cardinals created in 1350 seems to have come either from Burgundy or from Flanders.

[14] See Ricci, art. "Petrarca, Francesco," in *Enciclopedia cattolica*, IX (Città del Vaticano, 1952), col. 1292.

Carrara says that the consistory in question must have been the occasion for the writing of the Eclogue, and that some time must have elapsed between the consistory and the writing, so that Petrarch could have had a chance to learn of the vices of the new cardinals. In view of what has been said above as to the dating of the first part of the Eclogue, Carrara's statement cannot be regarded as valid for the Eclogue as a whole; but it is unquestionably valid for the portion of the Eclogue containing Epy's second long speech. The consistory was held on 17 December 1350 (not in September 1351, as stated by Carrara). Petrarch returned to Provence in June 1351: this speech must then have been written after that month.[15] Carrara states, with good reasons, that the Sixth Eclogue must have been written before the death of Clement VI (6 December 1352), and his reasons apply to the Seventh Eclogue as well as to the Sixth. The portion of the Seventh containing Epy's second long speech was therefore written in the second half of 1351 or in 1352.

III. *The Rejected Florentine*

After the conclusion of Epy's second long speech Mitio says to her (l. 132) that she has overlooked one good candidate:

> Hunc tamen oblita es; numeris ascribe merentem.

Epy replies:

> Invisa regione satum, quem florea vallis
> Paverit, et nostri spretorem miserit arvi:
> Pellicis imperio premimur; moribundus et unus
> Introeat, spatiumque brevis non expleat anni.

Mitio yields immediately:

---

[15] Rizzi 1, p. 256 (using Carrara's mistaken date for the consistory) suggests that the Eclogue may have been written before the consistory, the persons characterized in Epy's second long speech being, in this case, merely possible cardinals, in fact as well as in the fiction of the poem. This however disregards Mitio's acceptance (in ll. 129–131) of the candidates in question. It is in any case extremely unlikely that Petrarch could have known, before the consistory, the identities of the cardinals who were to be created—extremely unlikely, in particular, since the consistory was held while Petrarch was still in Italy.

Iram frange, precor: nil unquam tale iubebo.

The reference in ll. 133–134 is clearly to Florence, and to a man who is hostile to Avignon.

Roverella translates ll. 133–136 thus:

> In abborrita terra
> Nacque, e protervo spregiator de' nostri
> Campi lo diè fiorita valle a noi,
> Sì ci sforza il voler della rivale;
> Ei vegna pur, ma moribondo e solo
> Vegna, e non compia di breve anno il giro.[16]

The clause "Pellicis imperio premimur" is however certainly to be taken with what follows rather than with what precedes; and the meaning of ll. 135–136 appears to be: "a rival [a rival to Epy, that is, consequently a person or an entity comparable in influence to papal Avignon] presses so insistently for the appointment of this candidate that the appointment might better be made; but if so let it be made as a single appointment, and let the man die within a year." [17]

Rossetti states [18] that, in this candidate, Roverella "sospettò potervisi ravvisare il Petrarca medesimo": Roverella's suggestion is known only through this report. Honoring this suggestion as much as he can, Rossetti notes that ll. 132–134 certainly suggest Petrarch in these particulars: "Avignone che lo dimentica: Clemente che lo ricorda degno di onore sommo: l'Italia odiata da Avignone: la valle florida, ossia Firenze, che gli fu patria: il suo disprezzo per Avignone stessa."

---

[16] Roverella's translation of this Eclogue appears in Rossetti, I, 125–137.

[17] On the use of *pellex* in the sense of "rival," see Forcellini, *Totius latinitatis lexicon*, IV (Prato, 1868), *s.v. pellex*, 8. Clement's last previous nomination had been of a single cardinal (Pierre Roger de Beaufort, who was to become Gregory XI), and three of the nominations of John XXII (Eubel's XXI 9, 27, and 28) had been of single cardinals. Epy's "spatiumque brevis non expleat anni" is merely an imprecation, suggested perhaps by the fact that two of the cardinals named by Clement VI at his first consistory (Eubel's XXIV 4 and 8) had died within a year of their creation.

[18] In a long note on pp. 277–278.

Rossetti then goes on, however, to show why, in his opinion, the reference cannot be to Petrarch. Most of his arguments could readily be shown to have little or no weight (some of them have indeed been refuted by Rizzi[19]); but two are weighty, the second being, in my judgment, virtually conclusive. The first is that Petrarch's "amore d'indipendenza assoluta" renders it very improbable that he should ever have desired, much less tried to obtain, a cardinalate. Anyone familar with Petrarch's repeated protestations of his desire for freedom, and with the whole course of his life after, say, 1347, will recognize this argument as being very strong; but it is not accepted by Rizzi, and it is not absolutely conclusive—as will appear in the following chapter. Rossetti's second argument, based on l. 135, runs thus: "Quel *Pellicis imperio premimur* non può appartenergli nè in senso proprio nè in senso allegorico; non intendendosi quale donna o quale potenza fosse al Petrarca sì fattamente vincolata da farsi rivale d'Avignone o della Curia." The point is certainly well made. "Italy" was at this time a powerless and voiceless disunity. The two cities in which Petrarch had residences and had taken personal possession of benefices were Parma and Padua: there is no evidence that either one was in a position to bring any significant pressure upon the pope; Petrarch was at odds with Ugolino dei Rossi, Bishop and master of Parma; Jacopo da Carrara, Petrarch's Paduan patron, was assassinated on 21 December 1350; and Petrarch's friend Ildebrandino Conti, Bishop of Padua, urged him, in the Spring of 1351, not to return to Avignon.[20]

Rossetti then suggests that the Florentine candidate in question may have been Angelo Acciaiuoli, Bishop of Florence, a cousin (Rossetti mistakenly calls him a brother) of Niccolò Acciaiuoli. Rossetti notes that Niccolò and Angelo came to Avignon together in 1348 accompanying Queen Joan of Naples (a slightly inaccurate statement: they came not with the Queen, but with her second husband, Louis of Taranto, in order to act in the interests of both Louis and Joan); that Angelo might well have become acceptable to the Pope both because of his activity

---

[19] Rizzi 1, pp. 257–258.
[20] On Ildebrandino's remonstrances see below, p. 76.

on behalf of Joan and because of the importance of Niccolò; and that Angelo was again in Avignon in 1352.

Carrara [21] comments thus on the idea that in this eclogue Petrarch may have been referring to himself: "Figuratevi che in uno che Epi non vorrebbe eletto, e che solo è tollerato 'moribondo e morituro entro l'anno' si volle vedere il Poeta stesso!"

Rizzi,[22] endeavoring to prove that Petrarch desired a cardinalate, and assembling all data regarded as serving to support his important and in part well-argued thesis, asserts that the reference in the lines in question must be to Petrarch: "nessuno più di lui poteva esser detto da Epi 'nostri spretorem miseri arvi'; quel candidato escluso non può essere che il Petrarca." He refers to Roverella's suggestion, and refutes some of Rossetti's opposing arguments. With regard to Rossetti's argument that Petrarch's "amore d'indipendenza assoluta" renders it very improbable that he should ever have desired a cardinalate, Rizzi asserts that a cardinalate would have interfered with Petrarch's freedom much less than a bishopric or an apostolic secretaryship (offices that Petrarch repeatedly refused): but even if that were the case (which is debatable) the conclusion that a cardinalate would have involved *less* interference with his freedom than certain other offices does not indicate that it would not have involved a *substantial* interference with that freedom. And Rizzi ignores completely both Rossetti's argument from the clause "Pellicis imperio premimur" and Rossetti's suggestion that the candidate in question may have been Angelo Acciaiuoli. In Rizzi's own statement, quoted above, having said fairly enough that no one *more than* Petrarch could have been called "nostri spretorem arvi," he proceeds to draw the quite unwarranted conclusion that no one *else* could be so called.[23]

---

[21] Carrara 2, p. 101.

[22] Rizzi 1, pp. 257–258.

[23] Rizzi 2, pp. 46–48, confuses Rinaldo Orsini and the Florentine candidate (as is pointed out in n. 12); asserts that "l'implacabile spregiatore d'Avignone, venuto dall'Italia e da Firenze, è evidentemente il Petrarca"; and again ignores both the critically important "Pellicis imperio premimur" and Rossetti's suggestion that the candidate in question may have been Angelo Acciaiuoli.

In point of fact, Rossetti's suggestion that Petrarch's reference is to Angelo Acciaiuoli proves, on careful examination of all the circumstances concerned, to have a high degree of probability. Pressure for the advancement of Angelo would, in this case, have come from the Kingdom of Naples; and Clement would have been very susceptible to such pressure, since he, as Pope, was the feudal overlord of that Kingdom, and since he was constantly concerned for its integrity and in particular for the maintenance of the interests of Queen Joan—who was also, in her own right, the sovereign Countess of Provence.[24]

Niccolò Acciaiuoli, who had long been the mentor of Louis of Taranto, came into a position of great influence when Louis, in 1347, became the second husband of Queen Joan. In January 1348, when the King of Hungary invaded the Kingdom, Louis and Joan fled, separately, to Provence. Niccolò accompanied Louis, and in Tuscany they were joined by Angelo Acciaiuoli, who had been Bishop of Florence since 1342. When Louis and Joan reached Avignon, Clement was at first reluctant to receive them, since they had married without his authorization, and since they were still suspected—though no incriminating evidence was ever forthcoming—of complicity in the murder of Joan's first husband, Andrew of Hungary. Niccolò and Angelo went together to Clement, and prevailed upon him to receive Louis and Joan. In consequence, Clement authorized their marriage; and while he set up a commission of cardinals to examine the charges against Louis and Joan, he made no attempt to overcome their refusal to appear before the commission. It was doubtless Niccolò, furthermore, who engineered the sale of Avignon to the Pope, which brought Joan 80,000 florins; and it was Niccolò who, when the King of Hungary withdrew from Naples, made all the preparations for the return of Louis and Joan. In recognition of such services, Niccolò, while still in Avignon, was made Grand Seneschal of the Kingdom. While in Avignon, Niccolò

---

[24] The statements made in this paragraph and in the two following paragraphs are based (except for the items accounted for in nn. 26 and 27) upon Léonard 1, both volumes, *passim*. Léonard's index is serviceable.

petitioned the Pope for prebends for several members of his family.

From this time on, Niccolò was the power behind the Neapolitan throne. On 17 March 1349 Angelo was made Chancellor of the Kingdom—unquestionably on the recommendation of Niccolò—and was thereafter active not only as a high official but also as a member of the inner circle of Louis' counsellors. In 1350 and 1351, Louis in various ways brought pressure on Clement to authorize coronation for Joan and himself; but for a long time his efforts to this end were unavailing. Late in October 1351 Angelo went again to Avignon, as one of two Florentine envoys instructed in the first instance to win Clement to an alliance against the Visconti, and in the second instance to urge him to authorize the coronation of Louis and Joan. On 19 January 1352 Clement finally authorized the coronation. On the following 20 February Petrarch wrote *Fam.* xii 2 to Niccolò, congratulating him on the success of his efforts to secure the authorization [25] (Petrarch wrote also several other letters to Niccolò). On 24 May Angelo, then about to return to Italy, visited Petrarch at Vaucluse.[26] The coronation took place in Naples on 27 May.

On 15 March 1355 Angelo was transferred to the bishopric of Monte Cassino. With regard to this transfer, Moroni [27] says that Clement so transferred him "per le premure di Luigi I, secondo marito di Giovanna I," and continues: " Il re tutto doveva agli Acciaiuoli per avere rimessa in trono la moglie, onde volle gratificarli anco con questo pingue vescovato, avendo anzi ottenuto che fosse arcivescovato vivente fr. Angelo."

In view of all these facts it is clear that royal Neapolitan pressure might well have been brought to bear upon Clement to make Angelo a cardinal; and in view of Petrarch's relations both with Niccolò and with Angelo it is clear that Petrarch would have been greatly interested in such a possibility. It is then highly

---

[25] On this important letter see below, pp. 106 and 251–252.

[26] As related by Petrarch in *Fam.* xii 12.

[27] Gaetano Moroni, *Dizionario di erudizione storico-ecclesiastica,* xlvi (Venice, 1847), 176.

probable that the Florentine candidate referred to in ll. 132–137 of the Seventh Eclogue is Angelo Acciaiuoli.

The "unus" of l. 135 suggests that the proposal and rejection of the candidate in question took place after the consistory of 17 December 1350. It may have taken place either before or after Petrarch had written the second long speech of Epy: ll. 132–137 may then have been written either at the same time as that speech or, as an insert, at a somewhat later time.

CHAPTER IV

Petrarch and the Cardinalate

Students of Petrarch owe a debt of gratitude to Fortunato Rizzi for his championship [1] of the idea that Petrarch desired a cardinalate: for if that idea can be established as valid, or even as a definite possibility, it adds something of importance to our concept of Petrarch's ambitions and sense of values. In the course of the two preceding chapters I have shown that two of Rizzi's arguments are invalid; but what I have said in those chapters and what I have still to say in criticism of two of his four remaining arguments has been and will be said not only with full recognition of the fact that such arguments do not constitute the whole of his case, but also with a genuine appreciation of the value of his stimulating work upon this subject.

I

One of Rizzi's four remaining arguments is a renewal of a suggestion made by Mestica.

In 1345, when Petrarch had been in Italy for nearly two years, Sennuccio del Bene, doubtless on behalf of Cardinal Colonna, sent to Petrarch this sonnet:

> Oltra l'usato modo si rigira
> lo verde lauro hai qui, dov'io or seggio;
> e più attento e com' più la riveggio,
> di qui in qui con gli occhi fiso mira.
> È parmi omai ch'un dolor misto d'ira

---

[1] In Rizzi 1, pp. 195–201 and 245–260, and Rizzi 2. Three men have indicated, briefly and without comment, their acceptance of Rizzi's thesis: Giuseppe Petronio, in a review of Rizzi 1 in *Leonardo*, v (1934), 396; the author of a notice of Rizzi 2 in the "Spoglio dei periodici" in *GSLI*, cxii (1939), 350–351; and Ginori Conti, pp. 127–128.

l'affligga tanto che tacer no 'l deggio;
onde dall'atto suo io vi richeggio
ch'esso mi ditta, che troppo martira.
    E 'l signor nostro in desir sempre abonna
di vedervi seder nelli suoi scanni:
e 'n atto et in parlar questo distinsi.
    Mei fondata di lui trovar colonna
non potreste in cinqu'altri Sangiovanni,
la cui vigilia a scriver mi sospinsi.[2]

On the words *nelli suoi scanni* Mestica comments: " 'presso di sè,' e potrebbe anche significare un augurio al Petrarca per la dignità cardinalizia." [3]

But the first two lines of the sestet certainly mean simply this: "And our Lord [the Cardinal] still, as always, desires very much to see you sitting at his board." Compare the sentence in Fiammetta's story in the *Ameto:* "Le poste mense nullo altro aspettanti si riempierono d'uomini e di donne; e ciascuna tenne secondo il suo grado lo scanno." [4]

Mestica's suggestion, in any case, is completely out of key with the simple invitational character of the sonnet. The poem is too slight and playful to have carried any freight so weighty as the suggestion of a cardinalate; its message is simply this; "Laura wants you to come back, and so does the Cardinal." The normal interpretation of the words "i suoi scanni" would take the "scanni" to be seats possessed by the Cardinal. The idea that "nelli suoi scanni" might mean "among the cardinals" is very far-fetched indeed; the specific meaning would have to be "in a seat such as the cardinal's seat which he [Cardinal Colonna] occupies"—and the simple words can hardly bear that burden. Moreover, even if Cardinal Colonna had had such an idea, and had manifested it "in parlare" in Sennuccio's hearing, it is difficult to see how he could have manifested it in "atto," since "atto," here linked with "parlare," has certainly the sense of "looks"—as it does in the 7th line of this very sonnet, and as it does so often

[2] Quoted from *Le rime sparse e i trionfi*, ed. by Ezio Chiòrboli (Bari, 1930), p. 299.
[3] Mestica, p. 373.
[4] Boccaccio, *Ameto*, ed. by Nicola Bruscoli (Bari, 1940), p. 108.

in the poems of Petrarch. Nor is there in Petrarch's reply (addressed to the Cardinal)—the sonnet beginning

> Signor mio caro, ogni pensier mi tira
> Devoto a veder voi, cui sempre veggio—

any indication that Petrarch saw in Sennuccio's tercet anything more than an expression of a kindly desire that Petrarch should return to his familiar place in the Cardinal's household. Mestica's suggestion, accordingly, has no validity.

II

Another of Rizzi's arguments is based upon a passage in a letter (LAP 62) written to Petrarch after he had returned to Provence late in 1345, by Guglielmo da Pastrengo. Imagining Petrarch's activities in Avignon and in Vaucluse, Guglielmo writes:

nunc . . . ante revendissimorum (*sic*) patrum ora versaris, huic semita cedis, caput aperis, assurgis illi alteri, dexteram porrigis et nonnunquam de more patrio in oscula ruis; nunc in agricole nostri ede iactaris, vacas sacris, elisias circum agis sedes columne adherens paphice, sacras colis lauros, frondis delphice in umbra grataris. Gratulor et ego, nec livoris fele torqueor, sed exuberanti gaudio fartior. Vale foelixque vive, mi luce charior.[5]

Rizzi regards the passage "nunc . . . ruis" as indicating that Pastrengo thought of Petrarch as being now or in immediate prospect a cardinal among cardinals, and the sentence beginning "Gratulor" as a congratulation upon the receipt or the anticipation of a cardinalate: "Il Petrarca che stringe la mano e anzi bacia in volto i cardinali doveva dunque avere un posto tale che gli permettesse confidenza e familiarità con gli alteri porporati francesi. Forse aveva il poeta fatto all'amico qualche confidenza in proposito?" and "che si trattasse di qualche alto posto fatto balenare al Petr., si vede anche dalle congratulazioni gioiose, con cui la lettera si chiude." [6]

But in Guglielmo's picture of Petrarch in the papal court Petrarch appears *ante reverendissimorum patrum ora* rather than

---

[5] Avena, pp. 288–289.
[6] Rizzi 1, pp. 200–201.

as *inter reverendissimos patres unus*, and in respect to the several particular items mentioned Petrarch appears rather as an inferior than as an equal: "huic semita cedis, caput aperis, assurgis illi alteri, dexteram porrigis et nonnunquam de more patrio in oscula ruis." Nor do the congratulations imply elevation; they may be simply congratulations on Petrarch's opportunity of moving in so distinguished a company; or they may be congratulations on the freedom of Petrarch's life at Vaucluse. The *Gratulor*, indeed, resumes the idea of the *grataris*, which is used with regard to Vaucluse. The long *Met.* III 3, written from Avignon to Guglielmo, is devoted almost entirely to Vaucluse. Its only reference to the papal court is in ll. 23–26, which are as follows:

> Hic unus cum pace dies exactus aventi
> Vix totus; tot me laqueis, tot curia curis
> Implicat. Id meritum, qui vincula nota libenter
> Infelix, tritaque iugum cervice recepi.

III

Before considering Rizzi's two remaining and weighty arguments we may well consider Petrarch's attitude toward high ecclesiastical office in general.

Clement VI offered Petrarch a bishopric at least once before 1348 and at least once in 1351 or 1352, and an apostolic secretaryship in 1347 and again in 1351 or 1352; and Innocent VI offered him an apostolic secretaryship in 1359 and again in 1361; Petrarch, however, refused all these offers (see above, pp. 15–17).

The eighteen letters—several of them containing references to these offers—in which Petrarch indicates his attitude toward high ecclesiastical office will next be examined. These letters are listed herewith, in the order in which they were written:

Fam. III 20. 1346. To Laelius.
Fam. VII 6. 1347. To Socrates.
Fam. XI 14. 1351. To Philippe de Vitry.
Fam. IX 5. 1351. To Ugolino dei Rossi.
Invective contra medicum, I (originally a letter: see below, pp. 109–110). 1352. To a certain physician.
Fam. XIII 4. 1352. To Francesco Calvo.
Fam. XIII 5. 1352. To Francesco Nelli.

Fam. xiv 4. 1352. To Luca da Piacenza.
Fam. xvi 3. 1353. To Socrates.
Var. 64. 1354. To Philippe de Cabassoles.
Fam. xix 17. 1357. To Guido Sette.
Fam. xx 14. 1359. To Laelius.
Var. 55. 1361. To Philippe de Cabassoles.
Sen. i 4. 1361–1362. To Cardinal Talleyrand.
Sen. xi 3. 1368. To Francesco Bruni.
Var. 15. 1371. To Bruni.
Sen. xiii 13.[7] 1371–1372. To Bruni.
Sen. xiii 14. 1372. To Bruni.

These letters, as a whole, manifest a deep aversion to high ecclesiastical office, an aversion that rests mainly upon Petrarch's conviction that moderation in possessions and in status is better than wealth and eminence, and upon his exceedingly strong desire to preserve his personal liberty.

With reference to the principle of moderation Petrarch makes these statements:

hanc ipse michi legem statui: altiora me non querere, paria vero pauca quidem et modeste (*Fam.* iii 20, 10).

si optata michi mediocritas, quam iure Flaccus auream vocat . . . obvenerit . . . perliberaliter mecum agi dicam (*Fam.* vii 6, 4).

Honeste paupertatis appetens semper fui; nempe nullus melior, nullus tranquillior, nullus denique tutior vite modus (*Fam.* xx 14, 22).

Divitias alii, ego paupertatem appeto, sed non omnem profecto, non sordidam, non tristem, neque solicitam, sed tranquillam, sed pacificam, sed honestam (*Var.* 55).

Qui si scirent . . . quanto . . . mihi est melius cum mediocritate mea: quam eis cum omni eorum pompa atque inani magnitudine: desinerent forsitan aduersari. . . . Scito igitur . . . nihilo magis me magnis opibus gauisurum quam honesta paupertate. Quem paupertas animum quietaret: hunc mediocritas non quietabit? Ea vero mihi semper affuit: vnde usque ad hoc tempus sat liberaliter vixi (*Sen.* xiii 14).

Similar statements appear in *Fam.* vii 6, 2; *Fam.* ix 5, 24; *Var.* 64; and *Fam.* xix 17, 1–2 and 5. Specific disclaimers of avarice or envy or both appear in *Fam.* ix 5, 23; *Fam.* xiii 5, 1–2 and 6–7; *Fam.* xiv 4, 10–20; and *Sen.* xiii 14. Statements to the effect that

---

[7] The second half of this letter is merely a revision of the latter part of *Var.* 15: see above, p. 29.

Petrarch had in fact enough to live on occur in the sentence last quoted, and in *Fam.* vii 6, 4; *Fam.* xiii 5, 7 and 9; *Fam.* xvi 3, 5; *Fam.* xix 17, 2; *Fam.* xx 8, 15; and *Var.* 15.

With reference to the loss of personal liberty involved in the acceptance of high ecclesiastical office Petrarch makes these statements or portions of statements:

nunquam michi venit in animum . . . ut otium meum cum tuis negotiis, quietem meam cum tuis laboribus . . . commutasse cupiam (*Fam.* ix 5, 24).

splendide servituti libertatem humilem pretuli (*ibid.*, 29).

[me] Deique et hominum fidem contestante eripi michi libertatem atque otium, cuius appetitu nil natura melius, cuius successu nil michi fortuna felicius tribuisset; extorqueri michi gaudium et omnem vite dulcedinem atque has qualescunque literulas, sine quibus vivere posse diffiderem (*Fam.* xiii 5, 6).

cum in omnibus requiem quesiverim . . . et eam ab annis teneris usque ad desidie suspitionem semper amaverim—nunc penitus nichil quero, nichil amo aliud—, sine qua nulla michi vite conditio non molesta sit (*Fam.* xx 14, 20–21).

primum huiusce rei [the promotion of Philippe de Cabassoles to a cardinalate] nuncium letus audiui: mox ad me rediens misertus sum: domino autem nostro . . . quid latentis offense fecerit ignoro: quo in eum ultionis honorificum hoc genus inuenerit. Ut uelut aurea illum vinciens cathena dum maxime necessaria quies esset ac libertas omnem sibi spem quietis ac libertatis abstulerit (*Sen.* xi 3).

Similar statements appear in the *Invective contra medicum*, i, ll. 63–67, *Fam.* xiii 4, 4–5 and 20 ff., *Fam.* xiii 5, 19, and *Fam.* xiv 4, 9.

Petrarch's aversion to high ecclesiastical office is voiced most clearly in these statements:

omnis . . . michi altitudo suspecta est, et precipitii admonet omnis ascensus (*Fam.* vii 6, 3).

sin invisum illud et grave maioris officii honus imponitur, renuo, excutio. Pauper esse malim quam solicitus (*ibid.*, 4).

nemo usquam vivit tue sortis, cuius solio sedere vellem, imo vero non pertinacissime recusarem, si ultro etiam offerretur (*Fam.* ix 5, 24).

Siquidem non modo laborem illum magnum perpetuum inglorium tediosum . . . sed rubicundum quoque pilleum, non dico ambiendum precibus sed ultro etiam oblatum. si reciperem, ut modo res sunt et mores ordinis illius, abscisum gladio et rubenti sanguine madidum caput perdam (*Fam.* xx 14, 15–16).

mihi negetur [in a hypothetical case] episcopatus quem petendum duxero. immo vero plane mihi detur ut torquear: & si hac in parte delirauerim graui ac sollicito munere sera & insolita plectatur ambitio (*Sen.* xi 3).

Praelaturam itaque nullam volo, nec volui quidem unquam; similiter nec beneficium curatum quodcunque, quamvis opulentissimum; satis est mihi unius animae meae cura; atque utinam illi uni sufficiam! (*Var.* 15, *ad fin.*).

This last passage reappears, with slight verbal changes, in *Sen.* xiii 13. Similar statements appear in *Fam.* ix 5, 23 and *Fam.* xiii 5, 5.

IV

In the passage just quoted from *Fam.* xx 14 Petrarch expresses the imprecatory wish that he may be beheaded if under present conditions he should accept an offer of an apostolic secretaryship or even an offer of a cardinalate made without any request on his own part. Treatment of this passage as evidence in support of the theory that Petrarch desired and sought to obtain a cardinalate seems at first sight unjustifiable; but Rizzi, in one of his remaining arguments, comes close to justifying it. He first comments thus:

Il poeta ha voluto tenerci gelosamente nascosto il suo superbo desiderio; eppure, in un certo momento si è quasi tradito e s'è lasciato sfuggire una mezza rivelazione. . . . La testa sotto la scure! Vuol dire proprio che si rimestava un passato assai increscioso e amaro, e sempre vivo nell'animo suo così sensibile tanto alle gioie che alle avversità, tanto alle lodi che alle critiche. Oh ricevere il cappello cardinalizio spontaneamente profferto! Proprio quello che egli aveva sperato da Clemente VI, e che Clemente VI non aveva voluto o potuto fare.[8]

He then goes on to direct attention particularly to the clause "ut modo res sunt et mores ordinis illius," arguing, in my judgment rightly, that it implies that Petrarch would have accepted a cardinalate if it had been offered to him by Clement.

---

[8] Rizzi 2, p. 44.

V

Several of the letters listed in Section III contain evidence that Petrarch desired some papal benefaction which, at the time of the writing of the letter in question, had not been received. The nature of the desired benefaction is not stated in any one of the several cases. Upon this evidence Rizzi bases an argument that runs thus: Petrarch repeatedly refused offers of a bishopric and of an apostolic secretaryship, yet he frequently expressed a desire for some papal benefaction; the only still higher office that the Pope might have conferred on him was a cardinalate; Petrarch's desire must therefore have been a desire for a cardinalate. Rizzi assumes that the desired benefaction was the same in all cases: individual examination of the several letters will show, however, that this assumption is not justified.

Fam. III 20. In 1346, when this letter, addressed to Laelius, was written, Petrarch held canonries in Lombez and Pisa, and a minor benefice in Castiglione Fiorentino. Early in 1346 Pietro Marini, canon and archdeacon of the Cathedral of Parma, had died; and Petrarch had petitioned Clement VI for the canonry and the archdeaconate. His letter to Laelius contains these passages, in Sections 7 and 11: "queso ne pigeat apud comunem dominum pro felici rerum mearum exitu intercedere . . . ," and "Quamobrem per omnes te celicolas, frater, oro ab hac quamprimum perplexitate dissolvi . . ." The "comunem dominum" of the first passage is Cardinal Giovanni Colonna, whom both Petrarch and Laelius served as chaplains. It seems altogether probable that the matter with regard to which Petrarch was asking Laelius to prod the Cardinal was the matter of the double Parma appointment (see above, p. 12).

Fam. VII 6. In the following year, when this letter, addressed to Socrates, was written, Petrarch had received the Parma canonry, but not the archdeaconate. The letter closes with a statement which indicates that Clement, while offering Petrarch high offices that he could not accept, had denied him a "modicum" that he did desire. The last words of the letter are: "scimus ergo quia petenti modicum immensa porrigere, species est negandi."

The "immensa" are presumably offers of a bishopric and of an apostolic secretaryship: the "modicum" that is contrasted with these "immensa" cannot possibly have been a cardinalate. It was perhaps the archdeaconate of Parma, but there are other possibilities (see above, p. 17).

Var. 55. When this letter, addressed in 1361 to Philippe de Cabassoles, was written, Petrarch held his Parma canonry and archdeaconate, a canonry in Padua, and two minor benefices, but had resigned his canonries in Lombez and Pisa. Presumably his expenses were now increasing, as they certainly did toward the end of his life (see *Var.* 15). In *Var.* 55 Petrarch, who had just refused or was just refusing an offer, made by Innocent VI, of an apostolic secretaryship, asks Philippe to do everything he can to persuade Innocent to grant him (Petrarch) some benefaction. He insists, however, upon the modesty of his desires: "Familiariter olim tibi . . . studiorum finis et votorum meorum intellecta modestia est: utor enim fidenter hoc nomine, non superbe, conscius suae humilioris originis; quod unde modicum inde et modestia dicitur, et a modo nomen utrumque descendit." What he wants is just enough to assure him of a "paupertatem" that shall be "tranquillam," "pacificam," and "honestam." His desire in this instance, therefore, cannot possibly be for a cardinalate. His appeal seems to have been successful, for *Sen.* 1 2, written to Nelli in 1361 or early in 1362, contains this passage: "Nouissime uerum summus pontifex . . . me altis uocibus ad se uocat duobus iam nunc beneficijs collatis: pluribusque si paream oblatis."

Sen. 1 4. In this letter, written to Cardinal Talleyrand in 1361 or 1362, and referring to Petrarch's refusal of an apostolic secretaryship, there occur these general references to his desires: "Non quod aliquid ab eo [*i.e.*, from Innocent] magnopere cuperem. Ambitiones mee note tibi omnes sunt"; and "Quid uelim. quid optem. quid ambiam: quo suspirem non mihi notius quam tibi est." The desires thus referred to are clearly the same desires for a life of modest means so often expressed by Petrarch: the "Non . . . cuperem" excludes the possibility of reference to a cardinalate. It may be noted that at the point in this letter at which Petrarch refers to his refusal of an apostolic secretaryship his "etas deuexior laborum" is cited as one of the reasons for his refusal.

Var. 15. This extremely important letter was written to Francesco Bruni in 1371, not long after the election of Gregory XI, who soon after his election had sent to Petrarch a letter to which (in *Sen.* XIII 14) Petrarch refers as being "spei magne & pollicitationis multiplicis plena." In *Var.* 15 Petrarch draws a detailed picture of his way of life at Arquà: his income would be sufficient for the support of a canon without dependents, but he was maintaining a considerable household, and had frequently to entertain many guests. He would welcome, therefore, any benefaction that might come to him from Gregory:

> Si his [curis] ergo atque aliis, et quod mihi a praedecessore suo [the reference is presumably to Clement VI] promissum erat, ut nosti, dominus noster quieti meae consulere dignaretur, non teneretur, fateor, indigno et immerito, nisi ad imitationem forsan illius cuius vicem gerit . . . Et si quidem hoc velit, ut litterae eius indicant, potest perfacile profecto uno verbo.

Whatever Gregory's response might be, Petrarch would be content: "Sive enim multum faciat, sive nihil, sive modicum, contentabor." Petrarch will not himself make a specific request, and this for three reasons: "primum nempe quid petam prorsus nescio. . . . Deinde . . . ante . . . quam nuncius meus ad pedes Apostolicos perveniret, esset de facili idipsum petitum ab alio et concessum. . . . Postremo fieri posset ut aliquid peterem, quod eidem domino non placeret." If then the Pope wants to do something for Petrarch, let the Pope himself be at the same time "benefactor et consultor," and make any grant that may seem to him to be appropriate. This indeed would be just what Petrarch had asked Clement to do, many years before, when Petrarch had refused an offer of an apostolic secretaryship:

> Cum . . . continue recusassem, ultimo mihi dixit: *Pete quod vis et faciam tibi:* cui ego respondi: *si bene facere mihi vultis, non solum beneficentia sed electio, Pater sanctissime, vestra sit. Vos scitis optime quanti me facitis. Quando aliquid petente alio, vel quomodolibet ad notitiam vestram venit, quod me dignum videatur, mei si placet memoriam habetote:* quod ipse se facturum clementissime repromisit, et fecisset, non dubito, nisi eum mors multis, et inter alios mihi dam-

nosa, praevenisset. Ita ergo mihi expedit ut dominus noster faciat, si mihi aliquid vult facere.

The letter continues in the same tenor, repeating both expressions of desire and of contentment with any gratification or with no gratification, and indicating clearly what Petrarch does *not* want: "Praelaturam itaque nullam volo, nec volui quidem unquam; similiter nec beneficium curatum quodcunque, quamvis opulentissimum." Toward the end of the letter Petrarch writes: "Illud quoque sibi persuadeas quod, si quid mihi contulerit, idipsum cito alteri conferre poterit. *Ego enim iam delibor,* et ut aestimo, *tempus meae resolutionis instat.*" The benefaction desired from Gregory was then desired specifically in order that Petrarch might maintain more easily the kind of life he was living at Arquà; Petrarch's second reason for not making a specific request indicates that his desire would have been satisfied by the granting of a benefice such as others might naturally desire; and the concluding reference to the fact that the Pope would soon have the chance to confer on someone else whatever he might now confer on Petrarch indicates clearly that what Petrarch had actually in mind was a benefice. Moreover, that Petrarch in 1371, when he was settled in Arquà and rightly felt that the end of his life was drawing near, should have desired a cardinalate, with all that a cardinalate would necessarily have involved, is virtually unthinkable. The benefaction desired from Gregory, accordingly, can hardly have been a cardinalate.

With regard to the conversation with Clement, however, the case is different. That conversation certainly took place late in 1351. Petrarch at that time held canonries in Lombez, Pisa, Parma, and Padua, the archdeaconate of Parma, and a minor benefice in Castiglione Fiorentino, and was about to resign his canonries in Lombez and Pisa: he was therefore in no need of an additional benefice. He was talking face to face with a Pope who had already done much for him; and what he recalls having said to Clement would have been perfectly appropriate for him to say if he did in fact desire a cardinalate, but was unwilling to express that desire openly, even to his Pope.

Sen. XIII 13. In the first half of this letter, speaking of a cardinal who had been hostile to him, Petrarch writes: "Et o utinam ipse & ego simul equo in statu rerum temporalium non ego magnus ut ipse hoc enim nouit Christus nollem sed ipse paruus ut ego alicubi iustis sub iudicibus viueremus." The second half of this letter, as has been noted, is merely a revised form of the latter part of *Var.* 15, and contains accordingly, with minor variations, the "Praelaturam itaque nullam volo" passage, together with what immediately precedes it and what follows it.

Sen. XIII 14.   The appeal to Gregory brought no results; and in this letter Petrarch asks Bruni to make no further efforts in his behalf: his only remaining desire is to die a truly Christian death.

Rizzi's argument from these various expressions of desire is in effect reduced, therefore, to an argument based solely on the account given in *Var.* 15 of Petrarch's interview with Clement VI: but, thus reduced, the argument is strong.

VI

The circumstances attending Petrarch's return to Provence in 1351 have a definite bearing on the question as to whether he desired a cardinalate. He had been in Italy since December 1347, residing chiefly in Parma. He had received the archdeaconate of Parma in 1348; but his satisfaction with life there had been diminished by strained relations with the Bishop of Parma, Ugolino dei Rossi. In 1349 he had received a canonry in Padua, as the gift of Jacopo da Carrara, lord of Padua. Thereafter he had spent much of his time in Padua, happy in the patronage of Jacopo (which however came to a sudden end in December 1350, when Jacopo was assassinated) and in the friendship of the Bishop of Padua, Ildebrandino Conti.

At a consistory held on 17 December 1350 Clement created twelve new cardinals—nine Frenchmen, two Italians, and one Spaniard.[9] The news of this consistory must have reached Petrarch late in December 1350 or in January 1351. He must have been intensely interested, and indignant, though not surprised, at the continued packing of the College with Frenchmen and at the slight recognition given to Italians. But the fact that any Italians

---

[9] Eubel, pp. 18–19.

at all were included among the new cardinals may well have excited him. Both of the two Italians, Niccola Capocci and Rinaldo Orsini, seem to have been able men; but neither was of any great distinction. Capocci had been Bishop of Urgel; Orsini had been an apostolic notary. It would have been only natural if Petrarch, now well advanced in his own ecclesiastical career, had thought to himself: "If they have been made cardinals, why should not I be considered as a possible cardinal?" This is not to say that the idea that he might be so considered reached the stage of desire with him: against it there stood all his convictions as to moderation, all his intense desire for personal liberty, and all his hatred for Avignon. But a cardinalate would be a position of far greater dignity and influence than a bishopric or an apostolic secretaryship. Mental conflict would have been nothing new for him.

In the spring of 1351 he decided to return to Provence. His most explicit statement as to the occasion of that return is to be found in *Fam.* xiii 5. He was called to Avignon, he says, by two (unnamed) cardinals, speaking in the name of the Pope, but not stating the purpose for which they were calling him (the quotations are from Sects. 1–4):

> veni omnium que erga me agerentur ignarus . . .
> Duo illi principes Ecclesie me certatim evocabant, quos velut duos tauros validissimos lateque Cristi regnantes in pascuis grex dominicus nunc habet, quorum me alter veteribus beneficiis, alter insperata et nova ignoti hominis benivolentia, fame solius testimonium secutus, obstrinxerat. Superbia visa est voces illorum spernere quos reges et principes venerantur et presertim voces quibus summi pastoris inesse diceretur autoritas . . .

Though he did not know why he was being called, he knew only too well the state of things in the Papal court, and ought to have known better than to return to it: "michi nil penitus comune cum curia est; nunquam concordarunt mores . . ."; "veni autem loci gnarus, cause nescius . . ." It turned out that he had been called to Avignon in order that pressure might be brought to bear upon him to accept an apostolic secretaryship. If he had had any suspicion of this, he says, he would not have returned: "nunquam, siquid michi creditur, venturus sciens . . ."

Why then did he go? He must have engaged in speculation as to the purpose for which he was called, and he would hardly have gone at all unless he had foreseen as possible a purpose more attractive than that of appointment as apostolic secretary. Appointment as bishop would certainly have been equally unattractive to him. That would seem to leave but two possibilities: presentation to an additional benefice or benefices, or nomination to a cardinalate. He was at this time in no need of additional benefices; and if Clement had wanted to give him an additional benefice he could have done so without a call to Avignon. It looks very much as if Petrarch decided to return with the thought that he might be offered a cardinalate. It is worth noting in this connection that Clement might have promoted him to a cardinalate without creating other cardinals at the same time: Clement's last nomination to the cardinalate prior to the consistory of 17 December 1350 had been the nomination of a single cardinal (Pierre Roger, named in 1349).[10]

The idea that Petrarch returned to Provence thinking that he might be offered a cardinalate receives some support from consideration of *Sine nom.* 8, written to Bishop Ildebrandino Conti from Avignon in the autumn of 1351 or early in 1352. Ildebrandino had strongly advised Petrarch not to return to Provence:

> quotiens redit ad memoriam illa tua penitus paterna uox et salutaris admonitio, dum digressum paranti diceres: 'Quo abis? quid moliris? Que te tui immemorem trahit ambitio? Nescis quid petis, quid relinquis? An sciens ad indignum te laborem uadis? Vide, queso, acriter quid agas, quo properes! Si bene michi notus es, penitebit te profectionis tue. Curie laqueos expertus totiens non ignoras; in quos ubi semel incideris, absolui non poteris cum uoles.' Hec et his similia suadenti quid responderem? Aliud non erat nisi me caritate vinctum amicorum notas ad miserias reverti.

The sentence "Que te tui immemorem trahit ambitio?" is particularly to be noted.

Relevant also is *Fam.* xi 6, written to Boccaccio on 1 June 1351, as Petrarch was about to leave Italy for Provence. It adds

---

[10] *Ibid.*

no new fact, but its content is consistent with that of *Fam.* xiii 5, and its tones of suppressed excitement, secrecy, and uncertainty are consistent with the supposition that Petrarch was moved by an expectation that he did not wish to define. Petrarch says that he will soon be on his way to Vaucluse, though Vaucluse is far from Italy and close to Avignon; and continues thus:

Ferrem tamen utrunque, amara dulcibus leniens; sed alia quedam sunt que refugiunt stilum, ex quibus michi illic moram profecto brevissimam auguror, nisi quid novi forsan inciderit, quod ipsum quale suspicer ignoro. Id scio, nichil omnino non posse homini contingere. . . . Latet ergo rerum exitus, presens propositum animi non latet, quod et tibi et nostris non ignotum velim. Romanum nempe Pontificem quem ad ripam Tyberis querere consueverant patres nostri, nos ad ripam Rodani querimus. . . . Illum ergo nunc, quia ubi vellem nequeo, ubi possum querere est animus, simul ac sparsas dulcium reliquias amicorum; cumque omnibus supremum vale dixero . . . in prefato rure nostro [*i.e.,* Vaucluse] . . . quod superfuerit estatis solitaria quiete transigere . . . Autumnus me revehet, ut spero . . . (Sects. 6–9).

The words "alia quedam sunt que refugiunt stilum" presumably refer to the fact that the summoning cardinals had not told Petrarch why he was being summoned.

The element of secrecy with regard to Petrarch's return is mentioned also in *Fam.* xiv 4, 11: "Aliquid, puto, sed occultioris cause fuit, que me tot obstantibus urgeret retinentibusque convelleret."

Of interest, but of uncertain relevance, is the fact that immediately upon reaching Provence Petrarch sought and received from Philippe de Cabassoles commendatory letters to two (unnamed) cardinals. In *Fam.* xi 11, written on 29 June to thank Philippe for these letters, he says: "Que de me scribis, pater, duobus illis tam magnis apostolice cimbe remigibus, intenta mente perlegi; quam vera quidem, et qui dictavit illa viderit et qui legerit."

While the effective cause of Petrarch's decision to return to Provence was unquestionably the summons from the two cardinals, he was certainly influenced also by other considerations, which will be enumerated below (on pp. 82–86).

a conflict in Petrarch's own mind: I believe that he did desire a cardinalate, but that he dreaded it even while he desired it. Such a conflict would be nothing strange in the case of the man who wrote *I' vo pensando*, and wrote in *Var.* 55 (in another connection) the phrase "ita distrahor incertis affectibus."

I believe that his dread lest a cardinalate should put an end to his moderation and his personal liberty and should compel him to be much in Avignon prevented his desire from being very strong. I believe that he would have accepted a cardinalate if Clement had offered it to him; but I find no evidence that he ever actively sought a cardinalate, and I do not believe that he did so. I find no evidence that such desire as he may have had for a cardinalate became active before 1350 or continued after Clement's death in 1352. Finally, as I have indicated in Section VII, I believe that in so far as Petrarch thought of himself as a possible cardinal, he thought of himself as an active cardinal, fighting corruption, working for the return to Rome, and perhaps serving as a papal legate. It might have been well for the Church if Petrarch had been made a cardinal; but it is fortunate for the development of humanistic culture that he remained a devoted man of letters.

CHAPTER V

Petrarch in Provence, 1351-1353

After his return from Provence to Italy late in 1347 Petrarch had resided chiefly in his own pleasant home in Parma, where he held a canonry and, after August 1348, the archdeaconate. In the spring of 1349, however, Jacopo da Carrara, lord of Padua, had given him a canonry in that city, and thereafter he had spent much of his time in Padua, happy both in Jacopo's patronage and in the friendship of the Bishop of Padua, Ildebrandino Conti.

In the spring of 1351 he decided to return to Provence, at least for a short stay. He was not under any constraint to leave Italy. He might have remained in Padua: Jacopo had been assassinated in December 1350, but Jacopo's son and successor held Petrarch in affection and honor, as Petrarch states at the end of the *Epistola posteritati*. He might have resumed residence in Parma: he was not on the best of terms with the Bishop of Parma, Ugolino dei Rossi, but the strain had not at this time become serious. He might have moved to Florence: Boccaccio brought him, early in 1351, an urgent official invitation to settle in Florence, as a lecturer in the newly founded university, and to receive a full restoration of his confiscated patrimony. He acknowledged the invitation graciously, but he never accepted it.

He left Padua early in May, spent nearly a month in Verona, made shorter stays in Mantua and Parma, set out for Provence early in June, and reached Vaucluse on the 27th.

In *Fam.* xi 6, written shortly before he left Italy, Petrarch tells Boccaccio that he plans to remain in Provence only through the summer, and to return to Italy in the autumn. This letter, however, contains a passage which indicates that he already had in mind the possibility that circumstances might detain him for

81

a longer time; and in *Fam.* xi 12, written on 19 July to Luca
Cristiani, he says that he has decided to remain for about two
years. He did remain, in fact, until May 1353.

I. Reasons for the Return

Petrarch's most explicit statement as to the reason for his return appears in *Fam.* xiii 5. He was called to Avignon, he says,
by two cardinals, speaking in the name of the Pope, but not
stating the purpose for which they were calling him; and he felt
that he could not refuse the call, both because of the kindness of
the two cardinals and because disregard of their princely authority and of the pope's supreme authority would have rendered
him guilty of an unwarranted pride. He does not name the two
cardinals, but refers to them thus: "quorum me alter veteribus
beneficiis, alter insperata et nova ignoti hominis benivolentia,
fame solius testimonium secutus, obstrinxerat." It has been generally, and probably rightly, assumed that they were Gui de
Boulogne and Elie de Talleyrand. In 1349 Gui de Boulogne, on
his way to Hungary as Legate to King Louis, had stopped in
Padua, and it was he who, on 12 April, had installed Petrarch
in his Paduan canonry—"ita per manus domini Legati . . . prebendam ipsam . . . obtinui." [1] On his return, also, the Legate
had spent some time in Padua, where on 15 February 1350 he had
presided over the ceremony of the translation of the body of
St. Anthony of Padua (as Petrarch wrote, on that day, in *Fam.*
ix 13). He had then gone on to Rome, as one of the two cardinals designated as "Cardinals of the Jubilee"; and on his way
back from Rome to Avignon he had stopped again, in May, in
Padua.[2] The opening words of *Fam.* xiii 1, written in May
1352, to console the Cardinal for the death of his mother, prove
the existence of a warm friendship between the two men. Several
further references to their relations will be made in the course of
this study. There is no evidence that Petrarch had any acquaint-

---

[1] See the original form of the letter that ultimately became *Fam.*
viii 2–5, in Rossi 1, ii, 194–195.

[2] Baluze, pp. 345 and 399; Gregorovius, Book XI, Chap. VII, Sect. 1;
and Léonard 1, i, 196–228. The other "Cardinal of the Jubilee" was
Annibaldo di Ceccano.

ance with Cardinal Talleyrand before returning to Provence:
that they became closely associated thereafter will appear repeatedly below. Both cardinals were very influential: Froissart
says (speaking, to be sure, of things as they were some ten years
later) that they "estoient li plus grant de tout le collège." [3]

In *Fam.* xi 6 Petrarch indicates that he is returning to
Provence primarily to see the Pope—obviously because of the
fact that the two summoning cardinals had said that they were
speaking in the Pope's name.

In the preceding chapter I have shown that Petrarch had
some ground for thinking that Clement might have had it in
mind to make him a cardinal, and have indicated my opinion that
Petrarch did in fact desire a cardinalate, though dreading it even
while he desired it.

He was certainly moved also, in his decision to return to
Provence, by his longing for Vaucluse. It was presumably in the
spring of 1351 that he wrote his charming epigram on Vaucluse:

> Valle locus Clausa toto michi nullus in orbe
> gratior aut studiis aptior ora meis.
> Valle puer Clausa fueram iuvenemque reversum
> fovit in aprico vallis amena sinu.
> Valle vir in Clausa meliores dulciter annos
> exegi et vite candida fila mee.
> Valle senex Clausa supremum ducere tempus
> et Clausa cupio, te duce, Valle mori.

The "dux" of the last line is Philippe de Cabassoles, Bishop of
Cavaillon (the diocese in which Vaucluse is located), to whom
the epigram was sent in a brief covering letter, *Fam.* xi 4, in
which, as in the epigram itself, Petrarch expresses his desire to
return to Vaucluse.

In *Fam.* xi 6, also, he says that he would be glad to spend
the rest of his life in Vaucluse—where "libertas otium silentium
solitudo" were to be found—were it not for its distance from
Italy, its nearness to Avignon, and certain other impediments;
and that after he has seen the Pope, and such few friends as re-

---

[3] Jean Froissart, *Chroniques,* ed. by Siméon Luce, vi (Paris, 1876),
78 (Book I, Sect. 500).

main to him in Avignon, he will flee to Vaucluse, and there spend the summer "inter silvas ac flumina interque libellos varios, qui ibidem sub rustico custode vincti et taciti iam me quadriennium expectarunt."

His desire to revisit Vaucluse is set forth at some length and in some detail in *Fam.* xi 12 (a letter written to justify his decision to remain for two years), especially in these passages:

Cepit ecce impetus colles et specus et nemora revidendi virentique musco obsita atque ad famosum Sorgie fontem semper saxa sonantia.

Dulcedo quedam subiit locorum et latens animo calcar incussit; frenare illum ratio non potuit.

Impulit animum, ut dixi, non sine quadam dulcedine, memoria ruris abditi et silentis, ubi ab ineunte etate versatus sum.

Nichil autem me vehementius movit quam spes ingens supremam opusculis quibusdam meis imponendi manum, ut hic incepta Deo auspice, hic eodem duce finiantur. . . . Quantum ergo de preteritis futura conicio, biennii tempus ad id quod molior satis erit.

What were the "opuscula" that Petrarch thus hoped to complete? The four works (aside from the *Rerum memorandarum libri,* which he never touched after 1345) that had previously been largely written but had not yet been finished were the *De viris illustribus,* the *Africa,* the *De vita solitaria,* and the *De otio religiosorum.* The term "opuscula" might seem at first sight to be more appropriate for the *De vita* and the *De otio* than for the two major works; but it is properly to be taken simply as a deprecatory reference by Petrarch to works of his own, quite in line with other similar references.[4] Moreover, Petrarch could hardly

---

[4] In 1343 Petrarch received from Barbato da Sulmona a letter, now lost, in which Barbato, an avid collector of the writings of Petrarch, asked for more of them. In his reply—*Misc.* 16, the letter beginning *Inter varias*—Petrarch writes: "De opusculis quidem meis que maiori studio postulastis, quam vel illorum mereatur dignitas vel auctoris, excusari queso"; and in the course of the letter he promises to send the *Africa* as soon as it is finished (see below, p. 219). In the original form of the letter that became ultimately *Fam.* viii 2–5 Petrarch, developing the idea that Vaucluse had been the main scene of his literary inspirations, writes: "Illic . . . *Africam* cepi . . . ibi magna ex parte *Bucolica* mea scripsi . . . Nullus usquam locus aut plus otii opusculis meis dedit aut maius calcar ingenio" (Rossi 1, ii, 198). In *Fam.* xii 6 Petrarch speaks of the writings of his that were then at Vaucluse as "opuscula sive . . .

have thought that it would take him two years to do what little remained to be done on the two minor treatises. And the words "spes ingens" and the solemnity of the clause "ut hic incepta Deo auspice, hic eodem duce finiantur" point unmistakably to the *De viris* and the *Africa*.

At the end of the *Epistola posteritati*—in a passage, however, which was in all probability written many years afterward—Petrarch mentions his constant restlessness as the main cause of his return: "redii rursus in Gallias, stare nescius; non tam desiderio visa milies revisendi, quam studio, more aegrorum, loci mutatione taediis consulendi." [5]

Still other possible reasons for his return have been suggested. On his journey to Provence he took with him his son Giovanni, who had been at school in Parma (Petrarch had obtained his legitimation in 1347), and while in Provence he secured a benefice for him, as will appear below: the idea that he might succeed in doing this may well have been an element in his decision to return. Foresti, however, is certainly not justified in asserting that this was the "magna causa" of his return.[6]

Petrarch was interested, also, in the case of Don Ubertino, a Benedictine monk who was a friend of his. Appointment to the abbacy of the monastery of Cavanna—a dependency of the mon-

---

nugas meas." In *Fam.* xv 3 Petrarch speaks thus of the baggage he had planned to take with him to Italy: "Erat michi predulcis librorum sarcinula et veterum libris immixtum pauxillum nugarum mearum." In *Fam.* xvi 1 Petrarch says that his faithful but uneducated overseer, who in Petrarch's absence cared for his books as well as for his fields, "longo usu eo pervenerat ut et nomine nosset opera veterum et mea simul internosset opuscula." In the *Invective contra medicum*, ii, he says that his antagonist is offended because Petrarch has not written about him: "indignum te michi visum qui in meis opusculis scriberis."

[5] The *Epistola posteritati*, written in large part before 1350 (it is referred to in *Fam.* i 1), unquestionably received addenda in much later years. That the final passage is such an addendum is indicated both by the implications of the "semper" and of the perfect tense in the reference to Francesco da Carrara—"me carum semper et honoratum habuit"—and by the fact that, in view of the very definite reason or reasons for his return to Provence, only the perspective of a long intervening period could have justified him in attributing that return merely to restlessness.

[6] Foresti 1, p. 248; and "Il figlio di Francesco Petrarca," in *Archivio storico per le province parmensi*, N.S., xxxiv (1934), 363–390.

astery of Vallombrosa—had been promised to Don Ubertino by
the Abbot of Vallombrosa, who thereafter changed his mind, and
nominated another candidate.[7] While in Avignon Petrarch supported the claims of Don Ubertino, as will appear below: the
desire to do so may well have been an element in his decision to
return. Fracassetti, however, is certainly not justified in asserting
that desire to support the claims of Don Ubertino "sembra che
fosse la ragion principale, per la quale nel giugno del 1351, si
condusse in Avignone." [8]

II. The Dates of the Return

When Petrarch left Padua early in May 1351, he went first
(by way of Vicenza and Lonigo) to Verona. *Fam.* xi 6, which
he wrote, while there, to Boccaccio, contains this passage:

Promiseram tibi me Patavo digressurum ad XIV° Kalendas Maias;
vix V° Nonas inde . . . divulsus sum. Verone biduum aut triduum
agere decreveram; hic quoque iam procrastinando prope circumactus
est mensis . . . sed indulgentissimi amici blandis precum compedibus
explicari hactenus non potui . . . Hinc discedens hoc ipso die Man-
tuam peto . . . ibi me similis laqueus alter manet, sed ni fallor facilius
dissolvendus. Parme superioris amici frena non habeo . . . in ceteris
inde totius vie urbibus atque oppidis negotii nichil; itaque confestim
. . . e transalpino rure nostro ad te iterum scribam.

This letter, in its final form, is dated "Kalendis Iuniis" (1 June).
Of the six MSS of the original form of the letter, however, two
(one of them copied from the other) give the date as "III Kal.
Iulii," and two (one of them copied from the other) give it as
"II Kal. Iulii" (the other two omit the date). One of the many
MSS of the final form gives the date (apparently) as "Kal. Iulii."
Of these readings Rossi says:

La lezione 'Iulii' . . . è errore, perché comunque s'interpreti il

---

[7] Cochin 1, pp. 96–98 and 179–185; Cochin 2, pp. 7–9 and 57–60.
[8] Fracassetti 2, iii, 138 (in the notes on *Fam.* xii 5). For still other
possible reasons for the return see Rizzi 1, pp. 463–466.

'prope circumactus est mensis' . . . alla fine di giugno non si può certo arrivare.[9]

The document next to be considered is dated at Parma, "die xxv iunii." If the "iunii" is correct, as it probably is, it constitutes conclusive evidence that the letter just considered was written on or about 1 June rather than on or about 1 July.

While in Parma Petrarch had Corradino Corradi legally appointed to serve as his procurator during his absence. The document from which we learn of this appointment, as printed by Livi in 1878,[10] is one of several documents contained in a *quaderno* discovered by him in the Archivio Comunale of Reggio d'Emilia, and described by him in this sentence:

Non tardai a riconoscerlo per un protocollo, o più precisamente per uno di que' cosiddetti *libri imbreviaturarum* d'un notaio: non rare mi si mostrarono in esso le correzioni ed aggiunte in margine, e la scrittura mi apparve, come in simili libri, abbozzata e stesa per la prima volta.

The document in question (the fourth of those printed from the *quaderno* by Livi) begins thus (the parenthesis is Livi's):

Item eodem millesimo (1351), indictione et die xxv iunii, reverendus vir dominus Franciscus Petraccus, canonicus paduanus etc., fecit constituit et ordinavit suum certum nuncium, actorem, procuratorem et negotiorum gestorem, legiptimum defensorem Corradinum Corradi de Vuratislavia. . . .

It ends thus:

Actum Parme, in vicinia Sancti Stephani, in domo habitationis dicti Domini Francisci supradicti, presentibus dominis, dompno Luca presbitero Sancti Stephani parmensis, et Iohanne Petracco de Florentia, testibus vocatis et rogatis.

Fam. xi 7, written to Socrates and announcing Petrarch's

---

[9] Rossi 1, ii, 337. Rossi discusses the matter somewhere more fully in a note in Vol. I, p. xci. As to the day of the month he says, in that note, that the latter "è certo del 30 o 31 maggio." The omission of a numeral originally appearing before "Kal." was presumably merely scribal. For other instances of similar omission see Rossi's notes on the variants in the dates of *Fam.* i 3, ii 10, xii 3, 9, and 11, and xxii 5 and 13.

[10] Livi, pp. 289–299.

expectation of being soon at Vaucluse, is dated "III Idus Iunias, Placentie" (11 June, Piacenza).

Fam. xi 9, written to Giovanni Aghinolfi and saying that Petrarch expects an early visit from him at Vaucluse, is dated "XII Kal. Iulias, Gebenne montis e vertice" (20 June, from the summit—of the pass—of Mont Genèvre).

Fam. xi 10, written to Philippe de Cabassoles and saying that Petrarch has just arrived at Vaucluse and will come to Cavaillon (which is only six miles from Vaucluse) as soon as he has washed away the stains of his journey, is dated "V Kal. Iulias" (27 June).

Fam. xi 11, written to Philippe after Petrarch's return from Cavaillon, is dated "III Kal. Iulias" (29 June).

Fam. xi 12, written to Luca Cristiani after Petrarch had settled into his life at Vaucluse, is dated "XIV Kal. Augustas" (19 July).

There is an obvious discrepancy between the dating of the Parma document and the dating of the five letters just mentioned. If the date of 25 June is correct for the Parma document, then the dates for these five letters are erroneous, fanciful, or false. If the dates of the letters are correct, then the date of the Parma document is in some sense erroneous.

Rizzi [11] assumes the validity of the date in the document, and says, after quoting Petrarch's dates for *Fam.* xi 7 and 9:

Eppure il 25 Giugno il Petrarca era a Parma col figlio, che appare testimone in quell'atto di procura! Evidentemente il poeta appose a queste lettere date approssimative, più tardi, a memoria.

Fermi [12] echoes Rizzi, noting that acceptance of the date of the document involves also the conclusion that Petrarch's dates for *Fam.* xi 10 and 11 are also "inesatte e a memoria."

It is however by no means certain that the date given in the document as printed by Livi is correct. It seems to have been assumed not only that Livi's transcription was correct (as indeed it probably was, though he does not report the "correzioni" and "aggiunte" that he mentions), but also that the document he tran-

[11] Rizzi 1, pp. 474 and 480–483.
[12] Stefano Fermi, "Note piacentine su Francesco Petrarca," in *Bullettino storico piacentino*, xxxi (1936), 74–77.

scribed was an original document. But examination of the document as printed makes it clear that the document discovered by Livi was not an original document, but a transcript entered by a notary in a *quaderno* of his own. That this is the case is made evident by the very first words of the document as printed, "Item eodem millesimo, indictione": no original document could possibly have begun thus. It is indicated also by the abbreviated form of the reference to Petrarch, "canonicus paduanus etc." (unless the abbreviation is Livi's). It is indicated also by the clause, which occurs toward the end of the document, "Quod promisit mihi notario." It is made evident also by the fact that the presence of the witnesses is merely reported: no signatures appear. The date of the document as printed has then no such authority as has been attributed to it. If in the *quaderno* the date is actually "xxv iunii," the "xxv" is explicable as a scribal error or a notarial lapse of some sort, or as the date on which the notary transcribed the original document into his own *quaderno*, or as the date on which he placed the original document in the hands of the proper authorities.

It is indeed inherently improbable, in view of Petrarch's desire to make haste, as expressed in *Fam.* xi 6, that he should have been in Parma as late as 25 June.

Petrarch's memory was excellent. He was, to be sure, quite capable of altering dates, for special purposes, when he made up the collection of the *Familiares* (though the extent to which he did so has in my opinion been considerably exaggerated: see below, pp. 216–218 and 225–227); but it is impossible for me to imagine any reason that could have led him to the consistent alteration of the dates of *Fam.* xi 7, 9, 10, 11, and 12.

In view of the foregoing considerations it would seem that Petrarch's dates for these five letters should be accepted as valid, unless and until they should be impugned by convincing evidence not hitherto adduced.

III. *Vaucluse and Avignon*

Vaucluse and Avignon are only fifteen miles apart, and Petrarch could easily have ridden from one place to the other in a morning or afternoon. The evidence indicates, however, that during nearly all of his stay in Provence he dwelt for fairly long consecutive periods now in one place and now in the other, visiting only occasionally the place in which he was not dwelling. The following paragraphs concern only the distribution of Petrarch's time as between Vaucluse and Avignon, and disregard the brief visits to Cavaillon and to Montrieux that will be mentioned in the later course of this study.

There are extant four letters (*Fam.* xi 10–12 and xiii 11) that were certainly or probably written by Petrarch in the period 27 June–25 August 1351. All four are dated from Vaucluse; and there is no evidence indicating that Petrarch visited Avignon during this period. We may then conclude that he spent the summer of 1351 in Vaucluse—not excluding, however, the possibility of an occasional visit to Avignon.

A single letter (*Fam.* xi 13) written on 29 August is dated from Avignon; no other extant letter is known or thought to have been written in the period 29 August–22 October; letters written on 23 October and later are dated from Avignon. It may be that this single letter was written on a brief visit to Avignon, and that Petrarch thereafter resumed his stay at Vaucluse; or it may be that Petrarch had established himself in Avignon before the end of August. It is inherently probable that he had established himself there by about 1 October.

There are extant 25 letters (*Fam.* v 19; ix 5–7; xi 14–17; xii 1–7 and 9–10; xv 4; *Sine nom.* 6–11; and *Sine nom.* 5 plus *Fam.* xii 8, originally a single letter) that were certainly or probably written in the period October 1351–1 April 1352; and one other (*Fam.* ix 14) that may well have been written toward the end of the period. Nine of these 25 letters are dated from Avignon; six others were certainly written in Avignon; and nine others may have been written there. *Fam.* xv 4 was dated from Vaucluse on 26 February. We know from *Fam.* xii 8 that Petrarch spent ten days late in March in Vaucluse, and the same letter indicates that Petrarch had occasionally returned to Vaucluse before that time. We may then conclude that Petrarch spent this period in Avignon, except for the visits just mentioned.

There are extant 23 letters (*Fam.* xii 11–17; xiii 1 6 and 8–10; xv 5–10; and *Sine nom.* 13) that were certainly or probably written in the period 3 April–August 1352. Fourteen of these letters are dated from Vaucluse; three others were certainly written there; and four others may have been written there. One of the two remaining letters, *Fam.* xiii 1, was dated in Avignon on 14 May. The other, *Fam.* xii 11, dated 21 May, was certainly written in Avignon: its last words, however, make it clear that Petrarch planned to be in Vaucluse on the following day. We may then conclude that Petrarch spent this period in Vaucluse, except that he was in Avignon once or twice in May—not excluding the possibility of other occasional visits to Avignon.

All of the four letters that were certainly written in September 1352 (*Fam.* xiii 12 and xiv 1–3) were written in Vaucluse; but there is evidence (which will be presented in Section VIII of this chapter) that Petrarch was in Avignon at least once early in September and again at the very end of the month. We may then conclude that in this month Petrarch was at times in Vaucluse and at times in Avignon.

Two of the five letters that were certainly or probably written in the period October–7 November 1352 (*Fam.* xiv 4 and 5; xv 1; *Sine nom.* 4; and *Var.* 36) are dated from Avignon, and the others were certainly or probably written there; and there is evidence that Petrarch was continuously in Avignon throughout this period, returning to Vaucluse on 8 November.

There are extant 23 letters (*Fam.* vii 8; ix 14; xiii 7; xiv 6–8; xv 2, 3, and 11–14; xvi 1–10; and *Sine nom.* 12) that were certainly or probably written in the period 8 November 1352–May 1353. Of these 23 letters eleven are dated from Vaucluse, one other was certainly written there, and seven others were probably written there. *Fam.* xvi 1, written in Avignon on 5 January 1353, shows that Petrarch had come in from Vaucluse to Avignon on the 3rd and that he was returning to Vaucluse on the 5th. *Fam.* xvi 10, written in Avignon on 28 April, shows that Petrarch had come in from Vaucluse to Avignon two or three days earlier, to say his final farewells, and that he was returning at once to Vaucluse. These are the only indications that

Petrarch was ever in Avignon after 8 November 1352; and the temper of his references to Avignon in letters written on and after 8 November is such as to make it improbable that he returned to Avignon at all, after that date, except on the two occasions just mentioned. In May he started for Italy. We may then conclude that he spent this period in Vaucluse, visiting Avignon only on the two occasions just mentioned.

Thus Petrarch's last stay in Provence falls into these seven periods:

Summer 1351	Vaucluse
Late August and September 1351	Vaucluse or Avignon
October 1351–1 April 1352	Avignon
3 April–August 1352	Vaucluse
September 1352	Vaucluse and Avignon
October–8 November 1352	Avignon
8 November 1352–May 1353	Vaucluse

IV. Vaucluse: Summer 1351

On Monday, 27 June, the day of his arrival at Vaucluse,[13] Petrarch sent a message (*Fam.* xi 10) to Philippe de Cabassoles, saying that he had reached Vaucluse, and that he would come to Cavaillon (six miles to the south) after he had had a chance to remove the stains and the dust of travel. He evidently did go to Cavaillon on that same day or the next, and while he was there he seems to have asked Philippe for commendatory letters to two cardinals: for on 29 June he sent a note (*Fam.* xi 11) to Philippe, thanking him for the letters, which must therefore have been given to him while he was at Cavaillon or sent to him after his return to Vaucluse. He does not name the two cardinals. It has been generally assumed that they were Gui de Boulogne and Elie de Talleyrand: this assumption is probably correct, the probability being indicated, in the case of Cardinal Talleyrand, by cir-

---

[13] On Vaucluse and its surroundings see Flamini; also Jean Saint-Martin, *La fontaine de Vaucluse et ses souvenirs* (Paris, 1891: valuable chiefly for its illustrations). On Petrarch's house at Vaucluse see M. Mignon, "La maison de Pétrarque à Vaucluse," in *Etudes italiennes,* ix (1927), 215–235.

cumstances to be mentioned below (on p. 136). While at Cavaillon Petrarch presumably saw his friend Sansone Ponzio, Provost of Cavaillon, of whom he writes affectionately in the *De vita solitaria* (II 10, 1).

Immediately upon his arrival at Vaucluse Petrarch acquired a dog—characterized as "pice nigrior vento levior cane fidelior"— under circumstances reported in *Fam.* XIII 11 (Fracassetti's XII 17), written on 25 August to Matteo Longo. Matteo had been living at Vaucluse, but had left not long before Petrarch came, and had left his dog behind him: the dog's pitiful barking before the closed door served to inform Petrarch that Matteo had gone. The dog then, after a first suspicious hesitation, attached himself to Petrarch, and thereafter went with him on woodland walks: "Ut me autem ille conspexit, infremuit; mox tremula blanditiis cauda vocantem sponte consequitur; nunc mecum vadit in silvas, sub me militat, meis auspiciis ruit in beluas et michi sepe gratissimas predas agit."

Petrarch's fullest description of his life at Vaucluse is contained in a letter, *Fam.* XIII 8, which, though written in the summer of 1352, presumably applies equally well to his life there in the summer of 1351: it may therefore be summarized at this point.

I dress like a peasant and eat peasant food. In my own simple house I live with two menservants and a dog: close by is the house of my overseer, "villicus meus indulgentissimus familiaris," who can however be "saxeus" on my behalf. The overseer's wife—her heart as white as her face is black, her ugliness almost becoming to her—is an indefatigable worker, despite her years: she toils in the fields all day long, yet returns toward evening, ready to take care cheerfully of the needs of her children, her husband, my servants, and any guests I may have. Close to my house a rock formation makes a cave-like shelter in which I find defense against the summer heat: it is a place conducive to study. I have two gardens, "tam ingenio propositoque meo consentaneos ut nichil magis." One of the gardens is close to the point where the Sorgue gushes forth from under its high cliff: "Est . . . umbrosus solique studio aptus et nostro sacer Apollini," "locus . . . alta sub rupe ac mediis in undis, angustus quidem sed plenus stimulis ardentibus, quibus piger licet animus in altissimas curas possit assurgere." The other garden, on an island in the Sorgue, "aspectu

this writing was done "di un sol getto"; and that work on the *De viris* was going on in the early months of 1353, when Petrarch wrote, in Book II of the *Invective contra medicum,* "scribo de viris illustribus." [16] It does not necessarily follow, however, that the writing of the new preface and the twelve new lives was going on in 1353. It will indeed appear below (on p. 112), that the figures of Nimrod and Semiramis were active in Petrarch's mind in the autumn of 1351 and the following winter, a fact which suggests that Petrarch was then working on their lives or that he had recently been working on them. In view of Petrarch's statement of hope in *Fam.* XI 12, in view of the fact that he now again had access to his books, in view of the fact that he did actually work on the *De viris* in the course of this stay in Provence, and in view of the fact of his interest in Nimrod and Semiramis during the autumn of 1351 and the following winter, it is virtually certain that he began work on the completion of the *De viris* soon after he reached Vaucluse. It is possible, but improbable, that he worked on the *Africa,* or on the *De vita,* or on the *De otio* during his stay in Provence.[17]

During his stay in Provence Petrarch did much work on the formation of the collection of the *Familiares* (as will appear in Section XII of the present chapter): it may well be that some of this work was done in Vaucluse in the summer of 1351.

During this stay in Provence, also, Petrarch certainly wrote, in Vaucluse, the sixteen sonnets that were eventually included in the *Canzoniere* as Nos. 279–282, 288, 300–303, 305–306, 308, 310–311, and 320–321, and doubtless many of the other poems included in the second part of the *Canzoniere.* Presumably some, probably many, of these poems, were written during the summer

---

[16] Martellotti, pp. 51–80. For the continuity of the writing, see pp. 73 ff. For the quotation from the *Invective* (which appears in Ricci, p. 45) see pp. 70–71. For the date of Book II of the *Invective* see Bosco, pp. 103–104.

[17] For the *Africa* see the passage in *Fam.* XII 7 quoted below, and Martellotti, p. 64, n. 2 and p. 67, n. 1. For the *De vita* see B. L. Ullman, "The Composition of Petrarch's 'De vita solitaria' and the History of the Vatican Manuscript," in *Miscellanea Giovanni Mercati* (Città del Vaticano, 1946), IV, 107–142. For the *De otio* see Giuseppe Rotondi, "Le due redazioni del *De otio* del Petrarca," in *Aevum,* IX (1935), 27–77.

of 1351. Laura had died during Petrarch's absence in Italy; and the revisiting of scenes associated with his love for her may well have moved him very soon to the writing of such poems.

There is no evidence that Petrarch went in to Avignon before the end of August. From *Fam.* xi 6 it appears that he had originally planned to go there immediately; but in *Fam.* xi 9 (after inviting Aghinolfi to visit him in Vaucluse) he concludes: "illic aliquantulum respirabimus priusquam illud tartareum limen vicine Babilonis ingrediamur."

V. *Vaucluse or Avignon: Late August and September 1351*

The letter that Petrarch wrote in Avignon on 29 August, *Fam.* xi 13, was addressed to the Florentine Niccolò Acciaiuoli, now Grand Seneschal of the Kingdom of Naples and the driving force behind Louis of Taranto, who was the second husband of Queen Joan and the still uncrowned King of Naples. The affairs of the Kingdom were a matter of grave concern to the papacy, since the Kingdom was held as a fief under the sovereignty of the Pope. They were also a matter of great personal interest to Petrarch: he cherished his memories of his visit to Naples ten years before, when King Robert had pronounced him worthy of poetic coronation; in 1343, after the death of King Robert, he had been sent to Naples with missions from Cardinal Colonna and from the Pope, and though appalled by conditions at court he had greatly enjoyed the country around Naples, and had been made an honorary chaplain to Queen Joan; he had warm friends in Naples; and he abhorred the presence of "barbarian" troops in Italy.

Neapolitan difficulties were twofold: King Louis of Hungary, a claimant for the Neapolitan throne, had invaded the Kingdom (for the second time) in the spring of 1350; and Louis of Taranto and Queen Joan had been contending strenuously for the actual royal power, the Queen supported by the Pope, Louis by Acciaiuoli. In the summer of 1350 the intervention of papal emissaries led to a truce between invaders and defenders; the King of Hungary withdrew, leaving troops, largely mer-

cenaries, behind; in October Louis of Taranto, following a course
of action that had doubtless been planned by Acciaiuoli, won his
struggle with the Queen—Acciaiuoli's power being thereafter
recognized and respected even in Avignon; and in December
negotiations for a final settlement of the Hungarian-Neapolitan
claims began in Avignon. In February 1351 (the truce having
become a dead letter) Acciaiuoli made plans to drive out from
the Kingdom the troops that had been left there by the King of
Hungary, but (aside from trivial action on the Sorrentine peninsula) there was no clash of arms until the following September;
during the spring the negotiations carried on in Avignon pro-
gressed favorably—the King of Hungary was to renounce his
Neapolitan claims, but was to receive a huge indemnity; and on
14 June Acciaiuoli was able to say, in effect, in a letter to Florentine correspondents: "The general agreement between our
sovereigns and the King of Hungary has been made and accepted
by both parties . . . and we shall have peace." [18]

   Fam. xi 13 is in general devoted to praise and congratulation.
Two passages refer to recent or current events. The first refers
presumably to the success of the peace negotiations: "Accessit ad
uberiorem stili materiam recens regia fortuna tuis semper adiuta
consiliis, que michi letam spem restituit illo incolumi nunquam
barbaros in Italia regnaturos." [19] The second passage refers
clearly to Acciaiuoli's plans to drive out from the Kingdom the
troops left there by the King of Hungary—plans which Acciaiuoli began to carry out in September: [20] "et si . . . ceptis illustribus favor celestis affuerit, ut corpus italicum tabe barbarica
purgatum medullitus agnoscam, in quod iam nunc, ut fama est,
dulcia nostris amara hostibus confecistis . . ." If these plans are
successful, Petrarch concludes, he will be unable to resist his

---

[18] See Léonard 1, ii, 231–321. The quotation from the letter of 14
June appears on p. 313.

[19] Fracassetti's translation of "regia fortuna" as "il fortunato successo
delle armi regie" is certainly erroneous: except for the trivial action
on the Sorrentine peninsula there had been no fighting between the hostile
forces since the summer of 1350, and the fighting in that year had gone
against the Neapolitan troops.

[20] Léonard 1, ii, 299–300 and 320 ff.

desire to escape from the "retia" of his occupations in Avignon, to revisit Naples (that shore "cui non modo in Italia sed in toto etiam orbe terrarum scriptores rerum dant pulchritudinis principatum"), and to meet Acciaiuoli face to face.

In September Petrarch doubtless received Nelli's *Ep.* vi (LAP 28), written on 21 August, and *Ep.* iii (LAP 25), written on 27 August. *Ep.* vi concerns the case of Don Ubertino.[21]

VI. Avignon: c. 1 October 1351–1 April 1352

At some time after 25 August and before 23 October Petrarch established himself in Avignon; and there he remained until 1 April, except for the visit or visits to Vaucluse and Cavaillon to which reference has been and will be made.

The contrast between Vaucluse and Avignon was, for Petrarch, extremely great: Vaucluse, for him, was Helicon, Parnassus, Elysium; Avignon was Babylon, Tartarus, Avernus, Erebus, the Fifth Labyrinth, "Infernus viventium." Pierre Roger had been Pope, as Clement VI, since 1342. The College of Cardinals, in the autumn of 1351, consisted of 27 men: 24 Frenchmen, two Italians, and one Spaniard.[22] The conditions of life in the papal court, as they appeared to Petrarch, are depicted in lurid colors in his *Epistolae sine nomine* and in other writings of his.[23] Among the matters that were of concern both to the papal court in general and—as will appear presently—to Petrarch were the state of affairs in Rome, the state of affairs in the Kingdom of Naples, the policy of the Emperor, Charles IV, with regard to Italy, and, from December on, the serious illness of the Pope.

While in Avignon during the autumn and winter Petrarch was the guest of his friend Guido Sette, Archdeacon of Genoa, as we learn from a later reminiscent letter, *Fam.* xix 16. His son

---

[21] Cochin 1 and 2. For *Ep.* vi, see the references given above in n. 7. For *Ep.* iii, see Cochin 1, pp. 92–94 and 169–170, and Cochin 2, pp. 5–6 and 53–54.

[22] Those designated by Eubel, pp. 15–19, as xxi 4, 7, 12, and 27, xxii 2, 4, and 7, and xxiii 2, 5, 7, and 9–25.

[23] On conditions in Avignon see Piur 1, pp. 49–109; and Mollat, pp. 84–92 and 441–503.

Giovanni was with him, as we learn from *Sine nom.* 11. He saw much of many members of the papal court. In *Fam.* IX 5, 25, he says, speaking of the lack of happiness of those holding high ecclesiastical office: "Neque ego tam constanter hec dicerem, nisi romane sedis antistitem et hos romano cardine fulgidos atque alios urbium prelatos familiariter novissem; que familiaritas in illorum adumbrate felicitatis iudicio me non sinit errare." And *Fam.* XIII 5 contains the clause "quod a duobus [*i.e.*, the two cardinals who had called him to Avignon] audieram a multis ex eodem ordine conscriptis patribus audivi." As has already appeared or will appear below, he saw something, certainly or probably, of the following individual members of the papal court or persons connected directly or indirectly with that court: the Pope; Cardinals Gui de Boulogne, Elie de Talleyrand, Etienne Aubert and Niccola Capocci; the Apostolic Secretary Francesco Calvo; Pierre d'Auvergne, Abbot of St. Bénigne, an attaché of Gui de Boulogne; Stefano Colonna, Provost of Saint-Omer; and at least one of the Pope's attending physicians. He must have seen much of Guido Sette and of Socrates. As will appear below (on pp. 117–118), he saw something of the Italian musician Floriano da Rimini.

Petrarch must have seen much of two Florentines, Angelo Acciaiuoli and Forese Donati. Angelo (a cousin of Niccolò), Bishop of Florence and, since 1349, Chancellor of the Kingdom of Naples, was sent to Avignon late in October 1351 as one of two Florentine envoys instructed to win Clement to an alliance against the Visconti and to urge him to authorize the coronation of Louis and Joan.[24] He was interested also in the case of Don Ubertino.[25] Forese Donati, rector of S. Stefano in Botena near Florence, a devoted friend and admirer of Petrarch, was a member of Angelo's party. On 18 January Petrarch wrote to Nelli, in *Fam.* XII 5, "Forensem tuum, imo meum, imo nostrum, ut ait ille,

---

[24] The envoys received two sets of instructions: one, concerned only with the alliance against the Visconti, is published in full by Baldasseroni, pp. 85–89; the portion of the other which relates to the coronation is published in Léonard 1, II, 332, n. 2.

[25] Cochin 1, pp. 94–98 and 179–185; Cochin 2, pp. 6–9 and 57–60.

virum per se amari dignissimum, tota, ut iubes, mente suscipio." [26]

In *Fam.* xi 9, written on his way to Provence to Giovanni Aghinolfi, Chancellor of the Gonzaga, Petrarch had said: "tu me, oro, confestim sequere, et facies, scio . . . Ad fontem Sorgie te expecto." These words imply that Petrarch knew that Giovanni was soon to come to Avignon—doubtless on official business—in which case Petrarch, while in Avignon, would have seen something of him.

Presumably Petrarch carried out his intention to visit Philippe de Cabassoles at Cavaillon; and in that case he doubtless saw Sansone Ponzio there as well.

During the latter part of this period Petrarch suffered from ill health. *Sine nom.* 5, written on 1 April, ends thus:

Hic ita confectus et affectus et defectus sum, ut, iam sensim morbo animi in corpo translato, totus eger nil preter meros dolores ac rancores loqui possim . . . Vterque michi nunc stomachus dolet, nil ex me hodie placidum speres . . . Natura fert ut exulcerati pectoris infecta suspiria et offensi animi uerba sint acria.

Of his occupations in Avignon he speaks in general terms in several letters—thus, in *Sine nom.* 11: "Tam diuersa certatim et me urgent et se inuicem premunt impediuntque concursum. Non uacat omnibus obsequi. Infinita sunt enim." In *Fam.* ix 5 he asks and answers an imaginary question thus: " 'Quid facis in curia?' langueo crucior affligor indignor et . . . tempus . . . perdo . . . Denique si quid faciam roges, non tam facile possim respondere quid faciam quam quid non faciam." In *Fam.* ix 6 he speaks of

---

[26] On Forese, who is referred to also in *Fam.* xii 8 and is the addressee of the much later *Fam.* xviii 6, see Billanovich, pp. 161–162. Presumably Forese went to Avignon with Angelo. He was certainly there in December, since Nelli's *Ep.* iv, written on 4 January, must have been written after he had received a letter written by Forese in Avignon: see below, pp. 194–195. It may well have been Forese who brought to Avignon the gifts that Boccaccio sent to Petrarch at about this time: a copy of the *Divine Comedy*, with Boccaccio's accompanying *epistola metrica* beginning "Ytalie iam certus honos," and copies of Boccaccio's own *Amorosa visione* and *Caccia di Diana* and two minor poems: see Billanovich, pp. 147–150 and 163–164. Fracassetti's translation of the passage in *Fam.* xii 8 regarding Forese is erroneous.

being held "in hac tempestate negotiorum, que michi vix respirandi spatium prestat."

He had been called to Avignon by two cardinals, speaking in the name of the Pope, but not stating the purpose for which they were calling him. What that purpose was, Petrarch reports at length in *Fam.* xiii 5: they had hoped to persuade him to accept an apostolic secretaryship (although he had refused such an offer in 1347: see above, pp. 16–17). Petrarch was dismayed and distressed: if he had known that this was the purpose of the summons, he would never have come. Despite his obstinate resistance great pressure was brought to bear upon him to accept, even by the Pope:

> Et quid putas? omnis insidiarum scena primo michi patuit adventu. Quodsi omnes ambagum formas enumerem, quibus non sine indignatione mea . . . unus . . . annus effluxit, longa erit historia, summa cuntis ope tendentibus ut dives sed occupatus atque solicitus, imo quidem ut vere pauper miser et mestus fierem, me uno reluctante acriter ac recusante iugum aureum non aliter quam ligneum aut plumbeum . . .
> Talibus agebam sepe indignans, sepe vero flebiliter et prope cum lacrimis; contra autem amicorum obstinata acies et consilia . . . Veneram interea ad illius pedes qui digito celum pandit et temperat astra galero; is equidem adventu meo letare visus, multa dixit quibus satis apparet non libertati mee illum sed opinioni omnium favere.

He came very near to losing the struggle, but was saved by a circumstance to which he refers as "flebilem ridiculamque." Those who were urging his acceptance had only one fear: "Unum obstare dicebatur quod michi altior stilus esset quam romane sedis humilitas postularet"—and he contrived to convince them that he could not "lower" his style enough to meet their idea of apostolic propriety. Since it was for this purpose that Petrarch had been called from Italy, it is virtually certain that the struggle began, at least, by the autumn of 1351, and that Petrarch's interview with the Pope regarding the apostolic secretaryship took place in that season.

Passages in *Fam.* ix 5 and in *Var.* 15 show that Clement repeatedly offered Petrarch a bishopric, and that at least one such offer must have been made during Petrarch's last stay in

Provence.[27] Such an offer may or may not have been made during their interview with regard to the apostolic secretaryship. The end of an interview during which such an offer was made is reported in *Var.* 15, in a passage that has been quoted above (on pp. 72–73).

During the autumn and winter Petrarch doubtless was doing all he could to secure a benefice for his son. Success came on 20 March 1352, when the Pope granted Giovanni a canonry in Verona.

Of his strenuous efforts on behalf of Don Ubertino he writes thus in *Fam.* XII 13:

Ridiculum rancidulum stomaculo insidens, quod Umbrose Vallis arbiter instabili michi votorum alternatione pepererat . . . excutere nisus summa precum vi, quod michi nunquam fueram, fui alteri, ambitiosus sedulus solicitus. Vidisses iocundum simul et miserabile spectaculum: me solitudinis avidum atque otii et in silvis errare solitum, mutatis repente studiis, cum ingenti curialium catherva dies totos pontificum superbis liminibus oberrantem, mirantibus amicis, stomacantibus mecum Musis . . . qua in re et amicitia sibi profuit et meritum, sed nil magis quam inimicorum eius inexorabilis et implacata superbia et indignatio mea, que de segni me vigilantissimum fecerat: pati non potui tam licenter veritatem mendacio calcari.

Petrarch, also, had his enemies. Against the charge that he had come to Avignon in order to injure Ugolino dei Rossi, Bishop of Parma—a charge that Ugolino had been led to believe—he defends himself at great length in a masterly letter to Ugolino, *Fam.* IX 5. His anxiety about this matter is expressed also in two related letters, *Fam.* IX 6 and 7, written to Luca da Piacenza, rector of S. Stefano in Parma.[28]

In *Fam.* IX 5, also, Petrarch refers to the currency in certain quarters of the belief that he was a necromancer: "et fortasse— quod nescio qualiter venit ad aures meas inter magnos sepe iactatum . . . —multis iam nigromanticus ac magus appareo, quia

[27] See Carlo Cipolla, "La diplomazia fiorentina e il soggiorno di Francesco Petrarca in Avignone negli anni 1351–1352," in R. Accademia delle Scienze di Torino, *Memorie*, Ser. II, LIX (1909), Classe di scienze morali, storiche e filologiche, 163.

[28] On Petrarch's relations with Ugolino see Rizzi 1, pp. 475–480 and *passim* (see index). On Luca da Piacenza see Foresti 1, pp. 263–269.

sepe scilicet solus sum et—quod bilem risu mixtam eicit—quia
Virgilii libros lego." To this same experience Petrarch refers in
four later letters, briefly in *Fam.* xiii 6, *Sen.* i 2, and *Misc.* 2,
and in some detail in *Sen.* i 4, written to Cardinal Elie de Talleyrand. In this letter the originator of the calumny is characterized
as an influential cardinal, expert in the law, widely experienced,
and advanced in years: it has been shown to be probable that he
was Cardinal Pierre des Prez. His hatred was directed not against
Petrarch himself, but against "illum cui familiarissimum me fuisse
meminerat . . . sicut sepulto illi ipsius nec lenitus morte: ipsis
bellum cineribus indixerat"—the reference is presumably to Cardinal Giovanni Colonna, who had died in 1348. The same letter
makes it clear that among those who accepted the calumny
was Cardinal Etienne Aubert, who held firmly to it even though
Cardinal Talleyrand and Petrarch ridiculed it in his presence
(and even, for some years, after he had been made Pope as
Innocent VI).[29]

During the autumn and winter Petrarch took such action as
he could with regard to four matters of public concern that have
already been mentioned: affairs in Rome and in Naples, the policy of Charles IV with regard to Italy, and the illness of the Pope.

Gregorovius writes thus of the state of affairs in Rome at
this time:

Kaum war das Jubeljahr zu Ende gegangen, als Anarchie, frucht-
barer denn je, über Rom hereinbrach. Die Regierung der neuen
Senatoren . . . war kraftlos; der Adel achtete kein Gesetz, nahm
Räuber und Bravi in Gold, und erfüllte Stadt und Land mit Frevel-
thaten . . . Es gab keine Regierung mehr; die Republik schien auf-
gelöst.[30]

Cola di Rienzo was a prisoner in Bohemia: the Pope was pressing the Emperor to send him to Avignon, to be tried there for
heresy.[31] Before mid-November the Pope appointed a commission of four cardinals "to reform the government of the Roman

---

[29] On this episode see Carlo Segrè, "Chi accusò il Petrarca di magia,"
in his *Studi petrarcheschi* (Florence, 1903), pp. 199–224.
[30] Gregorovius, Book XI, Chap. VII, Sect. 2.
[31] Piur 2, Chap. VII.

Republic." The names of the four are not a matter of record. It is certain, however, that Niccola Capocci was one of them; and it is probable that the other three were Bertrand de Déaulx, Gui de Boulogne, and either Guillaume Court or Bertrand du Pouget.[32]

Petrarch's special interest in Roman affairs resulted from his sense of Rome's historic greatness, from his conviction that Rome alone was the proper seat of the papacy, from the deep impression made on him by his visits to Rome in 1337, 1341, and 1350, and in particular from the fact that Roman citizenship had been conferred upon him on the occasion of his coronation in 1341. One day in the autumn of 1351, standing in front of an ancient church, he had a memorable talk about the deplorable state of affairs in Rome with a man who seems to have been of high ecclesiastical status and a Roman citizen—probably Cardinal Niccola Capocci. This interview, as reported in *Sine nom.* 7, stirred in Petrarch a desire for action: "O! si unquam . . ."[33] O! si in diebus meis accidat! O! si tam clari operis et tante glorie sim particeps!" His opportunity came in November, with the appointment of the commission of four cardinals. Someone—again probably Cardinal Capocci—requested him to set down his views on the subject for the benefit of the commission: and he did so in the long and noble *Fam.* xi 16, addressed to the four cardinals on 18 November, in which he urged that the Colonna and the Orsini—the two great families, neither of them of Roman origin, whose struggle for power was the main cause of the plight of Rome—be excluded from the government of the city, and that membership in the Roman Senate be limited to those who were truly Roman citizens. Six days later Petrarch wrote to the four cardinals a second but much shorter letter, *Fam.* xi 17, on the same subject. The commission, however, accomplished nothing.

Negotiations for the settlement of the Hungarian-Neapolitan dispute had seemed to be close to conclusion in the summer of 1351; but difficulties had arisen, and during the autumn it was still not certain that either party would consent to new provisions

---

[32] On this point and on what follows see the next chapter.
[33] The suspension points are in this case a part of the text.

now found to be necessary. Meanwhile, from October to December, Niccolò Acciaiuoli and Louis of Taranto were engaged in a campaign to drive out the forces left in the Kingdom of Naples by the King of Hungary; and the Pope, with good reason, feared that this campaign would frustrate the negotiations. The campaign came to nothing, however, and peaceful settlement was finally reached in January 1352. This settlement opened the way for the Pope to authorize at last—on 19 January—the long desired and long deferred coronation of Louis and Joan as King and Queen of Naples.[34] On 20 February Petrarch sent to Niccolò a long and impressive letter, *Fam.* xii 2, in which, after congratulating him on the success of his efforts, he bids him now to devote redoubled efforts to the guidance of Louis in his kingship. The letter is in effect a treatise *de regimine principis*.[35]

Charles IV, emperor in fact since 1346, but not yet crowned as emperor, was too much a realist to think that he could establish actual imperial control over Italy; but he wished to maintain publicly his imperial claims in Italy, provided he could do so without fighting for them. Clement VI, though he had favored the election of Charles, was opposed to an imperial expedition to Rome, fearing, doubtless, that such an expedition might result in a conflict between papal and imperial claims.[36] Petrarch, however, was exceedingly eager to have Charles enter Italy, both because he hoped that the coming of the Emperor might bring peace and liberty to a land riven by local warfare and oppressed by local tyranny, and because, as a champion of the great Roman tradition and a citizen of Rome, he desired intensely the restoration of Rome to its rightful imperial state and dignity. In February 1351 he had written his first letter to Charles, *Fam.* x 1, urging him to enter Italy; but at the end of 1351 no answer to

---

[34] Léonard 1, ii, 307–335.

[35] An exposition of this letter by Barbato da Sulmona is printed in part by Faraglia: see below, pp. 251–252. A Catalan translation is printed, from a 15th-century MS, by E. Moliné y Brasés in his "La 'Letra de reyals custums' del Petrarca," in Institut d'Estudis Catalans, *Anuari*, i (1907), 345–351.

[36] Bede Jarrett, *The Emperor Charles IV* (New York, 1935), pp. 116–117 and 144–146; C. C. Bayley, "Petrarch, Charles IV, and the Renovatio Imperii," in *Speculum*, xvii (1942), 328–329; and Mollat, pp. 356–358.

that letter had been received.[37] Now, early in 1352, and certainly before the end of March,[38] he wrote to Charles a second letter, *Fam.* XII 1, repeating his urgent request that Charles should enter Italy:

pro honore Imperii, pro salute Italie, pro consolatione urbis Rome desolatissime sponse tue, pro amicorum gaudio, pro subiectorum commodis, pro quiete laborantium Cristianorum, pro maturando negotio Terre Sancte, pro adipiscendo in terris preclarissime et immortalis fame preconio, pro eterna beatitudine post huius fugacissime vite miserias promerenda, oro precor obsecro, toto nunc animo genibus tuis affusus, quatenus occasionem res maximas atque optimas gerendi oblatam incuntanter arripias.

He points out in particular that Tuscany, previously hostile to imperial claims, now desires the coming of the Emperor: presumably Petrarch knew (very possibly from Angelo Acciaiuoli) that negotiations were, or were soon to be, in process, looking toward the alliance between Charles and the Tuscan cities that was actually to be reached in Prague in May 1352.

Before the end of March—perhaps even before Petrarch wrote his letter to the Emperor—there existed a plan, of which we learn from *Fam.* XV 5, for Cardinal Gui de Boulogne to go to Italy to meet the Emperor, taking with him Petrarch, Pierre d'Auvergne,

---

[37] In point of fact the Emperor had drafted a reply, which was put into final form for him by Cola di Rienzo; but this letter (LAP 9) did not reach Petrarch until 1353, when he answered it in his third letter to Charles (*Fam.* XVIII 1), written certainly in Milan.

[38] That *Fam.* XII 1 was written in 1352 was shown by Piur, *Petrarcas Briefwechsel mit deutschen Zeitgenossen* (= Burdach, VII) (Berlin, 1933), p. 8; and that it was written before April is proved by the fact that it is referred to—in the sentence "Sperabam demens gemina exhortatione . . . movisse ne dicam inflammasse animum"—in *Fam.* XV 5, which was written on 3 April. In *Fam.* XII 1 Petrarch says that since writing his previous letter he has allowed "plusquam annuas indutias" to pass: since that previous letter, *Fam.* X 1, was written on 24 February 1351 this statement, if strictly accurate, would lead to the conclusion that *Fam.* XII 1 was written after 24 February 1352; but in view of Petrarch's tendency to exaggerate lengths of time one cannot take this statement too literally. The sentence quoted in part from *Fam.* XV 5 seems to indicate, but does not suffice to prove, that Petrarch had been hoping to receive an answer to *Fam.* XII 1, which would suggest that that letter had been written quite early in 1352. All in all, the sound conclusion would seem to be that *Fam.* XII 1 was written in the first quarter of 1352, probably before February 20.

and others. But Charles was not yet ready to undertake his coronation journey; *Fam.* xii 1, as far as we know, received no answer; and the plan for the Cardinal to go to Italy was dropped. Petrarch, greatly disappointed, writes, in *Fam.* xv 5, addressed to Pierre d'Auvergne on 3 April:

> In eo sane quod de nostri ducis [*i.e.*, Cardinal Gui de Boulogne] tuoque simul et omnium nostrum in Italiam transitu, quem proximum arbitrabar, certior literis tuis fio, falsam michi spem prereptam gaudeo, sed fuisse falsam doleo. Gloriosum enim iter videbatur et labor mundo utilis, sed "fata obstant," ut poete verbo utar, vereorque ne Cesari nostro vivere sit satis et sacro vertici debitum dyadema despiciens, nec imperii curam nec clarioris fame sentiat appetitum.

The illness of the Pope began early in December 1351 or shortly before. In a letter written on 17 December to Louis of Taranto Clement says: "Quidem tumor ex humorum collectione procedens, ex quo quedam febrilis discrasia causabatur, faciem nostram mirabiliter alteravit et diebus nos aliquibus vehementer afflixit." [39] Petrarch refers to the Pope's illness in *Fam.* xii 4, written to Nelli on 13 January 1352 in the words "morbus Pontificis Maximi diuturnus ac gravis"; and in *Fam.* xii 6, written to Philippe de Cabassoles on 1 February, in the words "papa noster a morte revertitur, quamvis redeundo eodem properet." Shortly before 12 March, as we learn from *Sen.* xvi 3, Petrarch sent an oral message to the Pope, urging him to beware of a multitude of doctors, and to choose a single doctor distinguished not by eloquence but by learning and trustworthiness. This message, however, was conveyed by a messenger of the Pope who was unable to deliver it clearly; and the Pope sent him back to Petrarch with the request that Petrarch put his message in writing. Petrarch, accordingly, addressed to the Pope on 12 March a letter, *Fam.* v 19, in which, while repeating his recommendation that the Pope choose a single learned and trustworthy doctor, he attacks the generality of physicians. He asserts that doctors traffic in human life, being free to cause death with impunity; that they disagree with each other deliberately, in order that each may seem individually authoritative; and that they disregard their own proper professional field in order to indulge in altisonant loquacity,

---

[39] Quoted by Léonard, 1, ii, 328, n. 2.

invading the fields of poets and rhetoricians. At three points in the letter Petrarch refers to Pliny as expressing opinions that confirm his own.

One of the doctors concerned immediately attacked Petrarch, in a letter that is not extant. In *Fam.* xv 6 (written on 17 April to Pierre d'Auvergne) Petrarch refers to this doctor—whom he does not identify—as "procax et insanus"; says of him "signa quedam pertinacis atque arrogantis inscitie in vultu hominis legi"; and says also that he has just learned that the doctor's letter had been written not by him but *for* him, and that it was the work "nescio cuius montani artificis." In Petrarch's rejoinder (which is presently to be considered) to the doctor's letter he calls that letter "inanem, sed ampullosam et tumidam plenamque convitiis"; and in a typical passage he says of its author: "In singulis . . . te verbis detegis nichil esse, nichil sapere, nichil nosse." The many references to the letter that are contained in Petrarch's rejoinder provide a considerable amount of information as to its contents. The doctor praised the art of medicine; asserted—according to Petrarch—that doctors are a "divinum et celeste genus"; and maintained that doctors do not disagree, and in particular that he and his colleagues had not disagreed as to the treatment of the Pope. He attacked Petrarch wrathfully, saying that Petrarch had been moved by envy and that he had deceived the Pope; and even included in his attack—according to Petrarch—a threat of death: "medicine nomine mortem michi literarum tuarum in fine denuncies." He attacked poets and poetry: "Tu autem non contentus in me multa dixisse, multa itidem contra poeticam ac poetas . . . evomuisti." He misrepresented Boethius as being hostile to poetry in general; spoke scornfully of Pliny: and implied—according to Petrarch—that Averroes is preferable to Christ.[40]

Petrarch's first impulse was to ignore the letter; but he tells us in *Sen.* xvi 5 that a cardinal—"vnus e principibus ecclesie cui familiarissimus fui"—urged him to reply, lest his silence be misconstrued. He accordingly replied in a very long letter, not extant in its original form, which was eventually revised, probably with little substantial change, and made into Book I of the

---

[40] The quotations in this paragraph are from Ricci, pp. 25, 32, 30, 38, and 33. Those in the next paragraph are from Ricci, p. 37.

Invective contra medicum. This rejoinder is comprehensive, violent, insultant, learned, and dialectically clever. The doctor's assertions and attacks are thoroughly answered. Petrarch maintains that he is attacking not medicine, nor doctors in general, but simply his particular antagonist and his ilk: "Hec non adversus medicinam . . . neque adversus excellentes medicos . . . sed adversus te delirantesque similiter dicta sint." The most important passages are those devoted to the defense of poetry. In the course of that defense, after quoting effectively from Cicero and Lactantius, Petrarch defines the poet's purpose thus: "poete . . . studium est veritatem rerum pulcris velaminibus adornare, ut vulgus insulsum . . . lateat, ingeniosis autem studiosisque lectoribus et quesitu difficilior et dulcior sit inventu." If you will but open your eyes, he says to his antagonist,

> videbis poetas raros quidem, natura rerum disponente ut rara quelibet cara simul et clara sint. Videbis eos gloria et nominis immortalitate fulgentes, quam non sibi tantum, sed et aliis peperere, ut quibus ante alios preituris consulere nominibus datum est, et quorum adminiculo ipsa etiam virtus eget, non equidem in se ipsa, sed in eo quod habet cum tempore et cum oblivione certamen.

Poetry is one of the *artes liberales:* medicine is one of the *artes mechanice.*

In spite of its length this rejoinder was written, as we are told in *Fam.* xv 5 (written on 3 April to Pierre d'Auvergne), in part of one day and part of one night—remaining thereafter in the hands of a copyist for several days. On or shortly before 22 March Petrarch left Avignon for a ten-day vacation at Vaucluse, as will appear below: since Pierre d'Auvergne witnessed the composition of at least part of Petrarch's letter to the doctor that letter must have been begun, at least, before Petrarch left Avignon. Presumably it was finished there, and left to be copied and delivered in Petrarch's absence. Later developments in this polemic will be referred to below (on pp. 120 and 151–153).[41]

---

[41] On this episode see the article by Bosco. In *Fam.* xv 5 Petrarch says also that he has been sorry to hear that delivery of the letter has been delayed: "destinato serius perventuram, invitus audio." Petrarch had been in Avignon again on 1 April, but had returned to

Throughout this stay in Avignon Petrarch, as usual, carried on an extensive correspondence. In *Fam.* xii 9 he speaks of the receipt of a great many—"plurime"—letters, which he felt he had to answer: "quamvis invitus, melioribus subductum curis non exiguum in his tempus expendo." Seven of the letters thus received are mentioned in Petrarch's replies, as will appear below: three from Nelli, two from Luca da Piacenza, and one each from Philippe de Cabassoles and Barbato da Sulmona. Only two of these letters, Nelli's *Ep.* iv and v (LAP 26 and 27) are extant. A letter, now lost, received in March from Niccolò Acciaiuoli is mentioned in *Fam.* xii 3, and a letter, now lost, received also in March from Petrarch's medical adversary is referred to, as has already been noted, in *Fam.* xv 6.

The most noteworthy of the 25 extant letters of Petrarch that were certainly or probably written during this stay in Avignon are—in addition to those addressed to the Emperor, the Pope, the four cardinals, Ugolino dei Rossi, and Niccolò Acciaiuoli—the seven that are included in the *Epistolae sine nomine* as Nos. 5–11.[42] One of these, No. 7, which has been referred to above, is devoted to the plight of Rome; and one, No. 9, is devoted to the plight of Italy. In this second letter Petrarch, anticipating the

_____

Vaucluse by 3 April: *Fam.* xv 5, written at Vaucluse on that day, is a reply to a letter received from Pierre d'Auvergne. It would seem that Petrarch's knowledge of the delay in delivery (which was presumably due to the scribal delay) came to him from Pierre's letter, which Petrarch presumably received at Vaucluse, either before or immediately after his brief return to Avignon.

[42] Nos. 6 and 5 were certainly written on 31 March and 1 April 1352 respectively. It will be shown below (on pp. 208–209) that No. 9 was written in November or the first half of December 1351 and that No. 10 was written on 13 January 1352, or soon afterward. No. 11 was clearly written late in 1351 or early in 1352, as both Piur and Foresti have shown. Foresti 1, pp. 253–256 dates No. 7 as of "ottobre del 1351 circa": it should be added that it must have been written before 18 November—the date of *Fam.* xi 16. Foresti (*ibid.*) dates No. 8 as of the autumn of 1351: it is equally possible, however, that it was written in the winter of 1351–1352, since it contains the motifs of Avignon as Babylon and Avignon as the Fifth Labyrinth, which were active in Petrarch's mind in December and January, and since its next-to-last sentence, "Hec tibi, pater, ne ante scriberem, pudor inhibuit," indicates that a considerable amount of time had passed after Petrarch's arrival in Avignon.

Risorgimento by five centuries, asserts that Italy can be free only if she is *one* in will:

> Hoc persecutionis fasce serua nostris temporibus suspirat Italia, tum demum finem habitura miserie, cum unum uelle ceperit. Difficilis plane conditio, sed nequaquam impossibilis. 'Vnum' dico, non studiis, sed studiorum termino tedioque seruitii indigni. Proh superi! dominari solebamus optimis. En! quo decidimus! nunc seruimus pessimis.

The other five letters constitute a terrific indictment of conditions in the papal court. These passages, from Nos. 10 and 11, are typical:

> Vna salutis spes in auro est. Auro placatur rex ferus, auro immane monstrum uincitur, auro salutare lorum texitur, auro durum limen ostenditur, auro uectes et saxa franguntur, auro tristis ianitor mollitur, auro celum panditur. Quid multa? Auro Cristus venditur.
>
> Vbi nulla pietas, nulla caritas, nulla fides habitat! Vbi tumor, liuor, luxus, auaritia cum artibus suis regnant, ubi pessimus quisque prouehitur et munificus predo ad celum tollitur, iustus pauper opprimitur, ubi simplicitas amentie, malitia sapientie nomen habet. Vbi Deus spernitur, adoratur nummus, calcantur leges, irridentur boni, usque adeo ut iam fere nullus qui irrideri possit appareat.

The motifs of Avignon as Babylon and Avignon as the Fifth Labyrinth are developed in No. 10, and appear singly or together in Nos. 5, 8, 9, and 11. Clement himself appears under the names of Nimrod (a reference to his building and his hunting) in Nos. 8 and 10, as Cambyses (a reference to his extravagance) in No. 10, and as Julian (the Apostate) in No. 6; and the Countess of Turenne appears under the name of Semiramis in Nos. 8 and 10 (and in No. 13, written a little later). Other references to Semiramis, not specific to the Countess of Turenne, occur in No. 10 (and in *Fam.* xii 11, written a little later). This series of references to Nimrod and Semiramis indicates clearly that the letters concerned were written at a time when Petrarch was working or had recently been working on the Lives of these two persons in the course of his effort to complete the *De viris*.

No. 5 is the first half of a letter written to Lapo da Castiglionchio, which Petrarch, in the making of his collections, split into two parts, entering the second part (which concerns Vaucluse) as *Fam.* XII 8. No. 6 shows that Petrarch had in mind the writing of a "tragicum carmen" on conditions in Avignon: as to this poem something will be said presently. No. 8 reveals the fact that before Petrarch had left Italy Bishop Ildebrandino of Padua had endeavored to dissuade him from going to Avignon. No. 11, addressed to Rinaldo Cavalchini, who had been a teacher of Petrarch's son Giovanni, refers to the presence of Giovanni in Avignon. The last two sentences of this letter show that Petrarch was not without concern as to the possible results of undue dissemination of some of these letters.

Six of the 25 letters, more than were sent to any other correspondent, were addressed to Francesco Nelli. Three of these appear among the *Sine nomine* as Nos. 6, 9, and 10. Two others, *Fam.* XII 4 and 5, are of interest chiefly because of their references to *Ep. met.* III 22 and to the illness of the Pope. *Fam.* XII 9 is a brief expression of friendship, with general references to conditions in Avignon. These six letters are to be considered in some detail below, in Chapters VII and VIII.

The remaining letters may now be briefly reviewed. *Fam.* XI 14, written on 23 October 1351 to congratulate Philippe de Vitry on his appointment to the bishopric of Meaux,[43] is in effect one of Petrarch's most emphatic statements of his conviction that the responsibilities of high ecclesiastical office involve well-nigh intolerable burdens.

Fam. XI 15, written on 25 October to Philippe de Cabassoles to express Petrarch's pleasure at his friend's return to Cavaillon after an absence of two months, contains an account of the hardships and perils of travel as experienced by Petrarch and by Philippe.

Fam. IX 6, written on 28 December to Luca da Piacenza, acknowledges the receipt of a welcome letter from Luca, and sends him *Fam.* IX 5—the long letter to Bishop Ugolino denying charges of envy and malice—asking him to deliver it to the Bishop, and to reënforce it by a confirming oral statement. *Fam.* IX 7, written to Luca two weeks later, recounts the fable of Fire,

---

[43] The appointment had been made on 3 January 1351 (see Eubel, p. 334): presumably Petrarch had not heard of it until he reached Avignon.

Wind, Water, and Suspicion, and asks Luca to observe carefully and to report the personal attitude of the Bishop with regard to Petrarch's denial.

Fam. xii 6, written on 1 February 1352 in reply to a letter from Philippe de Cabassoles, expostulates with him because, while Petrarch was in Avignon, Philippe had gone to Vaucluse without informing Petrarch, and had spent five days there. During that time he had devoted himself, day and night, to the reading of Petrarch's books—and not to the works of saints, historians, philosophers, and poets that he might have read, but to Petrarch's own writings—to which Petrarch, with his usual deprecation, refers as "opuscula sive . . . nugas meas."

Fam. xii 7, written on 20 February, is a reply to a letter from Barbato da Sulmona which had pursued Petrarch for almost a year before it reached him. In that letter Barbato had deplored the state of Naples since the death of King Robert; had referred regretfully to the fact that he and Petrarch had not succeeded in meeting in Rome in 1350; and had asked about the *Africa*. In his reply Petrarch speaks of the frustration, due to the death of King Robert, of his hope that he and Barbato might have lived as companions in Naples; refers to his treatment of this theme in *Ep. met.* i 1, the poem in which he is dedicating the collection of the *Metricae* (not yet complete) to Barbato; says that if they had met in Rome they would probably have spent more time in classicizing rambles than in churches; promises that when the *Africa* is finished Barbato shall be the first to see it; and reports that at the present time he is not working on it:

> Verum illa et morositate hospitis et innumeris fortune repagulis detinetur, que si cunta cessarent, tamen satius visum est illam domi manere et cum etate concoqui ac maturescere, ne si ante tempus exiisset . . . asperior evaderet nec ferret etatem, presertim cum nec reditus esset semel in publicum egresse, et ingenii mei incredibilis mutatio in dies fieret. Dehinc forte aliud consilii capiam incumbamque lima ultima . . .

Early in 1352 Petrarch had heard—we do not know how—that the Venetian Doge Andrea Dandolo (with whom Petrarch had exchanged letters before leaving Italy) had expressed astonishment at Petrarch's frequent changes of residence, and would like to see him settle down in the region of Venice; and on 26 February, being then in Vaucluse, he wrote to the Doge a long letter, *Fam.* xv 4, in which he seeks to justify himself for the unquestioned frequency of his changes, and says that although he would be glad to establish himself for the rest of his life in accordance with the Doge's suggestion he cannot yet see his way to do so.[44]

Ever since 1349 Niccolò Acciaiuoli had been trying to attract the Florentine schoolmaster Zanobi da Strada to Naples: Zanobi is nominated as a royal secretary in a Neapolitan document of 4 November of that year. But Zanobi was not disposed to leave Florence, where his presence is attested as late as 20 October 1351. Before the end of March 1352 Niccolò had sent to Petrarch a letter written "manu sua"—Niccolò was no stylist, and depended on Barbato da Sulmona and on Niccolò d'Alife for the writing of some of his letters—in which he asked Petrarch to urge Zanobi to give up his teaching and accept the invitation to come to Naples. With this request Petrarch complied in *Fam.* xII 3. By 11 April, the day on which that letter was written, Niccolò was expecting the arrival of both Zanobi and Nelli: a letter of 1 April contains the clause "Aspectto mastro Zenobio collo priore con lieto animo." What the basis of his expectation was, we do not know (Nelli did not come).[45]

On 1 April, also, Petrarch wrote to Lapo da Castiglionchio the letter which, in the making of his collections, he split into two parts, entering the first part in the *Epistolae sine nomine* as No. 5, and the second part in the *Epistolae familiares* as xII 8. This sec-

---

[44] *Fam.* xv 4 is dated "Ad fontem Sorgie, IV Kal. Martias." That it was written in 1352 is proved by the fact that in *Fam.* xv 8, which was certainly written on 24 April 1352, Petrarch, writing to Laelius about his restlessness, says "de quo ipse me nuper excusavi Venetiarum duci Andree," adding that he is sending Laelius a copy of his letter to the Doge. *Fam.* xv 4 and a later letter, *Fam.* xvII 16, written after Petrarch had left Provence, were both answered, in June 1354, by Dandolo's letter beginning "Amice dum singulare" (LAP 2).

[45] See Paola Guidotti, "Un amico del Petrarca e del Boccaccio: Zanobi da Strada, poeta laureato," in *ASI*, Ser. vII, xIII (1930), 249–293, and Léonard, 1, II, 222, 323, 373, 485, 489.

ond part, telling of ten days spent in Vaucluse, begins thus: "More meo nuper in Elicona transalpinum urbis invise strepitum fugiens secessi." The words "More meo" indicate that Petrarch had on other occasions fled from Avignon to Vaucluse for brief respites: it was evidently on such an occasion that he had written his letter to Dandolo. The letter to Lapo speaks of the charms of Vaucluse, but is devoted chiefly to an imaginative account of the pleasure that Lapo's Cicero—the personification of a MS, containing the *Pro Milone* and certain other orations, which Petrarch had borrowed and had not yet been able to get copied (he had apparently set his son to the task)—found in the company of other ancients there assembled: those mentioned by name are Brutus, Atticus, Herennius, Marcus Varro, Cotta, Velleius, Lucilius Balbus, Nigidius, Cratippus, Cicero's brother Quintus and son Marcus, Sulpicius, Crassus, Antonius, Cato the Censor, Lucius Torquatus, Cato Uticensis, Marcus Piso, Hortensius, Epicurus, Laelius, Scipio, Milo, Laterensis, Sulla, and Pompey. At the end of the letter Petrarch expresses the hope that he may soon return to Italy: he wants, however, to get Forese to Vaucluse before he leaves.

His desire to return soon to Italy is expressed also in *Fam.* xii 10, written on the same day to Boccaccio, in the words "vivi spes blanda colloquii teque in proximo revisendi propositum."

His various special efforts and the heavy burden of his correspondence could not prevent Petrarch from some continuance of the literary work that he regarded as his proper occupation—even the time spent on his letters was for him "melioribus subductum curis," as he wrote in *Fam.* xii 9. His intellectual industry was extraordinary; and he certainly found welcome relief in the hours that he could spend in literary pursuits. Probably he managed to continue his work on the completion of the *De viris*, although he must have been handicapped by the fact that his books were not in Avignon but in Vaucluse. The frequency of his references to Nimrod and Semiramis in letters of this period indicates, as has already been pointed out, that at this time he was working or had recently been working on the Lives of these two persons.

The three poems that were certainly written during these

months in Avignon are *Met.* III 21, 22, and 23. The two
latter poems are fully treated below, in Chapter VII. *Met.* III 21
is a short poem (13 lines), addressed to Giovanni Barrili, which,
like *Met.* III 22, develops the labyrinth motif:

> Quid singula verbis
> Expediam, coecumque chaos, labyrinthia claustra,
> Erroresque novos, et inextricabile septum
> Sollicito quod turba gradu miserabilis ambit? . . .
> Hic me declusum totiens, nunc sydere moesto
> Carcer habet . . .
> Rex tonat horrendus, stat sortibus urna malignis.
> Quis iussus prius ire mori? quem fata secundum
> Saeva vocent? Nec fila ferunt nec verba puellae
> Reginae miserantis opem, nec Daedalus usquam est.[46]

It corresponds closely to the treatment of the same motif in
Sine nom. 10, which contains this passage: "Non hic carcer horrendus, non tenebrose domus error, non fatalis urna humani
generis fata permiscens, denique non imperiosus Minos . . . defuerint, sed . . . fila perplexum iter tacita ope signantia, sed
Adriana, sed Dedalus." *Sine nom.* 10 was written on 13 January
1352 or soon afterward: *Met.* III 21 was presumably written at
about the same time.

Two other *epistolae metricae*, III 15 and 16, were certainly
written in Avignon during Petrarch's stay in Provence, and were
probably written at this time. Both poems concern an Italian
musician, Floriano da Rimini, of whom nothing else is known:
he may or may not be identical with a musician referred to in
two much later prose letters of Petrarch.[47] *Ep. met.* III 15, addressed to Floriano, refers to him as a modern Orpheus; says that
not even the original Orpheus could have made any impression
under conditions such as those now prevailing in Avignon; and
advises Floriano to return to Italy, where his musical abilities
will have some effect. The poem is full of characterizations of
Avignon, "mundi sentina," that are similar to those contained in
Ep. met. III 21–23. Lines 21–31 read:

---

[46] Rossetti, II, 106.
[47] See Magrini, pp. 148–149; and Nino Quarta, *Chi era Confortino?*
(Naples, 1938), and the references there given. The letters in question
are *Fam.* XIX 11 and *Sen.* XI 5.

Collibus his Rhodope multum, me iudice, multum
Impar erit feritate sua, nec thracius Hebrus
Certet aquis Rhodani. Sunt hic praedura metallum
Pectora; sunt silices animi; sunt viscera flammae.
Semiviros per prata boves, perque atria cernas
Semiboves errare viros. Non unus opacam
Minotaurus habet perplexi tramitis aulam;
Plurima permixtae, coecaeque libidinis extant
Signa per infames partus sobolemque nefandam
Et natos furor exagitat, rabiesque famesque
Dira, nec immites cessant a sangine fauces.[48]

The use of the labyrinth motif serves to indicate that this poem
is at least roughly contemporary with *Met.* III 21–23. It could
have been only in Avignon, not in Vaucluse, that Petrarch had
any association with Floriano. *Met.* III 16, a 10-line poem that is
hardly more than an epigram, states that "Orpheus," persuaded
by Petrarch's assiduous urging, had been intending to return to
Italy, but had been caught and held in Avignon by an unworthy
love affair. This poem is obviously somewhat later than III 15;
but it was certainly written in Avignon, and more probably in
the early months of 1352 than after Petrarch's return to Avignon
for some two months beginning in September 1352.

It is quite possible that *Met.* III 32 was written toward the
end of this stay in Avignon; but it seems to me more probable
that it was written somewhat later, and it is therefore treated at
the end of the following section.

It has been shown above (on pp. 54–56) that the portion of
Eclogue VII that contains Epy's second long speech (ll. 98–128),
in which she characterizes the cardinals created at the consistory
of 17 December 1350, was written within the last three months
of 1351 or in 1352, and that ll. 132–137, which probably refer to
Angelo Acciaiuoli as a rejected candidate for the cardinalate,
were written either at the same time or a little later—but still before the end of 1352.

From *Sine nom.* 6 we learn that Petrarch had in mind the
writing of a "tragicum carmen" on conditions in Avignon: this
would evidently have been a major work, in the course of which,

---

[48] Rossetti, II, 114.

he implies, he intended to deal with contemporary instances of crime and shame far more terrible than those recorded by ancient historians or treated as the subjects of ancient tragedies: "Non fabulas agam, etsi fabulis sint hec similiora quam uero. Dicam monstra que uidi, que audiui, quibus infectos oculos atque aures habeo. Non simplex insania, non unus furens Hercules, non una Thyestis cena . . . sed totus orbis euersus et lacer." But this carmen was never written.[49]

VII. Vaucluse: 3 April–August 1352

On the afternoon or evening of Sunday, the first of April, or, more probably, on one of the two following days, Petrarch established himself again at Vaucluse; and there he remained until the last week in September, except for occasional visits to Avignon. His return from the hated strenuousness of that city to the beloved quietness of Vaucluse brought him a considerable measure of relief; but even the delights of Vaucluse were impaired for him, now, by his fresh memories of his experiences in Avignon in the autumn and winter, and the continuance of unwelcome pressures.

On 3 April he wrote to Pierre d'Auvergne a letter, *Fam.* xv 5, to which reference has already been made. After thanking the Abbot "pro transmissis libris" he speaks first of his polemic with the Pope's physicians, and then of the abandonment of the plan for Cardinal Gui de Boulogne—with Petrarch, Pierre, and others —to meet the Emperor. The latter part of the letter castigates the Emperor for his failure to meet his imperial obligations. The last sentence of the letter proper reads: "Crede autem michi, pater: magnum est in sede Petri, magnum est in solio Cesaris sedere."

Sine nom. 13, addressed to an unknown person (who was probably in Avignon), was probably written very soon after the return to Vaucluse. It is exactly in the mood of *Sine nom.* 5, 6, 8, 10, and 11: there are references to Clement as a plundering Dionysius, and to the Countess of Turenne as Semiramis. Petrarch's flight to Vaucluse is referred to thus: "Prouideat domui

---

[49] Piur, 1, pp. 124–132.

sue Deus omnipotens, ego enim nichil habeo quod tam multis contranitentibus prestare possim preter commiserationem matri debitam et michi placitam, ut uides, fugam, qua oculos meos tam mesto liberem spectaculo." [50]

On 17 April Petrarch wrote again to Pierre d'Auvergne, who had shown his previous letter, *Fam.* xv 5, to the physician with whom Petrarch was in polemic. In this new letter, *Fam.* xv 6, Petrarch—evidently on the basis of a report from some correspondent or visitor other than Pierre d'Auvergne—says that he has learned that the reply sent by the physician to Petrarch's letter to the Pope (*Fam.* v 19) was actually the work "nescio cuius montani artificis"; that the physician, having received Petrarch's retort (the retort that ultimately became Book I of the *Invective contra medicum*) is now dismayed, and is going about the city looking for someone to help him; and in particular that the physician had become very much excited on reading the last sentence (quoted above) of *Fam.* xv 5, and had charged that Petrarch meant by that sentence that Rome was the only seat for a Pope: "Sed interpres iniquissimus quo rem trahit? dicit me dicere voluisse sedem Petri non alibi esse quam Rome." Petrarch defends himself at some length against this complicating charge.

At about the same time, and certainly before 24 April, Petrarch wrote to Stefano Colonna, Provost of Saint-Omer, a long

---

[50] There were three occasions—all in 1352—during Petrarch's last stay in Provence on which Petrarch fled from Avignon to Vaucluse: the first was the ten-day vacation in March, the second the return to Vaucluse in April, and the third the return on 8 November. The content of *Sine nom.* 13 implies that the return followed a stay of considerable length in Avignon; that the experiences of that stay had been very shocking to Petrarch, and that he expected to remain at Vaucluse for some time: these considerations serve to rule out the return of 8 November, when Petrarch had been in Avignon for not much more than a month; had known perfectly well what he would find when he went there; and was planning to return to Italy almost at once. The tone of the letter and in particular the reference to the Countess of Turenne as Semiramis serve also to place it close in time to *Sine nom.* 5, 6, 8, 10, and 11, written during the autumn and winter of 1351–1352. The passage quoted, moreover, clearly implies a flight for something more than a vacation of ten days. I conclude, therefore, that this letter was written soon after Petrarch's return to Vaucluse in April 1352.

and remarkable letter, *Fam.* xv 7, "de inquieto totius pene orbis statu," in which he surveys the current plights of Rome, all Northern Italy—between the Alps, the Apennines, and the Rubicon—Piedmont, Tuscany, the Marches, Campania, Southern Italy, Avignon (where Stefano was living), France, England, Germany, Spain, Majorca, Sardinia, Corsica, Sicily, Rhodes, Crete, Greece, Cyprus, Armenia, the Holy Land, and Asia and Africa. He concludes that "nullum quietis ac solatii locum" is to be found anywhere in the world, and indicates thus the only wise recourse: "Fac tibi in medio animi tui locum, ubi lateas ubi gaudeas ubi nullo interpellante requiescas ubi tecum Cristus habitet." [51]

On 24 April he wrote thus in *Fam.* xv 8, to Laelius (then in Rome) of his great restlessness:

Proinde quod ad locum attinet, vivere hic possem quietissime, nisi externis quaterer ventis. In ipso igitur portu timens multa circumspicio, sed ante omnia vicina Babilone deterreor . . . Huius certe vicinitas ac prospectus odorque terribilis et felicitati nimis infestus est; ille me vel solus hinc pelleret, ut omittam preteritarum reliquias tempestatum, que de tam propinquo usque in hunc portum conquassatam vite naviculam persequuntur.

He desires, therefore, to find an abode elsewhere, far from Avignon. The King of Sicily (Louis of Taranto) wants him to come to Naples, and the King of France wants him to come to Paris, but for various reasons these places do not appeal to him. His preference would be for Rome; but if Laelius dissuades him from seeking refuge there he will either return to Northern Italy or else make up his mind to stay in Vaucluse, despite the proximity of Avignon:

Hic quanquam urbis impie vicinus fragor et fumus impediant, obstruam tamen aures oculosque, gratoque otio, quod iam cepi, et optata fruor solitudine. Et siquis inde huc, quod vetare nequeo, turbator accesserit, sentiet me in silvis urbanarum oblitum atque immemorem curarum; surdo se locutum dicet; ita nichil omnino audiam, nichil loquar extra propositi mei fines; vagabor solus et liber ut nunc facio.

[51] Sections 16–18 of this letter are a later insert: see Wilkins 1, pp. 327–328.

Petrarch invited Bishop Angelo Acciaiuoli to visit him at Vaucluse before leaving Provence, and the Bishop agreed to come there on his return from a visit to the shrine of St. Anthony at Vienne.

Before the 21st Petrarch received letters from Niccolò Acciaiuoli and from Bartolommeo Carbone dei Papazurri, Bishop of Teano (near Naples). The substance of both letters is readily determinable from Petrarch's replies, *Fam.* xii 15 and 11, which are presently to be mentioned. Both Niccolò and Bartolommeo spoke of the preparations—"magnificus apparatus" is the term used by Petrarch in *Fam.* xii 11—that were being made by Niccolò: the reference is clearly to the preparations for the coronation of Louis of Taranto and Joan, which was to take place, with extraordinary pomp, on the 27th.[54] Niccolò's letter, which had been written for him by Barbato da Sulmona, contained a formal acknowledgment of Petrarch's *Fam.* xii 2, and an invitation to Petrarch to establish himself in Naples—an invitation referred to thus in *Fam.* xii 15: "esse tibi animum ut inter Vesevum Falernumque meo nomine posteris etiam profuturum novum suscites Parnasum." The Bishop's letter spoke of his contentment in a relatively minor bishopric, of his horror of Avignon, of his desire to see all his friends safely out of Avignon and back in Italy, and of the fact that as a result of Petrarch's good offices he (the Bishop) had found favor with Niccolò.

To the Bishop's letter Petrarch—again or still in Avignon—replied in *Fam.* xii 11, written on the 21st, "ad auroram." He commends the Bishop's moderation in respect to ecclesiastical preferment; and expresses his desire to return to Italy, but says that members of the papal court to whom he owes much are endeavoring to keep him in Avignon, or at least in Provence, and that if he cannot completely resist their pressure he will live in seclusion in Vaucluse. He then refers to the letter received from Niccolò, to whom, he says, he will send thanks either by letter or personally through Bishop Angelo, whom he expects to receive at Vaucluse on the very next day, on Angelo's return from his visit to the shrine of St. Anthony at Vienne.

---

[54] On the coronation see Léonard 1, ii, 354–361.

Before the 24th Petrarch had received from Zanobi a letter—
evidently a reply to *Fam.* xii 3—in which (judging from Petrarch's reply, *Fam.* xii 17, which is to be considered presently)
Zanobi had spoken of his need for Petrarch's advice, had asked
him to thank Niccolò Acciaiuoli on his (Zanobi's) behalf, and
had enclosed a Latin poem of his own composition. It is not clear
whether or not this letter informed Petrarch of Zanobi's decision
to go to Naples; but it is certain that by the 24th Petrarch knew,
from some source, of that decision, since *Fam.* xii 17, written on
that day, was sent to Naples, as will presently appear.

Before the 24th, also, and before Petrarch had answered the
letter recently received from Niccolò, he had learned, as will
presently appear, that the long-standing friendship between
Niccolò and Petrarch's friend Giovanni Barrili [55] had been, at
least, seriously strained.

In *Fam.* xii 12, addressed to Nelli, and dated from Vaucluse
on the 24th, "hora diei nona," Petrarch complains that Bishop
Angelo, who had promised to visit him, has not come; but adds
at the end: "Sane dum huc scribendo pervenissem et longius
eveherer, ingens clamor in foribus et epyscopus ipse adest." [56]
Fam. xii 13, also addressed to Nelli, and dated also from Vaucluse
on the 24th, reports the successful outcome of Petrarch's efforts
on behalf of Don Ubertino.

Four other letters, dated also from Vaucluse on the 24th, and

---

[55] On Barrili see Léonard 1, *passim* (see index) and Léonard 2; also
Francesco Torraca, "Giovanni Boccaccio a Napoli," in *Rassegna critica
della letteratura italiana*, xx (1915), 179–184. Barrili served as seneschal
of Provence for several months in 1348 and 1349.

[56] There is a discrepancy in dates as to the arrival of Bishop Angelo
in Vaucluse. In *Fam.* xii 11, dated on the 21st, Petrarch says that the
Bishop is due at Vaucluse on the next day: "crastino, igitur, ut pollicitus
est, ad fontem Sorgie poetico excipiendus prandio mecum erit"; but
Fam. xii 12, which reports his arrival, is dated not on the 22d, but on
the 24th. The most probable explanation would seem to be that the
Bishop actually came on the 22d, but later in the day than expected, and
that *Fam.* xii 12 was written on that same day, its date being changed
eventually from the 22d to the 24th as a result of the fact that another
letter to Nelli and four other letters were dated on that same day. Other
solutions, however, are possible. Whether or not Forese Donati ever
came to Vaucluse we do not know.

all sent to Naples, constitute Petrarch's very determined and
efficient effort to persuade Niccolò Acciaiuoli and Giovanni
Barrili to renew their friendship. The basic letter, *Fam.* xii 16
(Fracassetti's xiii 10), a long and impressive appeal, was addressed
to both men. On the outside of the letter Petrarch wrote, in
effect: "To be opened only by Niccolò or Giovanni, and only
when they are together"; and it was his intention and his hope
that it would be read by them while they were together. Instead
of sending this letter directly to one or the other of the two men
he sent it to Zanobi with a covering letter, *Fam.* xii 17 (Fracassetti's xii 18), in which he requests Zanobi to deliver *Fam.* xii 16
personally, in order that Zanobi may bring the two men together
to receive it and may add his own oral appeal. He wrote also
short separate letters, *Fam.* xii 14 and 15 (the latter Fracassetti's
xiii 9) to Giovanni and Niccolò, each letter containing a reference to the letter addressed to both men, and exhorting them to
renew their friendship.[57] The letter to Niccolò replies also to the
letter recently received from him, and acknowledges, grate-
fully but noncommittally, the invitation to settle in Naples: "Ego,
quod ad me attinet, etsi duos Parnasos me habere glorier, tamen
tertium non recuso, tuo sonorum Apolline tuis habitatum Musis,
tuis frondentem lauris, tuis demum auspiciis consecratum." The
letter to Zanobi, *Fam.* xii 17, served also as a reply to the letter
recently received from Zanobi. Before speaking of the letter to

---

[57] Léonard 1, ii, 371, assumes that the tension between Niccolò and
Giovanni had been of long duration, and that it had been due to the
fact that the two men had been on opposite sides in the quarrels between
Louis and the Queen. A careful reading of the letters concerned indicates rather that the tension was recent and personal. Its recency is implied by several passages which indicate that the friendship had been
of long duration, and by the "ut audio" in this passage in *Fam.* xii
14, 8: "Non effractam certe sed parumper, ut audio, dissutam amicitiam
vestram . . . reparare disposui." Its personal character is perhaps most
clearly indicated by this passage in *Fam.* xii 16, 18: "quenam levis of-
fensa seu potius offense suspitio potens erit tam solidam et tam sanctam
vestrarum mentium labefactare congeriem?" It is to be noted also that
these letters contain no reference to any public cause for the rift, and
that they were written four months after the authorization of the coronation, an authorization that had been followed by a new accord between
Louis and the Queen: see Léonard, 1, ii, 369 ff.

Niccolò and Giovanni, Petrarch says in effect that he has nothing
to add, in the way of advice, to what he had said in *Fam.* xii 3;
promises to convey Zanobi's thanks to Niccolò; and acknowledges the receipt of Zanobi's poem, which he calls a "carmen
eximium quod miror et laudo," but sends back to Zanobi with a
mark indicating that one of the lines is too long.[58]

June, July, and August

These were peaceful months for Petrarch. As far as we
know, he had no occasion to go into Avignon; and he was almost
wholly free from the exacting and distressing matters of concern
that had so pressed upon him during the winter. Even the volume of his correspondence seems to have diminished: there
survive only nine letters of his that were written certainly or
probably in these three months. Throughout the summer and
until mid-November the weather was perfect, though the lack
of rain caused a serious drought: this we learn from passages in
Fam. xv 2 and 3, written on 8 November and in the following
February respectively.

On 20 March, as has been said, the Pope had granted a Veronese canonry to Petrarch's son Giovanni. On Saturday, the 9th of
June, Petrarch sent Giovanni off to Verona, sending by him (or
perhaps by an accompanying servant or other companion) two
letters to Veronese friends—*Fam.* xiii 2 and 3, addressed to
Rinaldo Cavalchini and Guglielmo da Pastrengo respectively.
Both letters are dated 9 June: in the subscription of *Fam.* xiii 2
the date is followed by the phrase "quam festinanter, ipsa literarum facies indicio est." Both letters urge their addressees to do

---

[58] Léonard, 1, ii, 373, dates Zanobi's arrival in Naples between 1 April
(the date of Niccolò's letter referred to above, on p. 115) and 10 August
(the date of Petrarch's reply to Zanobi's reply to *Fam.* xii 17). But
Niccolò's letter of 1 April does not establish the date of Zanobi's actual
arrival in Naples, and the letter to which *Fam.* xii 17 (dated 24 May) is
a reply appears to have been written in Florence: it is probable, therefore, that Zanobi's arrival in Naples did not occur before May. And the
fact that *Fam.* xii 17 was sent to Naples proves that Petrarch had reason
to believe that Zanobi would be there by the time the letter reached
him, which would be early in June.

what they can for the boy: Rinaldo is asked in particular to do what he can for his "ingenium," and Guglielmo to do what he can for his "mores." *Fam.* XIII 2 contains a full characterization of Giovanni, and reveals Petrarch's sorely troubled but still paternally hopeful attitude toward him.

In 1347 Clement had offered Petrarch an apostolic secretaryship, which, on his refusal, was given to Francesco Calvo of Naples, who held it until his death in 1359. During the winter of 1351–1352 Petrarch must have seen much of him in Avignon; and on 10 June he wrote him a long letter, *Fam.* XIII 4, in which he contrasts the honorable and profitable but exhausting life of Francesco at the papal court with the humble quietness of his own life. This letter is one of Petrarch's most extensive and emphatic statements of his aversion to high ecclesiastical office (its very first sentence states that Clement himself, having heard Petrarch express himself on this point, had indicated his agreement: "quod dudum illi longe hominum maximo non sine ipsius assensu dixisse me recolo"); and its last pages provide one of his pleasantest accounts of his life at Vaucluse.

At some time in the summer, probably in June or July, Petrarch wrote to Nelli the delightful letter, *Fam.* XIII 8, in which he gives his fullest description of his life at Vaucluse: this letter has been summarized above (on pp. 93–94). In Vaucluse, he concludes, he might spend his life, "nisi vel tam procul Italia vel tam prope esset Avinio. . . . illius me amor mulcet ac vellicat, huius me odium pungit et asperat odorque gravissimus toti mundo pestifer; quid mirum si vicinitate nimia unius parvi ruris innocuam polluit puritatem? ille me hinc pellet, sentio enim." [59]

The Pope had long been pressing the Emperor to send Cola

---

[59] The letter opens with the words "Ad fontem Sorgie estatem ago," which would have been no news to Nelli unless this letter had been written before the two letters, *Fam.* XIII 5 and 6, which were written to Nelli from Vaucluse on 9 and 10 August and assume Nelli's knowledge that Petrarch was spending the summer there. The priority of *Fam.* XIII 8 is indicated also by the fact that its reference to a return to Italy is made in merely general terms, while in *Fam.* XIII 6 Petrarch says definitely "Hic vie comites opperior et autumni exitum. . ." I conclude that *Fam.* XIII 8 was written in June, July, or very early in August.

to Avignon, there to be tried; and he was finally sent in or about June 1352, arriving probably in July.[60] Soon thereafter Petrarch received letters from Avignon, from friends whom he does not name, telling of Cola's arrival and reporting current gossip as to his chances. Judging from *Fam.* XIII 6 (which is presently to be considered), the substance of these letters must have been very much as follows:

He came not in chains but between two guards, passing through a curious crowd. As he entered the city he asked whether you were now at the papal court. The Pope has appointed three cardinals to be his judges and to decide what his punishment shall be. His one hope lies in the spreading report that he is an illustrious poet, and should therefore be exempt from violence.

These letters must have been of the greatest interest to Petrarch.

At about the same time, apparently, Petrarch received from Zanobi da Strada and from Niccolò Acciaiuoli letters (written in reply to *Fam.* XII 15–17) which brought him the very welcome news that his efforts to reëstablish the friendship between Niccolò and Giovanni Barrili had proved successful.

On 9 August Petrarch wrote to Nelli the letter, *Fam.* XIII 5, already referred to (on pp. 82 and 102), in which he tells with much verve of his narrow escape from being made an apostolic secretary after his return to Provence. On the very next day he wrote to Nelli another letter, *Fam.* XIII 6, which contains a report, based upon the letters he had just received from Avignon, of Cola's arrival there, and reviews Cola's career and his own relations to it. His attitude toward Cola is very severe; but at the same time he is highly indignant that the real cause of Cola's being brought to trial is the fact that he had dared to desire the safety and the freedom of Rome and its reëstablishment as the seat of the Empire. In the course of the letter Petrarch refers to his letter of the preceding day, to the fact that he is planning to return to Italy, with companions, in the late autumn or early winter, and to his current endeavor "ut omnis dies, si fieri possit, aut aliquid maioribus ceptis adiciat aut minutum aliquid absolvat";

---

[60] Piur 2, Chapter VIII.

writes at length—led by the word that Cola's one hope lies in the spreading report that he is an illustrious poet—of the current and quite unintelligent vogue of poetry in Avignon; cites in this connection the case of a cardinal (not identified) who was constantly asking questions about poetry, and refers to the fact (already referred to in *Fam.* IX 5) that he himself had been thought to be a necromancer because of his familiarity with Virgil; and asks Nelli to send both letters on to Naples so that Zanobi and Barbato da Sulmona may also share his amusement and his indignation.

On the same day, 10 August, he wrote to Zanobi a letter, *Fam.* XIII 9 (Fracassetti's XII 15), in which he replies to the letter recently received from Zanobi, and expresses his gratification at the renewal of the friendship of Niccolò Acciaiuoli and Giovanni Barrili. He refers also to the letter recently received from Niccolò, to which, he says, he will reply, thanking Niccolò, on behalf of Zanobi, for Niccolò's liberality to Zanobi. No such letter, however, is extant. On 25 August he wrote again to Zanobi: this letter, *Fam.* XIII 10 (Fracassetti's XII 16), has reference only to a literary question as to a passage in *Fam.* XII 16.

Throughout the spring and summer Petrarch must have been busy with literary work. To such work he refers in the clause quoted above from *Fam.* XIII 6 in which he speaks of his constant endeavor "ut omnis dies . . . aut aliquid maioribus ceptis adiciat aut minutum aliquid absolvat." As *maiora cepta* he undoubtedly had in mind the *De viris* and the collection of the *Familiares*. The words "minutum aliquid" most naturally suggest poems, in Latin or in Italian.

It will be shown in Chapter VII that *Met.* III 33 was in all probability written within this period. It seems probable also that *Met.* III 32, addressed to Socrates,[61] was written in this period, although, as already noted, it may have been written before the end of March. It opens with the lines:

> Artibus ut variis, agitur brevis orbita vitae,
> Et per mille vias metam properamus ad unam!

After an introductory moralizing passage it does in fact review

---

[61] Rossetti II, 150–156.

various ways of life: those of the getter of wealth (ll. 18–21), the belly-god (22–28), the demagogue (29–30), the soldier (31–36), the tyrant (37–39), the pedant (40–41), the house-proud man (42–43), the henpeck (43–45), the peasant (46–49), the enter-priser (49–54), the sailor (55–58), the hunter (59–66), the fisherman (66–67), the taverner (68–69), the dicer (69), the cir-cus "fan" (70–71), and the amorist (72–80). The poem ends with these lines:

> Sic suus urit amor, sic fert sua quemque cupido;
> Sola iacet virtus: poterat quae sola beatos
> Efficere et vitae tranquillum sternere callem!

In its review of various ways of life this poem shows a very marked likeness to *Met.* III 23: it is however wider in its range and more systematic in its progression. In III 23 Petrarch, recall-ing his Muse from a dangerous digression on tyranny, had written:

> Maria horrida velo
> O mea Calliope, et remis fugiamus adactis,
> Securum carpamus iter, speciesque laborum
> Et cursus vitae varios, populumque canamus.

His reference is very possibly to the lines that follow immediately in III 23 itself; but it is also possible that his reference is to the proposed writing of such a poem as III 32, in which he does explicitly treat "species . . . laborum / Et cursus vitae varios" and the "populum" in general. In any case the relation of III 32 to III 23 is so very close as to indicate that the two poems are at least approximately contemporary. If the reference in III 23 is to III 32, then III 32 is later than III 23, which was written in the period 19 January–March 1352; and III 32 may have been written either before the end of March, or, somewhat more probably, I think, after the return to Vaucluse in April. The fact that in the collection of the *Epistolae metricae* III 32 stands next to III 33, which was in all probability written in the spring or summer, increases slightly the probability that III 32 also was written in the spring or summer.

It is inherently probable that the writing of the two *capitoli* of the *Triumph of Fame, Da poi che Morte* and *Pien d'infinita,* which were written to replace *Nel cor*, took place not long after the virtual completion of Petrarch's work on the pre-Romulean Lives, since it was work on those Lives that gave Petrarch material for the correction of some of the data that had been used in *Nel cor*. This probability carries with it the further probability that they were written in Vaucluse in the spring or summer of 1352: during the preceding winter Petrarch had been exceedingly busy and unhappy in Avignon, and after the summer of 1352, as will appear below, he was exceedingly restless and anxious to return to Italy (except perhaps for a brief period in or about February 1353).

VIII. *Vaucluse and Avignon: September 1352*

A brief letter, *Fam.* XIII 12 (Fracassetti's XIII 11), written in Vaucluse on Saturday, the 1st of September, Petrarch's one and only letter to an otherwise unknown Abbot of Corvara, is a reply to a letter in which the Abbot had asked him for a copy of the *Africa*. Petrarch's answer is courteous, but firm: "Atqui necdum Scipio meus ad summum meo perductus est carmine et Africa, diutius michi possessa et laboriosius exarata quam credidi, nondum tamen supremo sarculo culta est; nondum glebas inutiles rastris attrivi; nondum superductis cratibus scabrioris agelli cumulos coequavi; nondum frondator luxuriantes pampinos et hirsutam sepem falce compescui . . . "

On the same day Petrarch transacted a piece of ecclesiastical business in Avignon. He may either have written *Fam.* XIII 12 in Vaucluse in the morning and been in Avignon in the afternoon, or have been in Avignon in the morning and returned to Vaucluse in the afternoon or the evening. Since 22 May 1342 Petrarch had held a canonry in the cathedral of Pisa; but he had never taken personal possession of it, and had evidently received its income through procurators. His present business in Avignon consisted in the appointment of one Ugolino Martelli for this purpose. The document of appointment,[62] signed by a notary

---

[62] Published by Pagano Paganini, 212–214. The "habitatio domini francisci" is doubtless the home of Guido Sette. The "olim" has obviously its occasional medieval sense, "of long standing": see Du Cange, *s.v.*

who gives his name as "Testa filius Crescii," begins thus:

In nomine Christi Amen. Anno eiusdem a nativitate Millesimo trecentesimo Quinquagesimo secundo Indictione quinta. die prima mensis Septembris. . . . In presentia mei notarii et testium infra-scriptorum, Venerabilis et circumspectus Vir dominus franciscus Petracchi de florentia olim canonicus prebendatus Ecclesie Pisane . . . fecit constituit et ordinavit suum verum et legitimum procura-torem . . . Hugolinum Martelli Mercatorem florentinum . . .

Its last sentence (except for that containing the notarial signa-ture) is this:

Actum Avinione in hospitio habitationis suprascripti domini fran-cisci presentibus Baldino magistri Duttoli et Johanne Miglini Cambi florentinis testibus ad predicta Vocatis et Rogatis.

Early in September, in all probability, and necessarily in Avignon, Petrarch had with Cardinal Gui de Boulogne, who was about to leave, with Pierre d'Auvergne, for an absence not ex-pected to be very long,[63] a talk in which he (Petrarch) told the Cardinal of his desire to return to Italy, and received the Cardi-nal's permission to do so. This we know from *Fam.* xiv 7, written to the Cardinal on 8 November, and *Fam.* xiii 7, written to Pierre d'Auvergne soon thereafter. From these same letters we learn that the Cardinal after leaving Avignon wrote to Petrarch with-drawing the permission he had given and requesting Petrarch to await his (the Cardinal's) return—and apparently to wait for him in Avignon—before leaving Provence; and that Pierre also wrote to him, supporting the Cardinal's request. *Fam.* xiv 7 opens thus:

Licentiam abeundi, quam michi digrediens verbo dederas, remissis ex itinere literis abstulisti; in quibus . . . rogas ac consulis . . . ne me loco moveam donec vel ipse redeas vel rescribas quadam de re magna tangente, ut ais, statum meum, cui pro viribus provehendo te te offers humanitate simul ac liberalitate mirabili.

Petrarch was bound to comply with this request.

---

[63] We do not know the purpose, the destination, or the originally expected length of this absence. Fracassetti's assertion, in his note on *Fam.* xiii 7, that the Cardinal at this time went to Paris to carry on peace negotiations between France and England is erroneous: the Cardinal did not leave on this mission until January 1353, and he re-mained in Paris for more than a year: see Baluze, pp. 346–347.

Other references to the fact that Petrarch had been intending to return to Italy appear in xiv 7 in the passages "suspensum gressum tenui . . . [because] cum semel abiero, diu te . . . intervisurus sum" and "Novissime . . . iussionis tue pondus accessit motumque iam vinculis strinxit pedem," and in xiii 7 in the passage "cum michi iam moturo vestra incubuisset auctoritas, gressum cohibui."

The Cardinal must have been planning to arrange for the conferring of a substantial benefice on Petrarch: it was clear by this time that Petrarch would not accept an apostolic secretaryship. Petrarch, however, was not much interested in the receipt of an additional benefice. Though grateful, he writes, in xiv 7, "Michi enim uni pro hac brevissima vite via viatici satis est, abunde est, nimis est, nilque amplius requiro," and, in xiii 7, "gressum cohibui . . . nullam propter spem ipsis ex literis oblatam. Gloriari quidem apud te non vereor, nosse me hominem nullum minus illi deditum passioni; fere etenim nichil spero; scis causam: quia fere etiam nichil opto." He remained, as he indicates in both letters, only in deference to the Cardinal's request, and because he hoped to see the Cardinal's face once more before leaving for Italy.

Presumably the Cardinal's request was sent not long after his departure: otherwise it might have been too late to hold Petrarch in Provence.

In both xiv 7, written on 8 November—the very day on which Petrarch, unable to endure Avignon any longer, had returned to Vaucluse—and in xiii 7, written soon thereafter, Petrarch refers to his stay in Avignon as having been of two months' duration: the phrases "duobus necquicquam mensibus expectans" and "bimenstrem moram" occur in xiv 7, and the clause "Inter expectandum . . . bimestre tempus absumpsi" occurs in xiii 7. If these references were to be taken at their face value they would indicate that Petrarch had established himself in Avignon by 8 September; but Petrarch was given to exaggeration, and in this case he would certainly have been led to assign to his stay in Avignon the greatest length he could possibly assign to it: there is then no reason to think that it lasted for two full months. On the other hand, since the Cardinal knew when he had made his request to Petrarch, and presumably knew also when Petrarch had signified his acceptance, Petrarch's "two months" cannot be very far out of the way. Other conflicting considerations are afforded by the fact that *Fam.* xiv 1–3 were certainly written in Vaucluse, 1 and 2 on the 22d and 3 on the 25th, and by the fact that in *Var.* 36, written certainly in Avignon on 4 October, Petrarch speaks of himself as being "in praesens occupatior etiam fragiliorque quam soleo, quod et loci mutatio curas auxit et vires corporeas morbus imminuit"—which sounds as if it were some time since he had left Vaucluse for Avignon. It may be that Petrarch began his period of waiting in Avignon in the early or middle part of September, returning to Vaucluse for a few days including the 22d and the 25th, and returning then to Avignon; or it may be that he continued to live in Vaucluse until one of the very last days of the month, visiting Avignon for a day or more when business made it necessary. In the latter case he dated his "two months" either from the time of his acquiescence in the Cardinal's desire or from a visit to Avignon made soon after that acquiescence, finding justification for his "two months" in the fact that by 8 November he had spent in Avignon more than one month and parts of three calendar months.[64]

Evidence of the hostility of Bishop Ugolino must have been accumulating, and must have been convincingly presented to the Pope by Petrarch or on Petrarch's behalf; for on 15 September Clement addressed to Petrarch an extraordinary letter in which he decrees that, in order that "plena tranquillitas" may ensue to Petrarch, both he (Petrarch) and the archdeaconate of Parma shall be exempt, immune, and free "ab omni iurisdictione dominio ac ordinaria potestate episcopi Parmensis." And on the same day Clement addressed a corresponding letter to three clerics, directing them to see that the provisions of his decree be duly carried out (see above, pp. 20–21).

It was presumably in September, also, or possibly in the first

---

[64] This discussion supersedes the discussion of this matter in Wilkins 1, pp. 334–335, but serves to confirm the conclusion there reached that *Fam.* xiv 1–3 were written in 1352.

half of October, that Petrarch decided that he would resign his
canonries in Lombez and in Pisa, and declined the offer of a canonry in Modena (see above, pp. 24–25).

In Vaucluse Petrarch wrote, on the 22nd, *Fam.* xiv 1 and 2,
and, on the 25th, *Fam.* xiv 3. The first of these letters, addressed
to Cardinal Elie de Talleyrand, is a lengthy disquisition on the
perils of wealth and power. Instead of sending it directly to the
Cardinal, Petrarch sent it to Socrates, with xiv 2, in which he asks
Socrates to deliver it personally. That Petrarch's association with
Cardinal Talleyrand had become close is indicated in xiv 1, 37,
in this passage: "Novi ego quos ut nossem voluisti, ardentissimos
animi tui motus curasque pulcerrimas: studium literarum, exer-
citium ingenii, mediocritatis amorem, religionis affectum, solitudinis appetitum"; and in xiv 2 in this passage:

affectum vero eius ad me, narrare tibi velle superfluum fuerit, quo
non me solum sed te et meos omnes amplectitur. Hic vir tantus et
sic nostri amans, cum possit suo iure precipere, quotidie orat ut sibi
aliquid scribam, semper illud adiciens ut scribam clare, simulque illud
quod cum illa quam postulat vix claritate cohabitat, ut aliquid de
poetis interseram, quibus me hortante delectari cepit, non ut illis
inhereat sed ut eorum ope suis in finibus utatur pyeriisque coloribus
civilem facundiam, qua pollet eximie, condiat atque exornet.

Petrarch then indicates that what the Cardinal meant by clear
writing was in fact the legalistic style that he (Petrarch) so much
despised: and the development of this idea is such as to confirm
the general opinion that Cardinal Talleyrand had been one of
those who brought pressure upon him to accept an apostolic
secretaryship, as narrated in *Fam.* xiii 5, and, by the same token,
one of the two cardinals who had urged his return from Italy to
Provence. *Fam.* xiv 2 refers in passing, also, to an interview with
the Pope—presumably the same interview referred to in *Fam.*
xiii 5—in which Clement also had urged Petrarch to write, for
official purposes, in a simpler style. Toward the end of xiv 2
Petrarch states that he has tried to comply with Cardinal Talleyrand's desire to the extent of writing letters to him in a style that
he himself could not approve, and that he has not kept copies

of such letters: "sed ne displiceam multis, novo more usus, sic illi scribo ut exemplaria non reservem."

Fam. xiv 3, a reply to a letter received from Luca da Piacenza, expresses Petrarch's grief at the sudden death of a young mutual friend. There is a passing reference to the unreliability of medical claims.

At some time in September Petrarch received from Benedetto Colonna a letter containing the news that he (Benedetto) had been appointed administrator of the diocese of Chieti. (Guglielmo Capodiferro, Bishop of Chieti, had died earlier in 1352—the exact date is not known—and no immediate appointment of a successor was to be made.)

IX. *Avignon: October–8 November 1352*

By the end of September Petrarch was in Avignon, awaiting the return of Cardinal Gui de Boulogne, and there he remained until 8 November, when, unable to endure the city any longer—both *Fam.* xiv 7 and *Fam.* xiii 7, as well as other letters presently to be mentioned, contain passages that show that Avignon was at this time as hateful to him as ever—he returned to Vaucluse (where, on that very day, he wrote *Fam.* xiv 7 to the Cardinal).

That he was in poor health at this time is indicated by the passage in *Var.* 36 quoted above (on p. 135).

While in Avignon he was again beset by demands upon his time; he was again distressed by evidences of enmity; and he was again led to take epistolary action with regard to matters of public concern.

As to demands upon his time he writes, in *Fam.* xiii 7, "Quotidie epystolas, quotidie carmina omnis in caput hoc nostri orbis angulus pluit; nec satis est: peregrinis iam, nec Gallis modo sed Graiis et Theutonis et Britannis, tempestatibus literarum pulsor, omnium ingeniorum arbiter, mei ipsius ignarus." Furthermore, the current vogue of poetry, with regard to which he had written to Nelli in *Fam.* xii 6, was still raging in Avignon, and in *Fam.* xiii 7 he writes: "vix iam in publicum exire audeo; occurrunt enim omni ex parte frenetici, percontantur arripiunt docent disputant altercantur dicunt que nunquam mantuanus pastor, nunquam meonius senex novit."

The enmity that now distressed him was active, however, not in Avignon but in Italy, and presumably in Parma. A letter from Luca da Piacenza had informed him that the report of his intended return to Italy had stirred up new calumnies, against which Petrarch defends himself at length in the long *Fam.* xiv 4, written to Luca on 19 October. According to that letter four motives were being imputed to him as causes for his intended return: inconstancy, avarice, niggardliness, and lack of favor at the papal court. In the course of his defense against the charge of avarice Petrarch asserts, in a passage quoted in part above (on p. 24), that he has recently resigned two canonries, and that instead of accepting a canonry in Modena that had just been offered to him he has arranged to have it given to Don Luca.

The matters of public concern as to which Petrarch felt called upon at this time to say his say were the plight of Cola, conditions in Rome, and the warfare between Genoa and Venice.

Cola was now a prisoner in Avignon, confined in a tower of the papal palace.[65] On his arrival in Avignon, he had asked whether Petrarch were there, as has been said above; and Petrarch, then in Vaucluse, on learning of his arrival, had written to Nelli the letter, *Fam.* xiii 6, summarized above, in which he had spoken of Cola with great severity, while expressing his indignation that the real cause of the plight of the former Tribune was the fact that he had dared to desire the safety and the freedom of Rome and its reëstablishment as the seat of the Roman Empire. There is no evidence that Petrarch, while in Avignon in the autumn, made any effort to see Cola; but it was in all probability at this time that he wrote on Cola's behalf a long letter, *Sine nom.* 4, addressed to the Roman People. He writes as a Roman citizen, addressing the Roman People as "popule meus," [66] and stating "ciuem Romanum esse qui loquitur." He is writing,

---

[65] Piur 2, Chap. VIII.

[66] The quotations in this paragraph are from Piur 1, pp. 173–174 and 181–183.

he says, "cogente me ad calamum fide illa qua nos urbemque uestram inter omnes singulari quodam amore ac ueneratione complector." The particular purpose of the letter is to urge the Roman People to intervene on behalf of Cola by sending an embassy to Avignon to claim the right of jurisdiction over him as being a Roman citizen, or to demand at least that he be accorded legal advice and a public trial. The entire letter develops the position, already taken in *Fam.* xiii 6, that Cola's one great sin, in papal eyes, was in reality his endeavor to reëstablish Rome as the seat of the Roman Empire: "Illud sibi summum et crucibus expiandum scelus obicitur, quod affirmare presumpserit Romanum imperium nunc etiam Rome et penes populum Romanum esse." The entire central portion of the letter is devoted to a demonstration of the thesis that Rome and only Rome is indeed the proper seat of the Roman Empire. Petrarch blames Cola for having forsaken the task he had so well begun: "Est ille forte non indignus hec perpeti, qui suo ingenio suisque, ut ita dixerim, manibus plantatam et iam radicatam florentemque Rempublicam in ipso gloriosissimi successus flore destituit." But the tone of the letter, especially in its concluding pages, is much more sympathetic than the tone of *Fam.* xiii 6. Cola is generally and deservedly pitied: "Hominum pars magna compatitur; nemo fere est, qui non misereatur, preter eos, quibus maxime proprium erat misereri et parcere erroribus, non inuidere uirtutibus." He is generally and deservedly thought to merit reward rather than punishment: "Quodsi forte tribunus uester—quoniam multi, quin potius boni omnes ita sentiunt—non supplicio, sed premio dignus est . . ." The letter culminates in a glowing summary of Cola's efforts on behalf of Rome, a summary that ends thus: "Septem enim mensium non amplius spatio frena reipublice tenuit, ut uix ab origine mundi maius aliquid attentatum rear, et si successisset ut ceperat, diuinum potius quam humanum opus esse uideretur."

My belief that *Sine nom.* 4 was written during this stay in Avignon rather than while Petrarch was still in Vaucluse rests in part on the marked difference in tone between *Fam.* xiii 6 and *Sine nom.* 4, and in part on the obvious consideration that

neighborhood in Avignon to the imprisoned Cola would naturally have stirred Petrarch to an excitement on his behalf that he
could hardly have felt in his sylvan retreat.

On 26 December 1351 the Roman People, having wrested
control from the nobles, had elected one of their own number,
Giovanni Cerroni, as sole senator; but by September the nobles
had regained control, and Cerroni was driven from the city.
Stefanello Colonna and Bertoldo Orsini were then elected senators, their election being confirmed by the Guild of Merchants
on 10 October (they were never recognized by the Pope).[67]
Fam. xv 1, addressed to Laelius, shows that it was generally
believed in Avignon that Laelius was the effective counsellor of
the new senators: "quibus [*i.e.*, to the cardinals] ita persuasum
noveris, quicquid in novo geritur senatu quorumcunque opera,
consilio tuo fieri." Petrarch's letter expresses his hope that Laelius
will succeed in lifting Rome out of its fallen state: "ad attol-
lendam humo collapsam iacentemque rempublicam suffecturos
humeros tuos spero, modo et ipsa respublica credulam se consiliis
tuis prestet et tu proiectis affectibus propriis ad comune bonum
te convertas." To the papal court what Laelius was doing seems
improper and worthy of punishment: to Petrarch it seems praise-
worthy and conducive to eternal fame. If Laelius persists in his
enterprise, Petrarch will give him all the support he can. Meanwhile, he advises him to steer a middle course between "teporem
ac fervorem nimium," reminding him of Ovid's dictum, "medio
tutissimus ibis." The "novo" in the clause "quicquid in novo
geritur senatu" and the fact that the letter contains no reference
to later events indicate that *Fam.* xv 1 was written while Petrarch
was still in Avignon rather than at a later time.

In 1350 naval hostilities between Genoa and Venice had
begun on a small scale; and by the spring of 1351 Venice was
preparing to undertake warfare on a large scale. Petrarch then,
before leaving Padua, had written to Andrea Dandolo, Doge of
Venice, a long and very able letter, *Fam.* xi 8, in which he had
urged the Doge to make peace with Genoa. The Doge, however,

---

[67] Gregorovius, Book XI, Chap. VII, Sects. 2–3.

had replied [68] that the Venetian cause was just, and that Venice was undertaking war solely with a view to establishing an honorable peace. In July Clement VI made a futile offer of mediation. On 3 August Peter IV of Aragon declared war on Genoa; and the Greek Emperor then joined Venice and Aragon in an alliance against Genoa. In October Clement sent Fortanerio Vassalli, the Patriarch of Grado, to Italy in a futile effort to bring about peace. The first major battle of the war, fought in the Bosphorus on 13 February 1352, was a victory, though a costly one, for Genoa. Clement again sought to intervene, by summoning Genoa, Venice, and Aragon to send envoys to a conference in Avignon in September; but the conferees failed to reach any agreement.[69] On 1 November Petrarch again sought to promote a peaceful settlement, by sending to the Doge and Council of Genoa a long letter, *Fam.* xiv 5, in which, after referring to his earlier letter to the Doge of Venice, he urges Genoa, now victorious, to use her victory for the establishment of peace with Venice. For the Aragonese and for the Greeks he has no sympathy: he refers to the Aragonese as "venale genus ac fedifragum et insolens," and as the "infidos instigatores" of the war. Internecine warfare between Italian states should cease: let Genoa and Venice combine their forces, attack the perfidious Aragonese, and after an easy victory over them undertake the liberation of the Holy Land. In the latter part of the letter Petrarch, with good reason, warns Genoa against a renewal of the civil strife that has been so disastrous to her in the past. The letter contains a vivid account of the battle of the Bosphorus, and a fine description of the beauties of Genoa and its *riviera*.

The only other letter assignable to this particular period,

---

[68] In LAP 1. Petrarch's *Fam.* xi 8 and the Doge's reply are both referred to in a later letter to Dandolo, *Fam.* xviii 16.

[69] Jules Gay, *Le pape Clément VI et les affaires d'Orient* (Paris, 1904), pp. 123–124; Baluze, p. 468; and Odorico Rinaldi, *Annales ecclesiastici*, vi (Lucca, 1750), 561–562. De Sade, iii, 257, followed by Fracassetti (in his note on *Fam.* xiv 5), states that the conference in Avignon lasted through the month of October, and names four cardinals appointed by Clement as "Commissaires & médiateurs"; but he gives no reference in support of these statements.

Var. 36, written on 4 October, is a reply to the letter from Benedetto Colonna referred to above (on pp. 135 and 137). Petrarch congratulates Benedetto on his appointment as administrator of the diocese of Chieti. This letter contains the passage, quoted above (on p. 135), in which Petrarch speaks of his change of residence and of his poor health; and this characteristic reference to Avignon: "Itaque Tiberinos honores cuncta rodens Rhodanus vorat. Et quae spectacula, bone Iesu!"

X. *Vaucluse: 8 November 1352–May 1353*
November

On Thursday, the 8th of November, the very day of his return to Vaucluse, Petrarch wrote *Fam.* xiv 7 to Cardinal Gui de Boulogne, and within a few days thereafter he wrote *Fam.* xiii 7 to Pierre d'Auvergne: these letters are delayed replies to the letters from the Cardinal and from Pierre that have been referred to above (on pp. 133–138). Both these letters indicate that Petrarch was very impatient to start for Italy, and that he did not propose to wait long in Vaucluse for the Cardinal and the Abbot. In xiv 7 Petrarch writes: "nam quoad dabitur, ad fontem Sorgie subsistam . . . Hinc vero, si perstas, clam tacitus pergam amicos fallens"; and in xiii 7 he writes: "hic vos, dum sinet extrema necessitas, expectabo." As will presently appear, he actually started out for Italy on the 16th, but did not get very far. *Fam.* xiii 7, which was written after xiv 7 and before his start for Italy, must then have been written within the period 8–15 November.

One other letter, *Fam.* xv 11, addressed to Philippe de Cabassoles, was written within this same eight-day period. In this letter Petrarch reports his return to Vaucluse, and says that he is in a state of great perplexity, and that he is coming soon to Cavaillon in order to see Philippe, and in the hope of finding there a shelter from the besetting envy that has worn him out. The fact that the letter carries the news of his return to Vaucluse proves that it was written on or very soon after 8 November; and the fact that it does not announce a decision to start immediately for Italy proves that it was written some days before the 16th.

The story of Petrarch's unsuccessful start for Italy is told in three of his letters: *Fam.* xv 2, written to Nelli immediately afterward, on 18 November; *Fam.* xv 3, written on 22 February 1353 to Zanobi da Strada; and the reminiscent *Var.* 64, written to Philippe de Cabassoles, probably in the spring of 1354. When he had once made up his mind to leave immediately for Italy he decided to go by the coastal route, so that, stopping at Montrieux, he might see his brother Gherardo, whom he had not seen for five years. His baggage (as we learn from *Fam.* xv 3) consisted largely of books and his own papers: "Erat michi predulcis librorum sarcinula et veterum libris immixtum pauxillum nugarum mearum, quibus ipse quoque memphiticas papiros impleo." He set out on Friday the 16th, with several servants. There had been no rain for many months; but he had hardly left his house before it began to rain, at first lightly, then heavily. He went on, however, planning to stop briefly at Cavaillon to say farewell to Philippe de Cabassoles, and then to ford the Durance before sundown. At Cavaillon, however, he found Philippe sick, and at Philippe's urging he consented to spend the night there. The rain became a wild deluge, driving through the roofs; and there was little sleep in Philippe's household that night. In the course of the night word came that armed bands had come down from the mountains to Nice, making the coastal road impassable. Philippe urged Petrarch to give up his journey. Petrarch was reluctant to do so, and thought of changing his plans and taking the route that led over the pass of Mont Genèvre. But he feared that continuing rain would ruin his precious books; and for that reason—and with some feeling that the combination of obstacles might be a deterrent sign from Heaven—he yielded, and gave up the journey. He sent some of his servants on to Italy, one of them being instructed (as later developments indicate) to return with a report as to the state of affairs Petrarch might expect to find if he should return to Italy. As soon as the servants thus sent forward were beyond recall, the rain stopped. Night overtook him (as we learn from *Fam.* xiv 8) as he rode home, almost alone, to Vaucluse.

There, on the 18th, he wrote the letter to Nelli, *Fam.* xv 2, which contains the fullest account of this experience; and there, apparently soon after his return, he wrote to Sansone Ponzio a letter, *Fam.* xiv 8, in which he apologizes for having left Cavaillon without seeing Sansone, and tells him of his intention to start soon for Italy: "Da veniam, precor, neve novam querelarum habeas materiam, scito esse michi animum his proximis diebus in Italiam proficisci, et ut sepe fallunt cogitatus, quod autumno agere decreveram, hieme peragere."

Bishop Ildebrandino of Padua had died on 2 November; and the news must have reached Avignon, and in all probability Vaucluse, before the end of the month. It may then have been before the end of November, and under the first impact of what was for him a great personal loss, that Petrarch wrote, to the Paduan clergy, *Fam.* xv 14, a long and glowing eulogy of Ildebrandino, which contains also a deeply felt account of Petrarch's own friendship with Ildebrandino.[70] This letter must have been written before 15 December, since Petrarch sent a copy of it to Philippe de Cabassoles with *Fam.* xv 13, which was written on the morning of that day. The fact that xv 14 makes no reference to the death of Clement VI, which occurred on 6 December, indicates, though it does not prove, that it was written before that date. It was written, then, either late in November or early in December: the probabilities seem to me to favor late November.

December 1352

On the first day of the month Petrarch wrote to Giovanni Aghinolfi, who was still apparently in Avignon, a brief letter, *Fam.* vii 8, congratulating him on the improvements he had brought about—presumably through the success of his efforts as the representative of the Gonzaga in Avignon, and through advice sent directly to Luigi and Guido Gonzaga—in the internal status and the external relations of Mantua: "Gratulor ergo liber-

---

[70] On Ildebrandino see Paolo Sambin, "Ildebrandino Conti e l'introduzione dei monaci olivetani a Padova," in *Benedictina*, iii (1949), 249–277; "Note sull'attività politico-diplomatica di Ildebrandino Conti amico del Petrarca," in *Archivio Veneto*, xlvi–xlvii (1950), 16–44; and *Un amico del Petrarca: Ildebrandino Conti e la sua attività spirituale e culturale* (= Deputazione di Storia Patria per le Venezie, *Miscellanea di studi e memorie*, viii, i) (Venice, 1952).

tati patrie, principum nostrorum glorie, tranquillitati civium, religionis aumento, publice letitie, singulariter honori tuo, cuius manibus hactenus tenebrose urbi serenitas invehitur." Soon now, Petrarch hopes, they can both return to Italy: "casibus ipsis nostris atque difficultatibus gratulari incipio: uni scilicet motiuncule illi tui corporis . . . et viarum mearum impedimentis multis ac variis, quibus effectum spero ut ambo pariter in Italiam redeamus." [71]

Clement VI died on 6 December. He had done much for Petrarch. In 1342 he had appointed him to a canonry in the cathedral of Pisa; later in the same year he had appointed him to the priorate of S. Nicola di Migliarino, near Pisa; in 1343 (the appointment to S. Nicola having proved invalid) he had awarded him the rectory of S. Angelo in Castiglione Fiorentino; in 1346 he had appointed him to a canonry in the cathedral of Parma; in 1347 he had offered him a bishopric and an apostolic secretaryship; in 1348 he had appointed him to the archdeaconate of the cathedral of Parma; in 1351 (or, possibly, in 1352) he had again offered him a bishopric or an apostolic secretaryship; and on 15 September 1352 he had issued a letter exempting him from

[71] I quote from the missive form of the letter, which is dated "Ad fontem Sorgie, Kal. Decembris ante lucem." In the final form the specific clause "ut ambo pariter in Italiam redeamus" was replaced by the less definite "ut ambo simul in patriam revertamur," and the date was omitted: and in consequence Fracassetti dated the letter as of 1348—most of the letters of Book VII having been written in 1347 or 1348 (VII 16 and 17 are now thought to have been written early in 1351). But Luigi di Benedetto, in his *Da Giacomo da Lentino a Francesco Petrarca* (Naples, 1949), pp. 61–62, is clearly right in recognizing, on the basis of the variants of the missive form, that the letter was written in 1352 (though in error in asserting that the two persons for whom return to Italy is proposed are Petrarch and his son: see above, p. 127). The references to conditions in Mantua contained in the passage beginning "Gratulor" are too general to permit of confirmation by checking with the appropriate passages in the histories of Mantua available to me; but in connection with the phrase "religionis aumento" one may note the facts—reported by L. C. Volta in his *Compendio cronologico-storico della storia di Mantova*, II (Mantua, 1827), p. 72—that in 1350 the Gonzaga had rebuilt a convent and a church, adding to the church a "spedale per ricovero dei mendici," and that in 1351 Luigi Gonzaga had made a large distribution of alms.

the authority of the Bishop of Parma (see above, pp. 20–21). In the interview with Clement which had taken place in the autumn of 1351, or thereafter, the Pope, according to Petrarch's report of the interview in *Var.* 15 quoted above (on p. 72), had said to Petrarch: "Pete quod vis et faciam tibi"; and Petrarch had replied: "Quando aliquid . . . ad notitiam vestram venit, quod me dignum videatur, mei si placet memoriam habetote." And to this quotation Petrarch adds the comment: "quod ipse se facturum clementissime repromisit, et fecisset, non dubito, nisi eum mors multis, et inter alios mihi damnosa, praevenisset." Petrarch, on his part, had done what he could for Clement early in 1352, when the Pope lay ill, by advising him to beware of a multitude of doctors and to rely upon a single doctor distinguished not by eloquence but by learning and trustworthiness. Yet in spite of the cordiality of their personal relations Petrarch's judgment of Clement as Pope had been exceedingly severe—a judgment voiced in *Sine nom.* 6, 8, and 10, and most vehemently in the sixth and seventh Eclogues (see above, pp. 48–57).

Shortly before or almost immediately after the death of Clement Petrarch wrote a letter addressed to Philippe de Cabassoles, which he mentions in *Fam.* xv 12 and 13, and to which I shall refer as *Sine nom.* x. This letter is not extant, unless it is to be identified as *Sine nom.* 1: such identification is possible, but improbable.[72]

---

[72] *Sine nom.* 1 was written at a time when the death of a Pope was expected: the Pope in question must have been either Benedict XII or Clement VI. Piur, who has examined the evidence and all earlier discussions with great care, finds it probable that the reference is to Benedict; and the same opinion is expressed by Foresti and by Rizzi: see Piur 1, pp. 316–325; Foresti 1, pp. 89–90; and Rizzi 1, pp. 88–90. The only consideration not previously advanced that has occurred to me is this: what is almost certainly the first redaction of the collection of the *Sine nomine* (for which see below, pp. 179–180) opens with the letter that is now *Sine nom.* 4, which was written in all probability in October or November 1352 (see above, pp. 138–140); continues with the letter that is now *Sine nom.* 12, which was written in December 1352 or at the beginning of 1353, as will presently appear; and then continues with the letter that is now *Sine nom.* 1. This looks as if *Sine nom.* 1 were associated in Petrarch's mind with letters written late in 1352 or soon thereafter, and would therefore seem to suggest that the dying Pope of

On 14 December, before daybreak—"silentio noctis intempeste"—Petrarch wrote a brief letter, *Fam.* xv 12, to Philippe; and with that letter he sent three gifts: a fine fish caught in the Sorgue by a son of Petrarch's "villicus" (Raymond Monet); a fat duck, caught by Petrarch's dog; and *Sine nom. x.* The first two gifts were to be kept by Philippe, but *Sine nom. x* was to be returned:

hec venit ut redeat, neque diutius quam ut oculos tuos semel impleverit, tecum sit. Scis causam? quia veritas odium parit; quod si iam tempore Terrentii verum erat, quid hodie arbitraris? perlege ergo si libet, atque secretius, ac remitte donec sciamus quid mundo Deus aut fortuna paraverit; tunc consultabimus quid huic fiat, an danda sit flammis an sororibus ascribenda. Interim scito, et hinc fidem metire meam, nullis me oculis hanc aliis ostensurum fuisse quam tuis.[73]

The clause "donec . . . paraverit" obviously reflects Petrarch's anxious uncertainty as to the papal succession; and the phrase "an sororibus ascribenda" obviously indicates that Petrarch already had in mind the formation of the collection of the *Sine nomine.*

Philippe read *Sine nom. x* at once, and returned it, before the day was over, with a reply the tenor of which is indicated thus in Petrarch's acknowledgment, *Fam.* xv 13: "Legisti confestimque remisisti epystolam illam tibi inscriptam eo quod te capitalem hostem vitiorum noverim, quam quidem tibi valde placuisse gaudeo."

Fam. xv 13 was written before daybreak—"diluculo"—on the 15th. With it Petrarch sends to Philippe, as a fourth gift, a copy of his letter to the Paduan clergy on the death of Ildebrandino, and suggests that Philippe compare it with *Sine nom. x:* "Tu, pater, has invicem conferens epystolas, extimabis siqua huius

---

Sine nom. 1 was Clement rather than Benedict. This consideration, however, is by no means conclusive. Even if *Sine nom.* 1 had been written with reference to Benedict, Petrarch might have placed it after what is now *Sine nom.* 12 simply because, like that letter, it has reference to the death of a Pope; and if it had actually been written shortly before the death of Clement one might think that Petrarch would have placed it before rather than after *Sine nom.* 12.

[73] I quote from the missive form of the letter, using the variants recorded by Rossi.

calami vis est ad actus diversissimos, vituperandum scilicet ac laudandum."

On the following day, the 16th, the Cardinals met in conclave to elect a new Pope. It was a foregone conclusion that they would choose a Frenchman: Petrarch doubtless hoped, and not without reason, that their choice would fall upon either Gui de Boulogne or Elie de Talleyrand. It must have been with the utmost distress that he learned that, on the 18th, they had elected Etienne Aubert—who still held firmly to the belief that Petrarch was a necromancer, even though Cardinal Talleyrand and Petrarch had ridiculed that belief in his presence. The new Pope took the name of Innocent VI.

Petrarch's bitterness is vented in *Sine nom.* 12, which consists almost entirely of a long and violent outburst of psalmodic lamentation and argumentative reproach:

Ve populo tuo, Criste Jhesu! Ve populo tuo, Criste! Patere nos, misericordiarum fons, nostras tecum flere miserias!
. . . Certe si tu nos in honorem creatos in contumeliam uertis, quamuis id iuste facias, multo tamen quam soles acrius ulcisceris . . . Si uero non aspicis, ualde preter solitum factus es negligens tuorum.
. . . Eripuisti nos iugo graui et pessimo et obsceno: quid nobis ex eodem stipite iugum importabile reimponis?. . . Sperauimus enim in te quod motum fluctuum nostri maris, in quo feliciter senex ille piscatus tandem periit, tradita successori nauicula mitigares . . . quodque superbum humiliares et in brachio uirtutis tuo deponeres inimicos tuos, de ouibus lupos, de piscatoribus piratas, de pastoribus abactores. Nunc uero superbia eorum, qui te oderunt, ascendit semper.

Both Clement and Innocent are referred to in the question "Eripuisti . . . reimponis?" and in preceding questions not quoted here; Clement is referred to in the clause "in quo . . . periit"; and Innocent is referred to in what follows that clause. The sentence "Nunc . . . semper," the last sentence of the main portion of the letter, is followed by the sentence "Hactenus Deo hec," which is itself followed by a single final sentence addressed to a terrestrial "pater," who is certainly Philippe de Cabassoles:

Tu autem, pater, quem in primis dolorum meorum participem habeo, noli Fortune succumbere, sed donec illa, quod modo facturam sperabamus, meliorem in partem instabilem rotam uoluit, nitere ut uluas cι ualcas, uι, hinc postmodum nostro tempore discedentes, meliorem rumorem ad felices animas perferamus!

Piur is undoubtedly right in dating this letter as of the last days of December 1352 or the beginning of 1353 [74]: in view of the flaming quality of its indignation it seems to me probable, though by no means certain, that it was written very soon after Petrarch heard of the election of Innocent—that is, in December rather than in January.

January 1353

On 3 January (or possibly a day or two earlier) Petrarch, as we learn from *Fam.* xvi 1, received a message from Cardinals Elie de Talleyrand and Gui de Boulogne, asking him to come to Avignon. Their purpose in so asking him is not stated by Petrarch; but De Sade and Fracassetti are probably right in thinking that the two cardinals desired to present and recommend him to the new Pope.[75]

Petrarch accordingly went in to Avignon on Thursday the 3rd, leaving his faithful overseer Raymond Monet, as he thought, slightly ill. On the afternoon of the 4th, however, Raymond died; and the news of his death was brought to Petrarch late that night by one of his servants. On the 5th he wrote to the two cardinals a letter, *Fam.* xvi 1, in which he asks their permission to return to Vaucluse. The letter, quoted above, in small part (on p. 94), is, in substance, a touching tribute to Raymond, whom Petrarch, to the end of his life, remembered with grateful affection.

On 17 November, when Petrarch, then at Cavaillon, had given up his journey, he had sent some of his servants on to Italy. In less than two months—presumably, then, within the first half of January—one of them returned, bringing what was, for Petrarch, bad news. In *Fam.* xv 3, written in February to Zanobi, Petrarch represents his servant as saying to him, in effect:

Things would be even worse for you in Italy than in Avignon.

---

[74] Piur 1, pp. 371–373.
[75] De Sade, iii, 280; Fracassetti *ad loc.*

You have no idea what a mass of cares would await you; what troops of friends have been excited by the report of your intended return; how many distractions would beset you; how strenuously you would have to bestir yourself, if not for your own affairs, at least for the affairs of others, and how much time you would lose; what troubles you would have to endure in order to satisfy the desires of many men.

To these generalities the servant added convincing details: "singula diligenter explicuit, rationes afferens sole lucidiores." This report led Petrarch to give up his intention of returning to Italy in the course of the winter—the intention he had stated in *Fam.* XIV 8, written to Sansone Ponzio after his return from Cavaillon—and to settle down again in Vaucluse, at least for the time being:

> itaque mecum volvens ac multa recogitans et ubi portum esse credideram, suis fluctibus undosum mare conspiciens, moderatus ex ipsa rerum tempestate navigium animi, legi rudentes, ieci anchoram, clavum pressi, fessamque vite turbinibus carinam, donec portus appareat, hos inter scopulos alligavi, non rediturus ad curiam, neque nisi aliud audiero, Ausoniam petiturus.

When still in Padua, before coming to Provence in 1351, Petrarch, while supping with Bishop Ildebrandino, had learned from two other guests, monks of the Carthusian order, of his brother Gherardo's terrible and heroic experiences during the time of the Black Death: Gherardo, the sole survivor in his monastery, had done faithfully and singlehanded all that had to be done. In *Fam.* XVI 2, written to Gherardo after the death of Ildebrandino, Petrarch recounts the story as he had heard it so long before. The letter is not dated; but its reference to the Bishop's death shows that it was written after the news of that death had reached Petrarch, and since Petrarch actually went to Montrieux in mid-April to visit his brother it must have been written before he had decided to pay that visit. It must then have been written between mid-November and the end of March. It refers to the death of Ildebrandino as if it were well known; it contains no reference to Petrarch's intended November visit to Montrieux; and it does not in any way reflect the distress that overwhelmed Petrarch as a result of the election of Innocent VI. The probabilities are, then, that it was written either in January or in

February. That he had waited so long, after hearing the story, to write to Gherardo about it was presumably due to a combination of circumstances: when he had heard the story he was presumably planning to come to Provence and intending to visit Gherardo; he had presumably retained that intention after reaching Provence; and his final decision to write was presumably related to the death of Ildebrandino and to the failure of his own plan to visit Gherardo in November.[76]

Early in 1353, very probably in January or February, Petrarch's polemic with one of the physicians who had attended Clement VI became active again. Before 17 April 1352, according to *Fam.* xv 6 (see above, p. 120), that physician had been going about Avignon looking for someone to help him deal with the long rejoinder he had received from Petrarch—the rejoinder that ultimately became Book I of the *Invective contra medicum*. It was only after many months, as Petrarch says in Book III of the *Invective*, or a year, as Petrarch, perhaps exaggerating, implies in a passage in Book IV, that the physician produced his counter-rejoinder. Our information as to this document, which is not extant, comes from Petrarch's final counterblast, which, while not extant in its original form, is preserved, probably with little change, as Books II–IV of the *Invective*. The doctor's counter-rejoinder was long enough to be called a book, and was divided, formally or informally, into two or more parts. Petrarch writes: "O ridiculum animal . . . librum scribis; rectius dixerim . . . tabificos iocos scribis. Sed ut libri formam habeant, versutus opifex, distinguis in partes; et forsitan victor eris: apothecarii scripsisse te librum dicent. . . . Prima quidem libri tui pars de te ipso agit. . . . Secunda apologetici tui pars de me erat. . . ." According to Petrarch the doctor claimed to be a philosopher, and asserted that he could cure minds as well as bodies, and that often, by his skill, he had brought men back from the threshold of death: "homines velut a mortuis suscitatos." He accused Petrarch of arrogance, of adulation, of boasting of learning and fame, of being too proud to mention him (the doctor) by name, of speaking scornfully of old age, and of being no logician. He

---

[76] See Wilkins 1, pp. 337–338.

defended medicine, saying that by it "docemur recte vivere," and that the arts of speech are therefore properly subservient to it. He attacked poetry again, saying that its purpose is "mulcendo fallere"; that it is unnecessary, and therefore ignoble and unworthy; that whereas science is firm and immutable poetry makes use of metres and words that are variable; and that poets delight in obscurity because they hate the common folk. And he attacked Petrarch's attachment to solitude, praising the resources of city life.[77]

Petrarch's counterblast, which in its final and only extant form constitutes Books II–IV of the *Invective*, is a work of considerable length, covering sixty pages in Ricci's edition. Petrarch says of it, at the very end, "aliquot michi dies eripuit"; but he would have been inclined to belittle the amount of time it had taken him to write it. It is dated as of 1353 by a reference to the death of Clement and to the change in the papacy. It was doubtless written soon after the receipt of the physician's counter-retort—certainly before Petrarch left Provence, and almost certainly within the first quarter of the year. Two or three references show that it was written in Vaucluse. It was presumably divided into three Parts, which became Books II, III, and IV of the *Invective* respectively. The first of the three Parts demolishes various charges and assertions. Petrarch again makes it clear that he is not attacking all doctors: "Aliquot . . . medicos veros novi, et ingenio et ea que in omnium artium arte ponenda est discretione pollentes." In the second Part, an elaborate defense of poetry, Petrarch stresses the difference between the liberal and the mechanical arts; praises poets—

Quanta Virgilii integritas! quenam Statii urbanitas! que facetie Nasonis! que fides Ennii! que Pacuvii gravitas! quis Vari candor! que Flacci discretio! que Persii pietas! que modestia Lucani! que libertas atque constantia Iuvenalis!—

defends poetic obscurity, citing Augustine and Gregory, on the

[77] The quotations in this paragraph are from Ricci, pp. 39–42, 50, 76, and 59; and those in the next paragraph are from Ricci, pp. 98, 48, 69, 70, 75, 94, and 93. On the *Invective* see Ezio Raimondi's notable review of Ricci, in *Studi petrarcheschi*, IV (1951), 225–262.

ground that the solution of the difficulties of poetry enhances its value to the reader—

> Apud poetas . . . stili maiestas retinetur ac dignitas, nec capere valentibus invidetur, sed, dulci labore proposito, delectationi simul memorieque consulitur. Cariora sunt, enim, que cum difficultate quesivimus, accuratiusque servantur,—

and asserts that his writings are written for posterity: "sed scribo quod legant qui post me nascentur." The third Part is a defense of solitude, always a favorite theme with Petrarch. It contains, in the course of its main argument, a good many passages of incidental interest: references to Clement and to Innocent; a statement that he had written a "carmen breve" in answer to the doctor's "hymns," but had decided, because of its subject, not to inflict it upon the Muses; and another assertion that he is writing for posterity: "dum manus tua miserorum rimatur atque explicat purgamenta, mea aliquid scribit gratum postcris—ut spero—dum legetur." At the end he challenges the doctor to renew the argument, saying however that he will ignore any reply that he does not receive within a year: no reply, as far as we know, was ever forthcoming.

Book II of the *Invective* contains this passage:

> Scripsi aliqua, nec desino aut unquam desinam, dum hic digitus calamum ferat. Sed, omissis aliis . . . scribo de viris illustribus. . . . Illic, si tibi debitum locum putas, dic ubi vis inseri: parebitur; sed verendum est ne quos ex omnibus seculis illustres . . . in unum contraxi adventu tuo diffugiant, teque ibi solo remanente, mutandus libri titulus, neque *De Viris Illustribus* sed *De Insigni Fatuo* inscribendum sit.[78]

Petrarch, then, in the early months of 1353, was still working on the *De viris*. His work on the twelve pre-Romulean Lives had in all probability been completed before this time (see above, p. 116): it may well be that the work he was doing on the *De viris* early in 1353 was the composition of the final form of the Life of Scipio Africanus.[78a]

(left column, partially cut off)

inclusion in the
to Niccolò—ar
of his draft,
"transcripta in
multis mutatis
The letter
trarch's sympa
to come for re
Socrates noste
ope suffultus
animum serena
this point (at
draft ends) is
descriptions o
tyranny, no
no complainin
trumpets, no c
no servility,

> sed sobria
> inermis, regio
> aprica, fontes li
> roscida antra,
> que nimpharun

There too N
sanctis cum p
ricis."
On 22 Feb
on his letter to
already referr
an account of
of the return
the troubles th
settled down

[80] *Ibid.*
[81] III, 219.
[82] III, 192.
form, as record

[78] Ricci, p. 45.
[78a] See Martellotti's edition of this Life, *La vita di Scipione l'Africano* (Milan, 1954), pp. 18–22.

L
trarc
F
Vetu
abou
duer
V.L
origi
f. 15
tran
for t
cred
top
solis
This
to a

fille
he
V.I
the
of t
Tu
and
ther
use
of
As
cal

tair
wr
con
or

letter closes with an account of his life in Vaucluse and of his present frame of mind:

> media nocte consurgo, primo mane domo egredior, sed non aliter in campis quam domi studeo cogito lego scribo . . . aridos montes, roscidas valles atque antra circumeo, utranque Sorgie ripam sepe remetior, nullo qui obstrepat obvio, nullo comite, nullo duce, nisi curis meis minus in dies acribus ac molestis.

His one great consolation "in omni exilio" is that he can adapt himself to live anywhere—except in Avignon. He will remain in Vaucluse until fortune, "quod crebro solet, varium mutet edictum." He now regards Vaucluse as his Rome, his Athens, his "patria." Here he has gathered, in a sense, not only all his personal friends, but also friends of ancient times:

> hic omnes quos habeo amicos vel quos habui . . . [and those] qui multis ante me seculis obierunt, solo michi cognitos benificio literarum, quorum sive res gestas atque animum sive mores vitamque sive linguam et ingenium miror, ex omnibus locis atque omni evo in hanc exiguam vallem sepe contraho cupidiusque cum illis versor quam cum his qui sibi vivere videntur.[83]

Of the same period, as Foresti [84] has shown, is the poem in rhymed hexameters, addressed to Philippe de Cabassoles, which begins:

> Exul ab Italia furiis civilibus actus,
> Huc subii partimque volens partimque coactus.
> Hic nemus, hic amnes, hic ocia ruris amoeni,
> Sed fidi comites absunt vultusque sereni.

The poem is in fact a letter in verse; but Petrarch, doubtless because of its metrical form, did not include it in the collection of the *Epistolae metricae*.[85] Petrarch now plans to spend the rest

---

[83] One is reminded of Machiavelli's famous letter to Francesco Vettori.

[84] Foresti 1, pp. 270–278.

[85] Rossetti, ii, 60–66, wrongly includes it in the collection, giving it the number i 6. In a Riccardian MS the poem has this postscript (quoted in Foresti 1, p. 271): "Si alteri scriberem minus peculiari domino rescripsissem hec propter lituras; sed vobiscum, domine mi, non curo qualiter, sed quid scribam."

of his life in the peace of Vaucluse unless favorable news should come to him:

> Nam res, fama, novas properat nisi pandere laetas,
> Rure tuo statui quae restant tempora vitae
> Degere, nec bellis, nec tristi turbida lite.

Vaucluse is to be his Helicon, his "fons Aganippe." Here his books will yield forgetfulness of strife. Here there is no envy, no clamor of arms, no wealth, but the quiet life of poetry. Here there is no palatial furniture, or rare and injurious food; here

> Non tibi sollicito splendebit purpura lecto,
> Nec niveus thalamus fulgebit marmore secto,
> Non gemmas ostrumque premes, sed laeta virenti
> Gramine, sed fluvio circumdata prata recenti . . .
> Vmbra ex pomiferis veniet gratissima ramis,
> Dum curvos scopulos uncis scrutabimur hamis.
> Caetera clausa quidem Vallis praestabit abunde,
> Persica mala, pyra, mensae decus adde secundae . . .
> Haec tibi per sylvas scripsit, dignissime Praesul,
> Ille tuus, Sorgae dicam peregrinus an exul.

Foresti points out the resemblance of the poem, in certain respects, to Petrarch's letter of 22 February to Zanobi, and draws the sound conclusion that the poem is of about the same date as the letter. He notes in particular the exact correspondence between the letter and the poem with regard to Petrarch's remaining in Vaucluse: in each case Petrarch makes it clear that he is ready to remain in Vaucluse indefinitely, *unless circumstances should change*. In the letter he writes "fessamque vite turbinibus carinam, donec portus appareat, hos inter scopulos alligavi, non rediturus ad curiam, neque nisi aliud audiero, Ausoniam petiturus"; and says that he will remain in Vaucluse until Fortune, "quod crebro solet, varium mutet edictum." In the poem he writes:

> Nam res, fama, novas properat nisi pandere laetas,
> Rure tuo statui quae restant tempora vitae
> Degere . . .

and signs himself

> Ille tuus, Sorgae dicam peregrinus an exul.

The correspondences in detail between the letter and the poem
are indeed numerous: the motif of exile, for instance, appears, in
the letter, in the phrase "in omni exilio," and in the opening and
closing words of the poem. There are notable correspondences,
also, between the poem and the letter written on 15 February to
Bishop Niccolò of Viterbo, particularly the long series of oppo-
sites stated in balanced clauses introduced repeatedly by "non"
and "sed." [86]

Since 1326 Sardinia had been under the domination of Aragon, which, with some Sardinian support, had succeeded in
suppressing local uprisings and in beating off external attacks
by Genoa and other enemies. On 15 February 1353, however,
Genoa made an alliance with the powerful Sardinian rebel
Mariano IV d'Arborea, and warfare with Aragon began again.[87]
It was in all probability soon after Petrarch heard of this alliance
that he wrote to the Doge and Council of Genoa a letter, *Fam.*
xiv 6, beginning "Quod optabam video," in which he applauds
the action of Genoa, and urges a relentless prosecution of the
new war: "hoc pium hoc iustum hoc sanctum hoc minime italicum bellum est." *Fam.* xiv 6 is as bellicose as *Fam.* xiv 5 is pacific.

March 1353

Petrarch's statements of readiness to remain in Vaucluse, as
contained in *Fam.* xiv 3 and 6 and in the poem *Exul ab Italia*,
had been qualified by clauses such as "donec portus appareat."
His contentment in Vaucluse was impaired, as always, by the
proximity of Avignon; and he had by no means given up the idea
of returning to Italy. One of the servants he had sent on to Italy
in November had returned in January with an unfavorable report
of the conditions that would await Petrarch there; but Petrarch
now sent other messengers to Italy to find out what he might expect to find if he should now return. This we know from the clause
"Premissis enim rursus in Italiam exploratoribus nuntiis," which
occurs in *Fam.* xvi 10. Their report must have been received by

---

[86] It is just barely possible, though highly improbable, that *Met.*
iii 33 was written at about this time: see below, pp. 203–204.
[87] *Enciclopedia italiana*, s.v. "Sardegna."

18 April, since by that date, as will presently appear, Petrarch had decided definitely to return to Italy. It had taken Petrarch sixteen days, in 1351, to come from Piacenza to Vaucluse. One of the messengers sent in November had returned in somewhat less than two months. Presumably, therefore, the second set of messengers would have taken somewhat more, but probably not much more, than a month: probably, therefore, they were sent out about the first of March—perhaps a little earlier, perhaps a little later.

In the course of the month Petrarch received letters from Avignon, especially from one unnamed friend who was a friend of Socrates also, urging him to accept a remunerative papal appointment. A letter received from Socrates, also, while there is no indication that it urged such acceptance, reported evidently some possibility of a favor to be conferred on Petrarch by the new Pope. In this same letter, or in some other way, Socrates let Petrarch know that a certain friend, unnamed, would soon be coming to see Petrarch in Vaucluse.

With reference to a possible remunerative appointment Petrarch, on the 28th, wrote to Socrates a letter, *Fam.* xvi 3, which is one of the most detailed and emphatic of all Petrarch's refusals to incur any obligation that would involve him in the common and fatal struggle for wealth. He has all that he needs: "habeo ubi breve tempus, ubi longum habitem, quid edam, quid bibam, quid calciem, quid vestiam, qui michi serviat, qui me sotiet,[88] qui me vehat, quo tegar, ubi iaceam, ubi spatier, quo delecter; quid imperator plus romanus habet?"

He has his health—"Est preterea corpus sanum multo michi labore perdomitum, iamque non ita contumax animi mancipium ut solebat"—he has his books, his writing, his friends, his liberty, his freedom from enemies (except the envious), and he enjoys the general good will. All efforts to lead him to change his views on these matters will be utterly futile. The opening sentence of the letter shows that Petrarch was expecting to see Socrates soon. With reference to the report—the accuracy of which he doubts—that there is some possibility of a favor to be conferred upon him

---

[88] In this clause Petrarch is perhaps referring to his dog.

by the Pope he says, in the last sentence of the letter: "Esto equidem: Romanus novus Pontifex bonos amet, quid ad me? certe si non amat alios, paucos amat, quorum ex numero non sum et mallem esse quam pontifex."

On the following day, the 29th, Petrarch wrote a long letter, *Fam.* xvi 4, to an unknown friend, who was "in fide catholica hesitantem"—a noteworthy expression of the reasoned firmness of Petrarch's own faith. In the course of his argument he draws heavily on Augustine. The opening clause of the letter indicates that Petrarch hopes to have an opportunity to talk soon with this unknown friend.

On the same day, the 29th, Petrarch—as we learn from *Fam.* xvi 7 (written two days later)—received the visitor of whose intended coming he had had word from Socrates. Petrarch made him welcome, and showed him his house, his gardens, and his fields. The visitor then said that he would like to walk down to the island in the Sorgue (about three miles west of Vaucluse). Petrarch offered to send a servant with him, but he preferred to go alone. So he went—and never returned!

Fam. xvi 5, a letter written in all probability not long before or after the end of March, congratulates an unknown friend on his recovery from a serious illness, but warns him that all life is a continuous death, to be ended when one enters the gate of eternal life.[89]

April 1353

On the first day of the month Petrarch wrote to Socrates the letter, *Fam.* xvi 7, which tells the story of the visitor who started to walk to the island in the Sorgue, and never returned.

---

[89] This letter is undated. In the order of Book XVI it follows letters of 28 and 29 March, and is followed (after xvi 6, which, though written earlier, was doubtless placed at this point because, like xvi 5, it concerns recovery from a serious illness) by xvi 7, written on 1 April, and then by three letters written late in April. From 18 to 20 April, as will presently appear, Petrarch was away from Vaucluse, and he left for Italy in May. No letters written after his return to Italy precede xvi 11. *Fam.* xvi 5, then, was certainly written before Petrarch left Provence, and in all probability not long before or after the end of March.

It must have been about or before the middle of April that the messengers Petrarch had sent to Italy returned with a report to which he refers thus in *Fam.* xvi 10: "Premissis enim rursus in Italiam exploratoribus nuntiis, invenio, etsi nil usquam constet esse tranquillum, aliquam tamen fesso votivi portus effigiem non deesse." After receiving this report he decided definitely to return to Italy.

It was somewhat more probably at this time than at any earlier time during his stay in Provence that Petrarch received and answered a letter from Luca da Piacenza which reported troubles due, apparently, to Luca's friendship with Petrarch, but was devoted mainly to the praise of solitude. Petrarch's reply, *Fam.* ix 14, begins thus: "Sentio angores tuos, non magis quos loqueris quam quos taces. Scio: multi te quidem propter me persequuntur." Petrarch praises Luca's praise of solitude, and proposes that they find a solitary refuge together: "Ibimus et latebimus non sine gloria, nomenque nostrum, nisi fallor augurio, e latebris quam ex urbibus clarius audietur, undecunque torturum invidos. Ne dubites; recondet nos Deus in portu optimo."

Having decided to return to Italy, and to go by the pass of Mont Genèvre, Petrarch decided to make a special trip to Montrieux in order to see his brother Gherardo once more before leaving Provence. The convent is situated in the mountainous region northeast of Toulon. Its distance by road from Vaucluse was about eighty miles, the route leading south through Cavaillon and the ford of the Durance to the Avignon-Nice highroad, which passed through Aix and St. Maximin before reaching a point at which a road branching off to the south led, in about ten miles, to Montrieux. The journey, on horseback, would take two days.

Petrarch's account of his trip to Montrieux is contained in *Fam.* xvi 8, written on 24 April to Laelius, and *Fam.* xvi 9, addressed to Zanobi, and begun about the same time. He left Vaucluse early on Thursday the 18th, taking with him at least one companion, a youth to whom he refers thus in *Fam.* xviii 5, a letter sent to Gherardo a year later with a copy of the *Confessions* of St. Augustine transcribed by this same youth: "Familiaris

It was doubtless on one of these three days, also, that Petrarch had with a French cardinal—presumably Gui de Boulogne or Elie de Talleyrand—the extraordinary interview reported in *Sine nom.* 17 (written to Nelli in 1357). Petrarch said to the Cardinal, in effect:

> If it must be that the empire and the papacy are doomed to extinction within this present age, then I am glad that the blame rests, respectively, upon German and French barbarism ("quod . . . tante . . . culpe partem habet illa horrida et inmitis, partem hec mollis et eneruata barbaries"), while imperial and papal light and vigor remain in Italy ("cum in manibus nostris lux et uigor suus his manserit").

The letter then continues:

> Quibus ille auditis, libertate mea nichil offensus: 'Grauiter,' inquit, 'et libere et aliorum fortasse auribus importune, meis certe fidentissime et, ut te decuit, uerissime locutus es. Neu me forsan ueri inscium aut diuerse sententie arbitreris, duos Clementes nostros plus attriuisse Ecclesiam paucis annis quam septem Gregorii uestri multis seculis restaurare possent nec ego dubito nec dubitare aliquem existimo.' Ille quidem hec suspirans.[91]

On the 28th Petrarch finished the long letter to Zanobi that he had begun in Vaucluse, and wrote a short covering letter, *Fam.* XVI 10, in which he expresses his sympathy, apologizes for not expressing it at greater length, and vents again his hatred of Avignon. He hopes never to return to Babylon again. He will bear whatever he may have to bear, knowing that the world holds no place more turbulent or more evil than this Babylon, whose raging storms leave no room for peace in the surrounding region, not even in Vaucluse. The memory of what he has suffered here will console him, provided he is no longer here, for whatever fate may have in store for him. He will leave with the haste with which a prisoner leaves his prison; and once out of Avignon he will consider that the first and worse half of his journey is over. He expects to leave Avignon as soon as he has finished writing this letter, and to spend not more than eight days in Vaucluse before actually starting for Italy.

---

[91] Piur 1, p. 227.

XI. The Departure: May 1353

If in accordance with his stated intention Petrarch returned to Vaucluse on 28 April and spent not more than eight days there, he left for Italy by 7 May; and—in view both of his eagerness to be gone and of the fact that in November he had actually started for Italy, baggage and all, eight days after his return from Avignon to Vaucluse—it is highly probable that he did leave by 7 May, or within a very few days thereafter.

He left his home in Vaucluse—his fields, his gardens, his trees, his house, and some of his books—in the care of the sons of Raymond Monet, with the understanding that any friends of his who might come to visit there were to be made welcome.[92]

Of his journey we know only this: that he went by way of the pass of Mont Genèvre, and that as he crossed that pass there came to him at least the conception and in all probability some of the phrasing of his magnificent salutation to Italy (*Met.* III 24):

> Salve, cara Deo tellus sanctissima, salve
> tellus tuta bonis, tellus metuenda superbis,
> tellus nobilibus multum generosior oris,
> fertilior cunctis, terra formosior omni,
> cincta mari gemino, famoso splendida monte,
> armorum legumque eadem vereranda sacrarum
> Pyeridumque domus auroque opulenta virisque,
> cuius ad eximios ars et natura favores
> incubuere simul mundoque dedere magistram.
> Ad te nunc cupide post tempora longa revertor
> incola perpetuus: tu diversoria vite
> grata dabis fesse, tu quantam pallida tandem
> membra tegant prestabis humum. Te latus ab alto
> Italiam video frondentis colle Gebenne.
> Nubila post tergum remanent; ferit ora serenus
> spiritus et blandis assurgens motibus aer
> excipit. Agnosco patriam gaudensque saluto:
> Salve, pulcra parens, terrarum gloria, salve.

XI. The Letter Collections

Before 1350 Petrarch had decided to make a formal collection

---

[92] This we know from four later letters, *Fam.* XVII 5 and XXII 5, and *Sen.* VI 3 and X 2.

of his prose letters; but he had made little progress, before reaching Provence, with the enormous amount of work involved: selection, arrangement, revision, insertion, excision, and the occasional writing of fictional letters—letters, that is, that had not been actually written in earlier years and sent to the persons to whom they are ostensibly addressed, but were new compositions now written by Petrarch, for the specific purpose of enriching his collection. As he brought it with him to Provence, the collection, bearing the title *Familiarum rerum liber*, seems to have contained only a very few letters—some of those that stand in Book I, and some of the letters addressed to ancient writers that were to stand, and do stand, in the final Book of the collection.[93]

While in Provence he continued work on the collection, and completed the first three Books and part of the fourth. We do not know just when or where this work was done: probably it was done from time to time rather than continuously; and probably most of it, at least, was done in Vaucluse rather than in Avignon. In the course of this work, in all probability, he wrote a few additional fictional letters. It is probable, in particular, that he wrote at this time *Fam.* III 1 and 2, addressed ostensibly to Tommaso Caloiro, and—very possibly upon the basis of a much earlier actual missive form—the famous letter, *Fam.* IV 1, addressed to Dionigi da Borgo San Sepolcro, on his ascent of Mont Ventoux.

Since Petrarch now knew that many of the actual letters he was currently writing to his correspondents would ultimately find placement in the *Familiares*, he kept copies of the letters that he thought might prove to be appropriate for such placement. The evidence to be presented in the final Section of this study indicates that he kept them, exactly or almost exactly, in the order in which they were actually written.

Before leaving Provence, also, he had formed the idea of making a small special collection of letters dealing chiefly with

---

[93] Rossi, "Sulla formazione delle raccolte epistolari petrarchesche," in R. Accademia Petrarca di Lettere Arti e Scienze di Arezzo, *Annali della cattedra petrarchesca*, III (1932), 53–73; Billanovich, pp. 3–55; Wilkins 1, pp. 311–323. This note applies also to the next paragraph in the text.

the evils of Avignon, as we know from *Fam.* xv 12 (see above, p. 147); but we have no reason to think that he had begun work on the constitution and arrangement of such a collection.

XIII. *Fam.* x 6

This letter, addressed to the Czech humanist Jan ze Středa (usually referred to as Johann von Neumarkt), was written in 1352 or in 1353, perhaps before and perhaps after Petrarch left Provence.[94] It is an answer to Jan's first and undated letter to Petrarch, beginning "Vtinam Parnasei" (LAP 63), which asks that Petrarch favor him with some of his poetry: " . . . vobis supplicat scribentis affeccio vt musarum cantus dulcifluos . . . auris cancellarii imperialis recitacione suscipiens, inter magistralis mense vestre deliciosas epulas splendidis letetur conuiuiis et pregrato nectare poetalis facundie ebrietur." The superscription of Petrarch's reply reads thus: "Ad Iohannem Neumburgensem electum, imperialis aule cancellarium, responsio familiaris." Jan was named Bishop of Naumburg on 15 February 1352; but he never entered upon his bishopric, and therefore remained "Neumburgensis electus" until 9 October 1353, when he was named Bishop of Litomyšl. As far as this evidence goes, accordingly, Petrarch's letter might have been written either before or after Petrarch left Provence. Nor is the evidence suggested by the words "cancellarii imperialis" decisive. Jan entered the imperial chancellery in 1347, as one of several notaries, and even before promotion he was referred to, in certain documents, as "Dominus cancellarius." By 19 September 1352 he had been made Prothonotary, and by 26 December 1353 he had been made Chancellor: the exact dates of these promotions are not known,

---

[94] All of the letters exchanged by Jan ze Středa and Petrarch are published and discussed by Piur in his *Petrarcas Briefwechsel.* On Jan ze Středa see Jean Lulvès, *Die Summa cancellariae des Johann von Neumarkt*, Berlin, 1891, pp. 4–19; Alfred Hansel, "Johann von Neumarkts kirchliche Laufbahn," in *Jahrbücher für Kultur und Geschichte der Slaven*, N.F., ii (1927), 299–344; Joseph Klapper, "Johann von Neumarkt," in *Schlesische Jahrbuch*, i (1928), 49–88; and Burdach, *Aus Petrarcas ältestem deutschen Schülerkreise* (= Burdach, iv), Berlin, 1929, pp. 28–40. On the dates of Jan's nominations as bishop see Eubel, pp. 318 and 374.

but the probabilities are that they took place shortly before the dates just mentioned. In two documents written in January 1354 Jan is still referred to as Prothonotary.

Petrarch's letter can hardly have been written after Jan was made Chancellor, since that appointment was in all probability subsequent to his appointment as Bishop of Litomyšl. Petrarch's use of the title "imperialis aule cancellarium" is explicable on either of two grounds: it may be that the use of that title was permissible in the case of the imperial prothonotary; and it may be that this title did not appear in the original superscription but was added at a later time when Petrarch gave the letter its place in the collection of the *Familiares*.

Petrarch's letter contains the clause "benivolentiam tanti viri gloriabundus excipio." The combination of that clause and Jan's reference to himself as "cancellarius imperialis" serves to make it at least highly probable that both letters were written after Jan had been made Prothonotary—that is, in or after the autumn of 1352. Even so, however, Petrarch's letter may have been written either before or after he left Provence.

The possibility that Petrarch's letter was written in Milan is not ruled out by the fact of its inclusion in Book X of the *Familiares: Fam.* ix 15 was certainly written in Milan, and *Fam.* ix 16 was probably written there. Jan's next extant letter to Petrarch, beginning *Aureis redimita* (LAP 64), was written in the spring of 1354. Petrarch's next extant letter to Jan, *Fam.* xxi 2, was written in 1357.

XIV. *Writings Wrongly Assigned to Petrarch's Last Stay in Provence*

In my "Chronological Conspectus of the Writings of Petrarch" [95] *Fam.* ix 3 and *Sine nom.* 14 were erroneously assigned to Petrarch's last stay in Provence: they should have been assigned, respectively, to his third stay in Provence (1345–1347) and to his residence in Milan. [96]

---

[95] Wilkins 1, p. 55.

[96] See Foresti, art. cit. in n. 6, p. 365; and Piur 1, p. 380. Of the letters listed on p. 358 of Wilkins 1 as unassignable to any particular

In the same "Conspectus" *Met.* III 14, 20 and 30 were assigned to the last stay in Provence on the basis of earlier studies that I no longer regard as definitive. I now believe that Rizzi is right in assigning III 20 to the period of Petrarch's residence in Parma in 1343–1345, and that Calcaterra is right in assigning III 30 to the year 1340 or thereabouts.[97]

Met. III 14 is a brief poem of congratulation to Niccolò Acciaiuoli on the occasion of his being called to the control of the Neapolitan ship of state:

> Tibi carbasa cimbe
> et clavum lassata sue Trinacria tandem
> credidit.

The reference, as Rossetti, Miss Magrini, and Bianchi all recognize, is to Niccolò's appointment as Grand Seneschal of the Kingdom of Naples.[98] That appointment, however, was made not in 1349, as Rossetti states, nor in 1352, as Miss Magrini and Bianchi state, but on 3 June 1348 or a few days earlier.[99] Foresti[100] asserts, without argument, that the poem was composed in 1352, "quando il procacciante fiorentino si accinse all'impresa di Sicilia": this "impresa," however, was an abortive military expedition which took place not in 1352 but in 1354.[101]

On f. 12ᵛ of V.L. 3196 Petrarch, having entered an interlinear variant in the first stanza of his draft of the *canzone Che debb'io far* (No. 268 in the *Canzoniere*), made to the right of that variant this notation: "1351. decembris 28 nocte concubia." If this meant what it seems at first sight to mean—and Appel lists it without comment—it would indicate that Petrarch was working on this poem in Avignon on the night following the day on

---

period, the only ones that could possibly be of the last Provençal period are *Var.* 33 and 62, which however contain no elements that would make it in the least probable that they are of this period.

[97] Rizzi 1, p. 170; Calcaterra, pp. 155–161 and 201, n. 13.

[98] Rossetti, II, 110 and 397; Magrini, pp. 147–148; Bianchi, p. 793.

[99] Léonard 1, II, 137.

[100] P. 200. For "Trinacria" as a designation for the Kingdom of Naples see *Fam.* XII 3, 1, and Mascetta-Caracci, p. 532, n. 2.

[101] See Leopoldo Tanfani, *Niccola Acciaiuoli* (Florence, 1863), pp. 98–101 and 216.

which he had written his long letter to Bishop Ugolino and his covering letter to Luca da Piacenza (*Fam.* ix 5 and 6). But, as Appel himself has proved conclusively in the case of a similar entry, Petrarch, at this time at least, was beginning his years *a nativitate*. His "1351. decembris 28" was therefore, in terms of the common calendar, 28 December 1350.[102]

Among the many sonnets that are ascribed to Petrarch in certain MSS but may or may not be by him there is one, beginning

Io non posso dire, Italia mia,

which was evidently written by an Italian unhappily resident in France, anxious to return to Italy, and delayed in his hope for such a return. If this sonnet were by Petrarch it would fit the later circumstances of his last stay better than those of any one of his previous periods of residence in Provence. But the linguistic poverty of the sonnet and several of its particular phrases make it virtually certain that it is not by Petrarch. Cian classes it with other poems of which he says "l'attribuzione al Petrarca si presenta addirittura come inammissibile," calling them "componimenti attribuiti senz'alcuna ragione al Petrarca."[103]

XV. *The Eventual Placement of Letters Written in Provence*

When Petrarch left Provence for Italy he took with him his copies of the letters that he thought he might include in one or the other of his two collections—the large collection of the *Familiares*, and the small collection called eventually the *Epistolae sine nomine*.

The letters written in Provence that were to be considered for inclusion in the *Familiares* lay apparently, in the packet or packets that contained them, in a series, perfectly or almost per-

[102] Appel 1, pp. 85, 99, 189, and 190.
[103] This sonnet is printed in Angelo Solerti's edition of the *Rime disperse di Francesco Petrarca o a lui attribuite* (Florence, 1909), p. 161: Vittorio Cian's statement appears on p. xxxi of his introduction to this edition. The sonnet is printed in a better text by Di Benedetto, *op. cit.* in n. 71, p. 67: in n. 13 on p. 65 Di Benedetto indicates his belief that the sonnet is by Petrarch.

fectly chronological in its order, that consisted of the 75 letters now to be listed: interspersed, perhaps, were other letters (such as *Var.* 36) which he ultimately decided not to include in the collection. The 75 letters in question are as follows, in the order in which they were certainly or probably written, with dates that have been established previously or in this chapter, the names of their addressees, and numerals indicating the positions assigned to them in the *Familiares:*

	1351			
1.	27 June	Philippe de Cabassoles	XI	10
2.	29 June	Philippe de Cabassoles	XI	11
3.	19 July	Luca Cristiani	XI	12
4.	25 August	Matteo Longo	XIII	11
5.	29 August	Niccolò Acciaiuoli	XI	13
6.	23 October	Philippe de Vitry	XI	14
7.	25 October	Philippe de Cabassoles	XI	15
8.	18 November	The Four Cardinals	XI	16
9.	24 November	The Four Cardinals	XI	17
10.	28 December	Ugolino dei Rossi	IX	5
11.	28 December	Luca da Piacenza	IX	6
	1352			
12.	13 January	Luca da Piacenza	IX	7
13.	13 January	Francesco Nelli	XII	4
14.	18 January	Francesco Nelli	XII	5
15.	Jan.–March	Charles IV	XII	1
16.	1 February	Philippe de Cabassoles	XII	6
17.	20 February	Niccolò Acciaiuoli	XII	2
18.	20 February	Barbato da Sulmona	XII	7
19.	26 February	Andrea Dandolo	XV	4
20.	12 March	Clement VI	V	19
21.	1 April	Zanobi da Strada	XII	3
22.	1 April	Lapo da Castiglionchio	XII	8
23.	1 April	Nelli	XII	9
24.	1 April	Boccaccio	XII	10
25.	3 April	Pierre d'Auvergne	XV	5
26.	17 April	Pierre d'Auvergne	XV	6
27.	Before 24 April	Stefano Colonna	XV	7
28.	24 April	Laelius	XV	8
29.	A few days later	Laelius	XV	9
30.	April or early May	Sansone Ponzio	XV	10

31.	14 May	Gui de Boulogne	XIII	1
32.	21 May	Bartolommeo Carbone	XII	11
33.	24 May	Nelli	XII	12
34.	24 May	Nelli	XII	13
35.	24 May	Acciaiuoli and Giovanni Barrili	XII	16
36.	24 May	Barrili	XII	14
37.	24 May	Acciaiuoli	XII	15
38.	24 May	Zanobi	XII	17
39.	9 June	Rinaldo Cavalchini	XIII	2
40.	9 June	Guglielmo da Pastrengo	XIII	3
41.	10 June	Francesco Calvo	XIII	4
42.	June or July	Nelli	XIII	8
43.	9 August	Nelli	XIII	5
44.	10 August	Nelli	XIII	6
45.	10 August	Zanobi	XIII	9
46.	25 August	Zanobi	XIII	10
47.	1 September	Abbot of Corvara	XIII	12
48.	22 September	Elie de Talleyrand	XIV	1
49.	22 September	Socrates	XIV	2
50.	25 September	Luca da Piacenza	XIV	3
51.	19 October	Luca da Piacenza	XIV	4
52.	1 November	Doge and Council of Genoa	XIV	5
53.	Before 8 Nov.	Laelius	XV	1
54.	8 November	Gui de Boulogne	XIV	7
55.	A few days later	Pierre d'Auvergne	XIII	7
56.	A few days later	Philippe de Cabassoles	XV	11
57.	18 November	Nelli	XV	2
58.	18 Nov. or soon thereafter	Sansone Ponzio	XIV	8
59.	Late November	The Paduan Clergy	XV	14
60.	1 December	Giovanni Aghinolfi	VII	8
61.	14 December	Philippe de Cabassoles	XV	12
62.	15 December	Philippe de Cabassoles	XV	13
	1353			
63.	5 January	Elie de Talleyrand and Gui de Boulogne	XVI	1
64.	Jan.–February	Gherardo	XVI	2
65.	15 February	Bishop Niccolò	XVI	6
66.	22 February	Zanobi	XV	3
67.	Late February	Doge and Council of Genoa	XIV	6
68.	28 March	Socrates	XVI	3
69.	29 March	Unknown	XVI	4
70.	c. end of March	Unknown	XVI	5

71.	1 April	Socrates	XVI	7
72.	c. 1 April	Luca da Piacenza	IX	14
73.	24 April	Laelius	XVI	8
74.	c. 24–28 April	Zanobi	XVI	9
75.	28 April	Zanobi	XVI	10

It was doubtless soon after his establishment in Milan that Petrarch set about the continuation of work on the *Familiares*, beginning, naturally, with letters, still unused, that had been written *before* his return to Provence in 1351. These he arranged in an order that was roughly, but only roughly, chronological; and among them, as will presently appear, he placed six of the 75 letters written in Provence. Some of his variations from chronological order were evidently due to a desire to begin and end Books with particularly notable letters; and some others were evidently or apparently due to the fact that a letter placed out of chronological order was in some way associated with a letter the place of which was already fixed.

Of the letters Petrarch had written during his stay in Provence the first to find a place in the order of the *Familiares* was his letter to Clement VI, No. 20 in the list of 75, which he placed at the end of Book V, as v 19. In v 18 (written many years earlier), a reply to a letter in which Guido Sette had asked him for a report "de statu suo," Petrarch speaks first of the state of his mind and then of the state of his body, of which he says: "Quod ad corpus attinet, non sum quem reliquisti. Hospes corporis mei, secum male concordans, implacabilem litem agit. Hec iugis solicitudo faciem meam mutavit ante annos, ita ut iam vix primo me cognoscas occursu." The letter ends with this sentence: "Absit a me ut amore corporis aut huius lucis desiderio diem mortis horrescam, quoniam et hoc ab alio verissime dictum in usus meos verti, quod hec nostra que dicitur vita, mors est." But the letter did not make a very good ending for a Book of the *Familiares;* and Petrarch decided—probably at once, possibly at a later time— to complete the Book by ending it with his letter to Clement. That letter was in fact a notable letter, and it presumably stood out in Petrarch's memory not only because of the circumstances in which it had been written, but also because it had been the occasion for the beginning of his polemic with one of Clement's physicians; and it was very probably in his mind at this particular time because it was certainly soon after his establishment in Milan that he put the *Invective contra medicum* into its final form, combining its earlier and later elements. It may well be that the thing that brought his letter to Clement to his mind while he was working on v 18 was the fact that v 18 itself was concerned with failing health and with the idea of death.

After placing as the 7th letter of Book VII the letter of bitter reproach which he had written to Cola di Rienzo in November 1347 on hearing of his deplorable conduct as Tribune of Rome, Petrarch placed next, as *Fam.* vii 8, the letter—No. 60 in the foregoing list—which he had written to Giovanni Aghinolfi, on 1 December 1352, congratulating him on the extraordinary success of his efforts, as Chancellor of the Gonzaga, on behalf of Mantua and its princes. It may well be that Petrarch placed this letter immediately after his letter to Cola in order to provide a sharp contrast between the courses of action of two men in high political office, one of whom had misused his great responsibilities, while the other had made the most of those entrusted to him.

The next one of the letters written in Provence that appears in the order of the *Familiares* is the long letter to Bishop Ugolino, No. 10 in the list of 75, which was placed as ix 5. Petrarch's work on Book IX was quite certainly in progress in the autumn of 1356 or soon thereafter.[104] The first four letters placed in this Book are all letters in which Petrarch speaks of matters that distress him. The first begins: "Crebros insultus atque impetus fortune . . . his temporibus patior . . . Solebant leta tristibus, amaris dulcia miscere; nunc, heu, tristia et amara omnia." The second begins: "Ut compressis aliquando gemitibus sedatisque suspiriis atque animi turbinibus, infracta voce siccisque oculis te alloquar . . ." The third begins: "Reliquie nos malorum veterum exercent . . ." And the fourth: "Verba michi nunc metus

---

[104] See Billanovich, pp. 13–18. The long passage containing a brief reference to Semiramis which appears in the final form of *Fam.* ix 4, but not in the missive form, was doubtless inserted at this time: see Rossi 1, ii, 218 and 262–263.

ac dolor eliciunt . . . " It may well have been the prevailing mood of these four letters that brought to his mind one of the most grievous of all his distresses, the still unhealed breach between Bishop Ugolino and himself (see above, pp. 19–21 and 103), and thus led him to introduce his long letter to the Bishop at this point. Having done so, it was only natural that he should place immediately after it, as IX 6 and 7, his two closely related and chronologically immediately subsequent letters to Luca da Piacenza, Nos. 11 and 12 in the list of 75. And it is not strange that a much later letter to Luca, No. 72 in the same list, should have been placed, either at this time or later, near the end of the same Book, as IX 14.

The continuation of Petrarch's work on the *Familiares* brought him soon—quite probably in 1357 [105]—to the point in Book XI at which he was ready to begin to make systematic use of the letters he had written in Provence. The series of those letters, as now available for him, had been reduced by his use of No. 20 in Book V, of No. 60 in Book VII, and of Nos. 10–12 and perhaps No. 72 in Book IX. He next placed all of the remaining letters (except perhaps No. 72) in the range XI 10–XVI 10, nor did he introduce into this range any letter written either before or after his last stay in Provence. Within this range he placed in Book XI eight letters written in the period 27 June–24 November 1351; in Book XII seventeen letters written in the period 13 January–24 May 1352; in Book XIII nine letters written in the period 9 June–1 September 1352; in Book XIV five letters written in the period 22 September–1 November 1352; in Book XV five letters written in the period 9 November–15 December 1352; and in Book XVI ten letters written in the period 5 January–28 April 1353. Certain letters, however, were taken out of their chronological order and given special placement, for reasons identical with or similar to those that had led Petrarch to displace certain letters in the earlier portions of the *Familiares*.

As he started his work on the general mass of the letters he had written in Provence, he began, naturally, with Nos. 1–9,

---

[105] See Billanovich, pp. 19–22.

13–19, and 21–24, all of which, except Nos. 4 and 19, he placed
in the range xi 10–xii 10. Nos. 4 and 19 may have been placed in
that range at this time and transferred later to their present positions as xiii 11 and xv 4, or may have been omitted at this time,
because Petrarch may already have thought that they might more
suitably be located elsewhere. With regard to No. 4—the letter
about Matteo Longo's dog—my guess is that he did originally
enter it in Book XI, but decided at a later time to transfer it to
Book XIII, thinking that it would stand appropriately among the
Vaucluse letters contained in that Book. With regard to No. 19,
my guess is that, having begun Book XII with letters to the
Emperor and to Niccolò Acciaiuoli, he thought that proximity
to those two letters would not be desirable for No. 19, which is
addressed to the Doge Andrea Dandolo, and that he therefore
held this letter out for use at a later point. The remaining letters
of this group, Nos. 1–3, 5–9, 13–18, and 21–24, were then entered in the range indicated, where they stand as xi 10–17 and
xii 1–10. Nos. 1–3 and 5–9 were entered, in their chronological
order, as xi 10–17. At this point Petrarch was ready to begin a
new Book; and as he looked over the letters that stood next in
chronological order he saw one, No. 15, addressed to the Emperor Charles IV, which would obviously make a fine opening
letter for a new Book, and another, No. 17, his letter to Niccolò
Acciaiuoli on the guidance of a ruler, which seemed to him a
natural companion for his letter to the Emperor. He therefore
began his new Book, XII, with these two letters. Next, naturally
enough, he placed No. 21, a letter to Zanobi da Strada written
as a result of the receipt of a letter from Niccolò Acciaiuoli. He
now had left, of the group of letters with which he had been
working, Nos. 13–14, 16, 18, and 22–24: these he placed, in their
chronological order, as xii 4–10. In the case of No. 22, addressed
to Lapo da Castiglionchio, he broke the letter into two parts—
probably, but not necessarily, at this time—deciding to include
the first part, which was filled with bitter references to Avignon,
in the collection of the *Sine nomine*, while retaining the rest of
the letter for the *Familiares*.

The group of letters just considered was followed, in the

chronological order, by six letters, Nos. 25–30, all of which were written in Vaucluse in April or early May, 1352. Three of them, at least, Nos. 27–29, are letters of considerable importance. Petrarch, however, did not use these letters at this point. Their content suggests no reason for their temporary omission. Since they form in themselves a little block in perfect chronological order, it seems just possible that they may have been contained on a series of sheets that had become temporarily displaced.

The letters next in chronological order, Nos. 31–46, were then entered, together with one later letter, No. 55, in the range XII 11–XIII 10. No. 31, however, the consolatory letter to Cardinal Gui de Boulogne on the death of his mother, seemed to Petrarch to be a letter of such distinction as to call for its use as the opening letter of a new Book. Holding that letter, therefore, for use as XIII 1, he entered Nos. 32–38 as XII 11–17, in their chronological order (except perhaps in the case of the last four, all of which, however, are dated on the same day).

Having opened Book XIII with No. 31, Petrarch followed it with Nos. 39–41, in their chronological order, as XIII 2–4. Nos. 42–44 were all letters to Nelli, written in Vaucluse in the summer of 1352—No. 42 not dated, but probably written in June or July, Nos. 43 and 44 written on 9 and 10 August. He decided to place No. 42 after Nos. 43–44; but before No. 42 and immediately after No. 44, which discusses the rage for poetry then current in Avignon, he decided to place a later letter, No. 55, which discusses the same subject. Thus Nos. 43, 44, 55, and 42 stand as XIII 5, 6, 7, and 8. Nos. 45–46 follow, in their chronological order, as XIII 9 and 10. As XIII 11 Petrarch now placed No. 4, which, as noted above, he had not included in Book XI: he may well have felt that it added an appropriate element to the accounts of Vaucluse contained in Book XIII. He then closed Book XIII with No. 47, which thus became XIII 12.

He then began a new Book with the next five letters, Nos. 48–52, in their chronological order. After XIV 5 he placed, quite inevitably, a later letter, No. 67, which, like XIV 5, was addressed to the Doge and Council of Genoa. Passing over No. 53, which he evidently considered important enough to open a new Book, he continued with No. 54 as xiv 7; and then (No. 55 having already been used as xiii 7), passing over No. 56, which he preferred to group with other letters to Philippe de Cabassoles, and No. 57, which he apparently preferred to group with other letters to friends in Italy, he closed Book XIV with No. 58, which thus became xiv 8.

There now remained, of the letters written in Provence, No. 19, to Andrea Dandolo; Nos. 25–30, which Petrarch had not used when working on Book XI; No. 53, to Laelius; No. 56, to Philippe de Cabassoles; No. 57, to Nelli; and Nos. 59–75, with the exception of No. 67, already placed in Book XIV, and with the possible exception of No. 72, which may already have been placed in Book IX.

He began Book XV with No. 53, addressed to Laelius as the newly risen hope of Rome, and followed it with Nos. 57, 66, and 19, addressed to other friends in Italy; continued with Nos. 25–30, which he placed, in their chronological order, as xv 5–10; added, in their chronological order, Nos. 56, 61, and 62, all addressed to Philippe de Cabassoles, which now became xv 11–13; and closed the Book with No. 59, the notable letter addressed to the Paduan clergy after the death of Bishop Ildebrandino.

He now had left Nos. 63–75, with the exception of Nos. 66, which he had used in Book XV, and 67, which he had used in Book XIV, and with the possible exception of No. 72. He placed the ten remaining letters, Nos. 63–65, 68–71, and 73–75 as the first ten letters of Book XVI, retaining their original chronological order, except that No. 65, to Bishop Niccolò of Viterbo, was placed not in the 3rd but in the 6th position, probably because this letter, like xvi 5, was a moralizing letter of congratulation on a recovery from illness. It may have been either at this time or while he was working on Book IX that he decided to place No. 72 near the end of that Book, as ix 14: this letter, like ix 6 and 7, was addressed to Luca da Piacenza, and like these letters, though it was written considerably later, carries evidence of Petrarch's continuing concern over his breach with Bishop Ugolino.

One other extant letter written in Provence which might have been included in the *Familiares*, *Var*. 36, written to Benedetto Colonna on 4 October 1352, was not so included. Whether Petrarch's decision to exclude it was made before or after he left Provence we do not know. If it appeared in chronological order in the series of possible *Familiares* that Petrarch took with him from Provence to Italy, its position would have been between Nos. 50 and 51; and in that case his decision to exclude it would presumably have been made at about the time when he was considering those two letters.[106]

The letters that Petrarch took with him, when he left Provence, with a view to inclusion in the small special collection called eventually the *Epistolae sine nomine*, included, as far as we can tell, three letters written—two certainly and one probably— before his return to Provence in 1351, and ten, or perhaps eleven, written during his last stay in Provence.

The actual making of the collection took place during Petrarch's residence in Milan. It exists in what appears to be a first and superseded form,[107] and in a final form: each form contains thirteen letters written before Petrarch's return to Italy. These thirteen letters, with their certain or probable dates, the names of their certain or probable addressees, and the positions they received in the first form and in the final form of the collection, are as follows:

			Pos. in 1st form	Pos. in 2d form
a.	1342	Philippe de Cabassoles	3	1
b.	Early September 1347	Cola di Rienzo	11	2
c.	Mid-September 1347	Cola di Rienzo	10	3
d.	1351, about October, and before 18 Nov.	Niccola Capocci	12	7
e.	Autumn 1351	Bishop Ildebrandino	13	8

[106] This discussion supersedes the discussion of the order of the same letters in Wilkins 1, pp. 329–341. Its results are in accordance with the results there stated on pp. 338 and 341 insofar as the sequences as a whole are concerned; but it is now clear that there are several breaches of order within the sequences.

[107] See Piur 1, pp. 276–277.

f. November to mid-December 1351	Nelli	8	9
g. Late 1351–early 1352	Rinaldo Cavalchini	7	11
h. 13 January 1352 or soon afterward	Nelli	9	10
i. 31 March 1352	Nelli	5	6
j. 1 April 1352	Lapo da Castiglionchio	4	5
k. April–May 1352	Unknown	6	13
l. October–8 Nov. 1352	The Populus Romanus	1	4
m. Late December 1352–early 1353	Philippe de Cabassoles	2	12

Petrarch's procedure in the arrangement of the first form of the collection may be traced as follows. He began with two letters that may well have been associated in his mind with his plan for the making of the collection: *l*, an impressive letter dealing with the theme of Rome, and *m*, an equally impressive letter dealing with the theme of Avignon and specifically with the death of Clement and the election of his successor. After *m* he placed *a*, which, like *m*, concerned the death of a Pope. After *a* he placed six letters, *j, i, k, g, f*, and *h*, written at various times in the winter of 1351–1352 and the spring of 1352, all dealing with the theme of Avignon except that *f*, the first of two letters to Nelli, deals with the theme of Italy. After these he placed three letters, *c, b*, and *d*, which deal with the theme of Rome, the first two with Cola, the third with the reformation of the government of Rome. Last comes *e*, which deals again with the theme of Avignon.

In the revised form of the collection Petrarch placed first, in chronological order, the three letters, *a–c*, that had been written before 1351; after them he placed *l*, which, like *b* and *c*, concerns Cola; then follow seven letters written in Avignon at various times from the autumn of 1351 to the spring of 1352— *j* and *i* in the same order as in the first form, and *d, e, f, h*, and *g* in an order that is exactly or almost exactly chronological—and finally *m* and *k*, the two letters that were written thereafter in Vaucluse.

Sine nom. 5 (*j*) is merely the original beginning of *Fam.* XII 8 (see above, p. 115): the decision to break that letter into two parts, one for each of the two collections, was made probably in Milan, but possibly in Provence.

We know that Petrarch wrote also the letter that has been referred to above (on pp. 146–147) as *Sine nom. x*. While it is possible that that letter is to be identified with *Sine nom*. 1 (*a*), it is probable that it is not now extant—in which case Petrarch's decision not to include it in the collection was made perhaps in Provence, perhaps in Milan.

The collection was eventually completed by the addition of six letters written in Milan, *Sine nom*. 14–19, which stand, in both forms of the collection, in the order in which they were written.

CHAPTER VI

Petrarch and Cardinal Niccola Capocci

I

In the year 1351 conditions in Rome were extremely bad; [1] and late in the year Pope Clement appointed a commission of four cardinals to deal with the problem. Our only knowledge of this commission comes from the two noble letters, *Fam.* XI 16 and 17, which were written by Petrarch in response to a request, and were dated in Avignon on 18 and 24 November. The first is addressed "Ad quattuor cardinales reformando Romane Reipublice statui deputatos"; the second is addressed "Ad eosdem." [2] Petrarch does not give the names of the four cardinals, but refers to them thus, in XI 16, 6:

e quibus tres preter profundissimam sapientiam uberrimamque doctrinam, romanarum quoque rerum notitiam experientia docuisset; quartus vero non modo romane esset originis sed genus etiam, ut quidam putant, ex altissima ac vetustissima traheret gente Cornelia, et tamen—o vera pietas, o patrie dulcis amor!—adversus superbam nobilitatem athleta fortissimus indefense causam plebis ageret et oppresse patrocinium libertatis.

The only attempt made hitherto to identify the four cardinals is that of De Sade, who says: "Aucun Auteur que je sache, ne nomme ces Cardinaux; mais je crois pouvoir le faire avec confiance, & dire que ce fut Bertrand de Deux, Guillaume Curti, Gui

---

[1] Gregorovius, Book XI, Chap. VII, Sect. 2, quoted above, on p. 104. Cola di Rienzo was at this time in protective custody in Prague.

[2] These two letters, and *Sine nom.* 7, which also is to be considered in this chapter, are available in an excellent annotated English translation in M. E. Cosenza, *Francesco Petrarca and the Revolution of Cola di Rienzo* (Chicago, 1913).

de Boulogne & Nicolas Capoche." He adds, in a footnote: "Ce qui me le persuade, c'est que Pétrarque dit, que de ces quatre Cardinaux, il y en a trois qui connoissoient les affaires de Rome par expérience; le quatrieme étoit d'une grande & ancienne maison Romaine descendant des Corneliens. Ceci ne peut regarder que Nicolas Capoche. Les trois autres avoient été à Rome." [3] This identification is accepted by Fracassetti, Cosenza, and Foresti.[4]

De Sade is certainly right as to Niccola Capocci. The only other Roman (indeed, the only other Italian) member of the Sacred College at this time was Rinaldo Orsini: but the Orsini were one of the two great families (the Colonna being the other) attacked in *Fam.* XI 16 as being mainly responsible for the plight of Rome, and the same letter makes it clear that Petrarch thought that both families, far from being of Roman origin, were, from the Roman point of view, foreign interlopers.

As to Bertrand de Déaulx and Gui de Boulogne, De Sade is almost certainly right: as far as I can ascertain from Baluze, Gregorovius, Léonard, and Mollat, they were the only two French cardinals then living whose presence in Rome at any time before November 1351 is attested.

Bertrand de Déaulx served as papal nuncio in Italy in the years 1334–1337; and in January 1336, after being given the title of Syndic and Defender of the Republic by the people of Rome, he arranged a truce between the warring factions. He served in Italy again, this time as papal legate, in the years 1346–1348, first in Naples and then in Rome.[5]

Gui de Boulogne, who had been sent as Legate to the King of Hungary early in 1349, left Hungary at the end of that year or early in 1350; and, returning by way of Italy, was sent to Rome as one of two cardinals designated as "Cardinals of the Jubilee." On his way to Rome he stopped in Padua about the middle of February; and for three days early in March he

<hr/>

[3] De Sade, III, 157.
[4] Fracassetti 2, III, 99 (on p. 292, however, Fracassetti implies that he thinks that Elie de Talleyrand was one of the four cardinals); pp. 218–220; Cosenza, pp. 218–220; Foresti 1, p. 254. Gregorovius says only that Capocci was probably one of the four cardinals.
[5] For details and references see above, p. 52.

stopped in Perugia. On his return he stopped in Padua again in May, and reached Avignon in June.[6]

De Sade's identification of Guillaume Court as the fourth member of the commission is much less certain. Both he and Bertrand du Pouget had served as legates in Italy, but there seems to be no evidence that either one of them ever visited Rome. Guillaume Court served from October 1342 to October 1343 as legate in northern Italy, Dalmatia, Greece, and Crete. The Italian cities specified as falling within the scope of his legation were Genoa, Milan, Pavia, Piacenza, Ferrara, Parma, Modena, and Reggio Emilia.[7] Bertrand du Pouget served as legate in Italy from 1320 to 1334. Officially, the scope of his legation included the whole of Italy; but he was sent primarily to defend and to advance papal interests in the north. During most of his long service his headquarters were in Bologna; and there seems to be no evidence that his duties ever took him south of the Bolognese region. Of his last illness Petrarch wrote on 1 February 1352, in *Fam.* xii 6: "Ostiensis autem, dum hec tibi scriberam, animam agebat, quam dum hec leges, exhalaverit, qui ut michi videtur, matura sibi ac nature, sed acerba reipublice morte defungitur." He died two days later. He was then seventy-two or seventy-three years old.[8]

Two and only two other French cardinals who were living in November 1351 are known to have been in Italy before that time; but neither held a legateship, and there is no evidence that either one of them ever visited Rome. Either one or both

---

[6] Baluze, pp. 345 and 399; Gregorovius, Book XI, Chap. VII, Sect. 1; Léonard, 1, ii, 196–228. Fracassetti is mistaken in saying, and Foresti in repeating, that Gui de Boulogne went to Rome as a legate. The other "Cardinal of the Jubilee" was Annibaldo di Ceccano, who died in 1350.

[7] Baluze, pp. 322 and 367–368; Léonard, 1, i, 77–78. Fracassetti is mistaken in saying, and Foresti in repeating, that Guillaume Court went to Rome as a legate.

[8] Baluze, pp. 221–223; Gregorovius, Book XI, Chaps. III and IV; Edmond Albe, "Autour de Jean XXII: Jean XXII et les familles du Quercy," in *Annales de Saint-Louis-des-Français*, vii (1902), 206–220 (Chap. VI, Art. 3, Sect 1); Mollat, pp. 158–192; and Friedrich Bock, *Reichsidee und Nationalstaaten* (Munich, 1943), *passim* (I owe this last reference to the kindness of Professor T. E. Mommsen).

of them may well have done so, but not as a matter of official representation. Pasteur de Sarrats, who was made a cardinal on 17 December 1350, had held the bishopric of Assisi from October 1337 to January 1339. On his way to Assisi he had served as escort for a group of nuns who were being transferred from Provence to Naples.[9] Pierre Roger de Beaufort, who—at the age of nineteen—was made a cardinal in May 1348, went then at once to Perugia to study law under Baldo. There appears to be no record of his movements in Italy, or of the date of his return.[10]

Under all these circumstances it seems probable that the fourth member of the commission was either Guillaume Court or Bertrand du Pouget. Guillaume Court was the younger man, and his service in Italy was more recent. On the other hand the service of Bertrand du Pouget had been much more extensive, and he was not too old for commission membership. When his last illness began we do not know.

II

Fam. XI 16 begins thus:

Fragilibus humeris grande honus imponitur ab illo et pro illa quibus negare nil potui; nequid ergo reicerem, iussit anime dominus amor mee. Comunis patrie et parentis publice salus in ambiguo vertitur; non est filius quem pie matris non tangit iniuria. Accedit ad humani generis universale debitum singulare quoddam erga me meritum urbis Rome, que et suum me insigni privilegio civem vocat et fortasse non ultimum hoc tempore nominis sui et fame presidium senescentis in me repositum arbitratur.

The "illa" of the first clause is certainly Rome; but there is a fair question as to the identity of the person referred to in the words "ab illo [cui] . . . negare nil potui." It has been generally assumed that this person was one of the four cardinals, and that he was in all probability Gui de Boulogne.[11] That he was one of the four cardinals seems obvious; but that he was probably Gui de Boulogne is not so clear.

---

[9] Baluze, p. 404.
[10] Mollat, p. 122.
[11] See the references given in nn. 3 and 4.

It is quite true that the words "ab illo [cui] . . . negare nil potui" apply perfectly well to Petrarch's relations with Gui de Boulogne; but that fact does not suffice to prove that Petrarch might not have used them with reference to another cardinal. He could hardly have used them, however, with reference to Bertrand de Déaulx or to the other French member of the commission: there is no evidence that Petrarch was acquainted with Bertrand or with any of the other French cardinals named above.[12]

There is, however, no reason why he should not have used them with reference to Niccola Capocci, in view of the fact that Niccola was both a Roman and a cardinal. That Petrarch thought very highly of Niccola is indicated in the passage regarding the four cardinals quoted on the first page of this chapter—in which the words "o vera pietas, o patrie dulcis amor!" seem to echo the opening phrases of the letter. Petrarch refers to Niccola favorably also, though slightly, and in terms of pastoral allegory, in *Ecl.* vii, ll. 121–122, in the words "pratum ille modesto / dente metit" (see above, p. 55). Niccola was unquestionably more deeply concerned as to the fate of Rome than Gui de Boulogne could have been. It may be noted, also, that the clause "Rome, que . . . fortasse non ultimum hoc tempore nominis sui et fame presidium senescentis in me repositum arbitratur" is more readily justifiable on the theory that the request for the writing of the letter had come to Petrarch from a Roman source than it could be otherwise. It seems to me to be probable, therefore, that the person at whose request Petrarch wrote the letter was Cardinal Niccola Capocci.

III

The first of the *Epistolae sine nomine* was written in 1342; Nos. 2 and 3 (both addressed to Cola) were written in 1347; Nos. 4–6 and 8–13 were written during Petrarch's last stay in Provence; and Nos. 14–19 were written in later years.

---

[12] There is indeed evidence that Petrarch's private opinion of Bertrand de Déaulx was very unfavorable: see above, pp. 51–52.

The first half of *Sine nom.* 7 tells of a conversation Petrarch
has recently had with the addressee:

Dum sanctissimum grauissimumque sermonem repeto . . . con-
calesco acriter, et ita sum, ut . . . deum michi uidear audisse, non
hominem.   Adeo michi diuine presentem statum, imo casum ac
ruinam reipublice deplorare adeoque profunde digitos eloquii tui in
uulnera nostra demittere uisus eras, ut . . . cor meum, quod, dum
loquebaris, ardebat, nunc dum meminit, dum cogitat, dum prouidet,
resoluatur in lacrimas, non quidem femineas, sed uiriles, sed masculas
et, si detur, pium aliquid ausuras, proque uirili portione usque ad
iustitie patrocinium erupturas.

He then continues:

Cum sepe igitur antea, tum precipue post eum diem solito sepius
tecum sum; sepe subit desperatio, sepe spes, sepe autem inter utram-
que fluctuante animo mecum dico: O! si unquam . . . [13] O! si in
diebus meis accidat!   O! si tam clari operis et tante glorie sim
particeps!

The second half of the letter is an impassioned prayer for divine
intervention:

Ihesu bone et nimium mansuete, quid hoc est? . . . Quare faciem
tuam auertis? . . . Protector noster, aspice Deus! Vide quid patimur
et unde . . . Vide, et uindica: si minus, occurre, priusquam mortiferi
uis ueneni uitalia membra corripiat . . . Quamdiu oculos auertes,
quamdiu nostris non tangere miseriis . . . ? An mala nostra non
uides . . . ? An odio tibi sumus quos . . . amare consueueras . . . ?
. . . Adesto . . . et . . . in adiutorium nostrum intende ac festina!
Et uel tot mundi mala uel mundum ipsum finias precamur.

Fracassetti expressed the opinion that this letter was addressed
to Cola di Rienzo, that it had reference to Cola's plans for Rome,
and that it was written in 1343, while Cola was in Avignon as
leader of a Roman embassy: "E a chi altro se non a Cola, e su
qual altro subbietto da questo in fuori poteva scrivere il Petrarca
quelle calde parole?" [14] This opinion was in general accepted by
writers on Petrarch—as by Mézières, Carducci, Bartoli, Brizzo-
lara, Filippini, and Cosenza—up to and including Piur. Cesareo,

[13] The suspension points, in this case, are a part of the text.
[14] Fracassetti 2, II, 195.

however, noting the fact that in his collections of letters Petrarch customarily follows a chronological order, asserts—without special discussion of the letter in question—that *Sine nom.* 4–10 were all written during Petrarch's last stay in Provence.[15]

Filippini [16] notes the discrepancy between the attitude of distress ascribed to the addressee of the letter and the attitude of exultation expressed in the letters written by Cola in Avignon, early in 1343, to the Senate and the People of Rome: he seeks, however, to explain the discrepancy by assuming that a considerable amount of time had intervened between the writing of Cola's letters and the interview reported in *Sine nom.* 7 and that in the interim Cola had become disillusioned as to papal policy with regard to Rome. But the distress indicated in *Sine nom.* 7 is a distress arising from conditions in Rome itself; and in any case it is highly improbable that Cola's attitude could have changed so antipodally during his stay in Avignon. His two letters, the first written on 28 January 1343, and the second between 28 and 31 January, are concerned primarily with Clement's agreement to declare 1350 a year of Jubilee. The first of the two letters begins thus:

> Exultet in gloria virtus Altissimi, resultet beatorum spirituum ierarchia, iocundetur populorum turba fidelium et pro tanti doni leticia mundus gaudeat vniversus! Letetur et sancta mater Ecclesia sponsi sui decorata muneribus, et ex precordiis in mundum per omnes resonet graciarum accio et vox laudis!

The second letter begins thus:

> Exultent in circuitu vestro montes, induantur colles gaudio et vniverse planicies atque valles pacem germinent, ubertate fecundent et eterna leticia repleantur! Resurgat Romana civitas diuturne prostracionis a lapsu, solium solite maiestatis ascendens, vestitum viduitatis deponat et lugubre, sponsalem induat purpuram, liberum diadema capud exornet, colla monilibus muniat, resumat iusticie sceptrum.[17]

---

[15] "Su l'ordinamento delle poesie volgari di Francesco Petrarca," in *GSLI*, xix (1892), 290–291; and in Cesareo 1, p. 91.

[16] F. Filippini, "Cola di Rienzo e la curia avignonese," in *Studi storici*, xi (1902), 6.

[17] Burdach-Piur, Part III, pp. 1–8. Cola remained in Avignon until the

Piur [18] refers to the fact that previous writers have almost unanimously assumed that the letter was addressed to Cola and, consequently, written in 1343; and finds no adequate basis for rejecting that opinion. At the same time, however, he admits the lack of any completely convincing evidence in support of the identification of Cola as the addressee. He notes that the personal acquaintance of Petrarch and Cola dates back to 1343: but this of course does not constitute evidence that *Sine nom.* 7 was addressed to Cola. He then tries to explain away the difficulty arising from the position of the letter, in the *Sine nomine*, among letters written in 1351–1353 (if written in 1343 it would naturally have been placed as the second letter in the collection, and if addressed to Cola it would naturally have been grouped with *Sine nom.* 2–4). The only explanation Piur has to offer, however, is the theory that Petrarch separated 7 from 2–4 for "psychological" reasons—namely, because he may have felt, when he came to the making of the collection, that if 7 were grouped with 2–4 it would have revealed an early enthusiasm for Cola which he now preferred not to reveal. This argument, however, is exceedingly weak. If Petrarch had been moved by such considerations he would not have left 2–4 as an unbroken group in the emphatic position that they now occupy; and Petrarch's early enthusiasm for Cola is amply evident in 2–3 and is reflected even in 4. Piur mentions, in a footnote, the fact that in the first form of the collection 7 did follow 2–3 (these three letters stand as the 11th, 10th, and 12th letters in the first form, for which see the last pages of the preceding chapter): but that position is amply accounted for by the fact that 7, like 2–3, deals with the theme of Rome. It may be noted also that if 7 had been addressed to Cola and written in 1343, Petrarch, when making the first form of the collection, would naturally have placed it before rather than after

---

spring of 1344; but documents of 9 August 1343 and 13 April 1344 prove the continuance of friendly relations between Clement and Cola. In the first Clement commands the Roman senators Matteo Orsini and Paolo Conti to desist from actions aimed at Cola, and in the second he commissions three clerics to establish Cola in his office as notary of the Roman *camera urbana:* see Burdach-Piur, Part IV, pp. 3–5.

[18] Piur 1, pp. 342–345.

2–3, which were not written until 1347. Piur suggests, further, that the placement of 7 in its present position may have seemed appropriate on the ground that 7, like letters of 1351–1353, deals with the "Thema Avignon-Rome": but 7 does not deal with the theme of Avignon in the sense in which that theme is dealt with in 5, 6, 8, 10, and 11. With reference to the idea that 7 might have been written during Petrarch's last stay in Provence (in which case it could not have been addressed to Cola) Piur asks: "An wen sollte P. in jenen Jahren [1351–1353] einen solchen Brief mit solchen Hoffnungen gerichtet haben?" That question will be answered presently. Piur does not mention the discrepancy between the attitude of enthusiasm expressed in Cola's letters of January 1343 and the attitude of distress ascribed to the addressee of 7.

Foresti, in a study first published in 1926,[19] shows the weakness of Piur's attempt to explain away the natural implications of the position of 7 in the collection of the *Sine nomine;* stresses the discrepancy in attitudes already noted by Filippini; and points out the perfect appropriateness of the whole letter in relation to conditions in Rome in 1351. He concludes that it was written in that year, and that it is to be related to the appointment of the commission of the four cardinals and to the writing of Petrarch's letters to that commission. He suggests that the passage, quoted above, that begins with the words "Cum sepe igitur" and ends with the exclamation "O! si tam clari operis et tante glorie sim particeps!" may well have been written in the hope that it might lead to just such a request as the one that actually led to the writing of *Fam.* XI 16.

Foresti's argument seems to me conclusive; but I should like to confirm it by pointing out certain similarities between *Sine nom.* 7 and *Fam.* XI 16 and 17. With the latter part of the first passage quoted in this section, from "ut . . . cor meum" to the end, and with the immediately following passage, "Cum sepe . . . particeps!" compare this passage in *Fam.* XI 17: "sed delectat in comunis patrie questione loqui aliquid et pro parte viriliter me tangente, quia facta non possum, ad auxilium libertatis saltem

---

[19] In *La Rassegna,* XXXIV, 221 ff. Republished in Foresti 1, pp. 251–256.

verba conferre." And with the prayer of *Sine nom.* 7, portions
of which are quoted above, compare the prayer that appears in
Fam. xi 16, 12: "O bone Iesu, ubinam gentium habitamus? aspicis
ista, Salvator, aut quonam piaculis nostris offensus solite pietatis
oculos avertisti? Miserere iam et tanti maculas absterge dede-
coris."

Foresti infers that the addressee of *Sine nom.* 7 was one of the
four cardinals of the commission, and in this inference he is almost certainly right. Several of the elements of the first part of
the letter—"sanctissimum . . . sermonem"; "ut . . . deum michi
uidear audisse, non hominem"; "Adeo michi diuine presentem
statum . . . deplorare . . . uisus eras"—are certainly much more
appropriate for a highly placed ecclesiastic than for a layman.
Foresti adds, however, that the addressee was probably Gui de
Boulogne, "quello de' quattro cardinali di cui conosciamo gli
intimi rapporti col Petrarca in quel torno di tempo": but this, as
I shall point out presently, is improbable.

Piur, though acquainted with Foresti's arguments, has continued to maintain that 7 was addressed to Cola and written in
1343. In a chapter published in 1928 [20] he refers in a footnote
to Foresti's opinion that it was written in 1351 and addressed to
Gui de Boulogne, and says that Foresti's arguments are not convincing: but he does not attempt to refute them. In a chapter
published a year later [21] he says that the criticism of papal policy
with regard to Rome expressed in 7 seems not to be in accord
with Petrarch's enthusiasm for Clement's appointment of the
commission of four cardinals: but 7, while it deplores the condition of Rome, does not specifically blame papal policy for that
condition, and Piur's point loses all validity on the natural assumption that 7 was written before the appointment of the
commission. In his *Cola di Rienzo* [22] his opinion is expressed
again briefly, without argument and without reference to Foresti.

It seems to me highly probable that the addressee of *Sine*

[20] Burdach-Piur, Part II, pp. 116–117 (the chapter containing the passage in question was written by Piur).

[21] Burdach-Piur, Part V, pp. 79–80 (the passage in question is either
the work of Piur or that of Piur and Burdach together).

[22] Piur 2, Chap. III.

nom. 7 was Niccola Capocci rather than Gui de Boulogne. There is no reason to think that Gui de Boulogne would have had any such intensity of concern for the fate of Rome as is attributed to the addressee of this letter, whereas Niccola Capocci would certainly have had such concern; there is no reason to think that Gui de Boulogne, who as far as we know had been in Rome only once, and that briefly, in the spring of 1350, could have analyzed current conditions in Rome in such detail as is indicated in the passage "Adeo . . . uisus eras," whereas Niccola Capocci was doubtless in a position to do so; and the words "uulnera nostra" indicate a distress shared with a fellow citizen of Rome.

I conclude that the addressee of *Sine nom.* 7 was in all probability Niccola Capocci; and submit that this conclusion and the similar conclusion reached above at the end of Section II serve to reënforce each other.[23]

---

[23] On the career of Capocci see Baluze, pp. 409–411, and Alfonso Chacon, *Vitae et res gestae Pontificum Romanorum et S.R.E. Cardinalium*, revised by Agostino Oldoino (Rome, 1677), II, cols. 509–515. (Gregorovius, Book XII, Chap. VII, Sect. 2, 9th footnote, says: "Die Vita des Nicol. Capocci bei Mur. VIII, II. 65." I can make nothing of this reference: no such Life is to be found in Muratori.) A magnificent Bible given by Capocci about 1365 to the Olivetans of Perugia is now among the treasures of the Pierpont Morgan Library: see the *Census of Medieval and Renaissance Manuscripts in the United States and Canada*, ed. by Seymour De Ricci and W. J. Wilson (New York, 1937), II, 146; also *Italian Manuscripts in the Pierpont Morgan Library* (New York, 1953).

CHAPTER VII

Petrarch's Three Epistolae metricae
to Francesco Nelli

Met. III 22

The letters written by Nelli to Petrarch and the *Familiares* written by Petrarch to Nelli during the winter of 1351–1352 and the early spring of 1352 succeeded each other thus: [1]

Dates	Letters of Nelli	Letters of Petrarch
Probably late in December	A lost letter	
4 January	IV (LAP 26: received by Petrarch on 13 January after he had written *Fam.* XII 4)	
13 January		*Fam.* XII 4 (answers Nelli's lost letter)
18 January		*Fam.* XII 5 (answers Nelli's IV)
15 February	V (LAP 27: answers *Fam.* XII 4 and 5)	
1 April		*Fam.* XII 9 (answers Nelli's V)

At some time during this same period, it is agreed, Petrarch wrote *Met.* III 22, a poem of 35 lines on the theme of Avignon

---

[1] See Cochin 1, pp. 94–96 and 137, and Cochin 2, pp. 6–7 and 38. The dates of the five extant letters are definite (on the date of *Fam.* XII 4 see Wilkins 1, pp. 331–333). We know from *Fam.* XII 5 that Nelli's *Ep.* IV, written on 4 January, reached Petrarch on 13 January, after he had written *Fam.* XII 4 as a reply to Nelli's lost letter: it is highly probable, therefore, that that lost letter was written late in December.

as the Fifth Labyrinth. Its first 21 lines are devoted to the four ancient labyrinths—those of Egypt, Crete, Lemnos, and Clusium—and the last 14 to a characterization of Avignon written in the spirit of the *Epistolae sine nomine*. These last lines read as follows:

> Sed quorsum tibi nota trahens ignota profari
> Demoror? Vtque volans alium delatus in orbem
> Daedalus ad Rhodani laevam, nova monstra, novasque
> Ambagum formas, et plena doloribus antra
> Struxerit; ut nullus reduci vestigia filo
> Dux incerta regat; laquaeos ut nuper in istos
> Inciderim, nequeamve pedem cum laude referre.
> Non hinc Aegides, non hinc Minoïa proles
> Daedaleo ingenio freti, non ipse magister
> Exeat: ira viam faciet; dolor induet alas.
> Hinc ego vel nudus fugiam, nisi barbara busti
> Sors mihi servatur! Fugiam: similisque volanti,
> Iam Ligurum colles, facilemque remetior Alpem,
> Limina Pontificum toties damnata relinquens.[2]

The earliest reference to this poem occurs in Nelli's *Ep.* iv, in the sentence "Versus quosdam tuos per Forensem nostrum, michi promissos, egregium munus expecto, et quousque habeam affligitur anima." Forese Donati had been in Avignon presumably since November (see above, p. 100): the sentence just quoted shows that he must have been there early enough for Nelli to have heard from him by 4 January. The "per" means "through," and the clause as a whole indicates that it was through a letter from Forese that Nelli first heard of the poem. The sentence quoted gives no indication that Forese had reported the subject of the poem: the "quosdam" indeed suggests that when Nelli wrote his *Ep.* iv he did not know what the subject of the poem was.

On 13 January Petrarch, answering Nelli's lost letter, wrote

---

[2] Cochin 1, p. 137, and 2, p. 38, lists *Met.* iii 22, without argument, as written between 4 and 13 January. Since it was written before Christmas, as will presently appear, while Nelli's lost letter was probably written late in December, the writing of the poem presumably preceded the writing of Nelli's lost letter. The three *epistolae metricae* considered in this chapter are to be found in Rossetti ii, 254–264.

Fam. xii 4, in the course of which he makes his own first reference to the poem, in this passage:

ideoque parcius indignor hinc michi quoque longioris more causas texuisse fortunam, sed indignor tamen. De qua re carmen tibi breve iam scripsi, quod ideo nondum mitto quia ut ex ordine huius inextricabilis ergastuli mentionem facerem, de quattuor veteribus labyrinthis prius ibi mentio facta est, et de ordine dubito, neque modo quos consulam libri adsunt et parum fido memorie.

Nelli's *Ep.* iv was written on January 4; and Forese's letter must have been written at least some ten days earlier. *Met.* iii 22 must therefore have been written, substantially, before Christmas, 1351; and since Petrarch in *Fam.* xii 4 says of it "iam scripsi" it is probable that it was written not long before that time.

On 13 January, after he had written *Fam.* xii 4, Petrarch received Nelli's *Ep.* iv; and on that day or soon afterward he wrote *Sine nom.* 10 (see below, pp. 209–210), in which, after explaining to Nelli his reasons for dating an earlier letter (presumably *Sine nom.* 9) "super flumina Babilonis," he continues thus:

de quinque laberinthis potes etiam mirari, cum apud ceteros scriptores non nisi de quatuor mentionem inueneris ut puto. In quibus cum famam habeant Egiptus, Lemnos, Creta, et in Italia Clusium, laberinthum Rodani tacuerunt, omnium inextricabilissimum ac pessimum, siue quia nondum erat siue quia nondum noscebatur. Huius apud me mentio crebra est; quam iuste autem qui nosse cupit, huc properet. Non hic carcer horrendus, non tenebrose domus error, non fatalis urna humani generis fata permiscens, denique non imperiosus Minos, non Minotaurus uorax, non damnate *Veneris monimenta* defuerint, sed remedia, sed amor, sed caritas, sed promissorum fides, sed amica consilia, sed fila perplexum iter tacita ope signantia, sed Adriana, sed Dedalus. Vna salutis spes in auro est. Auro placatur rex ferus, auro immane monstrum uincitur, auro salutare lorum texitur, auro durum limen ostenditur, auro uectes et saxa franguntur, auro tristis ianitor mollitur, auro celum panditur. Quid multa? Auro Cristus uenditur.

This passage constitutes, in effect, Petrarch's own commentary on *Met.* iii 22.

The Labyrinth motif appears also, with mention of Daedalus, in *Met.* iii 23, as will presently appear, and in *Met.* iii 21 (addressed to Giovanni Barrili, and written presumably about the same time as III 23); and it appears, without mention of Daedalus, in *Sine nom.* 8 and 11, both written late in 1351 or early in 1352. It is echoed in *Sine nom.* 15 and 19, both written in later years.

The story of *Met.* III 22 is continued in *Fam.* XII 5, in a passage that begins thus:

> In versiculis autem ad te scriptis, quos tam ardenter efflagitas, scito Plinii Secundi consilio opus esse, quem Italia excedens in patria sua, Verone scilicet, ingenti virorum illustrium comitatum acie dimisi. Hic michi Plinius nusquam est, nec alteri, quod quidem noverim, nisi Romano Pontifici; is autem, ut fando audisti, ab ipso mortis vestibulo, quo dudum precipitanter accesserat, nunc pedetentim redit.

Petrarch then goes on to say that when the Pope has recovered he, Petrarch, will have a look at Pliny, and will then satisfy Nelli's desire to receive the poem.

Nelli's *Ep.* v, which answers both *Fam.* XII 4 and 5, refers to the poem in this sentence: "De carmine vero quod Plinium querit ante quam venit . . . superfluum reor aliquid dare laudis." *Fam.* v 19, written to the Pope on 12 March, contains several quotations from Pliny: presumably, therefore, Petrarch had been able to consult the Pope's Pliny before that date.[3] But it was only in 1355 that the poem was actually sent to Nelli, who acknowledged it in his *Ep.* XIII, written in that year on 16 August.

Met. III *23*

This poem reads thus:

> Scilicet, immensae quod Flaccus dixerat urbi:
> Bellua multorum es capitum: sibi vindicat omnis
> Villula. Fumosis sunt oppida moenibus, unde
> Pastor et hirsutus quondam veniebat arator,
> 5   Nunc vagus impostor quique omnia litora lustret;
> Insomnis mercator adest, quique omnia sulcet
> Aequora, et excisum patrio de stipite remum
> Ignotis qui verset aquis; qui sydere in atro
> Pervigil instantes mundo notet ante tumultus,
> 10   Publica presagis aut funera cernat in astris,
> Aut simulet; qui vel tristi radice paventem

---

[3] See Bosco, p. 108. Pliny's passage in *Nat. hist.* 36, 13 is quoted in Piur 1, p. 200.

Aegrotum, vel morte levet; qui pulvere et herbis
Improbus ex variis medicatum spondeat aurum;
Vulnera qui curet verbis et credula fallat
15 Artibus innumeris insani pectora vulgi;
Solvere qui legum laqueos et vincla professus,
Ludat, et attonitum teneat sub rostra clientem.
Quid loquor artifices scelerum, quos surgere passim
Cernimus, immites humili de stirpe tyrannos?
20 Iam quaecunque palus Syllas alit atque Nerones,
Portentum regale prius: sic flumine longo
Assyrium nostras defluxit virus in oras!
Nos miseri, venale pecus, vilisque lupinae
Praeda famis, sequimur dominos; dominarier orbi
25 Quos magni docuere patres. Nec tuta dolendi
Libertas, iustaeque sonant impune querelae.
Supplicium dolor ipse timet, nec parva gemendi
Materia est, non flere palam. Maria horrida velo,
O mea Calliope, et remis fugiamus adactis,
30 Securum carpamus iter, speciesque laborum
Et cursus vitae varios, populumque canamus;
Laeditur hic gratis, cuius discrimina mille,
Mille artes et mille viae, parque omnibus error.
Quaelibet ancipitem pariet sibi sylva sophistam;
35 Vepribus eliciet doctum nemus omne Platona;
Quolibet argutus procedet Tullius antro;
Aliger ex omni veniet tibi Daedalus alpe.
Si status hic ruris, quae nam confusio vasto
In populo, qualis magna labyrinthus in urbe?
40 Quae, si visa premunt animum, si dulcia turbant
Ocia; cunctamur tristes abrumpere nodos,
Ac laetam tentare fugam? Vestigia vulgus
Nota sequatur iners; at nos Helicone sub alto
Secretos longe nitamur carpere calles.

The theme of the poem is stated in ll. 1–3: Horace's characterization (in *Ep.* 1 1, 76) of the "urbs" as "Bellua multorum
capitum" now applies equally well to "omnis villula." After a
passing reference to the primitive simplicity of agricultural life,
the poem then proceeds, in ll. 5–21, to enumerate the human pests
by whom "omnis villula" is infected: the impostor; the peddler;
the sailor; the soothsayer; the quack; the gold-maker; the spell-
monger; the shyster lawyer; and swamp-born local tyrants. The
mention of this last pest leads the poet into a digression, in ll. 21–

28, on the evils of tyranny in general. From this horrific and dangerous digression he recalls his Muse, in ll. 28–31, to his main theme:

> Maria horrida velo,
> O mea Calliope, et remis fugiamus adactis,
> Securum carpamus iter, speciesque laborum
> Et cursus vitae varios, populumque canamus.

These lines, I take it, are hendiadic: what Petrarch really means appears to be "Let us sing of the various occupations and ways of life of the people." To the people he returns, accordingly, in ll. 32–37, speaking of their plight in general; their many contentions, devices, and ways of action; their common mistakenness; and their untrained and futile would-be leaders. If such conditions prevail in the "rus," he asks in ll. 38–39, how much worse must conditions be in the city? There is nothing left for him to do, as the concluding lines indicate, but to flee to Helicon.

The poem as a whole is obviously a companion piece to *Met.* III 22: as III 22 deals with the "urbs," so III 23 deals with the region around the "urbs"—indicated by the "omnis villula" and the (deprecatory) "oppida" of ll. 2–3 and the "rus" of line 38. Despite its obvious character, Melodia and Miss Magrini assume that it is a depiction of conditions in Avignon![4]

What actual experiences could have given Petrarch the basis for such a picture of the Provençal countryside? The words "omnis villula" are used in contrast to "urbs": they would therefore cover any group of habitations smaller than the "urbs" itself—small towns or villages. The human pests of ll. 5–21 and the would-be leaders of ll. 34–38 suggest small towns rather than villages; but even village incidents, supplemented by literary reminiscences and by his own imagination, would have sufficed to give Petrarch the material for his poem.

The village he knew best was, of course, Vaucluse. His own house stood outside the village, but not far from it. In his day the village (perhaps to be called rather a small town) appears to have been a place of some size and of some importance, derived in part, at least, from the fact that a castle belonging to the Bishop

---

[4] Melodia, pp. 87–88; and Magrini, p. 101.

of Cavaillon stood on a spur of the mountain that rises above the source of the Sorgue.[5] The idea of the village of Vaucluse as a place beset by such human pests as those enumerated in the poem does not fit well with one's natural idea of Petrarch's Vaucluse as a place of sylvan wanderings, nor does the idea of Vaucluse as a place of some size and importance fit in well with this sentence in *Fam.* XI 12: "Exilis glebule et felicioris vitis atque olee cultus vel flumineis hamis ac retibus intenta plebecula nullum vite sermonisque commercium habere mecum potest." The discrepancies, however, are perhaps explicable as due to selective emphasis, particularly if one allows for a considerable play of imagination in the poem.

Furthermore, as Petrarch rode between Vaucluse and Avignon, or between Vaucluse and Cavaillon, or between Avignon and Cavaillon, he would necessarily pass through several other villages or small towns—such as L'Isle-sur-Sorgue, Thor, Châteauneuf de Gadagne, Lagnes, and Caumont—in which he might well have seen and heard some of the sights and sounds that are reflected in the poem. The Pope and members of his court

---

[5] Gustave Bayle, in his "Le véritable emplacement de l'habitation de Pétrarque à Vaucluse" (Nîmes, 1897) (a reprint from the *Revue du midi*), pp. 4–5, writes thus: "On se ferait une fausse idée de ce qu'était ce village au XIVe siècle, si on en jugeait par ce qu'il est aujourd'hui, et même si on prenait à la lettre la description qu'en fait Pétrarque . . . Mais si on consulte les documents historiques que nous fournissent les registres des notaires et ceux de la cour seigneuriale, on voit qu'il y avait à Vaucluse, du temps de Pétrarque, en l'absence du seigneur, qui y faisait de rares apparitions, divers officiers civils, des magistrats, des ecclésiastiques, tels que châtelain, bailli, clavaire, procureur fiscal, notaire, greffier, juge de la cour seigneuriale, vicaire perpetuel, chapelains. On y comptait aussi plusieurs familles patriciennes, commes les Forcalquier, les Lagnes, les Esmivy, les Bruni, etc." Nino Quarta in his "La casa e i giardini del Petrarca a Valchiusa," in R. Accademia di Archeologia, Lettere e Belle Arti di Napoli, *Atti*, XXV (1908), 183, and Flamini, p. 90, both quote in part this statement of Bayle's without indicating reservations as to its validity; but I find it impossible to accept it without reservation. Bayle undoubtedly saw documents that gave him the material for his statement, but he does not cite them. We do not know their dates or their exact character, and cannot control the accuracy of Bayle's use of them. Tatham, II, 58, says that the existing remains of the castle "indicate only a small building."

spent much time in Villeneuve-lez-Avignon; and in possible visits
to that place Petrarch may well have received confirming impres-
sions. The very fact of the extraordinary importance of Avignon
in these years is indeed sufficient to account for the presence of
swarms of human pests in the region surrounding the papal city.

There appear to be in the poem a few minor reminiscences
of the concluding lines of Book II of the *Georgics*—lines that
might indeed have been introduced by words such as

speciesque laborum
Et cursus vitae varios, populumque canamus.

Before entering upon his final praise of country life Virgil reviews the inferior interests of men of various kinds, among them
those whom he characterizes thus (in lines 503–510):

> sollicitant alii remis freta caeca . . .
> condit opes alius defossoque incubat auro;
> hic stupet attonitus rostris; hunc plausus hiantem
> per cuneos geminatus enim plebisque patrumque
> corripuit.

There is a certain likeness, also—which may of course be
coincidental—between lines 18–20 of Petrarch's poem and *Purga-
torio* VI 124–126:

Chè le città d'Italia tutte piene
son di tiranni, e un Marcel diventa
ogni villan che parteggiando viene.

The lines

Maria horrida velo,
O mea Calliope, et remis fugiamus adactis,
Securum carpamus iter, speciesque laborum
Et cursus vitae varios, populumque canamus

call for extended comment. I have already stated my belief that
these lines serve to mark the end of the preceding digression and
the return to consideration of the "populus." This is indicated
by the fact that the words "populumque canamus" are followed
immediately by the lines—the first beginning "Laeditur hic gratis"
—that are devoted to the plight of the people. Melodia, however,

maintains that Petrarch is here referring to the *Triumphs*.[6]
Starting from the utterly mistaken idea that the poem is a depiction of conditions in Avignon, Melodia writes:

Vi albergano imposture, empietà, tirannia, frode, falso sapere ed
altri mali. . . . Volgerà pertanto, colla sua Calliope, le vele da quel
mare che fa orrore, si affiderà a corso sicuro, e canterà le varie specie
dei travagli, degli affanni mortali, le successive vicende di nostra vita,
i *Trionfi* [here Melodia quotes the four lines in question]. Questi
versi, che da noi per la prima volta si mettono in rilievo, sono
della massima importanza, perchè ci dipingono al vivo le condizioni
d'animo in cui il Petrarca concepì l'idea di scrivere, credo, i *Trionfi*:
dolore e sdegno per i mali d'Avignone.

He then continues:

E quei versi concordano (tranne che non v'è ricordata, e forse
non poteva essere ricordata la efficacia dell'amore) con le notizie,
diremmo quasi, storiche che il poeta ci dà in principio del poema:
          Amor gli sdegni e 'l pianto e la stagione
     Ricondotto m'aveano al chiuso loco
     Ov'ogni fascio il cor lasso ripone.
          Ivi fra l'erbe, già del pianger fioco,
     Vinto dal sonno, vidi una gran luce . . .

But the *Triumphs* are not concerned with "species . . .
laborum/Et cursus vitae varios, populumque": they are concerned with Love, Chastity, Death, Fame, Time, and Eternity.
The persons who appear in the *Triumphs* appear therein simply
and solely because of their relation to one or another of these
themes; and these persons, in their consistent distinction, are
antipodally different from the "populus." And the concordance
suggested by Melodia between the four Latin lines in question
and the five lines that he quotes from *Al tempo* is not discernible.
The idea that the lines in question have reference to the *Triumphs*
is then completely untenable.[7]
   To the word *Trionfi*, on its first occurrence in the passage just

---

[6] *Loc. cit.* in n. 4.
[7] Melodia's interpretation of the four lines was similarly refuted by
Volpi 2, pp. 420–421. Calcaterra, p. 164, still assumes that they refer to
the *Triumphs*, though he does not accept the argument that Melodia
bases upon that supposition.

Vaucluse. Since Petrarch did not meet Nelli until 1350, the poem must have been written during Petrarch's last stay in Provence, from June 1351 to May 1353. The periods that were spent—with occasional brief absences—in Vaucluse during that stay were, first, the summer and the early part of the autumn of 1351; second, the spring and summer of 1352; and third, the late autumn of 1352 and the following winter and early spring. The mournful tone of the poem, however, serves to exclude the first period, when Petrarch—as is indicated, for instance, in *Fam.* xi 12—was rejoicing in the resumption of his life in Vaucluse. While it is just barely possible that the poem was written in or about February 1353—within the weeks in which Petrarch wrote *Fam.* xvi 6, *Fam.* xv 3, and the poem *Exul ab Italia—Met.* iii 33 has so little in common with those letters and with *Exul ab Italia* that it remains highly probable that it was written in the spring or summer of 1352.[10]

---

[10] See above, pp. 154–158. Cochin 1, p. 148, and 2, p. 46, notes that the tone of this poem is that of the letters written during Petrarch's last stay in Provence, but does not regard it as certainly written at that time. Miss Magrini, p. 162, regards it as written soon after *Met.* iii 23.

CHAPTER VIII

On Part of the Correspondence Between Petrarch and Francesco Nelli

Henry Cochin, in his *Un ami de Pétrarque: Lettres de Francesco Nelli à Pétrarque*, published the thirty extant letters of Nelli to Petrarch, gave evidence as to certain lost letters, discussed dates, and endeavored to determine, as far as possible, the inter-relations of the letters of the two men. His conclusions are summarized in a list of 81 letters exchanged by the two men: [1] five written before Petrarch's return to Provence in 1351; nineteen written during Petrarch's last stay in Provence; and 57 written thereafter. This list is followed by brief statements regarding four other letters as to the dates of which Cochin is uncertain.

The present chapter is concerned only with the letters written, or wrongly supposed to have been written, during Petrarch's last stay in Provence. Cochin's list for this period is as follows (I have added parenthetical notes that are entirely in accordance with Cochin's findings):

Co-chin's Nos.	Dates	Letters of Petrarch	Letters of Nelli
	1351:		
6	Summer	A lost letter	
7	21 August		VI (LAP 28: answers Petrarch's lost letter)

---

[1] Cochin 1, pp. 134–148, and 2, pp. 36–46. Under No. 3, in both Cochin 1 and 2, 1350 is a misprint for 1351. Under No. 9 the *inviare* of Cochin 2 is a mistranslation of the *remettre* of Cochin 1. Under No. 17 of Cochin 2, 1353 is a misprint for 1352; and under No. 21 the figure 9 for the day of the month is omitted.

8	27 August		III (LAP 25)
9			A lost letter (referred to in Petrarch's *Var.* 44)
10	28 August		VII (LAP 29)
11		*Var.* 44 (answers Nelli's VII)	
12			A lost letter
	1352:		
13	4 January		IV (LAP 26: received by Petrarch on 13 January after he had written *Fam.* XII 4)
14		*Met.* III 22	
15	13 January	*Fam.* XII 4 (answers Nelli's lost letter—No. 12)	
16	18 January	*Fam.* XII 5 (answers Nelli's IV)	
17	15 February		V (LAP 27: answers *Fam.* XII 4 and 5)
18	1 April	*Fam.* XII 9 (answers Nelli's V)	
19	24 May	*Fam.* XII 12	
20	24 May	*Fam.* XII 13	
21	9 August	*Fam.* XIII 5	
22	10 August	*Fam.* XIII 6	
23	Summer	*Fam.* XIII 8	
24	18 November	*Fam.* XV 2	

This list now needs correction and supplementation.

Cochin's Nos. 9–11

Foresti has shown [2] that Nos. 10 and 11, assigned by Cochin to 1351, were actually written not in that year but in 1353. In No. 10 Nelli describes the very amusing messenger—whom he calls "Neophytus"—by whom he is sending the letter. In *Var.* 44 it appears that Neophytus, instead of waiting to deliver No. 10 himself, had sent it forward by another messenger who could and did reach Petrarch before he (Neophytus) could; and that

---

[2] Foresti 1, pp. 279–285.

some days after Petrarch had received No. 10 Neophytus himself arrived, bearing no letter, but inflicting upon Petrarch a
torrent of gossip, and apologizing for not being the bearer of
No. 10: "Nihil ille lentescere, sed enixe quemdam excusare quod
litteras ad me tuas quas afferre debuerat promisisset, nuncii celeri-
tate fortuiti, festinationi tuae consulueris." Cochin wrongly infers [3] that Neophytus himself delivered No. 10, and that Petrarch
had received, two days before the arrival of Neophytus, another
letter, listed by Cochin as No. 9, in which Neophytus was described: there is no basis for this in *Var*. 44. Cochin's idea that
No. 9 had been received by Petrarch precisely two days before
the arrival of Neophytus is derived from this passage: "posset ne
is esse Neophytus quem mihi pridie meus ille [*i.e.*, Nelli] sapi-
dissimo sale descripserat?" But the "pridie" in this passage refers
not to the time when Petrarch received the letter in question, but
to the time when Nelli had written it, and it is used here, as often,
not as a precise but as a general term.

Cochin fails to notice the fact that on the day when Neophytus arrived Petrarch had written to Nelli a letter (now lost),
which he sent to Nelli with *Var*. 44: "Neophytus quidem ille . . .
eo ipse die dum forte huius sociam scriberem ad me venit."

In Cochin's list, accordingly, No. 9 should disappear; No. 10
should be moved to a position just after Cochin's No. 29; and
Petrarch's lost letter (the "huius sociam") should be entered just
after Cochin's No. 32, and should be followed immediately by
Var. 44.

Cochin's Nos. 12–18

These letters all date from the winter of 1351–1352 or the
early spring of 1352. During this time Petrarch was in Avignon
(except for brief visits to Vaucluse and Cavaillon); [4] and circumstances facilitated promptness in the delivery of the letters
exchanged by Petrarch and Nelli. Nelli was a confidential ad-
viser of Angelo Acciaiuoli, Bishop of Florence; and late in
October 1351 Angelo had been sent to Avignon (where he
remained until May 1352) as one of two Florentine envoys

---

[3] Cochin 1, pp. 98–101, and 2, pp. 9–11.
[4] For the material of this paragraph, see above, pp. 100–101.

instructed to win Pope Clement VI to an alliance against Giovanni Visconti. Petrarch, as we learn from *Fam.* xii 4 and 5 and from certain later letters, was in close touch both with Angelo and with one of the members of his party, Forese Donati, who was a devoted friend and admirer of Petrarch. Under these circumstances letters exchanged between Nelli (who remained in Florence) and Petrarch, or between Nelli and Forese, would doubtless have been carried promptly by official couriers.

Cochin's No. 12

We know from *Fam.* xii 5 that Nelli's *Ep.* iv, written on 4 January, was received by Petrarch on 13 January—after he had, on that very day, written *Fam.* xii 4 as a reply to Nelli's lost letter (Cochin's No. 12): it is highly probable, therefore, this lost letter was written late in December.

The Three Epistolae metricae

It has been shown in the preceding chapter that *Met.* iii 22 must have been written, substantially, before Christmas, 1351, and probably not long before that time; and that it was presumably written before Nelli's lost letter (Cochin's No. 12). It should therefore precede that letter in the list.

In the same chapter it has been shown that *Met.* iii 23 was written early in 1352, probably after 18 January and before the end of March. We have no way of telling whether it was written before or after 15 February, the date of Nelli's *Ep.* v: the chances seem slightly to favor the later period, and the *epistola*, therefore, might well follow Nelli's *Ep.* v in the list.

In the same chapter it has been shown that *Met.* iii 33 was in all probability written in the spring or summer of 1352. While it may have been written at any time within that period, it seems very slightly more probable—since the poem appears to have been written after considerable reflection, and yet before the idea of returning to Italy had become dominant—that it was written in June or July rather than earlier or later; and it might well follow *Fam.* xii 13, therefore, in the list.

Sine nom. 6, 9, and 10

When Cochin wrote it was not known that these three letters

were addressed to Nelli. Piur has shown that *Sine nom.* 6 was so addressed on 31 March 1352, and that the other two letters were addressed either to Nelli or to Barbato da Sulmona; [5] and Foresti [6] has shown that these two letters were in fact addressed to Nelli. All three letters were written in Avignon.

Sine nom. 9 is concerned primarily with the plight of Italy, and only secondarily with conditions in Avignon. Its remarkable passage on the necessity of unity of will as a prerequisite for Italian liberty, quoted in large part above (on p. 112), ends thus: "Proh superi! dominari solebamus optimis. En! quo decidimus! nunc seruimus pessimis. Dura sors, intolleranda mutatio! Sed o semper stulta, nunc etiam demens et uesana barbaries, reginam rides Italiam!" While the "pessimi" and the "barbaries" undoubtedly included, in Petrarch's mind, the French members of the papal court, the only specific reference to Avignon is in the subscription of the letter: "Hec tibi raptim Hierosolymitanus exul inter et super flumina Babilonis indignans scripsi."

Piur dates the letter as of the latter part of 1351 or the first five months of 1352, and Foresti dates it as of a period ending 17 January 1352. A more exact dating appears to be possible. Since the letter is concerned primarily with the plight of Italy and only secondarily with conditions in Avignon, it is presumably prior to the series of violent outbursts regarding Avignon that begins with *Met.* III 22, and it is presumably at least roughly contemporary with Petrarch's extensive discussion of the plight of Rome in the two letters, *Fam.* XI 16 and 17, which he addressed on 18 and 24 November to the four cardinals appointed by Clement VI to reform the government of Rome. Petrarch was in Avignon on 26 October: he may have established himself there somewhat before that date, but we have no evidence to that effect (see above, p. 90). These considerations indicate that *Sine nom.* 9 was written in the latter part of 1351: confirmation of this tentative conclusion will follow presently.

Sine nom. 10, which Piur dates as of the latter part of 1351

---

[5] Piur 1, pp. 327–340 and 352–363.

[6] Foresti 1, pp. 257–262. These pages are reprinted from an article published in 1926.

or the early part of 1352 and Foresti dates as of 18 January 1352, begins with the words "Subscriptiones epistolarum mearum miraris. Nec immerito. Non nisi geminam Babilonem cum legeris, alteram quidem apud Assirios . . . alteram apud Egiptios . . . cuius nunc Babilonis inauditum tibi nomen ingeritur tecum uoluis." The first and main part of the letter is devoted to an explanation of the appropriateness of "Babylon" as an appellation for Avignon. The second part of the letter begins thus: "Atque ut hac admiratione succisa a radice aliam conuellam, de quinque laberinthis potes etiam mirari, cum apud ceteros scriptores non nisi de quatuor mentionem inueneris ut puto." *Sine nom.* 10 was written, then, after Petrarch had received from Nelli a letter expressing surprise at the subscription "Super flumina Babilonis"; and after he had mentioned to Nelli the theme of Avignon as the Fifth Labyrinth, but before any word of surprise had come to him from Nelli as to that theme. *Sine nom.* 9 had been subscribed "inter et super flumina Babilonis" and is the only extant letter of Petrarch presumably written before the end of 1351 that is so subscribed: presumably, then, since no reference to surprise at this subscription appears in any extant letter of Nelli, the letter in which he did express his surprise was the lost letter (Cochin's No. 12), written, in all probability, shortly before the end of December—the letter to which Petrarch replied on 13 January in *Fam.* xii 4, which also bears the subscription "super flumina Babilonis." It would seem that after writing that letter—and after the receipt, on that same day, of Nelli's *Ep.* iv—it occurred to Petrarch, who had mentioned the labyrinth theme for the first time in *Fam.* xii 4, that Nelli (who had referred to the promised poem in his *Ep.* iv, but had given no indication that he knew its subject) might be surprised at that theme also; and that he (Petrarch) accordingly gave him the explanation contained in the second part of *Sine nom.* 10. This would mean that *Sine nom.* 10 was written on or soon after 13 January.[7]

Furthermore, since the letter in which Nelli expressed his surprise at the subscription "super flumina Babilonis" was pre-

---

[7] Foresti's conclusion that *Sine nom.* 10 was written on 18 January may be right, but his argument is unsound: see Wilkins 2, pp. 331–333.

sumably the lost letter (Cochin's No. 12) written, in all probability, shortly before the end of December, and since his surprise
was presumably occasioned by the superscription of *Sine nom.* 9,
it follows that *Sine nom.* 9 was presumably written before the
end of December, and early enough in December to have reached
Nelli before he wrote his lost letter. Presumably, also, he had
received it not long before he wrote that letter. The combination
of these considerations with those advanced above as to the date
of *Sine nom.* 9 serves to make it virtually certain that *Sine nom.* 9
was written in November or in the first half of December, 1351.

A New Table

In view of the foregoing considerations the portion of
Cochin's table covering the period from the autumn of 1351
to 1 April 1352 should be reconstructed thus:

Co-chin's Nos.	Dates	Letters of Petrarch	Letters of Nelli
	1351:		
6	Summer	A lost letter	
7	21 August		VI (answers Petrarch's lost letter)
8	27 August		III
	November or the first half of December	*Sine nom.* 9	
14	December, before Christmas	*Met.* III 22	
12	December, late		A lost letter
	1352:		
13	4 January		IV (received by Petrarch on 13 January after he had written *Fam.* XII 4)
15	13 January	*Fam.* XII 4 (answers Nelli's lost letter)	
	13 January or soon afterward	*Sine nom.* 10	

16	18 January	*Fam.* XII 5	
		(answers Nelli's IV)	
17	15 February		v (answers *Fam.* XII
			4 and 5)
	Early in 1352	*Met.* III 23	
	31 March	*Sine nom.* 6	
18	1 April	*Fam.* XII 9	
		(answers Nelli's v)	
19	24 May	*Fam.* XII 12	
20	24 May	*Fam.* XII 13	
	Spring or	*Met.* III 33	
	Summer		
21	9 August	*Fam.* XIII 5	
22	10 August	*Fam.* XIII 6	
23	Summer	*Fam.* XIII 8	
24	18 November	*Fam.* XV 2	

CHAPTER IX

The Correspondence of Petrarch and Barbato da Sulmona

There are extant fifteen or sixteen prose letters and five letters in verse written by Petrarch to Barbato,[1] and four prose letters written by Barbato to Petrarch; and from some of these letters we learn of other letters, now lost, written by Barbato to Petrarch.

The chronological order of the several letters, with dates established previously or in the present chapter, appears to be as indicated in the following list.

Dates	Letters of Petrarch	Letters of Barbato
30 April 1341	*Fam.* IV 8	
Probably 29 May 1342; possibly *c.* 1 February 1343 or soon thereafter	*Fam.* V 1	
February–December 1342		A lost letter
February–August 1343	*Misc.* 16	
Mid-October–22 November 1343	*Met.* II 7	
Late November–mid-December 1343	*Met.* II 16	
25 February 1345 or possibly some days later	*Fam.* V 10	
Late September–December 1345		A lost letter?
1 August 1346	*Fam.* VI 5	
18 January 1347	*Var.* 49	
July–August 1347		A lost letter?
11 September 1347	*Fam.* VII 1	

---

[1] On Barbato see Faraglia; Weiss 2, and "Barbato da Sulmona, il Petrarca e la rivoluzione di Cola di Rienzo," in *Studi petrarcheschi*, III (1950), 13–22; and Léonard 1, I, pp. 6, 213, 239, 312, 338, and 489–490.

Not after summer 1355	*Misc.* 5?	
Summer 1348–spring 1351	*Met.* I 1	
18 October–late November 1350	*Misc.* 6	
March–June 1351		A lost letter
20 February 1352	*Fam.* xII 7	
March–mid-May 1352		A lost letter written for Acciaiuoli
May–December 1353	*Met.* III 18	
c. 1 January 1354	*Met.* III 19	
(1351–1355?		Packets of scissors)
September or slightly earlier, 1355		A lost letter beginning "Extremum Olimpiadis"; also LAP 5
4 October 1355	*Var.* 22; also *Misc.* 11	
November–December 1355		LAP 4
(1357	*Met.* I 1 and *Ecl.* I sent to Barbato)	
Spring–summer 1358		A lost letter
27 August 1358	*Fam.* xx 5	
Probably early 1360; possibly summer 1361–summer 1363	*Fam.* xxII 3	
27 April 1360	*Fam.* xxII 4	
Early 1361		LAP 3
Spring–early summer 1361		LAP 74
22 June 1361	*Misc.* 9	

Petrarch in Naples in 1341

On his way to Rome in the early spring of 1341 Petrarch spent four days in Naples, where he secured the sponsorship of King Robert for his coronation. While he was there King Robert presented him to high officials of the court, as we are told in *Met.* II 10 (lines 95–98):

Meque . . . tanto dignatus honore est,
Vt procerum primis sub regia tecta vocatis
Plurima nostrarum caneret praeconia laudum,
Vera utinam!

Among the high officials of the court were two, Barbato da Sulmona and Giovanni Barrili,[2] with whom he formed enduring friendships. Barbato, in a characterization of Petrarch contained in the introduction of his Commentary on Petrarch's *Fam.* xii 2,[3] refers thus to Petrarch's visit to Naples and to the beginning of their friendship:

et est praeter universas alias animi sui dotes magne fidelitatis, plene caritatis et perfecte humilitatis: magne fidelitatis in eo quod brevis consuetudinis causa quam infra quadriduum solum cum preclare memorie rege Roberto habere potuit, sic eum mortuum ut viventem in suis veneratur operibus . . . plene caritatis, adeo quod de Barbato sulmonensi, quem infra eandem actitudinem temporis amicum sibi coniunxerat, in quadam epistola . . . sibi transmissa dicat: Quid michi Barbato meo carius, quid dulcius? . . .

While Petrarch was in Naples King Robert appointed him to a chaplaincy, which can hardly have been more than honorary. According to an unconfirmed statement made by Boccaccio in his Life of Petrarch, King Robert, much impressed by Petrarch's exaltation of poetic studies, "sibi . . . in preceptorem ipsum Franciscum dummodo ibidem vellet remanere instantissime postulavit."[4] However that may be, plans were certainly made, while Petrarch was in Naples, for him to return and take up residence there, under the patronage of King Robert: to such plans, abandoned after King Robert's death, Petrarch refers in two letters written to Barbato in later years—each reference stressing the fact that such residence would have given their friendship an intimate character. *Met.* i 1 opens with the lines

Si michi seva pium servassent sidera regem,
pars animi Barbate mei, non litera cordis
nuntia per vastos tractus telluris et unde

[2] On Barrili see above, p. 125, n. 55.
[3] Part of the introduction of this Commentary and the beginning of the commentary proper are printed by Faraglia, pp. 353–357.
[4] See Wilkins 1, pp. 50–51.

ambiguum tentaret iter; tua lumina presens
aspicerem, vox viva tuas contingeret aures;

and refers to the particular hopes of Barbato and Petrarch in the
clause (ll. 18–19) "verum ordine vite / proposito excutimur."
In *Fam.* xii 7 Petrarch writes: "Ille qui nos vivens animo copu-
larat, corpore disiunxit moriens totumque propositum vite nostre
mesta rerum mutatione prevertit."

Fam. iv 8

This letter, Petrarch's first letter to Barbato, written in Pisa
on 30 April 1341, is a brief account of the coronation ceremony,
and of dangers incurred between Rome and Pisa. As to these
dangers, Petrarch writes, Barbato may learn fully from the messenger who bears the letter. On the same day Petrarch wrote to
King Robert a longer account of the coronation, *Fam.* iv 7: the
two letters were doubtless sent to Naples by the same messenger.

Fam. v 1

This letter, dated "IV Kal. Iunias," was written in Vaucluse
on the day following a day on which Petrarch, in Avignon, had
heard a report of the death of King Robert: "hec interea tibi flens
ad fontem Sorgie dictabam . . . quo heri ad vesperam solus fugi,
cum mane me Rodani ad ripam rumor mestissimus invenisset." At
one point in the letter Petrarch writes: "Duos ingenii duces habui:
utrunque michi annus hic abstulit, et de altero quidem, nuper,
dum adhuc essem in Italia . . . nostro cum Lelio questus sum."
The reference is undoubtedly to *Fam.* iv 13, a lament on the
death of Giacomo Colonna, which occurred not long before
1 October 1341.[5]

King Robert died on 19 or 20 January 1343.[6] The news of
his death must have been sent to Avignon by couriers travelling
with the utmost speed. The distance to be covered was 600 miles
or more; the latter part of the way led through the Alps; and it
was winter. Leaving Naples on the 20th, couriers could hardly

---

[5] His successor was appointed on that date: see Eubel, p. 310.
[6] The date is given as 19 January by Romolo Caggese, *Roberto d'Angiò
e i suoi tempi* (Florence, 1930), ii, 424, and as 20 January in Léonard 1,
i, 227.

have reached Avignon by the end of the month: they would certainly have arrived by the middle of February. Yet Petrarch's letter is dated 29 May.

De Sade [7] attempts to solve the difficulty by saying that the month named in the date should be February, not June—which would mean that the letter would have been written on 29 January, and that the news had reached Avignon on the 28th. This is mere guesswork: there would seem to be no reason why a scribe should have copied "Februarias" as "Iunias." Furthermore, it is all but impossible that the news of the King's death should have reached Avignon by the 28th.

Fracassetti [8] accepts De Sade's proposed date, and notes that if Petrarch had been writing in May 1343 he could hardly have used the words "utrunque michi annus hic abstulit" with reference to the death of Giacomo Colonna. Thinking, rightly, that Petrarch could hardly have written thus even in January 1343, Fracassetti suggests, "per via di congettura," that the death to which Petrarch was referring was not that of Giacomo Colonna, but that of Convenevole da Prato. This also is a poor guess: it is very unlikely that Petrarch, though he held the memory of Convenevole in grateful honor, should have bracketed him with King Robert as one of his two "ingenii duces"; we have no reason to suppose that Petrarch wrote to Lelius about the death of Convenevole; and the probabilities are that Convenevole died early in 1338.[9]

Tatham,[10] who says "The news of the sovereign's death would take at least a fortnight to reach his Provençal dominions," rejects De Sade's date, and suggests in its place "IV. Non. Febr." —that is, 2 February. Tatham's guess may be right, but it is nothing more than a guess. A double scribal error, "Kal." for "Non." and "Iunias" for "Febr." is inherently improbable; and Tatham's suggestion does not help matters with regard to the length of time elapsed since the death of Giacomo Colonna.

---

[7] De Sade, ii, 84.

[8] Fracassetti 2, ad loc.

[9] Giulio Ciani, Ser Convenevole da Prato (Prato, 1913), p. 83.

[10] Tatham, ii, 287.

mained there until the early part or the middle of December. During this stay in Naples he saw much of Barbato: a reminiscent passage in *Sen.* ii 1 contains the clause "neque mihi per id tempus absque illo dies ullus ageretur." In the course of this visit, as Petrarch tells in the same letter, Barbato succeeded, after repeated efforts, in getting Petrarch to give him a copy of thirty-four lines of the *Africa;* and, as we are told in *Sen.* xvi 1, Barbato gave Petrarch a small volume containing writings of Cicero. On 23 November, as we learn from *Fam.* v 4, Petrarch, Barbato, and Giovanni Barrili made an excursion together to Baia and other places on the northern shore of the Bay of Naples.

Met. ii 7

This *epistola*, written in Naples, urges Barbato to be his guide and companion in an excursion to Baia and near-by places. Since this excursion was actually made on 23 November this *epistola* must have been written before that day. Its proper dating is then "within the period mid-October–22 November 1343."

Met. ii 16

This epistola begins with the lines

> Dulcis amice, vale. Tua si michi semper imago
> it presens mecumque sedet mecumque quiescit,
> redde vices,

and contains the lines

> sed enim me dextera regis
> ripa Padi levumque patris latus Apennini
> arvaque pontifrago circum contermina Parme
> nunc reducem expectant Planeque umbracula Silve;
> namque ibi pyerius gelidum me contigit ardor.
> *Africa* nostra michi longum intermissa iacebat;
> excivit locus ingenium lapsumque repente
> restituit calamum.

In the latter part of the poem Petrarch refers again to the work he had done on the *Africa* at Selvapiana, and expresses the hope that he may now finish it:

Nunc revidere velim cepti michi conscius alti
extremamque manum longo imposuisse labori,
quem traxit fortuna diu. Si dextra favebunt
sidera, tum tandem incipiet secura vagari
Africa per Latium studio redimita supremo
Scipiadesque meus.

This *epistola* may have been written either just before
Petrarch left Naples, as Miss Magrini, Mascetta-Caracci, and
Bianchi think, or in the course of his journey from Naples to
Parma, as Cochin, Tatham, Foresti, and Rizzi think. The latter
opinion seems preferable in view of the words "Tua si michi
semper imago / it presens." Miss Magrini and Rizzi date the
epistola as of December 1343, and Cochin dates it as of that
month or the next. A more exact dating would be "within
the period late November–mid-December 1343." [13]

Fam. v 10

This letter tells of Petrarch's escape from Parma on the night
of 23 February 1345 and of the subsequent adventures that
brought him finally to Bologna on the 25th. The letter is dated
"V Kal. Martias, Bononia." After telling of the fall of Petrarch's
horse, on the night of the 23rd—a fall that left Petrarch "confractus ac pene exanimatus"—the letter continues: "Colligo tamen
in extremis animum et assurgo; quique multis iam diebus inter-
iectis ad os manum referre nondum valeo, tunc sublevante metu
in equum reinsilui." From the words "multis iam diebus inter-
iectis" D'Ovidio, Tatham, and Foresti have inferred that the
letter, despite its date, must have been written several days after
23 February.[14] D'Ovidio calls attention also to the last two
sentences of the letter—which read "Circa curam corporis, fit

---

[13] Magrini, p. 123; Mascetta-Caracci, pp. 524–529; Cochin, "Les 'Epistolae metricae' de Pétrarque," in *GSLI*, LXXIV (1919), 16; Tatham, II, 333;
Foresti 1, p. 156; and Rizzi 1, p. 53. Mascetta-Caracci's inherently improbable theory that Petrarch did not leave Naples and did not write this
epistola until the spring of 1344 is sufficiently disproved by the fact that he
wrote *Fam.* v 7 in Parma on 27 December 1343: see Foresti 1, p. 140.

[14] Francesco d'Ovidio, "Questioni di geografia petrarchesca," in R.
Accademia di Scienze Morali e Politiche di Napoli, *Atti*, XXIII (1889),
77–78; Tatham, II, 343; Foresti 1, p. 140.

quantum humano ingenio fieri potest; spes est potius certa, quam velox. Estatis opem medici, ego Dei omnipotentis auxilium expecto; interim torpens mihi dextra non obsequitur, animus fit promptior in adversis"—and remarks that they also indicate that Petrarch had been in Bologna "da un pezzo" when he wrote the letter. If that is the case, Petrarch, in dating the letter, must have been thinking of the date of his arrival in Bologna. But it seems to me more probable that the date given is the date when the letter was actually dictated; that the sending of the letter was delayed for several days for lack of a carrier or for some other cause; and that shortly before it was sent Petrarch added the last two sentences, and inserted the words "quique . . . valeo." It may well be that the sentence in which those words now appear was, as originally dictated, simply this: "Colligo tamen in extremis animum et assurgo; tunc sublevante metu in equum reinsilui." I should date the letter, then, as of "25 February 1345, or possibly some days later."

A Lost Letter of Barbato?

It may well be that *Fam.* VI 5, written on 1 August 1346, was written in response to a letter received from Barbato. If so, that letter must have concerned the murder of Andrew of Hungary, consort of Queen Joan of Naples, which occurred on 18 September 1345; and it must have been written before the end of 1345. A letter written by Barbato at that time might well have taken several months to reach Petrarch, who had returned from Italy to Provence late in 1345:[15] six years later, under similar conditions, a letter of Barbato took almost a year to reach Petrarch, as will appear below.

Fam. VI 5

To this long letter, when he placed it among the *Familiares*, Petrarch gave the title "Ad Barbatum Sulmonensem, de miserabili et indigna morte regis Andree." The first pages of the letter,

---

[15] He had been in Parma as late as 25 October—see Pierre de Nolhac, *Pétrarque et l'humanisme*, 2d ed. (Paris, 1907), II, 228—and had dated *Fam.* XXIV 4 as written in Avignon on 19 December 1345.

while they contain references to the fate of Andrew, are devoted chiefly to relatively restrained reflections on the bad conditions that had prevailed in Naples after the death of King Robert, as Petrarch had observed them on the occasion of his visit in 1343. The main portion of the letter, beginning shortly before the exclamation "O brevi multum mutata Neapolis, o infelix Aversa!" consists chiefly of an impassioned indictment of those responsible for the crime. The letter ends with this sentence: "Hec tibi quoque, Sorgie ad fontem, quo rursus e tanto Italie naufragio velut in portum fugi, et preteriti dolens et venturi trepidus, dictabam Kalendis Sextilibus, intempesta nocte." In view of the facts that the date in this case employs the distinctive word "Sextilibus," and that it is not abbreviated and appended to the letter in the usual way, but is written out in full and is incorporated in the text of the letter, there can be no reasonable doubt of its authenticity: the year must therefore be 1346. It is indeed strange that so long a time should have elapsed between the murder and the writing of this letter, but it is not inexplicable. It may be, for instance, that Petrarch, not having written immediately when the news first reached him, let the matter rest until the receipt of a delayed letter made an answer compulsory; or it may be that *Fam.* vi 5 was drafted not long after Petrarch learned of the murder, but was laid aside until the time came when he could complete and polish it, and could find a trusty messenger— the date 1 August being, on this hypothesis, the date of the finishing of the letter.[16]

Var. 49

This letter was "Data in inferno viventium, XVIII Januarii":

---

[16] De Sade, ii, 252–253, Fracassetti 2, *ad loc.*, and Tatham, ii, 369, being without knowledge of the actual text of the date, think it incredible that the letter could have been written as late as the summer following the murder: Fracassetti assigns it to the period October–December 1345, and Tatham (with a wild guess that the original date might have been "VI Kal. Nov.") to 27 October 1345. Rossetti, i, 255, is uncertain whether the letter should be assigned to the latter part of 1345 or to the summer of 1346. Rizzi 1, pp. 214–217, recognizes the validity of the reading "Kalendis Sextilibus."

it is agreed that the year was 1347.[17] The letter is in two parts: the first is a recommendation for Laelius; the second is a covering message for a copy of Petrarch's second Eclogue. In the first part Barbato is asked to give to Laelius (here called also Lellus Petri Stephani) such assistance as he can in the matters of which the Archbishop of Trani will have spoken to Barbato. The man referred to was certainly Guillaume de Rosières, who had been appointed to the archbishopric of Trani on 4 April 1343, and named early in October (just at the time when Petrarch arrived in Naples) as collector of papal revenues in the Kingdom of Naples. He had also the status of a papal nuncio, and until the summer of 1347 he remained an important and influential figure in Neapolitan affairs. On 28 February 1344 he was transferred to the archbishopric of Brindisi, and on 7 April 1346 to the bishopric of Montecassino: it is natural enough, however, that Petrarch should have referred to him by the title he held at the time of Petrarch's visit in 1343. There is no indication that his successor in the archbishopric of Trani, one Philippus de Neapoli, ever played any significant part in public affairs.[18] In the first part of the letter, also, Barbato is asked to see that "Iupiter noster egregius" (certainly Petrarch's other chief Neapolitan friend, Giovanni Barrili) regards it as addressed to himself also; and Petrarch refers to himself as "suum Mercurium." In the second part of the letter the three characters of the eclogue are identified in this passage: "per Idaeum Iovem nostrum, qui in Ida Cretensi altus est: per Pythiam Barbatum meum, propter insignem amicitiae gloriam, quam cum mihi non arrogem, non Damon elegi esse sed Silvius." Why it should be said that Barrili "in Ida Cretensi altus est" we do not know: he was a member of a prominent Neapolitan family. Barrili being called Jove, Petrarch's name of Mercury for himself would seem to have been suggested by *Acts* 14, 11: "Et vocabant Barnabam Jovem, Paulum vero Mercurium: quoniam ipse erat dux verbi."

---

[17] Fracassetti 2, *ad loc.*; Carrara 3, p. 142; Tatham, ii, 378; and Rizzi 1, p. 216. The single dissent, that of Cesareo 1, pp. 97–98, is based primarily on the dating "in inferno viventium," and is quite negligible.

[18] On Guillaume see Eubel, pp. 149, 169, and 491, and Léonard 1, *passim* (see index). Philippus de Neapoli is not mentioned by Léonard.

To this letter Petrarch appended the eight-line epigram—a tiny letter of recommendation in verse—that begins with the line

Laelius antiquis celebratum nomen amicis

and ends with the line

Faveris ergo mihi, si sibi, care, faves.

A Lost Letter of Barbato?

At one point in *Fam.* VII 1, written on 11 September 1347, Petrarch, recalling himself from a digression, writes: "et evehebar longius, nisi me expectans et crebro interpellans hic nuntius revocasset." This suggests, but does not prove, that *Fam.* VII 1 was written in response to a letter just received from Barbato. If so, Barbato's letter must have concerned the menace or the actuality of the Hungarian invasion, and must have been written in July or August 1347.

Fam. VII 1

In this letter, dated "Avinione, properanter atque anxie, III Idus Septembris," Petrarch refers to the belated approach of vengeance for the murder of Andrew of Hungary—"ecce iam pulvis italicus gressu quatitur barbarico—" and expresses his fear for the Kingdom of Naples and his distress on hearing that Sulmona has fallen:

In has terras amenissimas ab asperrimis Danubii ripis preceps ruit exercitus, et celi nostri serenitatem fedis nubibus involvit ab aquilone oriens procella, quam vereor ne, dum responsum tuum operior, cum ingenti fragore detonuerit. Sic omnia iam in extremum adducta referuntur; iam Sulmonem primo belli impetu calcatum in ditionem hostium pervenisse fama est.

Petrarch fears for Barbato, and makes him two offers: he will do anything he can for him through a request to Cola di Rienzo, in whose favor he (Petrarch) stands high; and he invites Barbato to come to live with him in Parma—he is himself planning to return to Italy: "me ab occidente reversurum."

The expressions of affection contained in this letter evidently meant much to Barbato: the introduction of his Commentary on

Met. 1 1

That this poem is the dedicatory poem for the *Epistolae metricae* as a whole is proved both by the very fact of its position and by its concluding clause:

nam dum maiora paramus
hunc tibi devoveo studii iuvenilis honorem.

The corresponding prose letter, *Fam.* 1 1 (Fracassetti's *Praefatio*), in which Petrarch dedicates the *Familiares* to his Socrates, contains this passage, which shows that both dedications were made in accordance with previous promises (the "Ea" are the "poemata" and prose letters that Petrarch had refrained from burning): "Ea vero duorum amicorum libranti ingenia hac lance partiri visum est, ut prosa tibi, carmen Barbato cederet; sic enim et vos olim optare solitos et me pollicitum esse memineram."

Met. 1 1 begins with the five lines expressive of friendship for Barbato that have been quoted above (on pp. 215–216), and continues with a tribute to the memory of King Robert, and then with a statement, in ll. 22–25, to the effect that Petrarch is writing in Northern Italy (very possibly in Mantua):

bustum tibi forte Maronis
obtigit in partem vatis, michi cessit origo,
amnibus ac toto disiungimur Apennino.
Hinc mea vox mittenda tibi est . . .[20]

The rest of the poem is as follows:

29   Memor ergo precum, dilecte, tuarum
institui exiguam sparsi tibi mittere partem
carminis, exacte percurrens otia vite.
(32–39: "As you read you will see that these poems are
youthful productions.")
40   Affectus animi varios bellumque sequacis
perlegis invidie curasque revolvis inanes,
quas humilis tenero stilus olim effudit in evo;

---

[20] Miss Magrini, p. 55, and Foresti 1, p. 349, think that these lines indicate that the poem was written in Mantua. Cochin, art. cit. in n. 13, p. 8, thinks that the reference is to Northern Italy in general. Rizzi 1, p. 400, is undecided. I agree with Cochin; but no definite decision appears to be possible.

perlegis et lacrimas et quod pharetratus acuta
ille puer puero fecit michi cuspide vulnus.
(45–59 are devoted to general moralization.[21])
60   Tempus edax minuit quem Mors exstinxit amorem,
flamma furens annis, tumulo cessere faville.
Nunc breve marmor habet longos quibus arsimus ignes,
pectore nunc gelido calidos miseramur amantes,
iamque arsisse pudet. Veteres tranquilla tumultus
65   mens horret, relegens alium putat ista locutum.
Sed iam nequicquam latebras circumspicit: ardens
turba premit comitum, quos par insania iactat,
dulce quibus conferre suis aliena; nec illos
submovisse sat est; acies nam maior apertam
70   protrahit in lucem. Durum, sed et ipse per urbes
iam populo plaudente legor, nec Musa regressum
secreti iam callis habet, vetitumque latere est.
Prodeat impexis ad te festina capillis
ac fluxo discincta sinu, veniamque precetur,
75   non laudem. Veniet tempus dum forte superbis
passibus atque alio redeat spectanda paratu.
Nunc tibi qualis erat sub prima etate, priusquam
figeret in thalamo speculum, vultumque comasque
inciperet cohibere vagas, occurrit, amice,
80   cui semper—rex quantus Amor!—non seria tantum
sed nuge placuere mee. Tu consule, queso,
parva licet, magni; nam dum maiora paramus
hunc tibi devoveo studii iuvenilis honorem.

In view of the fact that this poem is the dedicatory poem
for the *Epistolae metricae*, it seems obvious that the other poems
intended to be sent with it must have been individual *epistolae
metricae*. Recently, indeed, this opinion has prevailed without
challenge. Divergent and not altogether groundless opinions,
however, had formerly been advanced; and these opinions still
call for a critical review, especially since they have been thought
to carry implications that reach beyond the *Epistolae metricae*.

The idea that the poems in question were Italian poems rather
than *epistolae metricae* was first broached by Rossetti,[22] who

---

[21] Foresti 1, pp. 353–355, thinks that these lines are a later insertion.
Bianchi doubts this: see his "Le 'Epistolae metricae' del Petrarca," in R.
Scuola Normale di Pisa, *Annali*, Ser. II, IX (1940), 260–261.
[22] II, 3.

writes: "Con questa epistola mandava il Petrarca all'amico Barbato le sue rime amorose, cioè quello che noi appelliamo il suo
Canzoniere." He does not mention the fact that *Met.* i 1 is the
dedicatory letter for the *Epistolae metricae.*

Fracassetti,[23] disagreeing with Rossetti, expresses the opinion
that the poems in question were "le sue epistole poetiche alle
quali forse anche aggiunse le liriche italiane."

In two incidental remarks Gaspary [24] echoes Rossetti, without argument, and without recognition of the fact that i 1 is
the dedicatory letter for the *Epistolae metricae.*

Volpi,[25] however, maintains that the poems in question were
epistolae metricae, and supports his position by two arguments:
first, that the reference in *Fam.* i 1 shows that Petrarch was intending to dedicate the *Epistolae metricae* to Barbato, as he had
promised to do; and, second, that the words "bellumque sequacis
/ perlegis invidie" (ll. 40–41) prove that some of the poems in
question deal with the envy that beset Petrarch: no such poems
appear in the Canzoniere.

The idea that the poems in question were Italian was developed at some length by Melodia,[26] who refers to Volpi's argument without mentioning the fact of dedication, and attempts
to refute Volpi's second argument by saying that the envy referred to may have been envy incurred through Petrarch's fame
as the author of Italian poems (Melodia fails to realize the fact
that what Petrarch is saying in ll. 40–41 is that *some of the poems
in question deal with the envy that has beset him,* and the fact that
no such poems appear in the *Canzoniere*). Melodia's positive
arguments are, first, that the Italian poems in general, as against
only two of the *Epistolae metricae,* deal with love; second, that
poems dealing with love would have been welcome to lovers in
general and to Barbato, to whom, among the writings of Petrarch,
"non seria tantum / sed nuge placuere" (ll. 80–81: Melodia sug-

---

[23] In his note on *Fam.* xii 7.
[24] Adolf Gaspary, *Geschichte der Italienischen Literatur* (Berlin,
1885), i, 461 and 473.
[25] Volpi 1, p. 262.
[26] Melodia, pp. 90–91.

gests that the "seria" may have been *epistolae metricae*); and, third, that the references to the poems in question in the words "sparsi" (l. 30) and "nuge" correspond to Petrarch's well-known uses of the same or similar words with reference to his Italian poems.

In a review of Melodia's book Carrara,[27] without recognition of the fact that I 1 is the dedicatory letter for the *Epistolae metricae*, indicates his agreement with Melodia, adding (with reference to ll. 66–68): "A che, meglio che ai versi d'amore, converrebbe l'aspettazione ansiosa dei compagni di sventura?"

Miss Magrini[28] discusses the problem at considerable length and very well indeed, coming to the conclusion that the poems in question must have been *epistolae metricae* and *epistolae metricae* only. She insists upon the implications of the fact that I 1 is the dedicatory letter for the *Epistolae metricae* as a whole; she reënforces Volpi's first argument by reference to *Fam.* XXII 3 (written to Barbato in or after 1360), which begins thus: "Diu multumque dubius fui, Barbate carissime, an epystolas metricas olim tibi inscriptas aliquando mitterem an vero supprimerem et penitus abderem"; she reënforces Volpi's second argument by pointing out that the "invidia" of which Petrarch writes is precisely the subject of the two *epistolae metricae* (II 10 and 17) that are addressed to "Zoilus"; she notes that the references in I 1 to the poems in question as being youthful productions are matched by similar references in *Fam.* XXII 3 which are applied specifically to the *Epistolae metricae;* she notes that the references in I 1 to poems dealing with love are explicable as referring to *Met.* I 7 and 8; she points out that the clause in I 1, "Durum, sed et ipse per urbes / iam populo plaudente legor" (ll. 70–71) is matched by Petrarch's statement, in *Fam.* XXII 3, that he would have decided to destroy the *epistolae metricae* "nisi . . . ferme omnia in publicum exivissent"; and she suggests that one might concede that when Petrarch wrote ll. 70 ff. his Italian poems were present to his mind and still not infer that the poems to be sent with I 1 were Italian poems.

---

[27] In *Giornale dantesco*, VII (1899), 129–132.
[28] Pp. 51–55.

Cochin [29] recognizes clearly the dedicatory character of I 1 and the consequence that the poems in question were *epistolae metricae*: "Il faut considérer d'abord l'épître dédicatoire, qui est en tête du recueil: le poète offre ses Épîtres latines en vers au fidèle ami." But he is impressed by the passages in which the poems in question are referred to as youthful productions, as poems dealing with love, as "nuge," and as widely sought and read. On the first of these points, however, he notes that Petrarch's use of terms of age was far from precise, that in *Sen.* III 4 Petrarch refers to the *Epistolae metricae* as a "juvenile opus," and that more of them were written in the years 1341–1343 than at any later time; and on the fourth point he says: "Le public lettré rechercha les Épîtres, où il voyait renaître la muse antique; il les rechercha avec avidité," citing as an example a marginal note by Lapo da Castiglionchio, appended to a group of four *epistolae metricae*, which reads in part: "Has epistolas et quedam alia . . . per me non sine labore quesita . . . in hoc eodem libello scribi et collocari feci." In fine, Cochin thinks it possible that as Petrarch wrote certain passages he had his Italian poems in mind; but this does not lead him to any questioning of the fact that the poems referred to as to be sent with I 1 were *epistolae metricae*.

Both Foresti and Rizzi [30] refer to I 1 as the dedicatory letter for the *Epistolae metricae*. Neither one discusses the problem of the poems in question; but both write evidently in the belief that those poems were *epistolae metricae*.

Bianchi [31] is certain that those poems were *epistolae metricae*: he does not discuss the problem, however, except to point out that the references in I 1 to the fewness, the youthfulness, and the themes of the poems in question are readily explicable on the theory that when Petrarch wrote I 1 the collection was much smaller than it ultimately became, and that it consisted largely of early poems.

It may be noted that critical envy is referred to not only in *Met.* II 10 and 17 but also in II 13 and in III 26, and that II 10 is,

[29] Art. cit., pp. 7–9.
[30] Foresti 1, pp. 321 and 349–350; Rizzi 1, pp. 400–402.
[31] *Loc. cit.* in n. 21.

with one exception (II 14), the longest of the *Epistolae metricae;* also that the theme of Laura is treated not only in I 7 and 8 but also in III 27, and that I 7 is one of the longest of the *Epistolae metricae*, and perhaps the most striking of them all.

The last part of I 1, from l. 75 to the end, speaks of a greater poetic enterprise that Petrarch has in preparation. The time will come, perhaps, when his Muse will appear not in humble and careless guise, as at present, but "superbis / passibus atque alio . . . spectanda paratu." And the poem ends with the clause

> nam dum maiora paramus
> hunc tibi devoveo studii iuvenilis honorem.

Since the poems intended to be sent with I 1 were Latin poems, the greater enterprise here referred to must have been an enterprise in Latin verse. It was in all probability, as both Carrara and Miss Magrini suggest, the *Africa*. To the *Africa*, and to the *Africa* only, the phrases "superbis passibus," "alio spectanda paratu," and "dum maiora paramus" would seem to apply perfectly; and Barbato's known desire to possess the *Africa* was very strong indeed. The only other possibilities, both extremely unlikely, are the *Bucolicum carmen*, which has not by any means the stateliness of the *Africa*, or some project of which we have no knowledge.

Melodia, moving from his mistaken premise that the poems intended to be sent with I 1 were Italian poems, asserts further that the greater enterprise must also have been an enterprise in Italian verse, and that it must therefore have been the *Triumphs*. But even Carrara, though accepting Melodia's first premise, rejects this further idea as being completely untenable. It is indeed impossible that all the poems referred to in the dedicatory poem for the *Epistolae metricae* should have been Italian poems; and it is impossible that in I 1, in which Petrarch writes of his love for Laura as something of which he was ashamed, he could have referred to the *Triumphs*, in which Laura is exalted, in the terms in which he refers to this greater enterprise.

Since the poem was written after Petrarch learned of the death of Laura (the news of which reached him on 19 May 1348)

nostri sonantem calamum recognovi." Since *Fam.* xii 2 was written on 20 February and the acknowledgment written by Barbato had reached Petrarch before 21 May (on which date it is referred to in another letter of Petrarch, *Fam.* xii 11, addressed to Bartolomeo Carbone dei Papazurri), the acknowledgment must have been written within the period March–mid-May 1352.

Met. iii 18

This brief poem expresses Petrarch's contentment in the tranquil home he had found in Milan. It begins:

> Rus michi tranquillum media contingit in urbe,
> rure vel urbs medio,

and contains the lines (12–16):

> Hic mihi tanta quies, quantam nec valle sonora
> Parnasi nec cecropie per menia ville
> invenit studiosa cohors heremoque silenti
> vix Egiptiace cives, nisi fallor, arene
> angelici sensere patres.

It was doubtless written, as Miss Magrini, Foresti, and Bianchi all think, soon after Petrarch, returning from Provence to Italy in May, 1353, took up his abode in Milan.[35]

Met. iii 19

This poem begins with a statement that Petrarch has been bidden to go to his hated Avignon, as he has so often gone before, and that this journey is to be made in winter:

---

[35] Magrini, pp. 151–152; Foresti 1, p. 309; Bianchi, p. 797. Omero Masnovo, in his "La data di due epistole metriche di F. Petrarca," in *Archivio storico per le provincie parmensi*, Ser. iii, i (1936), 70–80, attempts to prove that this *epistola* was written in Parma in the period 1349–1351; but his arguments have little weight as compared with the close correspondence of the *epistola* to the account of Petrarch's situation in Milan as reported to Nelli in *Fam.* xvi 11 (wrongly referred to by Miss Magrini as xvi 12 and by Bianchi as xvi 2), which was certainly written in August 1353. The phrase "in maxima frequentissimaque urbe solitudinem," which occurs in that letter, constitutes the very theme of the *epistola*.

Sors sua quenque vocat: rigidam transire per Alpem
sole nivem radio nondum frangente iubemur,
obscenosque locos informia claustra malorum
atque feram Rodani totiens contingere ripam.

Fate whirls him relentlessly from place to place (ll. 14–16):

huc volvis et illuc,
nullaque iam tellus, nullus michi permanet aer;
incola ceu nusquam, sic sum peregrinus ubique.

He has not much longer to live (ll. 20–21 and 26–27):

patere hanc in rure reposto
etatem transire brevem. Iam proxima mors est . . .
qualem sperare senectam
linquitur?

The fact that he has refused a proffered high position has not
sufficed to win him freedom from interference (ll. 37–38):

sic nil michi profuit altum
solicite vitasse locum.

So he must go again by a way already trodden, by the Trentino
and the headwaters of the Danube and the Rhine and the German lakes, since hostilities close the direct way (ll. 40–45):

Sors igitur mea me repetit, tritumque viator
prendere iussus iter carosque relinquere amicos,
urgeor alpinum raptim penetrare Tridentum
Danubiumque novum iuvenemque ab origine Rhenum
germanosque lacus; claudit namque hostis apertas
ense vias.

He must obey (ll. 45–46):

Quid agam? Rebus parere coactum
durius est, et ferre iugum sine murmure prestat.

He has been enjoying a rare period of tranquillity, but must now
undertake a difficult task (ll. 47–52):

Pareo. Tranquillum dulcis michi fluxerat annus,
sed brevis heu nimiumque fugax, oblitaque forte
tantisper fortuna mei, dum cetera gaudet
precipiti versare rota, michi grata reliquit
otia; nunc eadem sphingosa negotia reddit,
et labor invitus placidam fugat ecce quietem.

In the concluding line (53) Barbato is advised not to leave his quiet home (in Sulmona):

Tu, felix Barbato, tuum ne desere nidum.

Thrice and only thrice, after he had become acquainted with Barbato, did Petrarch return from Italy to Provence—in 1342, in 1345, and in 1351—and the data of the poem do not correspond to the conditions of any one of these three returns. In 1342 Petrarch could not have used the word "totiens" with reference to previous returns to Avignon; in 1342 (being then, in the first half of the year, 37 years of age) he could not have said of himself, "Iam proxima mors est"; in 1342 he had not refused any proffered high position; and in 1342 Cardinal Colonna (who alone, at that time, could have called him back to Avignon) would certainly not have employed him to carry on "sphingosa negotia" ("sphingosa" means "sphinx-like") at the papal court. Furthermore (though these considerations are in themselves less decisive) it is very unlikely that in 1342, when Petrarch's relations with Cardinal Colonna were still cordial, he should have referred to these relations in such words as "Rebus parere coactum / durius est, et ferre iugum sine murmure prestat"; no other expression of Petrarch's hatred for Avignon is of so early a date (and it is to be remembered that Laura was still living in 1342); and it is probable that the return in 1342 took place in the spring rather than in the winter, since in *Var.* 57, written in Parma on 31 January 1342 to Giovanni Barrili, then in Naples, Petrarch, after saying that he is eager to return to Naples, continues: "sed catena multiplicis obligationis, qua domino Azoni sum constrictus, me hucusque detinuit."

In 1345, the year of his perilous escape from Parma, he could not possibly have spoken of a preceding period of tranquillity; and in 1351 he returned to Provence in June, and by way of Piacenza and Mont Genèvre.

Foresti [36] (who disposes adequately of earlier discussions of the date of this poem) points out that in the winter of 1353–1354, according to *Fam.* XVII 6 and 10 (this latter letter being dated

---

[36] Foresti 1, pp. 300–311.

1 January), Petrarch, then living in Milan, was designated, certainly by Archbishop Giovanni Visconti (who had previously sent Petrarch on an embassy to Venice), as a member of an embassy to Avignon, concerned with the establishment of peace between Genoa and Venice; and that the data of the poem correspond perfectly to the conditions of the proposed embassy (which, for reasons indicated by Foresti, was never actually sent). In 1352 Petrarch had for the second time refused an apostolic secretaryship; the year 1353 had certainly brought to him, in Milan, a tranquillity that was in striking contrast with the strenuous experiences of the two preceding years in Provence; in the order of the *Epistolae metricae* the poem immediately follows III 18, written in Milan in 1353; and that poem, in its very first line, expresses Petrarch's relief in the tranquillity he has found:

Rus michi tranquillum media contingit in urbe.

Foresti might have noted also the correspondence between the "quies" of III 18 (l. 13) and the "quietem" of III 19 (l. 52), and he might have noted also the fact that since in 1345 Petrarch had returned by way of the Trentino he might well have referred to that route, in III 19, as a "tritum . . . iter."

Foresti's argument is in fact conclusive; yet Rizzi [37] (who, like Foresti, refutes effectively certain earlier arguments) maintains that the poem relates to the return of 1342—an opinion that has already been shown to be untenable. Rizzi attacks Foresti's argument, first, on the ground that Petrarch could not have considered 1353 a year of tranquillity, since it had witnessed both Petrarch's abandonment of Vaucluse and Avignon and the protests of Florentine friends against his establishment in Milan (Rizzi fails to note the tranquillity that is the theme of III 18), and, second, because III 19 refers to the command as compulsory and entirely unwelcome, whereas the tone of *Fam.* XVII 6 in this regard is quite different. In point of fact the passage in question in *Fam.* XVII 6 reads thus:

Parebo tamen ut qui iubenti nil penitus negare velim idque eo promptius, quoniam, ut propie dixerim, non iubet ille sed rogat,

---

[37] Rizzi 1, pp. 80–86.

fortunam suam quamvis altissimam humanitate illa notissima super-
gressus. Quantum preterea viarum rigor et brumalis terret asperitas,
tantum profectionis causa delectat; eo enim ad pacem inter potentis-
simos duos Italie populos reformandam, tam feliciter utinam quam
libenter.

The differences, however, are in fact "sfumature diverse," as
Foresti calls them, matters of emphasis appropriate for the two
addressees: Barbato was an intimate friend; Bernardo Anguissola,
the addressee of *Fam.* xvii 6, was an official in the service of the
Visconti. The striking likenesses between the two prose letters
and *Met.* iii 19 far outweigh these slight differences.

Barbato's Packets of Scissors

Misc. 11, which, as will presently appear, was written in
Milan on 4 October 1355, contains this passage:

Forficulas tuas licteris ad me missis inclusas habui, et anno altero
sine licteris sex paria ab Avenione receperam, de quibus partem feci
illi qui tunc in Liguria participem non habebat, nunc partem ibi non
habet, nisi quantum corpore occupat.[38] Audieram etiam te prius
alia quinque paria misisse, que ad me non pervenerunt, Florentie, ut
dicitur, intercepta; nec minus ideo gratias ago.

From this passage it appears (1) that a pair of scissors had been
sent with Barbato's letter "Extremum Olimpiadis," which Petrarch, as will presently appear, had received just before writing
Misc. 11; (2) that in the course of the year 1354—and before
5 October, the date of the death of Archbishop Giovanni
Visconti—there had been forwarded to Petrarch, from Avignon,
a packet from Barbato containing six pairs of scissors and not
accompanied by any letter; and (3) that Barbato had previously
sent him a packet, containing five pairs, which had never reached
him, having been held, according to report, in Florence. The
six-pair packet would seem to have been sent at a time when
Barbato thought that Petrarch was in Provence: probably, then,
not later than 1353. Interception of the five-pair packet in

---

[38] The reference is clearly to the Archbishop Giovanni Visconti, who
died on 5 October 1354: see Marco Vattasso, *Del Petrarca e di alcuni suoi
amici* (=*Studi e testi*, 14) (Rome, 1904), p. 31, n. 1.

Florence would have been slightly more probable if Petrarch were in Provence than if he were in Italy: there is then some slight probability that this packet was sent in 1351 or 1352. The fact that Petrarch gave some of the scissors to the Archbishop indicates that they were of some rarity and of fine craftmanship— similar, doubtless, to some of those illustrated in the *Enciclopedia italiana* article on "Forbici." It is quite possible that such scissors were a specialty of Sulmona industry.

Barbato's Lost "Extremum Olimpiadis"

In September 1355, or slightly earlier, Barbato wrote to Petrarch a letter, now lost, with regard to which a considerable amount of information is preserved in Petrarch's *Var.* 22 and *Misc.* 11 and in a note prefixed to *Var.* 22 in a Vatican MS. From that note we know that the letter began with the words "Extremum Olimpiadis." From *Var.* 22 we know that it was brought to Petrarch by a monk to whom he refers as "religiosum hunc virum" and "sanctum hunc et devotum hominem"; that the superscription designated Petrarch as "poetarum rex"; that it contained a reference to Barbato's eagerness to possess works of Petrarch (the relevant passage in *Var.* 22 reads: "amicitiae vis . . . quae te adeo solicitum ardentemque coacervandis opusculis meis fecit, quae ut memoras, ab innumeris et mirum in modum patria, moribus ac professione distantibus mendicasti"); that it made particular mention of the letters of Petrarch, reporting that Barbato had gathered a little collection of them, and that he found them all pleasing; that it referred to the monk who carried the letter as authority for the statement that Petrarch was referred to, in the region where he dwelt, as "poetarum rex"; and that he was again so referred to at the end of the letter. From *Misc.* 11 we know that it asked for full information as to Petrarch's health and activities; that it reported the admiration of one Francesco Sanità, a man unknown to Petrarch; and that there came with it a pair of scissors.

Var. 22 was written on 4 October 1355, which was, Petrarch says, the day following that on which he received Barbato's letter. We cannot tell how long a time the monk spent on his

evidently felt that *Var.* 22 should be entrusted to the Celestines, who would see that it was delivered to Barbato whether he was in Naples or in Sulmona, he decided to take advantage of the fact that Matteo was going to Naples by giving him a brief second letter to be delivered to Barbato if Matteo, "incertus an te ibi reperturus, an omnino visurus sit," should find him there. In this letter, after referring to the circumstances in which it was written, Petrarch thanks Barbato for the scissors, says that Matteo will give Barbato all the personal information he wants ("omnem statum meum . . . omnem vite mee ordinem, quid agam, quid cogitem, quid optem, quid moliar, quid expectem, ab hoc audies"); and sends his greetings to Francesco Sanità.

Barbato's "In maximis lacrimarum" (LAP 4)

At the end of this letter Barbato says that he has received Petrarch's brief letter (*Misc.* 11) from the hand of Niccolò himself, but has not yet received the longer letter (*Var.* 22). The main purpose of Barbato's letter is to convey to Petrarch the news of the death of their mutual friend Giovanni Barrili (Barbato encloses the letter, written by a jurist and man of letters named as Petrus—identified by Vattasso as Pietro di Monteforte [41]—which had brought the sad news to him); and to ask Petrarch, apparently at the suggestion of Pietro, to write an epitaph for Giovanni. Barbato's letter, as Vattasso shows, must have been written in November or December 1355.

Met. I 1 and Ecl. I sent to Barbato

From *Fam.* xx 5, written on 27 August 1358, we know, thanks to Foresti's convincing study [42] of the contents and the date of that letter, that at some time in 1357 Petrarch, finding that a Bolognese acquaintance of his was going into Southern Italy, gave him, for transmission to Barbato, copies of *Met.* I 1 and of *Ecl.* I.

---

[41] On Pietro di Monteforte see Faraglia, pp. 343–345, and a forthcoming article by Billanovich.

[42] Foresti 1, pp. 348–353.

A Lost Letter of Barbato

Fam. xx 5, which is a reply to a lost letter of Barbato, makes it clear that that lost letter had contained a pleasant reference to Niccolò Acciaiuoli, and that it reported a visit in the course of the preceding year (1357) from two men, one a Bolognese and the other from beyond the Alps, who represented themselves as friends of Petrarch and asked and received money from Barbato; and gives some basis for thinking that the lost letter indicated that Barbato had expected one or both of his visitors, returning to Northern Italy, to convey messages to Petrarch. It is evident, also, that Barbato's letter did not mention receipt of the two poems—presumably because he had expected that his thanks would be conveyed orally to Petrarch by one or both of the two visitors. Since *Fam.* xx 5 was written by Petrarch—then in Milan—on 27 August 1358, it follows that Barbato's letter was written in the spring or summer of that year.

Fam. xx 5

In *Fam.* xx 5 Petrarch refers pleasantly to Niccolò Acciaiuoli; says that he knew the Bolognese but not Barbato's other visitor; cautions Barbato against being imposed upon by men representing themselves as his (Petrarch's) friends; reports that the Bolognese had not returned to Milan, but had died; refers to the fact that the Bolognese was to have delivered the two poems to Barbato; states that he has been hoping and is still hoping to settle in Rome, and that if he succeeds in doing so he will have some other writings for Barbato, whom he will either call to Rome or, possibly, visit in Sulmona; and sends his greetings to Francesco Sanità.

Fam. xxii 3

This letter, written to accompany the collection of *Epistolae metricae*, is in effect a brief preface to the collection. Petrarch speaks of his long uncertainty as to whether he should send the poems, long since dedicated to Barbato, or suppress them; refers to them as youthful productions and depreciates them;

waiting impatiently for him to finish it; reports the joy of
Francesco Sanità on receiving Petrarch's greeting; and expresses his pleasure on seeing that Petrarch's letter was written
in Venice, and his (ill-founded) hope that Petrarch has broken
away entirely from Milan.

The Christmas Day on which Barbato received *Fam.* xxii 4
must have been that of 1360—the long delay being explicable
as due to the difficulty of finding a prompt messenger; and
Barbato's reply must have been written early in 1361.   In
Petrarch's *Misc.* 9, written on 22 June 1361, he states that he
had received Barbato's letter on the preceding day: the long
delay may have resulted from the usual difficulty as to messengers, or from Petrarch's removal from Milan to Padua, or
from both causes.

Barbato's "Convenientibus nobis"
(*LAP* 74)

From Barbato's letter "Magna, vir doctiloque," written to
Boccaccio some time after the death of Zanobi da Strada, who
died in late July or early August 1361, we learn that before
Zanobi's death Niccolò Acciaiuoli, Napoleone Orsini, and Nicola
Orsini met with Barbato in Barbato's garden in Sulmona, where
they read one of the *epistolae* of Petrarch; and that after the
reading "decreverunt dicti domini, pro conmuni omnium parte,
dicto domino Laureato de publicanda *Africa* scribere, dictusque
Magnus Senescallus promisit faciendas mihi licteras de Neapoli,
quo tunc accessurus erat, transmictere."

Barbato accordingly wrote the letter "Convenientibus
nobis," to which he gave the heading "Domino Francisco
Petracho de Florentia laureato poete preclaro viro amico
reverendo Nicolaus de Azayolis magnus Senescallus Melfie,
Neapolio Logotheta Manuppelli de filijs Ursi, Nicolaus Nolanus
et Palatinus, comites."

The letter is an urgent and well-reasoned plea that the *Africa*
—which, it is assumed, is now finished and polished—be released
by Petrarch immediately, rather than held for release after his
death. Petrarch himself may desire further delay; but such

delay would be a cause of regret to many, and a cause of offense to Scipio. If Petrarch insists on holding the poem for
further retouching, "erit in infinitum procedere, et res exitum
non habebit." If he releases the *Africa* he will be free to devote
himself to other tasks. Copies should be sent "per diversas
Ausonie partes . . . ut tot amicorum et devotorum tuorum
desideria conpleas, qui arrectis auribus et cupidis animis id in dies
expectant." Petrarch's delay has already had the effect of
depriving King Robert and other now deceased friends of the
pleasure of reading the poem. If it is to be held until after
Petrarch's own death it may be lost entirely: "Quid autem scis
an casus aliquis sicut tot urbes absorsit, sic etiam tuos labores
auferat, et expectantium spem eludat?"

The original plan that this letter should be transmitted by
Niccolò Acciaiuoli had been prevented—so Barbato writes in
his covering letter to Boccaccio—by the death of Zanobi, which
had led Niccolò to replace his interest in the *Africa* by interest
in the possibility of persuading Petrarch to move to Naples. It
is for this reason that Barbato now sends his letter to Boccaccio,
to be transmitted with a supporting letter to be written by
Boccaccio himself to Petrarch, "Qui, lectis eis, spero, si Deus
faverit, quod vel nos voti conpotes faciet, vel notabilem prorsus
epistolam de negatione transmictet." The death of Zanobi occurred, as has been said, in late July or early August 1361: evidently the letter "Convenientibus nobis" had been written not
long before Zanobi died, doubtless in the spring or early summer of that year.[44] Barbato's letter to Boccaccio was written after

[44] Foresti 1, pp. 404–407, thinks that this letter was written after Barbato had received *Misc.* 9, and that *Misc.* 9 was the letter read by the four
men in Barbato's garden. He may be right; but it seems to me very
unlikely that *Misc.* 9, a letter of only fifteen lines, should have been the
object of the garden discussion, or that it should have been referred to in
the phrase "ad aliquam operum tuorum particulam perlegendam" which
appears in "Convenientibus" or in the clause "ubi quamdam ex epistolis
domini nostri Laureati legimus" which appears in Barbato's letter to
Boccaccio. *Misc.* 9 was written on 22 June: "Convenientibus" was written
before Barbato had heard of the death of Zanobi, which occurred in late
July or early August, as has been said. Nicola Festa, in his edition of the
Africa (Florence, 1926), p. xxxv, n. 4, noting that the opening words of

the death of Zanobi, but before the following May. Boccaccio's reply was written on 13 May 1362.[45]

In that reply—beginning "Suscepi, dilectissime vir"—Boccaccio says that while he will do as Barbato asks he has no hope of a favorable result: "Hijs certiorem te facio, quod quantumcumque suasiones tuas libens volensque suscipiam, huc usque non expectassem quod suades." In the course of his letter Boccaccio promises that he will himself bring or send to Barbato copies of Petrarch's *Bucolicum carmen* and *Invective contra medicum*.

It may well be, as Foresti thinks, that the receipt of Barbato's "Convenientibus nobis" with a covering letter from Boccaccio was the occasion for Petrarch's writing to Boccaccio, on 13 March 1363, the long *Sen.* II 1, in which he goes bitterly into detail as to the criticisms heaped upon him because of alleged but non-existent faults in the single passage of the *Africa* that he had given to Barbato long before, on Barbato's promise, soon broken, that he would keep it for himself alone.

Misc. 9

In this brief letter, beginning "Multa se offerunt," and written in Padua on 22 June 1361, Petrarch reports the receipt, on the preceding day, of Barbato's "In die nativitatis"; and says that he would gladly comply with Barbato's requests were it not for difficulties with servants and copyists, and that he will do what he can: "nitar tamen." The main purpose of this letter, however, is to ask Barbato to endeavor to avert an injurious action by which Petrarch's friend Bartolomeo Carbone dei Papazurri, Bishop of Chieti, is threatened. Petrarch is writing

---

the letter, "Convenientibus nobis in unum non quidem in templo Domini ad cenam manducandum dominicarum . . . " reflect *I Corinthians* XI 20, conjectures that the letter was written on Maundy Thursday (which fell, in 1361, on 25 March): I agree with Foresti in thinking this conjecture unjustified.

[45] Barbato's letter to Boccaccio and Boccaccio's reply are published by Vattasso, *Del Petrarca . . .* , pp. 17–20 and 23–28. Boccaccio's reply is published also in his *Opere latine minori*, ed. by A. F. Massèra (Bari, 1928), pp. 144–146. Barbato's acknowledgment (which has no importance for the present chapter) is published by Vattasso, pp. 28–29.

to the same effect to Niccolò Acciaiuoli and to Niccolò d'Alife (neither letter is extant), and asks Barbato to confer with them.

Barbato's Commentary on Fam. XII 2

Barbato's long and elaborate commentary on *Fam.* XII 2 (Petrarch's immediately famous letter to Niccolò Acciaiuoli on the guidance of Louis of Taranto as king), entitled *Expositio epistolae "Iam tandem,"* is preserved in a single MS in the Bibliothèque Nationale (where it bears the number Lat. 14845). The introduction, from which several passages have been quoted (on pp. 215, 226, 227, and 234), consists mainly of a characterization of Petrarch as being "magne fidelitatis, plene caritatis et perfecte humilitatis." The commentary proper is preceded by this passage: "Intencio . . . est . . . docet dictum Magnum Senescalum, ut et ipse regem, tanquam dux et magister eius, doceat, qualiter collapsum regnum virtutibus reparent, ac in tranquillitate gubernent . . ." As far as one can judge from the portion of the Commentary printed by Faraglia, Barbato quotes every single phrase of Petrarch's letter, and comments on each phrase—the proportionate length of comment to text being roughly ten to one. His comments are partly stylistic and partly historical: his historical comments, based on his experience as an eyewitness of the Neapolitan troubles, are of interest and importance. Faraglia states that in the course of the Commentary Barbato cites St. Augustine, St. Ambrose, St. Gregory the Great, Terence, Virgil, Cicero, Sallust, Livy, Ovid, Seneca, Valerius Maximus, and Florus.

The form of *Fam.* XII 2 quoted by Barbato piecemeal but in its entirety was undoubtedly the missive form. The MS should be examined throughout for the collection of missive variants both for *Fam.* XII 2 itself and for Barbato's quotations from other letters of Petrarch.[46]

Sooner or later after the completion of the Commentary Barbato sent it "for correction" to Pietro di Monteforte, with an undated covering letter that begins thus:

---

[46] See the variants for *Fam.* VII 1 quoted above, on p. 226.

Amplissimo Pyeridum hospiti, domino Petro de Monte forti, curie vicarie regni judici reverentissimo et precarissimo sibi: Barbatus sulmonensis salutem hominis utriusque. Estate retro proxima cum preter solitum nullam domini nostri laureati Petrarchi novam habuissem epistolam, libuit illam de reformacione ac regimine regni dudum magno senescallo quam nosti directam cunctantius revisere.[47]

The Commentary, then, was written in the course of a summer which, judging from the "dudum," was not long subsequent to Petrarch's writing—on 20 February 1352—of *Fam.* xii 7 to Barbato. As far as we know, Petrarch's next letter to Barbato was *Var.* 22, written on 4 October 1355. It would seem probable, therefore, that the Commentary was written in the summer of one of the years 1352–1355—less probably in 1352 than in some one of the three later years.

Petrarch's Other References to Barbato

References to Barbato occur in thirteen prose letters and one *epistola metrica* addressed by Petrarch to men other than Barbato. *Fam.* i 1 mentions Petrarch's decision to dedicate the *Metricae* to Barbato; *Fam.* v 4 reports his excursion to Baia with Barbato and Giovanni Barrili; the first form of *Fam.* viii 2–5 mentions Barbato as a friend, as do *Fam.* ix 2 and *Var.* 36; *Fam.* xii 3 and 15 speak of him as one to whom Niccolò Acciaiuoli turned for the writing of letters; in *Fam.* xiii 6 Petrarch suggests that Nelli show the letter to Barbato; and *Fam.* xxiv 12 mentions him as a friend of Homer. *Sen.* ii 1 tells of Barbato's obtaining and releasing a passage from the *Africa; Sen.* iii 4 is a brief affectionate eulogy written after Barbato's death; and *Sen.* xvi 1 mentions Barbato's gift of a volume of writings of Cicero. *Met.* ii 10 (to "Zoilus") refers to Barbato as an appreciative reader of Petrarch's verse.

Sen. iii 4 is addressed to a man to whom Petrarch refers thus: "Tu qui sub illius magisterio creuisti: cui conuictu continuo ac longevo rerum illius atque actuum plena notitia est: cui etas: ocium: ingenium favet . . ." Very possibly this

---

[47] Published by Attilio Hortis in his *Studj sulle opere latine del Boccaccio* (Trieste, 1879), pp. 347–348.

addressee was the Francesco Sanità referred to in some of the
letters that have been considered above. Petrarch's final characterization of his devoted friend reads thus:

Nihil mitius: nihil integrius: nihilque candidius: sol vidit, nihil
amantius literarum Quibus ut lautissimis vescebatur cibis huius ap-
petentissimus: reliquarum omnium negligens voluptatum.   Inanis
glorie fugitans. Insolentie nescius ac liuoris. Ad hec & ingenio acer
& stilo dulcis: & doctrina uber: & memoria promptus fuit.

CHAPTER X

On the Chronology of the Triumphs

Each of the six *Triumphs* consists of one or more *capitoli*. There exist 15 such *capitoli* (one of them a mere fragment and another incomplete), which belong to the several *Triumphs* as follows:

Triumphus cupidinis
Al tempo che rinnova i mie' sospiri.
Stanco giá di mirar, non sazio ancóra.
Era sí pieno il cor di meraviglie.
Poscia che mia fortuna in forza altrui.

Triumphus pudicitie
Quando ad un giogo et in un tempo quivi.

Triumphus pudicitie or *Triumphus mortis*
Quanti giá ne l'etá matura et acra (fragment).

Triumphus mortis
Quella leggiadra e gloriosa donna.
La notte che seguí l'orribil caso.

Triumphus fame
Nel cor pien d'amarissima dolcezza.
Da poi che Morte triumfò nel vólto.
Pien d'infinita e nobil meraviglia.
Io non sapea da tal vista levarme.
Poi che la bella e gloriosa donna (incomplete).

Triumphus temporis
De l'aureo albergo, co l'Aurora inanzi.

Triumphus eternitatis
Da poi che sotto 'l ciel cosa non vidi.

Petrarch certainly thought of *Al tempo*, *Era sí pieno*, and *Poscia che* as being respectively the first *capitolo*, the next-to-last *capitolo*, and the last *capitolo* of the *Triumphus cupidinis*. How *Stanco già* stood in Petrarch's final thought we do not know: he may have decided to retain it, in which case it would necessarily have been placed between *Al tempo* and *Era sí pieno;* he may have decided to discard it; he may never have made up his mind.

The fragment *Quanti già* was certainly discarded. It may have been intended as the beginning of a second *capitolo* of the *Triumphus pudicitie* or as the beginning of the *Triumphus mortis:* the latter possibility appears to be the more probable.

Petrarch certainly thought of *Quella leggiadra* as the first *capitolo* of the *Triumphus mortis:* whether he ever made up his mind as to the retention of *La notte* we do not know.

Nel cor, which is continuous with *La notte*, was certainly discarded, being replaced by *Da poi che Morte* and *Pien d'infinita*. *Poi che la bella* was drafted as a possible substitute for *Io non sapea*, but was never completed.

I

Petrarch's habits of work on his Italian poems are known to us through some hundreds of cancellations, emendations, and notes and signs of various kinds that appear on the twenty precious work sheets preserved as V.L. 3196, and through some hundreds of other variants and notes that are derived directly or indirectly from twenty or thirty other work sheets that are now lost.[1] From this evidence we know that even in the first drafting of poems or parts of poems Petrarch revised freely; that he returned again and again to poems already written, retouching them here and there or revising them thoroughly; and that he copied and recopied them (or had a scribe do so).

---

[1] The data used in this section and in the last section of this chapter are derived from Appel 1, from Weiss 1, and from the photographic reproductions of V.L. 3196. In quoting Petrarch's abbreviated notations I use the expanded forms given by Mestica, modifying them, when clearly desirable, by reference to Appel's edition of the *Triumphs* (Halle, 1901), pp. 109–115; to the diplomatic reproduction of V.L. 3196 by Mario Pelaez in *Bullettino dell'Archivio paleografico italiano*, II (1910), 163–216; or to the photographic reproductions of V.L. 3196.

Some sixty of the many hundreds of variants and notes are dated; and these dated entries suffice to prove that Petrarch's concern for the perfection of a given poem continued, in a number of cases, for many years, and that in some cases his retouching or revision followed a long period during which the poem had lain untouched. The *canzone Nel dolce tempo de la prima etade,* for instance, of which Petrarch himself wrote "et est de primis inventionibus nostris," was copied in part on 3 April 1350; was marked on 28 April 1351 as needing correction; and was copied on 4 November 1356 and again on 10 November. The note in V.L. 3196 recording this last copying reads: "transcripta in ordine post multos et multos annos . quibusdam mutatis .1356. Iouis in vesperis . 10. nouembris mediolani."

Above the (already somewhat revised) copy of Stanzas 1–2 and 4–5 of the *canzone Amor, se vuo' ch'i' torni al giogo antico* that appears on f. 12ʳ of V.L. 3196 Petrarch wrote first

> 1350 . mercurij . 9 . Junij . post vesperos;

to this he presently added the words

> voluj incipere . sed vocor ad cenam,

and on the next day or soon thereafter the words

> proxime mane prosequi cepi.

In the following spring he wrote, in the margin opposite the first stanza,

> hanc transcripsi et correxi et dedi Bastardino. 1351 . die sabati. .XXV . martii;

then, just below that,

> mane rescribo iterum;

then, just below that,

> Rescripsi eam .XXVIII. martii mane et illam inscribi dedi;

and finally, at the top of the page, above his first note,

> Transcripta in alia papiro . 1351 . aprilis 20 sero per me scilicet per Bastardinum.

Many of Petrarch's work sheets—most of them, indeed—must have been lost. Only 54 of the 366 poems of the *Canzoniere* appear in V.L. 3196; and as far as I am aware there are among the remaining 312 lyrics only two for which Petrarch's own variants and notes are recorded elsewhere.

Only two of the *capitoli* of the *Triumphs* are contained in V.L. 3196: the *capitolo Era sí pieno* (in large part) and the single *capitolo* of the *Triumphus eternitatis:* they show many variants and notes. Many variants and notes preserved by collators exist for *Al tempo*, the rest of *Era sí pieno, Stanco giá, Da poi che Morte,* and *Poi che la bella;* and one or two or a very few more exist for each of the other *capitoli* (except *Quanti giá*).

The earliest dated notes that concern the *Triumphs*—notes preserved not in V.L. 3196 but mainly in Casanatensis A. III. 31—have reference to the *capitoli Al tempo* and *Era sí pieno.* Above the copy of *Al tempo* that begins on f. 149[r] of that MS there stands a note that reads

Triumphus cupidinis &c. 1357. veneris hora vesper. 8. sept. hragnani.[2] unde abitum meditor membris fessus occurrit hoc vaganti valde animo.

In the margin to the left stands this later note:

transcriptus totus quaternus sic 1360. 12. sept.

At the end of f. 149[v] there stand these three notes, of which the first has reference (possibly the others also) to line 73 of *Al tempo:*

Lune ante matutinum. protho.

anno sequenti fuit die martis id festum & eram pagaz. ubi sum & hodie mercurij 12. sept. mane dum hoc scribo et ista percurro fastidio potius quam studio (the rest of the note is not relevant to the *Triumphs*).

hoc additum nihil ad rem nisi quod tunc ista relegebam 1360 sept. 3. ita res vadit de septembri in septembrem. nec incepi hoc de bona littera scribere.

---

[2] *Hragnani* is Garegnano; and *pagaz.* (just below) is Pagazzano. Both places are near Milan.

By a careful process of reasoning Appel reaches the conclusion that the *mercurij 12. sept.* must have been 12 September 1358, the *die martis* 12 September 1357, and the *Lune* 12 September 1356.

These and other similar notes give us this record of Petrarch's work on the *Triumphs* in the years 1356–1360:

12 September 1356	*Al tempo*	retouched
8 September 1357	*Al tempo*	reread
12 September 1357	*Al tempo*	retouched
13 September 1357	*Era sí pieno*	retouched
16 September 1357	*Era sí pieno*	retouched
30 April 1358	*Al tempo*	retouched
12 September 1358	*Al tempo*	retouched
12 September 1358	*Era sí pieno*	retouched
4 November 1358	*Al tempo*	retouched
3 September 1360	*Al tempo*	reread
12 September 1360	*Al tempo*	recopied.

All the later dated notes that concern the *Triumphs* will be reported in the last section of this chapter.

II

In the 16th century Lodovico Beccadelli, who saw the work sheet, now lost, that bore at the head of *Al tempo* the note, quoted above, which says of that *capitolo* that on 8 September 1357 "occurrit hoc vaganti valde animo," drew from that note the obviously erroneous conclusion that it recorded the beginning of the writing of the *Triumphs:* "Nelli Trionfi sono un mondo di mutationi, solo ne dirò alcune come per saggio, nè lascerò d'avvertire che a quello che si vede dalli suoi ricordi, gli cominciò a scrivere del 357." [3]

The first influential statement of the still common idea that the writing of the *Triumphs* was begun during Petrarch's last stay in Provence was made by Mestica.[4] After pointing out the erroneousness of Beccadelli's inference Mestica continues (referring, at the start, to Appel's conclusion that the day referred to in the note "Lune ante matutinum" was a day in 1356):

---

[3] Appel 1, p. 6.
[4] Mestica, pp. xiv–xv.

E difatti si raccoglie da un'altra postilla che esso lavorava in quel Canto anche l'anno precedente, e si può con buon fondamento credere che la concezione e forse il cominciamento del poemetto risalgono alla primavera del 1352, durante il suo ultimo soggiorno a Valchiusa, che nelle prime terzine è bellamente rappresentata, e dove è immaginato il principio della visione.

But Mestica's inference is as erroneous as Beccadelli's. There is absolutely no reason to suppose that the particular copy of *Al tempo* that bore the notes in question—the copy seen by Beccadelli in the 16th century—was the original copy of that *capitolo*. The original copy might perfectly well have been written many years earlier and been destroyed or lost. It is indeed perfectly possible that two or three copies had intervened between the original copy and the one that survived into the 16th century. The existence of the notes in question, therefore, does not constitute evidence that the writing of the *Triumphs* was begun during Petrarch's last stay in Provence.

While the consideration just advanced is in itself sufficient to dismiss Mestica's argument, three other points may be noted. (1) The particular copy seen by Beccadelli might have been made long before 1352 and kept by Petrarch for many years before he returned to it on 12 September 1356. (2) Many of the notes and variants that occurred in the copy in question might have been made long before 1356: there are in all about 150 such notes and variants, and only ten are dated. (3) Even if Mestica is right, as he may well be, in assuming that work on the *Triumphs* was begun at Vaucluse, it might perfectly well have been begun not in Petrarch's last stay in Vaucluse, but in one of his three earlier stays.

The first general discussion of the chronology of the *Triumphs* appears in Melodia's *Studio su i Trionfi del Petrarca*, published in 1898.[5] Melodia maintains that the inspiration and the beginning of work on the *Triumphs* are to be dated as of the spring of 1352 or the spring of 1353, probably the former. To Mestica he refers merely in passing: "Anche il Mestica ha accennato alla data del 1352." Melodia supports his opinion by

---

[5] Melodia, pp. 87–96.

the two arguments which will be summarized and discussed in the two following paragraphs.

(1) Petrarch's *Met.* III 22, 23, and 33, written not long after 5 January 1352, deplore conditions in Avignon. Having in mind III 22, Melodia writes:

Avignone è un labirinto da cui non saprebbero uscire nemmeno Teseo ed Arianna, anche aiutati dall'arte di Dedalo:

. . . ira viam faciet, dolor induet alas.

Then, considering only ll. 28–31 of *Met.* III 23—

Maria horrida velo,
O mea Calliope, et remis fugiamus adactis,
Securum carpamus iter, speciesque laborum
Et cursus vitae varios, populumque canamus—

he argues that the reference in these lines is to the *Triumphs*. This argument has been thoroughly refuted above (on pp. 200–202).

(2) Melodia's second argument runs thus: (a) in the *Epistola posteritati* Petrarch says "Per dirlo in poche parole, *tutti* [italics Melodia's] gli opuscoli miei, se non per intero composti, furono cominciati o per lo meno orditi in quel luogo [Vaucluse]"; (b) therefore the *Triumphs* were begun in Vaucluse; (c) therefore they were begun in 1352 or 1353. It is likely enough that the *Triumphs* were begun in Vaucluse, though the passage in the letter *Posteritati* does not prove it: Melodia was quoting Fracassetti's translation, but the Latin text reads "quicquid *fere* [italics mine] opusculorum" etc. But even on the assumption that the *Triumphs* were begun there, it does not follow that they may not have been begun in one of Petrarch's earlier stays there rather than in his last stay.

Having argued that the inspiration and the beginning of the *Triumphs* are to be dated as of the spring of 1352 or, less probably, the spring of 1353, Melodia next presents an argument which, if valid, would lead to the conclusion that some sort of preliminary idea of the *Triumphs* was presumably in Petrarch's mind by 1349. This argument, in its main lines, runs thus:

(a) *Met.* I 1, addressed to Barbato da Sulmona, accompanies a gift of poems;

(b) these poems were apparently Italian lyrics;

(c) at the end of the *epistola* there is a reference to a further and greater poetic enterprise;

(d) since the poems referred to in the body of the *epistola* were apparently in Italian, this further poetic enterprise was presumably also an enterprise in the field of Italian poetry—perhaps the *Triumphs*, or "un poema che poi fu quello de' *Trionfi*";

(e) the *epistola* was written after the death of Laura, and probably in 1349; and

(f) some sort of preliminary idea of the *Triumphs* was therefore presumably in Petrarch's mind by that time.

It has been shown in the preceding chapter that since *Met.* I 1 is unquestionably the dedicatory letter for a collection of *epistolae metricae*, the poems referred to in the body of the *epistola* must have been *epistolae metricae;* also that the poetic enterprise referred to at the end of the *epistola* cannot possibly have been the *Triumphs*, and was probably the *Africa*.

Melodia then adds a final argument which, if valid, would lead to the conclusion that *La notte, Nel cor,* and *Stanco già* were composed before the idea of the *Triumphs* as a whole had become clear in Petrarch's mind and before he had composed any of the other *capitoli;* and further—though Melodia apparently does not see this outcome—that since, in his opinion, the formation of a clear idea of what the *Triumphs* were to be and the writing of *Al tempo* and other *capitoli* occurred in the spring of 1352, *La notte, Nel cor,* and *Stanco già* would have been written before that time. This final argument is based on the fact—which does not by any means serve to support it—that in many MSS of the *Triumphs* these three *capitoli* precede the others; on the very doubtful theory that *La notte*, as being in effect a triumph of Laura's virtue, must have been written before *Quella leggiadra;* and on the very doubtful theory that lines 13–18 of *Nel cor*, beginning

O Polimnia, or prego che m'aiti,

were designed as invocation and proposition for the *Triumphs* as a whole. But this argument is broken down completely by the fact that *Stanco giá*, which begins with the tercet

> Stanco giá di mirar, non sazio ancóra,
> or quinci or quindi mi volgea, guardando
> cose ch'a ricontarle è breve l'ora,

obviously assumes the earlier existence of at least one preceding *capitolo*, and cannot possibly, therefore, have been an initial *capitolo* for the *Triumphus amoris*.

Appel, in his critical edition of the *Triumphs*, published in 1901, argues thus as to the date of the beginning of Petrarch's work:

(a) "es ist . . . selbstverständlich, dass die Vision nach dem Tode Lauras stattfindet, d.h. nach dem 6. April 1348";

(b) a MS notation proves that *Al tempo* existed in 1356;

(c) the poem was therefore begun between 1348 and 1356;

(d) the action of *Al tempo* begins in Vaucluse and in the spring;

(e) on the hypothesis "dass die im Gedichte angegebenen zeitlichen und örtlichen Umstände mit den bei seiner Entstehung wirklich vorliegenden übereinstimmten" the poem must have been begun in Vaucluse and in the spring;

(f) the only possibilities are therefore 1352 and 1353; and

(g) the *ricondotto* of l. 8 of *Al tempo* suggests 1352 rather than 1353.[6]

But Appel's first premise, on which his whole argument rests, is entirely baseless: there is abolutely nothing in any of the *capitoli* of the *Triumphus amoris* or in the single *capitolo* of the *Triumphus pudicitie* to indicate that they were written after the death of Laura. Appel's hypothesis of a correspondence between fictional and actual time and place is questionable; but even if it were sound it would not follow that the spring in question was that of 1352 or that of 1353, since Petrarch was in Vaucluse in the spring of each of these earlier years: 1338, 1339, 1340, 1342, 1343, 1346, and 1347.

Thus the arguments of Mestica, Melodia, and Appel to the effect that Petrarch began the writing of the *Triumphs* during his last stay in Provence are all invalid; and the demonstration

---

[6] Ed. cit. in n. 1, pp. xx–xxi.

of their invalidity opens the way for a new approach to the question of the chronology of the *Triumphs*. A new approach was indeed made by Calcaterra in 1942. His argument will be reported in Section V of this chapter; but before reporting it I am offering two arguments of my own as to the time when the first *capitoli* were written.

III

The *capitolo Al tempo* reports fictional events, sights, and a conversation that are represented as being wholly of the past. All the main verbs of the *capitolo* (all the verbs, that is, that are not grammatically subordinate) are in past tenses, except those that occur in sentences spoken by Petrarch to his guide or by the guide to Petrarch, and the present *trovo* that occurs in the parenthetical tercet consisting of ll. 61–63. The complete series of main verbs, except for those just mentioned, is as follows: *scaldava, correa, ricondotto aveano, vidi, Vidi, mirai, temea, misi, strinsi, riconobbi, avea cangiata, venne, chiamò, dissi, scoverson, assidemmo, cominciò, dissi, disse, intesi, demandai, rispose.* The *capitolo Stanco già* is of the same narrative character. All of its main verbs are in past tenses, except those that occur in sentences spoken by Petrarch, Masinissa, Sophonisba, Seleucus, or the guide.

The first 88 lines of *Era sí pieno* are of the same narrative character. All of the main verbs are in past tenses, except those that occur in sentences spoken by Petrarch or the guide. The complete series is: *Era, disse, risposi, parlava, avea.* In ll. 89–90 Laura appears:

> quando una giovenetta ebbi dallato,
> pura assai piú che candida colomba.

The narrative then continues, through l. 111, in the same manner: the main verbs, except for one occurring in a sentence spoken by the guide, are *prese, fui, fece, disse, era, torcea,* and *era.*

With l. 112 the whole character of the *capitolo* changes: from this point on Petrarch is no longer reporting what he saw. Lines 112–117 are as follows:

> Da quel tempo ebbi gli occhi umidi e bassi,
> e 'l cor pensoso, e solitario albergo
> fonti, fiumi, montagne, boschi e sassi;
> da indi in qua cotante carte aspergo
> di penseri, e di lagrime, e d'inchiostro,
> tante ne squarcio, e n'apparecchio, e vergo.

The *ebbi* means "I have had and I still have." All the remaining main verbs of the *capitolo*, except the merely exclamatory *poria* (which is present in effect) of line 139, are in the present tense: *so, mostro, veggio, teme, è, suole, è, infiamman, trovo, è, prego, ascolta*, and *so* repeated thirteen times. This verbal analysis is merely a mechanical demonstration of a fact that *saute aux yeux* when one reads ll. 112–184 as a whole. In those lines Petrarch is reporting his present state—his state, that is, at the time when he is writing—and that present state is beyond all question one in which Laura is still alive. Consider in particular these lines:

> E veggio andar quella leggiadra fera,
> non curando di me né di mie pene (121–122).

> questo signor, che tutto 'l mondo sforza,
> teme di lei, ond'io son fuor di spene (125–126).

> Costei non è chi tanto o quanto stringa,
> cosí selvaggia e rebellante suole
> da le 'nsegne d'Amore andar solinga (130–132).

> gli occhi ch'accesi d'un celeste lume
> m'infiamman sí ch'i' son d'arder contento (137–138).

> Cosí preso mi trovo, et ella è sciolta;
> io prego giorno e notte (o stella iniqua!),
> et ella a pena di mille uno ascolta (145–147).

The entire passage serves to prove the point, and receives a new light and a new freshness when it is read in the realization that it was written during Laura's lifetime. The fact that the point has been so generally missed has presumably been due in part to respect for the opinions expressed by Mestica, Melodia, and Appel, but mainly to the assumption that most of the *Triumphs* were written continuously and that the existence of the account of the death of Laura in the *Triumphus mortis* proves therefore that the *Triumphus cupidinis* and the *Triumphus pudicitie* were also written after her death. But that assumption is utterly unwarranted. It is indeed inconsistent with our general knowledge of Petrarch's habits of composition.

That *Al tempo* also was written during the lifetime of Laura is indicated not only by the sufficient fact that, as the initial *capitolo*, it clearly precedes *Era sí pieno*, which assumes the earlier "meraviglie" and the presence of the guide, but also by ll. 61–63:

> Io no' l'intesi allor; ma or sí fisse
> sue parole mi trovo entro la testa,
> che mai piú saldo in marmo non si scrisse.

That *Poscia che* also was written during the lifetime of Laura is indicated by lines 82–84:

> Ma pur di lei che 'l cor di pensier m'empie,
> non potei coglier mai ramo né foglia,
> sí fûr le sue radici acerbe et empie.

Indication that this *capitolo* is of relatively early date is afforded also by the reference in ll. 59–64 to the death of Tommaso Caloiro, which occurred in 1341. Line 64 reads:

> dove se' or, che meco eri pur dianzi?

That the *Triumphus pudicitie* also was written during the lifetime of Laura is indicated by ll. 7–18, which read, in part, thus:

> ché s'io veggio d'un arco e d'uno strale
> Febo percosso e 'l giovene d'Abido . . .
> non mi debb'io doler s'altri mi vinse
> giovene, incauto, disarmato e solo.
> E se la mia nemica Amor non strinse,
>   non è ancor giusta assai cagion di duolo,
> ché 'n abito il revidi ch'io ne piansi;

also by ll. 41–42:

> tanto Amor pronto venne a lei ferire
> ch'al vólto ha le faville ond'io tutto ardo;

also by ll. 79–81:

Onestate e Vergogna a la fronte era,
nobile par de le vertú divine,
che fan costei sopra le donne altèra.

IV

Martellotti has demonstrated, beyond the shadow of a doubt,
that the twelve pre-Romulean Lives of the *De viris illustribus*
were written after *Nel cor* and before the two *capitoli*, *Da poi
che morte* and *Pien d'infinita*, by which *Nel cor* was replaced;
and I have shown above (on pp. 95–96) that the composition
of those pre-Romulean Lives was quite certainly begun immediately upon Petrarch's return to Provence. It follows that
Nel cor was written before that return.

Nel cor, in turn, which opens with the lines

Nel cor pien d'amarissima dolcezza
risonavano ancor gli ultimi accenti
del ragionar ch'e' sol brama et apprezza,
    e volea dir—O dí miei tristi e lenti!—
e piú cose altre, quand'io vidi allegra
girsene lei fra belle alme lucenti.
    Avea giá il Sol la benda umida e negra
tolta dal duro vólto della Terra,
riposo della gente mortale egra;
    il sonno, e quella ch'ancor apre e serra
il mio cor lasso, a pena eran partiti,
ch'io vidi incominciar un'altra guerra,

is obviously continuous with *La notte*, which ends thus (Laura
is speaking in the first eight of the lines now to be quoted):

Ma per tuo diletto
tu non t'accorgi del fuggir de l'ore;
    vedi l'Aurora de l'aurato letto
rimenar a i mortali il giorno, e 'l Sole
giá fuor de l'oceáno in fin al petto:
    questa vien per partirne, onde mi dole;
s'a dire hai altro, studia d'esser breve,
e col tempo dispensa le parole.—
    —Quant'io soffersi mai, soave e leve
—dissi —m'ha fatto il parlar dolce e pio;
ma 'l viver senza voi m'è duro e greve.

Però saper vorrei, madonna, s'io
son per tardi seguirvi, o se per tempo.—
Ella, giá mossa, disse: —Al creder mio,
tu starai in terra senza me gran tempo.—

It follows, therefore, that *La notte* was written before *Nel cor*, and before Petrarch's return to Provence.

La notte, moreover, which begins

La notte che seguí l'orribil caso
che spense il sole, anzi 'l ripose in cielo,
di ch'io son qui come uom cieco rimaso,
    spargea per l'aere il dolce estivo gelo . . .
    quando donna sembiante a la stagione,
di gemme orientali incoronata,
mosse vèr me da mille altre corone,

can never have been conceived as an opening *capitolo* for the *Triumphus mortis:* it follows further, therefore, that *Quella leggiadra*, the main and only other *capitolo* of that *Triumph*, was written before *La notte*.

One has then, from the considerations advanced in the preceding section and in the present section, this picture of the earlier phases of the composition of the *Triumphs:* the *Triumphus cupidinis* and the *Triumphus pudicitie* were written while Laura was still living; the two *capitoli* of the *Triumphus mortis* were written after her death but before the return to Provence; and *Nel cor*, written as a first *capitolo* for the *Triumphus fame*, was also written before the return to Provence.

V

Calcaterra [7] argues that the first two *Triumphs* were composed early in the 1340's. His arguments are as follows:

(1) (a) *Met.* III 30, addressed to Guido Gonzaga, was written to accompany a copy of the *Roman de la rose* sent to Guido by Petrarch in response to a request for a copy of some French work highly esteemed in France; (b) several passages in the first two *Triumphs* are closely related to passages in *Met.* III 30 (ll. 79–81 of *Era sí pieno* to ll. 6 and 14–15 of the *epistola;* ll. 151–165 of *Era sí pieno* to ll. 7–12 of the *epistola;* and ll. 19–24 of

---

[7] Calcaterra, pp. 153–176 and 200–205.

Poscia che to ll. 16–21 of the *epistola*) or to the *Roman de la rose* itself (both poems are springtime dreams, and both make notable use of personifications, as in ll. 115–119 of *Poscia che* and ll. 76–90 of the *Triumphus pudicitie*); (c) the guide of the *Triumphs* is Giovanni Aghinolfi, the chancellor of the Gonzaga (this point is argued at great length); and (d) *Met.* III 30 was written about 1340, since it is closely related to *Fam.* III 11, which was written before 1340.

(2) The *capitolo Stanco giá*, "in cui è introdotto quasi in compendio l'episodio di Sofonisba e Massinissa, fu certamente concepito quando in lui non era spenta l'ispirazione che gli aveva dettato il libro V dell'Africa, vale a dire nel 1341 o poco dopo."

(3) The death of Tommaso Caloiro (which occurred in 1341) is referred to as recent in ll. 58–64 of *Poscia che*.

(4) The *Triumphus pudicitie* is to be dated as of 1343 or 1344: (a) because of its close relations with the *Penitential Psalms* and the *Secretum*, which are of those years, and (b) because lines 163–177, in which the triumphal procession visits Baia and then, passing between Monte Barbaro and the Cave of the Cumaean Sibyl, goes to the villa of Scipio at Linterno, reflect recent memories of Petrarch's own visit to the same scenes in November 1343—a visit reported in detail in *Fam.* V 4, written on 23 November to Cardinal Giovanni Colonna.

These considerations lead Calcaterra to believe and to maintain that in these early years Petrarch thought of the *capitoli* he was then writing as constituting a twofold poem, complete in itself, on the theme of love—specifically, as a poem on "Amore trionfante" and "Amore trionfato"; and that in writing it he was intending "di metter a paragone la sobria e incisiva arte italiana e quella gallica piú stemperata e ridondante," "di contrapporre alla narrazione stemperata e svagata del libro francese una raffigurazione storicamente piú concreta e fantasticamente piú salda della potenza dell'Iddio, che vince e strema tutti i cuori degli uomini." Doubtless, also—it may be added —he thought of his own poem as superior because of its wealth of classic personages and references, and, ethically, because of its assertion that chastity may triumph over love.

At the start of a detailed review of Calcaterra's arguments Goffis [8] calls them "Argomenti interessanti, ma che avrebbero bisogno di essere rincalzati da altri più probanti." In the course of his examination of the several arguments Goffis maintains that the parallels noted in (1b) are not sufficiently precise to be weighty; that (1c) is not substantiated; that (3) and (4a) are not justifiable; and that (4b) is not necessarily valid.

Raimondi,[9] discussing Goffis' book in a review that is in itself an important contribution to the study of the *Triumphs*, accepts Calcaterra's (1b) as valid, and reënforces it; he does not consider that Goffis has disproved (1c); he agrees with Goffis that (3) and (4b) are weak; and he does not attach much weight to (4a), though he does not dismiss it. He accepts and approves Calcaterra's conclusions: that the first two *Triumphs* were composed early in the 1340's; that Petrarch then thought of them as constituting a twofold poem, complete in itself; and that in writing them Petrarch was intending to demonstrate the superiority of Italian poetic art to that of France.

Bosco speaks thus of Calcaterra's argument: "La tesi filologica, pur suggestiva, ha bisogno di essere approfondita nei suoi precisi termini, sebbene molti, e anche chi scrive, pensino, per altre ragioni, alla necessità di una retrodatazione del poema." [10]

For my part, I agree with Raimondi as to the strength of Calcaterra's (1b), especially as reënforced by Raimondi; and I do not regard any of Calcaterra's later arguments as necessary for the support of his conclusion. His (1c) seems to me to be probably but not certainly sound; his (1d), (2), (3), and (4a) seem to me weak; but his (4b) still seems to me to be weighty. I agree wholeheartedly with Raimondi as to the soundness of Calcaterra's conclusions; and I believe those conclusions to

---

[8] C. F. Goffis, *Originalità dei "Trionfi"* (Florence, 1951), pp. 1–9. Goffis discusses at length, also, the theory that the *Triumphs* were modelled on the *Amorosa visione* of Boccaccio, received by Petrarch in or after 1351, and finds no validity in that theory. Raimondi, in the review referred to in the next note, agrees with him.

[9] Ezio Raimondi, in *Studi petrarcheschi*, iv (1951), 262–283.

[10] Umberto Bosco, "Gli studi petrarcheschi del Calcaterra," in *Studi petrarcheschi*, v (1952), 8.

be strongly reëforced by the considerations advanced in the two preceding sections of the present chapter.

VI

It was presumably the death of Laura that gave Petrarch the vision of a vaster work. As Calcaterra puts it,

> La scomparsa della donna amata, sommovendo nel profondo l'animo del poeta, fu il vero motivo dell'ampliamento e della trasfigurazione di tutta l'opera. Il *Triumphus Cupidinis* e il *Triumphus Pudicitiae* divennero le prime parti di poema piú vasto, in cui fossero raffigurate tutte le labili vicende umane e fosse mostrato all'evidenza che supremo interesse dell'uomo è "fondare in loco stabile sua speme," vale a dire raggiungere ciò che non passa a traverso ciò che passa.[11]

The *Triumphus mortis*, then, as Calcaterra sees it, represents a start toward a newer and a greater goal, the first two *Triumphs* being now conceived as the first two elements in a more comprehensive work.

Calcaterra notes an evident lack of continuity between the first two *Triumphs*, on the one hand, and the *Triumphus mortis*:

> Ora è evidente che la prima parte [*i.e.*, the first two *Triumphs*] reca implicito qualche cosa dello spirito occasionale, polemico e in certo modo "ad rem," da cui è stata originata, e che le altre [*i.e.*, the last four *Triumphs*] . . . spaziano sulla prima col respiro di una piú larga e pacata contemplazione cosmica, del tutto svincolata dagl'intendimenti occasionali, da cui artisticamento erano nati il *Trionfo d'Amore* e il *Trionfo della Pudicizia* . . . [12]

He then notes that there are signs of discontinuity, also, within the last four *Triumphs*, but concludes: "Ma in nessun luogo l'intervallo logico e formale è rimasto cosí lampante come fra il *Trionfo della Pudicizia* e il *Trionfo della Morte*."

Discontinuity between these two *Triumphs* is indicated also by the fact that whereas the *Triumphus pudicitie* celebrates the triumph of chastity over love, the *Triumphus fame* the triumph of fame over death, the *Triumphus temporis* the triumph of time over fame, and the *Triumphus eternitatis* the triumph of

---

[11] Calcaterra, p. 176.
[12] P. 197.

eternity over time, the *Triumphus mortis* does not celebrate the triumph of death over chastity.

Goffis advances the inherently improbable thesis that in Petrarch's original concept of the *Triumphs* the *Triumphus fame* followed immediately upon the *Triumphus pudicitie*, and that the *Triumphus mortis* was inserted, after the death of Laura, between the *Triumphus pudicitie* and the *Triumphus fame*.[13] His argument, however, is thoroughly refuted by Raimondi and is indeed invalidated by the fact (for which see above, pp. 266–267) that *Nel cor*, the rejected draft of an opening *capitolo* for the *Triumphus fame*, is continuous with *La notte*, the second *capitolo* of the *Triumphus mortis*.[14]

VII

It is inherently probable that the writing of *Da poi che Morte* and *Pien d'infinita* took place not long after the virtual completion of Petrarch's work on the pre-Romulean Lives, since it was work on those Lives that gave Petrarch some of the data that were to correct data that had been used in *Nel cor;* and it is probable, specifically, that they were written in Vaucluse in the spring or summer of 1352 (see above, pp. 131–132).

VIII

The MS evidence as to dates when Petrarch in the years 1356–1360 retouched or recopied *Al tempo* and *Era sí pieno* has been reported in Section I of this study. The corresponding evidence for the later years of Petrarch's life, for these and other *capitoli*, is as follows.[15]

---

[13] Goffis, pp. 19–27.

[14] In the course of his discussion Goffis attempts to prove also that the fragment *Quanti giá* was written as a beginning not for a second *capitolo* of the *Triumphus pudicitie* nor for the *Triumphus mortis* but for the *Triumphus fame*, and that the incomplete *Poi che la bella* was not drafted as a late substitute for *Io non sapea*, but was an early draft which had the same preliminary status as *Nel cor* and was later replaced by *Io non sapea*. His arguments are thoroughly refuted by Raimondi.

[15] The sources of this evidence and the method followed in the expansion of Petrarch's notes are as indicated in n. 1.

On 1 July 1363 Petrarch retouched *Io non sapea*.

On 19 January 1364 he wrote at the head of a copy of *Da poi che Morte* four notes which (not without some uncertainties) may be expanded and interpreted thus:

(1) 1364. veneris. mane. 19. Januarij dum inuitus patauii ferior. quartus Triumphus.

(2) . . . auroram [the rest is illegible].

(3) aut lacrimis movetur Deus e contrito corde manantibus aut nulla penitus re movetur.

(4) Dum quid sum cogito. pudet hec scribere. sed dum quid fieri cupio animum subit creuit pudor torporque omnis abscedit. Scribo enim, non quasi ego sed quasi alius nescio quis unquam transformari studeo.

On 19 February 1364 he retouched *Io non sapea*.

On 1 September 1369 he retouched *Quando ad un giogo*.

On 2 September 1370 he wrote the date above a copy of *Al tempo*.

On 9 July 1371 he began work on *Poi che la bella*, as a possible substitute for *Io non sapea*, and at the head of his work sheet he wrote *1371 Mercurii post somnum diuinum Julij. 9.;* and on 13 August he retouched this new *capitolo*.

On 1 July 1373 he retouched *Poscia che;* and on the next day he retouched *Al tempo*.

On 15 January 1374 he wrote, at the head of an autograph copy of the *Triumphus eternitatis* that is preserved in V.L. 3196, the note ".1374. dominica ante cenam. 15. Januarij. vltimus cantus."

On 12 February, opposite

> che pora essere a vederla in cielo,

which was then the last line of the poem, he wrote the words "explicit. Dominica carnis priuii. 12. februarii. 1374. post cenam."

Below that line he soon wrote

> or che fia dunque a riuederla in cielo,

and at the right of this new line he recorded his final poetic satisfaction, by adding the words "hoc placet."

CHAPTER XI

Petrarch and Giacomo de' Rossi

Petrarch's *Sen.* XIII 2 was written to Philippe de Mézières in reply to a letter, not now extant, written on the occasion of the death of a mutual friend, whom Petrarch calls only "Jacobus." Passages in Petrarch's letter show that this Jacobus had served with King Peter I of Cyprus, and in particular that he had taken part in the capture of Alexandria. Fracassetti and Mas Latrie were unable to identify him; [1] but he was identified as Giacomo de' Rossi of Parma by Jorga, who found in MS 499 of the Bibliothèque de l'Arsenal—a manuscript of the late fourteenth century, containing a collection of letters written by or to Mézières—a sequence of three letters, of which the first is a letter by Mézières headed *Epistola pie lamentacionis cancellarii domino bonifacio de lupis directa de morte magnifici et strenuissimi militis domini Jacobi de rubeis de Parma;* the second, though headed *Epistola responsiua domini bonifacii de lupis ad epistolam cancellarii super mortem domini Jacobi de rubeis de Parma*, is in fact Petrarch's *Sen.* XIII 2; and the third, headed *Iterum alia epistola responsiua domini bonifacii de lupis ad cancellarium super mortem domini Jacobi de rubeis de parma*, is Bonifazio's reply to Mézières. [2]

---

[1] Fracassetti 3, II, 279–280.

[2] N. Jorga, "Une collection de lettres de Philippe de Mézières (Notice sur le ms. 499 de la bibl. de l'Arsenal)," in *Revue historique*, XLIX (1892), 312–314. A later but still early hand added at the head of Petrarch's letter the notation "hanc epistolam dictauit clare memorie admirabilis et catholicus poeta franciscus" (followed by one or more words now undecipherable); and a much later hand added at the end, presumably from one of the 16th-century collective editions of the works of Petrarch, the date, "Pataui pridie nonas nouembris." For Bonifazio de' Lupi see below, p. 277 and n. 10. My quotations from the three letters are based upon photostatic copies of ff. 141–143 of the manuscript.

Petrarch's letter shows that he esteemed Giacomo very highly indeed, and that he regarded him as a dear and intimate friend. The statements of esteem, frequent throughout the letter, culminate in this passage:

> omnia perfecit que ad veram gloriam pertinerent. plura facere poterat non maiora. ea fuit in iuuentute grauitas in grauitate iocunditas in iocunditate seueritas in seueritate clementia ea demum virtus in animo in proposito constancia in consilio acumen in presentibus circunspeccio in futuris prouidencia in conuersacione suauitas in verbis fides in rebus atque actibus industria, cum amicis caritas, cum hostibus leue odium et placabile, cum superioribus obsequium cum subditis humanitas cum omni genere hominum Justicia.

The warmth of Petrarch's friendship for Giacomo is evidenced by his repeated expressions of personal grief for his loss, and by such phrases as these: *tanta amicicia et affinitate coniunctus* and *de illo quem dileximus ymmo vero quem diligimus.*

In view of Petrarch's admiration and friendship for Giacomo it would seem to be desirable that a gathering of the scanty data as to his career and personality should be attempted.[3]

Since the portion of Giacomo's life of which we have most knowledge was spent in the service of King Peter I of Cyprus, a brief reminder of some of the circumstances and events of Peter's reign may be in order. He succeeded to the throne in 1359. Philippe de Mézières was his chancellor; Pierre Thomas was the papal legate at his court. Cyprus was close to the dominions of the sultan; and Peter was convinced that he had a divinely attested crusading mission. Within the first three years of his reign he attacked Asia Minor, capturing Adalia. He spent most of the years 1362–1365 in Europe, seeking financial and military support: his journeyings took him to Italy, France, Flanders, Brabant, Germany, England, Bohemia, Poland, and Austria, and again to Italy, where he spent, in Venice, the first half of the year 1365. He then returned to

---

[3] Most of the sources I have used have come to my attention, directly or indirectly, through references given by Jorga, either in the article already cited or in his *Philippe de Mézières, 1327–1405, et la croisade au XIVe siècle* (Paris, 1896), pp. 253, 280, 314, 317, and 320. This book is cited hereafter as Jorga, *PM.*

Cyprus; and in October 1365 he attacked and captured Alexandria, which was disgracefully plundered by his troops. The chancellor, the legate, and others urged him to hold the city, despite the certainty of a counterattack by the sultan; but at a council of war there was a strong majority for evacuation, and the king, bitterly disappointed, gave way. The last four years of his reign were spent in negotiations with the sultan, which were, however, accompanied by occasional raids on Egypt and on Syria. Peter visited Italy again in 1368. As a result of scandalous personal conduct he was murdered, in Cyprus, on 17 January 1369.[4]

Giacomo's first recorded experience is as a knight, in the forces of Bernabò Visconti, captured at the battle of Solara, in April 1363, by the forces of the Church and its allies. Several chroniclers speak of the battle: the only two who mention Giacomo are Johannes de Mussis, author of the *Chronicon placentinum*, and the unknown author of the *Annales mediolanenses*. The former, after telling of the battle, continues: "Sed demum fere totus exercitus Domini Bernabovis ibi remansit . . . Et ibi tunc capti fuerunt de gentibus dicti Domini Bernabovis certi Nobiles Lombardi subditi sui, videlicet Dominus Jacobus Rubeus . . ." Then come other names, and then the words "omnes de Parma," which are followed by the names of several other captives. This passage reappears *verbatim* in the *Annales mediolaneneses*.[5]

His next appearances are at Alexandria, in the taking of the city and in the discussions that followed. Of these matters Mézières writes thus in his letter to Bonifazio:

Quam admirabilis est deus in suis militibus. & maxime in magnifico Jacobo milite suo perelecto qui pro fide saluatoris tanquam athleta fidelis sanctum passagium adimpleuit ac pro re publica fidei non modicum zelauit. mirabili victoria alexandrie perprobante et precium eius demonstrante. Ipse quidem velud fortis leo cum clippeo

---

[4] Sir George Hill, *A History of Cyprus*, II (Cambridge, England, 1948), 308–369. Petrarch refers to King Peter in *Sen.* VIII 8 as well as in XIII 2.

[5] Muratori, XVI, cols. 507 and 734. On this battle see Jorga, *PM*, pp. 211–212.

fratres suos defendebat confortando legem dando intrepidus cuneos phalangarum infidelium penetrabat. & victoria adeo plena obtenta in consilio regio aliis militibus vaxillantibus miles egregius Jacobus inventus est fidelissimus. ac pro custodia ciuitatis iocunde paratus miliciam suam expendere corpus et animam ponere in obsequium sancte crucis resistendo fidei inimicis. Egyptum et siriam possidentibus.

Petrarch refers thus to the same events:

O felices igitur oculi tui qui viderunt que ab illo viro ante non multum tempus apud alexandriam gesta sunt. . . . felices quoque aures tue que audierunt forcia illa et salubria et gloriosa consilia quibus si creditum fuisset hodie quantum ego arbitror et petrus inclitus Cipri rex indigni vir exitus sed sacre memorie uiueret neque in conuentum malignancium et manus impias cecidisset.[6]

Giacomo's next recorded appearances are at the deathbed and the reopened tomb of the legate, who was taken ill soon after the return from Alexandria, and died in the evening of 6 January 1366. Late in the afternoon Giacomo had come to see him: this visit is reported thus by Mézières in his *Vita S. Petri Thomasii:*

Quibus peractis venit magnificus Dominus Jacobus de Rubeis ejus dilectus, stetitque coram eo. Pater vero meus ipsum Dominum Jacobum tristem caussa sua respiciens, dixit sibi: O fili bene sto, ne doleas. Multi sunt vocati, pauci vero electi. Ego vero sum vocatus, et de electis; Christus vocat me; ego vado ad Christum. Ne doleas fili mi, ne doleas, deditque sibi suam benedictionem et recessit.[7]

Mézières, convinced that miraculous phenomena had attended the legate's death and burial, caused evidence to be gathered from several witnesses, and on 8 May caused the tomb to be opened in the presence of witnesses, of whom Giacomo was one. The body was found to be in an extraordinary state of preservation.[8]

Very shortly after this, Giacomo and Mézières left with the

---

[6] On the capture and abandonment of Alexandria see Jorga, *PM*, pp. 277–303, and Hill, pp. 328–335.

[7] *Acta Sanctorum*, III, including lives for 29 January (Paris, 1863), p. 635 (Chapter XX, Paragraph 124). On the death and burial of the legate see Jorga, *PM*, pp. 311–316.

[8] Jorga, *PM*, pp. 316–317. Jorga states that the procès-verbal drawn up after the opening of the tomb is printed in Daniel de Sainte-Marie's edition of the *Vita S. Petri Thomasii* by Jean Carmesson (Antwerp, 1666): this work is not accessible to me.

Cypriote fleet for a series of raids along the southern coast of
Asia Minor. Giacomo's last recorded appearance is as a heroic
participant in a raid at Candelore (Alaia). Of this raid Mézières
writes thus, in his letter to Bonifazio:

> cristianis castrum de candelor debellantibus. magnanimus Jacobus
> firmiter stetit. nec tela turchorum timuit artem sue milicie demon-
> strando. ac viriliter dimicando. strenuitate eius non defuit nec latuit.
> nostris etenim inportune terga vertentibus. meis oculis videntibus.
> quasi solus iacobus firmiter stetit . . . [9]

Toward the end of his letter Mézières refers to Giacomo's
children, and to his own intention to undertake responsibility
for them. Mézières must have mentioned this same intention in
his lost letter to Petrarch, for Petrarch applauds it toward the
end of his letter to Mézières.

The main statements of Mézières with regard to the character of Giacomo are these: "hic certe a iuuentute. amator veri-
tatis. equitatis & prudencie. clemencie magnanimitatis et dux
Justicie ac in tribulacione continua. magister. paciencie contra
agarenos. bellator fortis velut alter ionata"; and "quod non sit
in etate sua ei similis in milicia in virtute & mansuetudine in
longnanimitate et paciencia coronata."

The main attempt at characterization in the letter of Bonifazio (which is obscure at several points) is this: "Dic mihi
amice virtutis ubi gayus (?) humati corporis gestus ubi militaris
astucia viri, ubi sagax industria facti. ubi compta verecundia
voltus ubi verborum parcitas cum pudore, ubi [here an illegible
word] expressio, ubi tranquilla voluntas eiusdem."

Giacomo was a kinsman of Bonifazio: Mézières in his letter
to Bonifazio speaks of Giacomo as "tui dilecti consanguinei,"
and Bonifazio in his reply speaks of Giacomo as "magnifici consanguinei." Bonifazio served for a time in 1363 as commander
of the Florentine forces in the war against Pisa: Matteo Villani
speaks of him several times, always favorably.[10]

---

[9] The scribe then repeats the words "nec tela . . . dimicando." On
this raid see Jorga, *PM*, pp. 211–212, and Hill, pp. 338–339.

[10] *Cronaca*, xi, 2, 6, 13 and 15. For a general notice of Bonifazio's
serviceable and beneficent career see B. Gonzati, *La basilica di S. Antonio
di Padova*, ii (Padua, 1853), 93–94. Bonifazio is referred to also in a

The reference in Petrarch's letter to the death of King Peter makes it clear that all three letters were written, and that the death of Giacomo occurred, after the murder, which took place, as has been stated, on 17 January 1369. The letter of Mézières is not dated; Petrarch's letter bears, in the first edition of the *Seniles*, the date "Pataui: pridie nonas nouembris"; and Bonifazio's letter bears in the manuscript the date "datum padue die primo nouembris." In November 1369 Petrarch was living in Padua; in the late spring of 1370 he moved to Arquà; and while he visited Padua occasionally there is no reason to think that he was ever there again for any length of time except from 15 November 1372 to the spring of 1373, when he took refuge in Padua from the current local warfare. It follows that the three letters were written in the autumn of 1369, and that the death of Giacomo occurred in the summer or autumn of that year. It may be noted that Petrarch speaks of the capture of Alexandria as having occurred "ante non multum tempus"; also that he speaks of Giacomo as having died in the flower of his strength: "in ipso flore extinctum."

The correspondences in content between the letter of Mézières and that of Petrarch suffice to indicate that the lost letter of Mézières to Petrarch must have been similar, in general, to the letter sent by Mézières to Bonifazio; but they do not suffice to indicate that the letter sent by Mézières to Petrarch was identical with his letter to Bonifazio.[11]

As the presence of Petrarch's letter in a manuscript collection of letters by and to Mézières would lead one to expect, Petrarch's letter as contained in the Arsenal manuscript represents not the final form of the letter, as revised by Petrarch for inclusion among the *Seniles*, but its missive form. The differences, however, are slight. Those that are clearly more than scribal and go beyond the omission or insertion of a single word, or a slight change in order, are as follows:

---

document published by G. Verci in his *Storia della Marca Trivigiana e Veronese*, xiv (Venice, 1789), 62, in the documentary section at the end of the volume.

[11] On the relations of Petrarch and Mézières see Billanovich, 129–130.

Arsenal MS 499	*Edition of 1501*
omnipotentem esse facundiam	omnipotentem ut sic dixerim esse facundiam
si quo die plato rebus humanis excessit vt scriptum est. sol celo cecidisse. visus est Jacobi obitus mesta eclipsi vt ille philosophie sic iste milicie lumen pressit.	mors illius mesta eclipsi militie lumen pressit.
nil ad iram difficilius: nil facilius ad veniam	nil ad iram tardius: nil promptius ad veniam
suarum florida prata virtutum pii amoris dulcibus imbribus irrigasti	suarum florida prata ubi tutum (*lege* virtutum) magni amoris piis imbribus irrigasti
inexausto eterni amoris fonte	inexhausto summi amoris fonte

CHAPTER XII

A General Survey of Renaissance Petrarchism

The field of Renaissance Petrarchism is so vast that it would take a series of volumes to cover it adequately. My purpose, in the present chapter, is simply to attempt a very general survey of the field, hoping thereby to throw some helpful light on some of the main trends, groupings, and relationships that appear within it.

The word "Petrarchism" may properly be used, if the widest possible application is desired, to mean "productive activity in literature, art, or music under the direct or indirect influence of the writings of Petrarch, the expression of admiration for him, and the study of his works and of their influence." The word may properly be used, also, in a large variety of more or less restricted meanings.

After a brief survey of the general features of literary activity under the influence of Petrarch during the Renaissance, I shall limit the scope of this chapter to consideration of the influence of Petrarch on Renaissance lyric verse.

The writings of Petrarch may be classified thus: (1) the Latin works; (2) the *Triumphs;* (3) the *Canzoniere.* There exist also, outside the *Canzoniere,* some Italian lyrics that are certainly by Petrarch, and a good many that may or may not be his.[1]

From each of the three divisions of his work there proceeded, beginning in his lifetime, a specific wave of influence. While these waves were virtually simultaneous in respect to their time

---

[1] These poems, called *rime disperse* or *rime estravaganti,* are far less important than the *Canzoniere,* but they should not be disregarded in any serious study of Petrarchism, especially since a few of them are included as addenda in a good many sixteenth-century editions of the *Canzoniere.*

of origin, they were by no means equal in their original strength or in their periods of greatest strength. Generally speaking, the first wave, in point of original strength and in respect to the time when it reached its peak, was the wave that proceeded from the Latin works; next came the wave from the *Triumphs;* and last the wave from the *Canzoniere.*

In Italy the wave from the Latin works reached its peak in the late fourteenth and early fifteenth centuries, diminished thereafter, and virtually disappeared in the seventeenth century. The wave from the *Triumphs* reached its peak in the fifteenth century, diminished thereafter, and virtually disappeared in the sixteenth century. The wave from the *Canzoniere*, of lesser strength, until the latter part of the fifteenth century, than the wave from the *Triumphs*, thereafter gained strength swiftly, rose to a tremendous peak in the sixteenth century, and has diminished gradually since that time, though occasionally resurgent and still existent.[2]

In other European countries the order of the three divisions in respect to influence was, broadly speaking, the same. The three waves overlap; but, in terms of the times of original impact and of peak of interest, the wave from the Latin works generally came first, the wave from the *Triumphs* next, and the wave from the *Canzoniere* last.

From this point on I shall limit my attention to the third wave—redefining Renaissance Petrarchism, accordingly, as "the writing of lyric verse under the direct or indirect influence of Petrarch in a period beginning in his lifetime and ending about 1600."

The main manifestations of Renaissance Petrarchism are the use of Petrarchan words, phrases, lines, metaphors, conceits, and ideas, and the adoption, for poetic purposes, of the typical

---

[2] Most fourteenth- and fifteenth-century MSS of the Italian poems of Petrarch contain both the *Triumphs* and the *Canzoniere:* but among the many that contain only one of the two works those that contain the *Triumphs* are far more numerous than those that contain the *Canzoniere*. Similarly, most fifteenth-century editions of the Italian poems of Petrarch contain both works; but, while there are several separate editions of the *Triumphs*, there is no separate edition of the *Canzoniere*.

Petrarchan experiences and attitudes. In countries other than Italy, Petrarchism manifests itself also in translations and paraphrases. Among the poets who were in some sense Petrarchistic there is wide variation with respect to the intensity of their Petrarchism. Some are subservient and purely imitative; some, though they make use of Petrarchan materials, have something of their own to say; and there are some in whose verse the Petrarchistic elements are merely secondary and incidental.

Most of the headings of the numbered sections of the rest of this survey begin with the name of just one poet. The men whose names are thus selected are in general either the initiators or the most notable representatives of the phase of Petrarchism concerned; in all such cases, however—except that of Chaucer— it is to be understood that other poets were also writing Petrarchistic verse in the same period. It is to be understood, also, that in many cases activity on the part of some members of the group of poets concerned continued into a period following that in which most of their work was done.

Petrarchism began, of course, in Italy; and we may first consider its development in its homeland.

Italian Petrarchism

(1) *Boccaccio: The Middle of the Fourteenth Century.* By making use of two of the sonnets of Petrarch in certain stanzas of the *Filostrato*, which he wrote about 1340, Boccaccio—always a devotee of Petrarch—qualified as the first Petrarchist. In Boccaccio's own lyrics the influence of Petrarch appears merely as one of three strains, the other two being the influence of Dante and that of certain followers of Dante and Cavalcanti. The same triple influence persists in other Italian poets of the fourteenth century.

(2) *Minor Poets of the First Half of the Fifteenth Century.* In Giusto de' Conti and some of his contemporaries the influence of Petrarch became dominant: these men, themselves quite uninspired, are the first group of thoroughgoing Petrarchists.

(3) *Boiardo: The Second Half of the Fifteenth Century.*

Boiardo and Lorenzo de' Medici, the major lyrists of this period, both derived much from Petrarch; but their own lyric gifts enabled them to absorb and re-create what they derived. Boiardo, close to Petrarch, is nevertheless a fine and spirited poet in his own right. Lorenzo's Petrarchism is held to the status of a resource to be drawn upon or disregarded at his princely pleasure. Other writers—among them Pico della Mirandola, disappointingly feeble as lyrist—represent subservient Petrarchism.

(4) *Il Chariteo: The Late Fifteenth Century*. None of the poets of the first three periods of Italian Petrarchism had any considerable influence on the later lyric, Italian or foreign; but in the last decades of the fifteenth century there developed a new phase of Petrarchism which was destined to have great influence, both in Italy and abroad. The responsibility for the initiation of this new phase lies with the Catalan Benedicto Gareth, who came to Naples in his early youth and became, to all intents and purposes, an Italian: he was known, in Italy, as Il Chariteo. Petrarch himself, from time to time, indulges in conceits, antitheses, and other rhetorical devices—which, however, constitute a secondary group of characteristics within the general body of his rich and beautiful and living verse. Il Chariteo—though by no means without artistic gifts of his own —devotes too much attention to these rhetorical devices, and exploits them energetically. His cardinal and most infectious sin is the materialization of Petrarchan metaphors, to which he gives an existential literality they were never meant to bear. His two chief companions and followers in flamboyance were Tebaldeo and the devastatingly popular Serafino dell'Aquila. Others whose verse, though in itself insignificant, proved to be very influential were Sasso and Filosseno. The Chariteans, especially Serafino, made extensive use of the eight-line *strambotto*—a form not found in Petrarch.

(5) *Bembo: The First Half of the Sixteenth Century*. From such flamboyant aberration Italian lyrism was rescued, for the time being, by the Venetian patrician, Pietro Bembo, of whom an admirer wrote:

Che se non eri tu, mastron di tutti,
Tutti sariemo stati Tebaldei!

Bembo, in his attainment and lordly exercise of literary dictator-
ship, was to the Italian sixteenth century what Malherbe was to
the early French seventeenth century and Dr. Johnson to the
late English eighteenth. Partly because he was a humanist, and
partly because his own creative gift was very slight, the main
literary law he announced was that of imitation; and in the field
of Italian poetry the one adequate and compulsory object of
imitation was Petrarch. So Bembo himself wrote imitative
Petrarchistic verse, with extreme fidelity, impeccable good taste,
and not much else. In his train hosts of Italian poets and poetesses
strove to imitate Petrarch—or Bembo—or each other. Among
them were Alamanni, Ariosto, Caro, Castiglione, Vittoria Colonna, Della Casa, Veronica Gambara, Guidiccioni, Molza, Navagero, Sannazaro, and Bernardo Tasso. Castiglione and Guidiccioni wrote admirable patriotic verse—still within the Petrarchan
tradition. The one great Italian lyrist of this period, Michelangelo,
made some use of Petrarchan material in his highly individual
poetry, but he never bowed the knee to Bembo—or to anyone else.

The sixteenth century saw the prolific production of two
kinds of books that were influential both for contemporary and
for later Petrarchism: editions of the *Canzoniere* and lyric anthologies. More than 130 editions of the *Canzoniere* were published in Italy in the course of the century. Some of them
contained the text alone; others contained voluminous commentaries, among which that of Vellutello was the one most frequently reprinted. In 1545 the enterprising Venetian publisher,
Giolito, brought out a well-made little volume entitled *Rime
diverse di molti eccellentiss. Auttori nuovamente raccolte, Libro
primo*. About a hundred poets, most of them Petrarchistic in
the Bembist sense, were represented in this volume, some by
one or two poems only, some by several or by many poems. The
success of this anthology led Giolito and a number of rival
publishers to print many similar volumes. In the earlier anthologies poetry of the Bembist type predominated.

(6) *The Neapolitans: The Mid-Sixteenth Century*. Toward the middle of the century there appeared in Italy a new lyric movement which was in part a reaction against the puristic restraint of Bembo, in part a reversion to the flamboyance of the Chariteans, and in part a manifestation of true lyric energy. The leaders of this movement were—like Il Chariteo—men of the Neapolitan region: Angelo di Costanzo, Rota, Tansillo, and Galeazzo di Tarsia. Fortunately, they were better poets than the Chariteans. Their flamboyance was in general less violent; they retained something of Bembo's stylistic carefulness; and some of them, at least, were more distinctive than either the Chariteans or the Bembists in their poetic experiences and utterances. Tansillo, the best Italian lyrist between Michelangelo and Tasso, is notably successful as a poet of nature. The verse of these men was made known chiefly in some of the later anthologies, first in the *Rime di diversi illustri napoletani et d'altri nobiliss. intelleti, nuovamente raccolte e non piu stampate, Terzo libro*, published by Giolito in 1552, but most emphatically in *I fiori delle rime de' poeti illustri nuovamente raccolti et ordinati*, published by Sessa in 1558.

(7) *Torquato Tasso: The Second Half of the Sixteenth Century*. Tasso's 2,000 lyrics are similar, on the whole, to those of the Neapolitans; but the best of them shine with an inner and an outer beauty denied to lesser men.

Marino, through whom the returning Chariteanism was to attain the still more startling triumphs of Marinism, began the writing of his lyrics before 1600; but their publication and their influence belong to the history of the following century.

From Italy Petrarchism spread westward into Catalonia, the rest of Spain, Portugal, and France; northward into England, Scotland, the Netherlands, and Germany; and eastward into Dalmatia, Hungary, Poland, and Cyprus. We may now survey its development in each of these regions.

Catalan Petrarchism

Toward the end of the fourteenth century Lorenz Mallol imitated Petrarch's *canzone* beginning *S'i' 'l dissi mai*; and early in the fifteenth century Jordi de Sent Jordi paraphrased Petrarch's sonnet *Pace non trovo*. The chief Catalan lyrist of the fifteenth century, Ausias March, is regarded by some scholars as an imitator of Petrarch; others believe that the resemblances in the poems of the two men are due to independent derivations, direct or indirect, from the Provençal lyric.

Spanish Petrarchism

(1) The Marquis of Santillana: The Mid-Fifteenth Century. The forty-two sonnets *fechos al itálico modo* in 1444 and thereafter by the Marquis of Santillana are of interest as constituting the first instance of Spanish Petrarchism. The Marquis, however, poet though he proved himself in other writings, did not, in these sonnets, attain either smoothness of form or distinction in content; and they did not serve to establish a Petrarchistic tradition in Spain.

(2) Boscán: The First Half of the Sixteenth Century. The early years of the sixteenth century, made distressful for Italy by French and Spanish invasions and by Franco-Spanish conflicts in Italy, were inevitably years in which many warring French and Spanish courtiers received an immediate and impressive revelation of Italian culture. Among the Spaniards thus impressed were Boscán and Garcilaso de la Vega, both of whom served in Italy. But the torch of Petrarchism was passed to Boscán not in Italy, but after his return to Spain. In Granada, in 1526, he met the Venetian ambassador Navagero, humanist and poet; and Spanish Petrarchism, as an effective and continuing movement, appears to stem directly from their conversation.[3]

---

[3] In the dedicatory letter of his *Sonetos y canciones a manera de los italianos*, Boscán writes thus of his conversation with Navagero and its consequences:

"Porque estando un día en Granada con el Navagero . . . tratando con él en cosas de ingenio y letras, me dixo por qué no probaba en lengua Castellana Sonetos y otras artes de trovas usadas por los buenos autores de Italia; y no solamente me lo dixo así livianamente, mas aun me rogó que lo hiciese. Partíme pocos días después para mi casa, y con la largueza y soledad del camino discurriendo por diversas cosas, fuí á dar muchas veces

The Petrarchistic results of Boscán's experiment were a hundred sonnets and *canciones*, based chiefly on the poems of Petrarch himself, but with some minor Bembist reflections. They have little poetic value; but they gave a new and enduring orientation to the Spanish lyric. Boscán (whose prose was better than his verse) translated the *Cortegiano*. His comrade in arms and in verse, Garcilaso de la Vega, darling of the annals of Spanish heroism, exemplified the perfect courtier. Bembo called him the best-loved Spaniard who ever came to Italy. Garcilaso's Petrarchan poems, not very numerous, are of a refined and idyllic beauty that has proved to be perennial in its charm. Petrarch was his main model; but he shows acquaintance also with the poems of Sannazaro and of the young Tansillo. It was presumably the character of the Italian poets whom they came to know personally that saved Boscán and Garcilaso from the Chariteam infection. The Petrarchistic tradition thus initiated was presently confirmed by the example of the humanistic diplomat, Diego Hurtado de Mendoza, who wrote a number of Petrarchistic sonnets.

(3) *Herrera: The Second Half of the Sixteenth Century.* The writers of this period constitute a varied group, distinguished from their predecessors not only in date but by the fact that these later poets made extensive use of the Italian lyric anthologies of the middle of the century. Cetina and Acuña, soldiers both, linked the earlier and later groups.[4] Fray Luis de León, the noblest Spanish poet of his time, translated poems by Petrarch and by Bembo; but his Petrarchism was hardly more than incidental. The outstanding and most influential Petrarchist of the group was Fernando de Herrera, whose verse, replete with Petrarchistic phrases and images, is spirited and magniloquent.

---

en lo que el Navagero me había dicho; y así comencé á tentar este género de verso. En el qual al principio hallé alguna dificultad, por ser muy artificioso y tener muchas particularidades diferentes del nuestro. Pero después pareciéndome, quizá con el amor de las cosas propias, que esto comenzaba á sucederme bien, fuí poco á poco metiéndome en calor con ello."

[4] Cetina came to the New World. He was killed while serenading in Los Angeles on 1 April 1554.

Portuguese Petrarchism

(1) *The Cancioneiro geral: The Late Fifteenth Century and the Early Sixteenth.* Petrarchan influence makes its first Portuguese appearance in a few of the thousand poems of this very miscellaneous collection, put together by Garcia de Resende.

(2) *Sá de Miranda: The First Half of the Sixteenth Century.* Sá de Miranda, humanist and courtier, the first noteworthy Portuguese Petrarchist, spent some time, in and after 1521, in Italy, where he probably came to know Bembo, Ariosto, Sannazaro, and Vittoria Colonna. He was an enthusiastic admirer of Boscán and Garcilaso. He wrote Petrarchistic poems both in Portuguese and in Spanish, and in some cases acknowledged his source by the notation "feita seguindo Petrarca." But his Petrarchism, partly direct, is also mediated in part by Boscán and Garcilaso. Sá de Miranda was followed by a considerable group of Petrarchistic poets, among whom Ferreira was the most vocal.

(3) *Camões: The Second Half of the Sixteenth Century.* Camões, great by reason of his lyrics as well as by reason of his epic, manifests a thorough and appreciative acquaintance with Petrarch. He made extensive use of both the sonnet and *canzone* forms. Several of his poems reflect particular Petrarchan poems, and many others are in some measure Petrarchistic in their content. He shows knowledge also of the poetry of Bembo. Camões, like Sá de Miranda, was followed by a group of minor Petrarchists.

French Petrarchism

(1) *Marot: The First Half of the Sixteenth Century.* Unlike Boscán, Garcilaso, and Sá de Miranda, the first French imitators of Italian verse took as their main models not Petrarch and the Bembists, but the Chariteans, especially Serafino; and the form they chiefly imitated was not the sonnet but the *strambotto*. And whereas the Iberians had some personal acquaintance with Bembo and the Bembists, the transmission of the Charitean influence to the French poets was a matter of the printed page: Il Chariteo and Serafino had died long before Marot first went to Italy, and Tebaldeo, though still alive at that time, had long out-

lived his poetic self. Petrarchan and Bembist influence, however, is not absent. Marot translated seven of the poems of Petrarch, six sonnets and one *canzone*, *Standomi un giorno solo a la fenestra*, headed: *Des visions de Petrarque*. Saint-Gelais, who occasionally shows direct knowledge of Petrarch, Bembo, and Sannazaro, wrote several sonnets. Scève, when he rose above his Chariteans, was more Platonic than Petrarchistic.

In 1545 Jean de Tournes published at Lyons an edition of the Italian text of the poems of Petrarch. This edition was reprinted in 1547 and 1550. In the latter year another Lyonese publisher, Roville, brought out a similar edition, of which reprints or revisions appeared in 1551, 1558, 1564, and 1574.

(2) The *Pléiade: The Mid-Sixteenth Century*. Du Bellay refers to Petrarch five times in *La Deffence et illustration de la langue françoyse* (1548), most notably in this passage:

Sonne moy ces beaux sonnetz, non moins docte que plaisante invention italienne, conforme de nom à l'ode, et differente d'elle seulement pource que le sonnet a certains vers reiglez et limitez, et l'ode peut courir par toutes manieres de vers librement . . . Pour le sonnet donques tu as Petrarque et quelques modernes Italiens.

There is also a laudatory reference to Bembo.

The publication of the *Deffence* was followed by a spate of Petrarchistic lyrics. In the preface to the first edition (1549) of the *Olive* Du Bellay states frankly that he has used Italian models. Of the 115 sonnets of the second edition (1550), the majority are derived—some almost literally, some freely—from Italian sources: about ten from Petrarch, about twenty from Ariosto, and about thirty from the first two Bembist anthologies. The *Erreurs amoureuses* of Tyard (1549) are modelled mainly on Scève and the Chariteans. Ronsard, Baïf, and Magny, in their respective *Amours* (1552, 1552, and 1553), find their models most frequently in Petrarch, Bembo, and the first two Bembist anthologies—Ronsard re-creating whatever he touches. In the collections published by Baïf and Ronsard in 1555 and 1556, however, there are intrusions of Chariten influence. Du Bellay's *Antiquitez de Rome* (1558), written after his return from a four years' stay in Italy, echoes certain patriotic poems of

Petrarch and the Bembists. To the *Antiquitez* Du Bellay added, under the title *Songe ou vision sur Rome*, a series of fifteen sonnets in which he follows the general idea, but not the content, of Petrarch's *canzone* of the six visions.

In these same years Vasquin Philieul, a jurist of Carpentras, produced a verse translation of the Italian poems of Petrarch—first, in 1548, a collection of about 200 translations, under the title *Laure d'Avignon,* and finally, in 1555, *Toutes les euvres vulgaires de Françoys Petrarque.*

(3) *Desportes: The Second Half of the Sixteenth Century.* Olivier de Magny, who had been in Italy at the same time as Du Bellay, brought back, in his *Soupirs,* a very different type of influence; for, though a few of the poems of this collection reflect poems of Petrarch and some of the Bembists, the main influence is that of the Chariteans—an influence resurgent, just then, in Italian Petrarchism. The same influence is dominant also in the sonnets of Belleau, and is discernible in the later verse of Ronsard. It is strong in Desportes as well; but Desportes drew heavily, also, upon Petrarch himself, and derived much from the Neapolitans—especially Angelo di Costanzo—and from other poets represented in the Italian lyric anthologies. With Bertaut the influence of the Chariteans fades out; the influence of the Neapolitans, especially that of Tansillo, becomes very strong; and the influence of Torquato Tasso appears for the first time. *Enfin Malherbe vint:* but in his earliest poems he too is a follower of of the Neapolitans and of Tasso.

Flemish Petrarchism

Vander Noot: The Second Half of the Sixteenth Century. The lyrics of Jan Vander Noot, the first Renaissance poet of the Netherlands, were strongly influenced by Marot and the poets of the Pléiade. He knew and admired the work of Petrarch, and translated two of his sonnets. He refers often to Boscán, an edition of whose poems was published in Antwerp in 1576; but it is not clear that he derived any poetic material from him. Vander Noot was an ardent Calvinist, and in 1567 had to take refuge in London. There, in 1568, he brought out an antipapal tract with a long title beginning *Het Theatre oft Toon-neel.* To the prose body of the tract he prefixed, as texts, three poems: first, under the heading *Epigrammen*, a translation, based in part on the Italian and in part on Marot's version, of Petrarch's *canzone* of the six visions; second, under the heading *Sonnetten naar du Bellay*, a translation of eleven of the fifteen sonnets of Du Bellay's *Songe*—which, as has been noted, was patterned on the same Petrarchan *canzone;* and third, four similar stanzas of his own, based on the Apocalypse. Each stanza or sonnet is illustrated by an engraving.[5] He brought out, in the same year, a French edition of the *Theatre*, in which the poems of Marot and Du Bellay appear in their original French, and, in the following year, an English edition, entitled in part, *A Theatre wherein be represented . . . the miseries & calamities that follow the voluptuous Worldlings:* this English edition will be referred to presently. Three years later a German edition was published in Cologne; the poems were translated, from the Flemish, by one Balthasar Froe.

English Petrarchism

(1) *Chaucer: The Late Fourteenth Century.* Chaucer's *Cantus Troili*—lines 400–420 of Book I of the *Troilus and Criseyde*, which was completed in the period 1385–1387—is a close adaptation of Petrarch's sonnet *S'amor non è.*

(2) *Wyatt: The First Half of the Sixteenth Century.* Sir Thomas Wyatt, who visited Italy in 1527, returned to England with a considerable knowledge of Petrarch and a determination to imitate him. Among Wyatt's hundred poems there are some thirty sonnets—the first English sonnets. About twenty-five of his poems are derived wholly or in part from Petrarch, several being translations: the Petrarchan poems concerned include *canzoni* as well as sonnets. Wyatt makes use of Petrarchan poems not only in his sonnets but also in several of the poems he wrote in other forms. One of his sonnets is a

---

[5] These engravings have their importance in the history of emblem books. They reappear in the French, English, and German editions of the *Theatre*.

translation of a sonnet by Sannazaro. Wyatt's versification is very rough. The Earl of Surrey, a junior contemporary and a great admirer of Wyatt, was much more successful in his adaptation of Italian forms. About half of his two-score poems are sonnets. A few of them are translations or adaptations of particular Petrarchan poems: more of them—some sonnets, some in other forms—show brief Petrarchan borrowings.[6] The poems of Wyatt and Surrey were first published, posthumously, in 1557, in Tottel's *Miscellany*, which opens with these words, addressed by "The Printer to the Reader":

> That to haue wel written in verse, yea & in small parcelles, de-
> serueth great praise, the workes of diuers Latines, Italians, and other,
> doe proue sufficiently. That our tong is able in that kynde to do as
> praiseworthely as y rest, the honorable stile of the noble earle of
> Surrey, and the weightinesse of the depewitted sir Thomas Wyat
> the elders verse, with seuerall graces in sondry good Englishe writers,
> doe show abundantly.

The poems of Wyatt and Surrey make up about two-thirds of the collection, which contains also about a hundred poems by "Vncertain auctours."[7] A few contain Petrarchan borrow-ings. Two of these poems are entitled respectively "A praise of Petrarke and of Lawra his ladie" and "That Petrark cannot be passed but notwithstanding that Laura is far surpassed." The first of the two is worth quotation:

> O Petrarke hed and prince of poets all,
>   Whose liuely gift of flowyng eloquence,
> Wel may we seke, but finde not how or whence
> So rare a gift with thee did rise and fall,
> Peace to thy bones, and glory immortall
> Be to thy name, and to her excellence.
> Whose beauty lighted in thy time and sence
> So to be set forth as none other shall.
> Why hath not our pens rimes so parfit wrought
> Ne why our time forth bringeth beauty such
> To trye our wittes as golde is by the touche,

---

[6] The general parallelism between the Spanish pair, Boscán and Gar-cilaso, and the English pair, Wyatt and Surrey, is extraordinarily close.

[7] A similar section of poems by "incerti autori" appears in the Giolito anthology of 1547—the *Rime di diversi nobili huomini . . . Libro secondo*.

If to the stile the matter aided ought.
But ther was neuer Laura more than one,
And her had petrarke for his paragone.

(3) *The Early Elizabethans: The Second Half of the Sixteenth Century.* Gascoigne (who owned a copy of the edition of Petrarch with the Gesualdo commentary published by Giglio in 1552) and other early Elizabethans occasionally wrote sonnets and occasionally used Petrarchistic material. Some of their poems are translations or imitations from the French Petrarchists. In the English edition of Vander Noot's *Theatre* the stanzas that represent Petrarch's *canzone* are headed *Epigrams:* the first and third are sonnets; the others, also rhymed, are of twelve lines. The sonnets taken from Du Bellay's *Songe* and those on the Apocalypse are headed *Sonets:* each consists of fourteen lines in blank verse. The first two poems—and presumably the third— were translated directly from the French. It seems probable that these translations were made by Spenser, though he was then only sixteen or seventeen years old. The *Complaints . . . by Ed. Sp.* published in 1591 contains as its last two items *The Visions of Bellay* and *The Visions of Petrarch formerly translated.* The text of the *Visions of Petrarch* corresponds *verbatim* to that of the translation in the *Theatre*, except for a few minor variants and the fact that the twelve-line stanzas are now extended to sonnet length by expansion of the concluding lines. The text of the *Visions of Bellay* corresponds in a great many phrases to that of the translation in the *Theatre*, but is in rhymed sonnets, and includes the four sonnets of the *Songe* that were not included in the *Theatre*. Spenser translated also the *Antiquitez de Rome*, as *Ruines of Rome: by Bellay;* and upon the *Antiquitez* he based his own *Ruines of Time.*[8]

---

[8] The Harvard copy of the edition of Petrarch with the commentary of Vellutello published by Griffio in 1554 was owned by an Englishman at least as early as 1574. That date is written on f. 62ᵛ, beside the first line of the sonnet *Ben sapeva io.* On f. 89ʳ the entire sonnet *S'una fede amorosa* is underlined, and above it is written the date ". 9 . ffe: 1577." There are many marginal translations in a slightly later hand: on f. 1ᵛ, for instance, "guai" is translated as "sorowes"; on f. 3ʳ "s'agghiaccia" is translated as "waxeth colde"; and on f. 205ᵛ "speglio" is translated as "mirrour or looking glasse."

(4) The Later Elizabethans: The Late Sixteenth Century.
The typical form of English lyric activity in the last two decades
of the century was the writing of sonnet sequences. The first
to be published was Watson's *Hecatompathia* (1582). Sidney's
Astrophel and Stella, published posthumously in 1591, was
probably written in large part in 1582. The years 1592–1597
saw the publication of nearly a score of sequences: among the
more notable are Daniel's *Delia* (1592), Constable's *Diana*
(1592), Lodge's *Phillis* (1593), and Spenser's *Amoretti* (1595).
Nearly all the sequences are, in varying degrees, Petrarchistic.
The sources appear to be about equally Italian and French; the
latest authors derive much also from their immediate English
predecessors. The Italian sources include Petrarch, Il Chariteo
and the Chariteans, Bembo and the Bembists, the Neapolitans,
and Tasso. Many of the Italian poems in question seem to have
become known through the Italian lyric anthologies. The
French sources include Scève, the Pléiade, and Desportes. All
of the English sonneteers are more or less eclectic. Desportes
is a favorite source for Constable, Ronsard for Lodge, and
Tasso for Spenser.

No convincing evidences of specific Petrarchistic derivation
are to be found (though there has been much seeking) in the
sonnets of Shakespeare.

Scotch Petrarchism

Several Scotch poets, in the last decades of the century,
wrote verse in which there is a Petrarchistic strain. Alexander
Montgomery and some others wrote in Scotch; the Earl of
Stirling and others wrote in English. Their sources, naturally
enough, are mainly French, but some use is made of Petrarch
and of Italian Petrarchists, and there are some borrowings from
English contemporaries.

German Petrarchism

Aside from Balthasar Froe's translation of Vander Noot's
translation of Petrarch's *canzone* of the six visions, there is no

certain evidence of any German use of the *Canzoniere* before 1601. *The Schönes Blumenfeldt* of Theobald Höck, published in that year, opens with a poem which is largely an adaptation of the opening sonnet of the *Canzoniere;* and there are a few more or less certain Petrarchan echoes in some of Höck's other poems.

Dalmatian Petrarchism

(*1*) *Menčetić and Gjora Držić: The Late Fifteenth Century.* These were the first two lyric poets of the thriving republic of Ragusa, which had close commercial and cultural relations with Italy. They took as models both Petrarch himself and their contemporary Chariteans, especially Serafino.

(*2*) *Minor Poets of the First Half of the Sixteenth Century.* A few poets of this period, some of them Ragusans, some from the Dalmatian islands, continued the Petrarchistic tradition. Bembo and Ariosto appear among the poets imitated.

(*3*) *Ranjina: The Second Half of the Sixteenth Century.* Ranjina, of a leading merchant family of Ragusa, came to Messina in 1559, lived there until 1563, and in those four years seems to have written most or all of his Croatian poems. The Chariteans, especially Serafino, were his early models. In 1563 he moved to Florence where, called Ragnina, he was warmly welcomed into literary society. His Croatian poems, *Piesni razlike*, were published in Florence in 1563. He then wrote a number of poems in Italian, taking as new models Petrarch, Bembo, and some of the Neapolitans. Twenty-seven of his Italian sonnets were included in the 1565 edition of Giolito's *Secondo volume delle rime scelte di diversi eccellenti autori.* This was one of the favorite sources of Desportes; and three, at least, of the sonnets he derived from it are based upon sonnets by Ranjina. Zlatarić, a Ragusan poet of greater originality and distinction, adapted material from Petrarch, Bembo, some of the Bembists, and some of the Neapolitans. Several other men, including Marin Držić and Naljesković, wrote Petrarchistic verse in the same half-century.

Hungarian Petrarchism

The first great Hungarian lyric poet, Balassa, whose writing was done mainly in the last quarter of the sixteenth century, enriched his genuinely personal poems with elements drawn from many sources, among them the *Canzoniere* of Petrarch. The *Canzoniere* as a whole seems to have served Balassa as a model, in a very general sense, for his Julia cycle; and specific Petrarchan influences appear in certain poems.

Polish Petrarchism

The influence of Petrarch is present, though as a minor strain, among the many influences, largely classic, that affected the vigorous lyrics of the first great Polish poet, Kochanowski, who wrote in the second half of the sixteenth century.

Cypriote Petrarchism

A sixteenth-century MS now in the Library of St. Mark's contains a collection of some 200 poems in the Greek dialect of Cyprus. Twenty-two of these poems are sonnets, and these are in general Petrarchistic in form and content. Several are translations or adaptations of particular poems of the *Canzoniere*. In an adaptation of the sonnet *Quand'io veggio* the first, fifth, ninth, and twelfth lines of Petrarch's sonnet are incorporated in their Italian form. The name of the author is not known, but there is evidence that he was a man of culture and of noble family. The MS once belonged to the humanist Natale Conti.

BIBLIOGRAPHICAL NOTE

The bibliography of Petrarchism is, of course, vast. Many of the most important discussions are to be found in general histories of the literatures concerned, in editions of particular poets, and in books or articles dealing with particular poets. The following is a list of a few publications that deal with Petrarchism and (except in a very few cases) cover the works of more than one man.

Petrarchism (General)

C. Calcaterra, "Petrarca e il petrarchismo," in *Problemi ed orientamenti critici di lingua e di letteratura italiana*, ed. A. Momigliano, III (Milan, 1949), 198–213, 253–273.

H. Hauvette, *Les Poésies lyriques de Pétrarque* (Paris, 1931), Part II, "La Fortune des poésies de Pétrarque."

Italian Petrarchism

V. Cian, "Il maggior petrarchista del Cinquecento, Pietro Bembo," in R. Accademia Petrarca di Lettere Arti Scienze di Arezzo, *Annali della cattedra petrarchesca*, VIII (1938), 1–42.

G. G. Ferrero, *Il petrarchismo del Bembo e le rime di Michelangelo* (Turin, 1935).

A. Graf, *Attraverso il Cinquecento*, 2nd ed. (Turin, 1926), pp. 3–86, "Petrarchismo ed antipetrarchismo."

F. Rizzi, *L'anima del Cinquecento e la lirica volgare* (Milan, 1928).

L. Tonelli, *L'amore nella poesia e nel pensiero del rinascimento* (Florence, 1933), pp. 15–132, "La lirica."

H. Vaganay, *Le Sonnet en Italie et en France au XVIᵉ siècle* (Lyons, 1907).

J. Vianey, *op. cit.* below, under French Petrarchism.

Foreign Petrarchism (General)

A. Meozzi, *Azione e diffusione della letteratura italiana in Europa (sec. XV–XVII)* (Pisa, 1932–1934). Vol. I, *Contatti di uomini e idee;* vol. II, Part I, *Il petrarchismo europeo.*

Catalan Petrarchism

A. Farinelli, *Italia e Spagna* (Turin, 1929), I, 1–88, "Petrarca in Ispagna (nell'età media)."

A. Pagès, *Ausias March et ses prédécesseurs* (Paris, 1912).

B. Sanvisenti, *I primi influssi di Dante, del Petrarca, e del Boccaccio sulla letteratura spagnuola* (Milan, 1902).

Spanish Petrarchism

A. Farinelli, *op. cit.;* also "Il Petrarca fra gli Ispani e i Lusitani," *Studi petrarcheschi*, I (1948), 225–239.

J. G. Fucilla, many articles, especially "Two Generations of Petrarchism and Petrarchists in Spain," in *Modern Philology*, XXVII (1929–1930), 277–295.

A. Meozzi, *Lirica della rinascita italiana in Spagna e Portogallo (sec. XV–XVII)* (Florence, 1943).

B. Sanvisenti, *op. cit.* above, under Catalan Petrarchism.

Portuguese Petrarchism

J. G. Fucilla, several articles, especially "A Miscellany of Portuguese Imitations," in *Hispanic Review*, III (1935), 45–55.

A. Meozzi, *op. cit.* above, under Spanish Petrarchism.

G. C. Rossi, "La poesia del Petrarca in Portogallo," in *Cultura neolatina*, III (1943), 175–190.

French Petrarchism

H. Chamard, *Histoire de la Pléiade*, 4 vols. (Paris, 1939–1940).
F. Flamini, *Studi di storia letteraria italiana e straniera* (Leghorn, 1895), pp. 197–381.
M. Françon, "Sur l'influence de Pétrarque en France aux XVe et XVIe siècles," in *Italica*, xix (1942), 105–110.
H. Gambier, *Italie et renaissance poétique en France* (Padua, 1936).
P. Laumonier, *Ronsard, poète lyrique* (Paris, 1909).
C. Pellegrini, "Il Petrarca nella cultura francese," *Rivista di letterature moderne*, i (1946), 75–84.
A. Pizzorusso, "Il petrarchismo di Desportes," in *Studi petrarcheschi*, v (1952), 237–297.
H. Vaganay, *op. cit.* above, under Italian Petrarchism.
J. Vianey, *Le Pétrarquisme en France au XVIe siècle* (Montpellier, 1909).

Flemish Petrarchism

R. Galland, "Un Poète errant de la Renaissance: Jean Van der Noot et l'Angleterre," in *Revue de Littérature comparée*, ii (1922), 337–350.
R. O. J. Van Nuffel, "Il Petrarca nell'opera di Jan Vander Noot," in *Studi petrarcheschi*, iii (1950), 183–196.
A. Vermeylen, *Leven en Werken van Jonker Jan Van der Noot* (Antwerp, 1899).
Catharina Ypes, *Petrarca in de Nederlandse Letterkunde* (Amsterdam, 1934), pp. 35–69.

English Petrarchism

L. Einstein, *The Italian Renaissance in England* (3rd ed., New York, 1935), Chap. VIII.
H. K. Hasselkuss, *Der Petrarkismus in der Sprache der englischen Sonettdichter der Renaissance* (Münster, 1927).
Lisle C. John, *The Elizabethan Sonnet Sequences* (New York, 1938).
H. E. Rollins, ed., *Tottel's Miscellany (1557–1587)*, 2 vols. (Cambridge, 1928–1929).
H. E. Rollins, ed., *The Sonnets*, in *A New Variorum Edition of Shakespeare* (Philadelphia and London, 1944), ii, 125–132.
Janet G. Scott, *Les Sonnets élisabéthains* (Paris, 1929).
C. Segrè, *Relazioni letterarie fra Italia e Inghilterra* (Florence, 1911), pp. 53–159, "Due petrarchisti inglesi del secolo XVI."

Scotch Petrarchism

Janet G. Scott, *op. cit.* above, under English Petrarchism, Chap. XV.

German Petrarchism

H. Souvageol, *Petrarka in der deutschen Lyrik des 17. Jahrhunderts* (Anspach, 1911), pp. 1–9.

Dalmatian Petrarchism

A. Cronia, "La fortuna del Petrarca fra gli slavi meridionali," in R. Accademia Petrarca di Lettere Arti e Scienze di Arezzo, *Convegno petrarchesco dell'11–13 ottobre 1931*, Part II (Arezzo, 1932), pp. 101–113; also "Il petrarchismo nel Cinquecento serbo-croato," in *Studi petrarcheschi*, I (1948), 241–255.

M. Deanović, "Les Influences italiennes sur la littérature croate du littoral adriatique jusqu'à la fin du XVIIIᵉ siècle," in *Revue de Littérature comparée*, XIV (1934), 30–52.

G. Surdich, " 'Traduzioni' dal Petrarca nell'antica letteratura serbo-croata di Dalmazia," in *Studi petrarcheschi*, II (1949), 231–242.

J. Torbarina, *Italian Influences on the Poets of the Ragusan Republic* (London, 1931).

Hungarian Petrarchism

A. Eckhardt, "Valentino Balassa e Petrarca," in *Corvina*, I (1921), 59–71.

Polish Petrarchism

M. Brahmer, *Petrarkizm w poezji XVI wieku* (Cracow, 1927).
J. Langlade, *Jean Kochanowski* (Paris, 1932).

Cypriote Petrarchism

A. Cosattini, "Un petrarchista greco," in *Atene e Roma*, VII (1904), 115–120.

Appendix

PETRARCH'S CORONATION ORATION

The oration delivered by Petrarch on the occasion of his coronation on 8 April 1341 illuminates more clearly than does any other existing document the gradual transition from the Middle Ages to the Renaissance. With all its mingling of elements old and new it is the first manifesto of the Renaissance. Yet it is almost unknown. The Latin text is available only in the *Scritti inediti di Francesco Petrarca* edited by Attilio Hortis (Trieste, 1874). A French translation by Victor Develay, which I have found useful, especially because of Develay's identification of the sources of Petrarch's quotations, appeared in *Le Livre*, VI (1885), 278–288. No English translation has appeared hitherto. The present translation follows the Latin text faithfully. The use of the numerals I, II and III to mark the main divisions of the oration is merely editorial.[1]

THE ORATION

> Sed me Parnasi deserta per ardua dulcis
> raptat amor.[2]

Today, magnificent and venerable sirs, I must follow in my speech the ways of poetry, and I have therefore taken my text from a poetic source. For the same reason I shall do without those minute distinctions that are usually to be found in theological declamations, and I shall make my speech as brief as possible. Yet I must first invoke the divine favor; and to win this, despite my desire to be brief, I must not fail to offer salutation to the glorious Virgin.

---

[1] The coronation and the oration are discussed in a chapter in Wilkins 1, pp. 9–69.

[2] "But a sweet longing urges me upward over the lonely slopes of Parnassus" (Virgil, *Georgics* III 291–292).

I

> Sed me Parnasi deserta per ardua dulcis
> raptat amor.

These words are written in the third book of the *Georgics* of the greatest and most illustrious of all poets. The phrase "me Parnasi deserta per ardua" suggests the difficulty of the task I have set myself [3]—and we should note the force of the several words "Parnasi" and "ardua" and "deserta." The phrase "dulcis raptat amor" suggests the ardent eagerness of a studious mind—and we should note the force of "amor" in itself, of "dulcis amor," and of "amor" having the power to urge one upward. This difficulty and this eagerness are closely related, and are dependent each upon the other: for he who undertakes to climb the "ardua deserta Parnasi" must indeed long intensely for that which he seeks to attain; and he who loves to climb is doubtless the better prepared thereby to attain through study that in which his mind delights. For study without longing and without great mental pleasure and delight cannot attain the desired results. This may be gathered from the opinion of the Peripatetic philosophers, as set forth so well by Cicero in the fourth book of the *Tusculans*, and is clear also from the very definition of study as "an assiduous and eager concentration of mind directed with great pleasure toward some particular object": a definition which corresponds to Cicero's definition of philosophy, poetry, and the other arts in the first book of his treatise *On Invention*.

So then, to be brief, as I have promised to be, and as befits my profession, I declare first that the difficulty of the task I have set myself is rendered great by three circumstances: the very nature of the task; the ill fortune that has relentlessly beset me; and the fact that in times like these the minds of men are set upon material things, and are adverse to such studies. Of each of these three circumstances I must now speak briefly.

The inherent difficulty of the poet's task lies in this, that whereas in the other arts one may attain his goal through sheer toil and study, it is far otherwise with the art of poetry, in which nothing can be accomplished unless a certain inner and divinely given energy is infused in the poet's spirit. Take not my word for this, but Cicero's, who in his oration for Aulus Licinius Archias has this to say of poets: "We have it upon the authority of the most learned men that whereas attainment in other activities depends upon talent, learning, and skill, the poet attains through his very nature, is moved by the energy that is within his mind, and is as it were inspired by a divine inbreathing—so that Ennius fairly calls poets sacred in their own right, since they

---

[3] That is, the poet's task.

appear to be commended to us by the possession of a divine gift."
In his reference to "the most learned men" Cicero, I believe, was
thinking of Marcus Varro, by far the most learned of all the Romans,
who is believed to have expressed this very idea in the first book of
his treatise *On Poets*. It is in view of this same difficulty that the
Satirist says:

> Magnae mentis opus, nec de lodice paranda
> attonitae, currus et equos faciesque deorum
> aspicere et qualis Rutulum confundat Erinys.[4]

Lucan also in his ninth book exclaims: "O sacer et magnus vatum
labor." [5] Does it not seem to you that the inherent difficulty of my
task has been established sufficiently and by suitable authorities?
With regard to other activities, however, the poet writes, in the first
book of his *Georgics:* "Labor omnia vincit / improbus." [6] Hence
come the foolish efforts of those who to the very end of their lives
toil uselessly and ineffectively in verse, as the books on Scholastic
Discipline bear witness.

How hard and inexorable fortune has been to me, with what
labors she has oppressed me from my youth up, how many blows I
have endured from her, God knows, and they also know who have
been my close companions. But this I pass over, lest with sorrowful
words I hinder the rejoicing of this day. Everyone, to be sure, who
has made trial of the poetic task knows what impediments are placed
in his way by the bitterness of fortune. Aware of this, and thinking
not only of poets in general, but even of Virgil, the very father of
poets, the Satirist writes:

> Nam si Vergilio puer et tolerabile desset
> hospitium, caderent omnes a crinibus hydri,
> surda nihil gemeret grave bucina,[7]

and again:

> Sed vatem egregium, cui non sit publica vena,
> qui nil expositum soleat deducere nec qui
> communi feriat carmen triviale moneta,
> hunc, qualem nequeo monstrare et sentio tantum,
> anxietate carens animus facit, omnis acerbi
> impatiens, cupidus silvarum aptusque bibendis

---

[4] "It takes a noble mind, not one dismayed by the cost of a coverlet,
to behold the chariots, the horses, and the faces of the gods, and such a
fury as could confound the Rutulian" (Juvenal, *Satire* VII 66–68).

[5] "Sacred and great is the task of poets" (*Pharsalia* IX 980).

[6] "Relentless toil overcomes all difficulties" (I 145).

[7] "For if Virgil had had no boy to serve him and no tolerable dwelling,
all the snakes would have fallen from her hair, and her trumpet, silent,
would have sounded no dread note." These lines follow immediately
those quoted above from Juvenal.

fontibus Aonidum. Neque enim cantare sub antro
Pierio thyrsumve potest contingere maesta
paupertas atque aeris inops, quo nocte dieque
corpus eget.[8]

Of the third difficulty I will say only this, that, as we all read and
know, there was a time, there was an age, that was happier for poets,
an age when they were held in the highest honor, first in Greece and
then in Italy, and especially when Caesar Augustus held imperial
sway, under whom there flourished excellent poets, Virgil, Varus,[9]
Ovid, Horace, and many others. Of this time the Satirist writes:
"Tunc par ingenio pretium, tunc utile multis / pallere et vinum
toto nescire Decembri." [10] But today, as you well know, all this is
changed. This is obvious, and needs no proof, so that one may rightly
say today what the Satirist, distressed by a change in the times, said
long ago:

Frange miser calamum vigilataque proelia dele,
qui facis in parva sublimia carmina cella,
ut dignus venias hederis et imagine macra.
Spes nulla ulterior; didicit iam dives avarus
tantum admirari, tantum laudare disertos,
ut pueri Iunonis avem. Sed defluit aetas
et pelagi patiens et cassidis atque ligonis.
Taedia tunc subeunt animo, tunc seque suamque
Terpsichoren odit facunda et nuda senectus.[11]

These, then, are the three difficulties of which I spoke: the first

---

[8] "But the good poet, whose line is not commonplace, who does not
deal in the reworking of old stuff, nor stamp his songs in a common mint
(I cannot show him to you, I can only imagine him) must have a spirit
free from anxiety, untouched by any bitterness, eager for the woods, and
ready to drink at the fountain of the Muses. For none can sing in the
Pierian cave or wield the thyrsus who is oppressed by sad poverty and
lacks the coin to meet the body's daily and nightly needs" (VII 53–62).

[9] Petrarch had in mind the Augustan poet Varius, mentioned by
Horace and Virgil. His name appears as Varus in some MSS, including
Petrarch's own MS of Virgil.

[10] "Then genius found its due reward; then it was worth while for
many to grow pale and to abstain from wine for all December" (VII
96–97).

[11] "Break your pen, poor fellow, and destroy the battles over which
you have toiled in the night hours, writing sublime songs in your poor
little room, hoping to earn a meagre bust, bedecked with ivy. There is
nothing more to hope for: the rich miser has now learned to admire and
praise only the fluent, as boys admire the bird of Juno. The time is past
that could endure the sea, the helmet, and the mattock. Weariness overcomes the spirit; and old age, eloquent but naked, hates itself and its own
Muse" (VII 27–35).

two show how arduous are the heights of Parnassus which I have set out to climb; the third shows how lonely they are.

Someone then might say: "What is all this, my friend? Have you determined to revive a custom that is beset with inherent difficulty and has long since fallen into desuetude? and this in the face of a hostile and recalcitrant fortune? Whence do you draw such confidence that you would decorate the Roman Capitol with new and unaccustomed laurels? Do you not see what a task you have undertaken in attempting to attain the lonely steeps of Parnassus and the inaccessible grove of the Muses?" Yes, I do see, oh my dear sirs; I do indeed see this, oh Roman citizens, "Sed me Parnasi deserta per ardua dulcis / raptat amor," as I said at the outset. For the intensity of my longing is so great that it seems to me sufficient to enable me to overcome all the difficulties that are involved in my present task.

The second portion of my first theme springs from this, that after the reference to the toilsome ascent "per ardua deserta Parnasi" there follows the mention of the effective cause of that ascent: "dulcis raptat amor." And here it is to be noted that just as the difficulty has been shown to rise, as it were, from three roots, so the disposition of the spirit which is victorious over that difficulty rises also from three roots, which are, first, the honor of the Republic; second, the charm of personal glory; and third, the stimulation of other men to a like endeavor.

The honor of the Republic stirs my heart when I recall that in this very city of Rome—the capital of the world, as Cicero calls it—in this very Roman Capitol where we now are gathered, so many and such great poets, having attained to the highest and most illustrious mastery of their art, have received the laurel crown they had deserved, but that now this custom seems rather to have been lost than to have been merely laid aside, and not lost merely, but reduced to a matter of strange legendry, and discontinued for more than twelve hundred years. For we do not read that anyone has been decorated with this honor since the illustrious poet Statius, who flourished in the time of Domitian. I am moved also by the hope that, if God wills, I may renew in the now aged Republic a beauteous custom of its flourishing youth. And here, not as a matter of vain boasting, but for the sake of the truth, I venture to relate that at one and the same time, a year or so ago, I was invited both to Rome and to Paris, rivalling each other in their invitations to receive this honor—to Rome by the Senate that was then in office and by certain noblemen of Rome, some of whom are present in this gathering, and to Paris by that excellent man and Master, Robert, Chancellor of the University of Paris, and by other well-known men of that city and that university. And although I hesitated for a time because of the present fame of that university, I finally decided to come hither—why, I ask you, if not for the very reason that Virgil gives, "Vicit amor patriae." [12] I was much moved also toward this decision by a certain affection and reverence for those ancient poets of excellent genius who flourished in this very city, who lived here, who are buried here—even as Cicero well says in the second book of his *Laws:* "I regard this as a sound reason for your coming here by preference and for your loving this place," and continuing: "Our emotions are somehow stirred in those places in which the feet of those whom we love and admire have trodden. Wherefore even Athens delights us not so much through its magnificent buildings and its exquisite works of ancient art as through the memory of its great men: 'twas here they dwelt, 'twas here they sat, 'twas here they engaged in their philosophical discussions. And with reverence I contemplate their tombs." [13] This, I confess, was not the least of the causes for my coming to Rome. But whatever the cause, I trust that my coming, because of the novelty of the occasion if for no other reason, may serve to bring some glory to this city, to the city whence I come, and to all Italy.

On the second point, namely the charm of personal glory, many and various things might be said which for the sake of my promised brevity I shall pass over. Let this one truth suffice: that the desire for glory is innate not merely in the generality of men but in greatest measure in those who are of some wisdom and some excellence. Hence it is that although many philosophers have much to say in contempt of glory, few or none can be found who really condemn it. Which is shown most clearly by the fact that "they have inscribed their names at the beginning of the very works they have written in contempt of glory," as Cicero says in the first book of the *Tusculans.* Consider also what he said in this very hall in the presence of Julius Caesar: "You will not deny that you crave glory most eagerly." [14] Is there any need of further quotations? Most true is that which Cicero says elsewhere: "There is hardly anyone who after the completion of a laborious task or the meeting of perils does not desire glory as a reward for what he has accomplished." [15] True also are these lines of Ovid: "Excitat auditor studium, laudataque virtus / crescit, et immensum gloria calcar habet." [16]

To join the first point and the second, let me now quote in its

---

[12] "Love of his fatherland has conquered" (*Aeneid* vi 823).

[13] *Laws* ii 2.

[14] *Oration for Marcus Marcellus,* 8.

[15] *Offices* xix.

[16] "The thought of the listener excites the toiling writer; excellence grows when it is praised; and the thought of glory is a powerful spur" (*Epistles from Pontus* iv 2, 35–36).

entirety that line of Virgil the first half of which I have already quoted: "Vicit amor patriae laudumque immensa cupido." [17]

As to the third point, namely the stimulation of the activity of others, I will say only this: while there are some who think it shameful to follow in the footsteps of others, there are far more who fear to essay a hard road unless they have a sure guide. Many such men I have known, especially in Italy: learned and gifted men, devoted to the same studies, thirsting with the same desires, who as yet—whether from a sense of shame, or from sluggishness, or from diffidence, or, as I prefer to think, from modesty and humility—have not entered upon this road. Boldly, therefore, perhaps, but—to the best of my belief—with no unworthy intention, since others are holding back I am venturing to offer myself as guide for this toilsome and dangerous path; and I trust that there may be many followers.

So then the triple difficulty is overcome by its triple opposite. And I do not deny that in the struggle I have had the advantage of a certain genius given to me from on high by the giver of all good things, by God himself—that God who may rightly be called, in the words of Persius, "Magister artis ingeniique largitor." [18]

II

Now, since with God's help I have in some fashion come through the opposing difficulties to the desired goal, it remains for me to express the hope that I may receive a reward for all my labors. But I judge it fitting that before I close I should say something as to the nature of the profession of poetry, and as to the character of the reward that is desired.

With regard to the first of these matters a few words will suffice. You must know, illustrious sirs, that the office and the profession of the poet are not by any means what they are commonly believed to be. For as Lactantius says so well in the first book of his *Institutes:* "They know not the limits of poetic license or how far they may go in fictional composition. For the office of the poet consists in this, that he should take things that have really come to pass and transform them by means of subtle figures [19] into things of a different sort. To make up all that one writes is to be a fool and a liar rather than a poet." Whence Macrobius, in the second book of his commentary on the sixth book of the *Republic:* "And they maintain that Homer, the fount and source of all divine inventions, was setting truth before the wise under the cloud of a poetic fiction when he spoke of

---

[17] "Love of his fatherland has conquered, and the immense desire for praise."

[18] "Master of the arts and bestower of genius" (*Satires*, Prologue, 10).

[19] The Latin words are "obliquis figurationibus."

Jove as going to the ocean with the other gods, that is, with the stars, to attend a feast to which the Ethiops had invited him. They maintain that by this fabulous image Homer meant to signify that the stars draw their nourishment from the ocean. And he represents the Ethiop kings as participants in the feast of the gods because none dwell on the ocean shores save the Ethiops, whose nearness to the sun has burned them into the semblance of blackness."

It would take me too long to discourse upon this theme; but if time were not lacking and I did not fear to weary you I could readily prove to you that poets under the veil of fictions have set forth truths physical, moral, and historical—thus bearing out a statement I often make, that the difference between a poet on the one hand and a historian or a moral or physical philosopher on the other is the same as the difference between a clouded sky and a clear sky, since in each case the same light exists in the object of vision, but is perceived in different degrees according to the capacity of the observers. Poetry, furthermore, is all the sweeter since a truth that must be sought out with some care gives all the more delight when it is discovered. Let this suffice as a statement not so much about myself as about the poetic profession. For while poets are wont to find pleasure in a certain playfulness, I should not wish to appear to be a poet and nothing more.

III

It remains for me now to speak of the reward for which, however undeservingly, I hope.

The poet's reward is beyond question multiple, for it consists, firstly, in the charm of personal glory, of which enough has been said already, and secondly, in the immortality of one's name. This immortality is itself twofold, for it includes both the immortality of the poet's own name and the immortality of the names of those whom he celebrates. Concerning the first of these two kinds of immortality Ovid speaks with assurance at the end of the *Metamorphoses:* "Iamque opus exegi, quod nec Iovis ira nec ignis / nec poterit ferrum nec edax abolere vetustas," [20] and so on to the end. So also Statius at the end of the *Thebaid:*

> Durabisne procul dominoque legere superstes,
> O mihi bissenos multum vigilata per annos
> Thebai? [21]

---

[20] "And now I have finished my work, which neither the wrath of Jove nor fire nor sword nor the ravages of time can destroy" (xv 871–872).

[21] "Wilt thou long endure and be read, surviving thine author, oh my *Thebaid*, whereon for twelve long years I have toiled through the night watches?" (xii 811–813).

Of the second kind of immortality Virgil speaks thus in his ninth book:

> Fortunati ambo! si quid mea carmina possunt,
> nulla dies umquam memori vos eximet aevo,
> dum domus Aeneae Capitoli immobile saxum
> accolet imperiumque pater romanus habebit.[22]

So also Statius in the *Thebaid:* "Vos quoque sacrati, quamvis mea carmina surgant / inferiore lyra, memores superabitis annos." [23] And of both kinds together Lucan speaks in his ninth book: "Venturi me teque legent; Pharsalia nostra / vivet, et a nullo tenebris damnabitur aevo." [24]

There have indeed been many men who in their lifetime were glorious and memorable for what they wrought in writings or in arms, whose names have nevertheless fallen into oblivion for this one reason, that they did not succeed in expressing in the stable and enduring style of a true man of letters what it was that they really had in their minds and spirits. For as Cicero says in the first book of the *Tusculans:* "It may happen that a man may think rightly and yet be unable to express effectively what he thinks, or to attract the reader by any charm. To fail thus is to make poor use of leisure and of letters." Many mighty men and warriors, and others who have deserved eternal memory have passed into oblivion simply because they had not the good fortune to be recorded by capable authors, as Horace says so well in his *Odes:*

> Vixere fortes ante Agamemnona
> multi; sed omnes inlacrimabili
> nocte premuntur,

and the reason follows: "carent quia vate sacro." [25] Certain illustrious men, foreseeing such a possibility, have kept poets with them and held them in high honor, so that there might be someone who would hand down their praises to posterity—a matter carefully set forth by Cicero in his oration for Aulus Licinius Archias, to which I have already referred. Nor is it to be wondered at if famous warriors have held famous poets dear, according to Claudian's rule:

---

[22] "Fortunate are ye both! If my verses have any power, no day shall ever cancel you from the memory of the ages, as long as the progeny of Aeneas dwells on the unshakable rock of the Capitol, and the Roman father holds imperial sway" (*Aeneid* IX 446–449).

[23] "You too, now consecrate, shall survive the unforgetting years, even though my songs rise from a less lofty lyre" (X 445–446).

[24] "Posterity shall read of me and thee; and our *Pharsalia* shall live, and shall not by any age be condemned to oblivion" (IX 985–986).

[25] Many mighty men lived before Agamemnon, but all are buried in a tearless night . . . since they lack an inspired bard" (IV 9, 25–28).

"Gaudet enim virtus testes sibi iungere Musas; / carmen amat quisquis carmine digna gerit." [26] And in so far as mundane glory is
concerned the saying of Horace is certainly true: "Paulum sepultae
distat inertiae / celata virtus." [27] Hence comes that famous exclamation of Alexander of Macedon, of whom it is related that when
he came to the tomb of Achilles he sighed, and said: "Oh fortunate
youth, that didst find so great a herald for thy valor!"—referring to
Homer, the prince of poets, who is known to have conferred fame
upon Achilles by his noble songs.[28]

Other rewards, also, come to poets; but passing over these I come
to the laurel crown. This crown, the due reward of Caesars and of
poets, is a wreath made of the leaves of the laurel—though the poet's
crown is sometimes made of myrtle and sometimes of ivy and is
sometimes a simple fillet, variations which I have brought into one
of my epistles in these two lines: "Nunc tamen et lauri mirtusque
hedereque silentur, / sacraque temporibus debita vitta tuis." [29]

And now, lest I continue at too great length, I shall treat briefly
of the properties of the laurel.

The laurel, first of all, is fragrant, as our own senses tell us, as
does Virgil in the sixth of the *Aeneid:* "Inter odoratum lauri nemus," [30] and in the second Eclogue of his *Bucolics:* "Et vos, o lauri,
carpam et te, proxima myrte, / sic positae quoniam suaves miscetis
odores." [31] This first property we may take to signify the fragrance
of good repute which both Caesars and poets seek; also, that as we
consist of both body and spirit, two ways of seeking glory are set
before us, namely the way of the body and the way of the spirit—
though in this life each needs the help of the other. Nor is there any
doubt that Caesars strive toward glory by the first of these two ways,
and poets by the second. So then, since both Caesars and poets move
toward the same goal, though by different paths, it is fitting that one
and the same reward be prepared for both, namely, a wreath from a
fragrant tree, symbolizing the fragrance of good fame and of glory.

In the second place, the laurel tree is shady, and affords a resting

---

[26] "For valor delights to win alliance with the Muses: he loves song
whose deeds are worthy of song" (*On the Consulate of Stilicho* III 5–6).

[27] "There is little difference between buried indolence and hidden excellence" (*Odes* IV 9, 29–30).

[28] This anecdote is derived from Cicero's *Oration for Archias*, 24.

[29] "But laurel now and myrtle and ivy are still, and the sacred fillet
that your brows should bear." The poem from which these two lines
are quoted is not otherwise known.

[30] "Within a fragrant laurel grove" (VI 658).

[31] "And you, oh laurels, I will pluck, and thee, myrtle, therewith, since
thus combined ye mingle sweet fragrances" (II 54–55).

place for those who labor. Whence come the lines of Horace in his 44th *Ode:* "Spissa ramis laurea fervidos / excludet ictus solis," [32] and in his 46th: "Longaque fessum militia latus / depone sub lauru mea." [33] Not inappropriately is this property of the laurel associated with Caesars and with poets: for it may symbolize the rest that is in store for the former after their toils in warfare, and for the latter after their toils in study.

It is said that the leaves of this tree are not only themselves incorruptible, but preserve from corruption also those books and other things on which they are placed: which is singularly appropriate for poets, whose work serves assuredly to preserve from corruption both their own fame and the fame of others.

The laurel is moreover a sacred tree, to be held in awe, and to be reverenced. Whence Virgil, in the seventh book of the *Aeneid:* "Laurus erat tecti medio in penetralibus altis, / sacra comam multosque metu servata per annos." [34] Beside the laurel they were wont to erect altars, as is indicated in the second book of the *Aeneid:*

> Aedibus in mediis nudoque sub aetheris axe
> ingens ara fuit iuxtaque veterrima laurus,
> incumbens arae.[35]

It was appropriate for the service of sacrifice, whence Virgil in the third book of the *Aeneid:* "Phoebique sacerdos / vittis et sacra redimitus tempora lauro," [36] and Lucan in his sixth book: "Unde et Thessalicae veniunt ad Pythia laurus." [37] It is an adornment, moreover, not for temples only but for the Capitol itself, as Lucan says in his first book: "Sacras poscunt Capitolia laurus." [38] The day would fail me if I should continue with quotations. In many other instances, indeed, the laurel is equally appropriate for Caesars and for poets, since I could show that both were wont to be called sacred—

---

[32] The thickly-branched laurel will shut out the hot shafts of the sun" (II 15, 9–10).

[33] "Rest under my laurel tree thy body wearied with long campaigning" (II 7, 18–19).

[34] "There was a laurel tree in the midst of the palace, in a high inner court, sacred in its leafage, and reverently guarded for many years" (VII 59–60).

[35] "In the midst of the palace, under the open sky, there was a great altar, and beside it an ancient laurel tree overhanging the altar" (II 512–514).

[36] "A priest of Apollo, his brows bound with fillets and the sacred laurel" (III 80–81).

[37] "Whence the laurels of Thessaly are brought to the Pythian games" (VI 409).

[38] "The Capitol calls for the sacred laurel" (I 287).

were I not mindful of Cicero's remark that evidence is superfluous in a case in which there is no ground for doubt.

There remain three properties possessed by the laurel that cannot be passed over in silence. The first is this, that when a person who is asleep is touched with laurel his dreams come true. Which makes it singularly appropriate for poets, who are said to be wont to sleep upon Parnassus, as Persius has it: "Nec in bicipiti somniasse Parnaso" [39] and the rest. This is said covertly to show that truth is contained in poetic writings which to the foolish seem to be but dreams—the poet's head being wreathed with the leaves that make dreams come true. It is appropriate in another respect also, for in so far as it promises foreknowledge of the future it is fitting for Apollo as the god of prophecy—whence, as I shall say presently, he is feigned to have loved the laurel tree. Accordingly, since Apollo was held to be the god of poets, it is no wonder that deserving poets were crowned with the very leafage of their own god, whom they regarded as their sustaining helper, whom they called the god of genius.

The second of these last three qualities of the laurel is its eternal verdure, with reference to which someone has well said: "Winter harms not the laurel, even as the pyre harms not gold." [40] . . . it is said to be beloved by Apollo and sacred to him. Whence Virgil says in the *Bucolics*: "Formosae myrtus Veneri, sua laurea Phoebo," [41] and again in the seventh book of the *Aeneid:* "Quam pater inventam, primas dum conderet arces, / ipse ferebatur Phoebo sacrasse Latinus." [42] And this gave rise to the story that Apollo loved Daphne, for according to Uguiccione [43] the Greek word *daphne* has the same meaning as the Latin *laurus:* this story may be read in full in the first book of the *Metamorphoses* of Ovid. Nor is this poetic fiction without a basis, for though every tree is dear to the sun, from which all life and growth descend, the one tree that is adorned with an eternal verdure most worthily holds the title of the loved one. And the immortality of this verdure, which symbolizes the immortality of fame sought through warfare or through genius, was perhaps a reason why both Caesars and poets were crowned most usually with a laurel wreath.

The third and last of these properties is this: that, as all agree who

---

[39] "Nor to have slept on twin-peaked Parnassus" (Prologue, 2–3).

[40] The single MS of the oration is defective at this point.

[41] "To lovely Venus the myrtle, to Apollo his own laurel" (vii 62).

[42] "Which Father Latinus, it is said, found while he was building the first citadel, and consecrated to Apollo" (vii 61–62).

[43] The 12th-century lexicographer, Uguiccione of Pisa.

have written on natural history, the laurel is immune to lightning.[44] A great and notable prerogative! And this—to continue as we began— was the hidden reason why this tree . . .[45] for in the affairs of men what thunderbolt is more terrible than the diuturnity of time, which consumes all the works of men, all their possessions, all their fame? Rightly, therefore, since the laurel fears not the thunderbolt, is a crown of laurel given to those whose glory fears not the ages that like a thunderbolt lay all things low.

You have heard the considerations that have occurred to me without long meditation and, as it were, on the spur of the moment. The fact that Caesars and poets were indeed crowned with laurel could be proved by innumerable testimonies, and for each by separate declarations. As to Caesars, Horace speaks sufficiently in his 40th *Ode:* "Cui laurus aeternos honores / Dalmatico peperit triumpho." [46] As to poets, Statius in the *Thebaid:* "Tempus erit, cum laurigero tua fortior oestro / facta canam." [47] And as to both together, Statius in the *Achilleid:* "Cui geminae florent vatumque ducumque / certatim laurus." [48]

Much might still be said as to the origins of poetry, the kinds and varieties of poets, and other related and very interesting matters: but the greater the attention you give me, the more careful I must be not to impair it by excessive speaking, nor to offend thereby your patient ears.

Thus then I conclude. Whether the first two kinds of reward shall come to me, God and my fortune know; you too shall know, my lords and friends; they too shall know who are still unborn, whose judgment will be, I hope, the surer and the more equitable since, as Cicero says, "They will judge without love or partiality, and without hatred or envy." [49] But however I may fare with regard to those two awards, the third award, namely the poet's laurel crown, I humbly seek to receive at your hands, illustrious Senator.[50] To

---

[44] This idea is derived from Suetonius' *Life of Tiberius*, 69: see Billanovich, "Uno Svetonio della biblioteca del Petrarca," in *Studi petrarcheschi*, VI (1954).

[45] The MS is defective at this point.

[46] "For whom the laurel won eternal honors by thy Dalmatian triumph" (II 1, 15–16).

[47] "A time will come when, stronger through an inspiration laurel-wreathed, I shall sing of thy deeds" (I 32–33).

[48] "For whom the twin laurels of poet and warrior flourish in rivalry" (I 15–16).

[49] *Oration for Marcus Marcellus*, 9.

[50] At this point Petrarch is addressing directly his friend Orso dell' Anguillara, one of the two Roman Senators then in office.

you also there have been conveyed the requests, in this regard, of the most illustrious King of Sicily,[51] by whose high and profound judgment I, though unworthy, have been approved—to whom, moreover, by ancient custom the power of approval has been entrusted by the Roman people.

---

[51] Robert of Anjou, King of Naples and Sicily, who a few days earlier had given Petrarch a three-day oral examination, at the end of which he had pronounced him qualified to receive the laurel crown.

Index of Persons

Entries are made for all persons mentioned by name in the several chapters and the Appendix of this book except the following: Petrarch; persons mentioned only in "A General Survey of Renaissance Petrarchism"; persons of the 18th and later centuries; persons mentioned only in titles; fictional or mythological characters (those who are subjects of Lives in the *De viris* are, however, included); and divinities. Names ending in a prepositional phrase are entered under the initial of the last element of that phrase.

Index of Letters

Epistolae familiares

Letters Addressed to Petrarch

Epistola metrica addressed to Petrarch